# PHILOSOPHY OF GOD
## Course Reader

Younan

ISBN-13: 978-1519130839
ISBN-10: 151913083X

# TABLE OF CONTENTS

# From the *Timaeus*
## By Plato
## Translated by Benjamin Jowett

SOCRATES: I see that I shall receive in my turn a perfect and splendid feast of reason. And now, Timaeus, you, I suppose, should speak next, after duly calling upon the Gods.

TIMAEUS: All men, Socrates, who have any degree of right feeling, at the beginning of every enterprise, whether small or great, always call upon God. And we, too, who are going to discourse of the nature of the universe, how created or how existing without creation, if we be not altogether out of our wits, must invoke the aid of Gods and Goddesses and pray that our words may be acceptable to them and consistent with themselves. Let this, then, be our invocation of the Gods, to which I add an exhortation of myself to speak in such manner as will be most intelligible to you, and will most accord with my own intent.

First then, in my judgment, we must make a distinction and ask, What is that which always is and has no becoming; and what is that which is always becoming and never is? That which is apprehended by intelligence and reason is always in the same state; but that which is conceived by opinion with the help of sensation and without reason, is always in a process of becoming and perishing and never really is. Now everything that becomes or is created must of necessity be created by some cause, for without a cause nothing can be created. The work of the creator, whenever he looks to the unchangeable and fashions the form and nature of his work after an unchangeable pattern, must necessarily be made fair and perfect; but when he looks to the created only, and uses a created pattern, it is not fair or perfect. Was the heaven then or the world, whether called by this or by any other more appropriate name—assuming the name, I am asking a question which has to be asked at the beginning of an enquiry about anything—was the world, I say, always in existence and without beginning? or created, and had it a beginning? Created, I reply, being visible and tangible and having a body, and therefore sensible; and all sensible things are apprehended by opinion and sense and are in a process of creation and created. Now that which is created must, as we affirm, of necessity be created by a cause. But the father and maker of all this universe is past finding out; and even if we found him, to tell of him to all men would be impossible. And there is still a question to be asked about him: Which of the patterns had the artificer in view when he made the world—the pattern of the unchangeable, or of that which is created? If the world be indeed fair and the artificer good, it is manifest that he must have looked to that which is eternal; but if what cannot be said without blasphemy is true, then to the created pattern. Every one will see that he must have looked to the eternal; for the world is the fairest of creations and he is the best of causes. And having been created in this way, the world has been framed in the likeness of that which is apprehended by reason and mind and is unchangeable, and must therefore of necessity, if this is admitted, be a copy of something. Now it is all-important that the beginning of everything should be according to nature. And in speaking of the copy and the original we may assume that words are akin to the matter which they describe; when they relate to the lasting and permanent and intelligible, they ought to be lasting and unalterable, and, as far as their nature allows, irrefutable and immovable—nothing less. But when they express only the copy or likeness and not the eternal things themselves, they need only be likely and analogous to the real words. As being is to becoming, so is truth to belief. If then, Socrates, amid the many opinions about the gods and the generation of the universe, we are not able to give notions which are altogether and in every respect exact and consistent with one another, do not be surprised. Enough, if we adduce probabilities as likely as any others; for we must remember that I who am the speaker, and you who are the judges, are only mortal men, and we ought to accept the tale which is probable and enquire no further.

SOCRATES: Excellent, Timaeus; and we will do precisely as you bid us. The prelude is charming, and is already accepted by us— may we beg of you to proceed to the strain?

TIMAEUS: Let me tell you then why the creator made this world of generation. He was good, and the good can never have any jealousy of anything. And being free from jealousy, he desired that all things should be as like himself as they could be. This is in the truest sense the origin of creation and of the world, as we shall do well in believing on the testimony of wise men: God desired that all things should be good and nothing bad, so far as this was attainable. Wherefore also finding the whole visible sphere not at rest, but moving in an irregular and disorderly fashion, out of disorder he brought order, considering that this was in every way better than the other. Now the deeds of the best could never be or have been other than the fairest; and the creator, reflecting on the things which are by nature visible, found that no unintelligent creature taken as a whole was fairer than the intelligent taken as a whole; and that intelligence could not be present in anything which was devoid of soul. For which reason, when he was framing the universe, he put intelligence in soul, and soul in body, that he might be the creator of a work which was by nature fairest and best. Wherefore, using the language of probability, we may say that the world became a living creature truly endowed with soul and intelligence by the providence of God.

This being supposed, let us proceed to the next stage: In the likeness of what animal did the Creator make the world? It would be an unworthy thing to liken it to any nature which exists as a part only; for nothing can be beautiful which is like any imperfect thing; but let us suppose the world to be the very image of that whole of which all other animals both individually and in their tribes are portions. For the original of the universe contains in itself all intelligible beings, just as this world comprehends us and all other visible creatures. For the Deity, intending to make this world like the fairest and most perfect of intelligible beings, framed one visible animal comprehending within itself all other animals of a kindred nature. Are we right in saying that there is one world, or that they are many and infinite? There must be one only, if the created copy is to accord with the original. For that which includes all other intelligible creatures cannot have a second or companion; in that case there would be need of another living being which would include both, and of which they would be parts, and the likeness would be more truly said to resemble not them, but that other which included them. In order then that the world might be solitary, like the perfect animal, the creator made not two worlds or an infinite number of them; but there is and ever will be one only-begotten and created heaven.

Now that which is created is of necessity corporeal, and also visible and tangible. And nothing is visible where there is no fire, or tangible which has no solidity, and nothing is solid without earth. Wherefore also God in the beginning of creation made the body of the universe to consist of fire and earth. But two things cannot be rightly put together without a third; there must be some bond of union between them. And the fairest bond is that which makes the most complete fusion of itself and the things which it combines; and proportion is best adapted to effect such a union. For whenever in any three numbers, whether cube or square, there is a mean, which is to the last term what the first term is to it; and again, when the mean is to the first term as the last term is to the mean—then the mean becoming first and last, and the first and last both becoming means, they will all of them of necessity come to be the same, and having become the same with one another will be all one. If the universal frame had been created a surface only and having no depth, a single mean would have sufficed to bind together itself and the other terms; but now, as the world must be solid, and solid bodies are always compacted not by one mean but by two, God placed water and air in the mean between fire and earth, and made them to have the same proportion so far as was possible (as fire is to air so is air to water, and as air is to water so is water to earth); and thus he bound and put together a visible and tangible heaven. And for these reasons, and out of such elements which are in number four, the body of the world was created, and it was harmonized by proportion, and therefore has the spirit of friendship; and having been reconciled to itself, it was indissoluble by the hand of any other than the framer.

Now the creation took up the whole of each of the four elements; for the Creator compounded the world out of all the fire and all the water and all the air and all the earth, leaving no part of any of them nor any power of them outside. His intention was, in the first place, that the animal should be as far as possible a perfect whole and of perfect parts: secondly, that it should be one, leaving no remnants out of which another such world might be created: and also that it should be free from old age and unaffected by disease. Considering that if heat and cold and other powerful forces which unite bodies surround and attack them from without when they are unprepared, they decompose them, and by bringing diseases and old age upon them, make them waste away—for this cause and on these grounds he made the world one whole, having every part entire, and being therefore perfect and not liable to old age and disease. And he gave to the world the figure which was suitable and also natural. Now to the animal which was to comprehend all animals, that figure was suitable which comprehends within itself all other figures. Wherefore he made the world in the form of a globe, round as from a lathe, having its extremes in every direction equidistant from the centre, the most perfect and the most like itself of all figures; for he considered that the like is infinitely fairer than the unlike. This he finished off, making the surface smooth all round for many reasons; in the first place, because the living being had no need of eyes when there was nothing remaining outside him to be seen; nor of ears when there was nothing to be heard; and there was no surrounding atmosphere to be breathed; nor would there have been any use of organs by the help of which he might receive his food or get rid of what he had already digested, since there was nothing which went from him or came into him: for there was nothing beside him. Of design he was created thus, his own waste providing his own food, and all that he did or suffered taking place in and by himself. For the Creator conceived that a being which was self-sufficient would be far more excellent than one which lacked anything; and, as he had no need to take anything or defend himself against any one, the Creator did not think it necessary to bestow upon him hands: nor had he any need of feet, nor of the whole apparatus of walking; but the movement suited to his spherical form was assigned to him, being of all the seven that which is most appropriate to mind and intelligence; and he was made to move in the same manner and on the same spot, within his own limits revolving in a circle. All the other six motions were taken away from him, and he was made not to partake of their deviations. And as this circular movement required no feet, the universe was created without legs and without feet.

Such was the whole plan of the eternal God about the god that was to be, to whom for this reason he gave a body, smooth and even, having a surface in every direction equidistant from the centre, a body entire and perfect, and formed out of perfect bodies. And in the centre he put the soul, which he diffused throughout the body, making it also to be the exterior environment of it; and he made the universe a circle moving in a circle, one and solitary, yet by reason of its excellence able to converse with itself, and needing no other friendship or acquaintance. Having these purposes in view he created the world a blessed god.

Now God did not make the soul after the body, although we are speaking of them in this order; for having brought them together he would never have allowed that the elder should be ruled by the younger; but this is a random manner of speaking which we have, because somehow we ourselves too are very much under the dominion of chance. Whereas he made the soul in origin and excellence prior to and older than the body, to be the ruler and mistress, of whom the body was to be the subject. And he made her out of the following elements and on this wise: Out of the indivisible and unchangeable, and also out of that which is divisible and has to do with material bodies, he compounded a third and intermediate kind of essence, partaking of the nature of the same and of the other, and this compound he placed accordingly in a mean between the indivisible, and the divisible and material. He took the three elements of the same, the other, and the essence, and mingled them into one form, compressing by force the reluctant and unsociable nature of the other into the same. When he had mingled them with the essence and out of three made one, he again divided this whole into as many portions as was fitting, each portion being a compound of the same, the other, and the essence. And he proceeded to divide after this manner:—First of all, he took away one part of the whole (1), and then he separated a second part which was double the first (2), and then he took away a third part which was half as much again as the second and three times as much as the first (3), and then he took a fourth part which was twice as much as the second (4), and a fifth part which was three times the third (9), and a sixth part which was eight times the first (8), and a seventh part which was twenty-seven times the first (27). After this he filled up the double intervals (i.e. between 1, 2, 4, 8) and the triple (i.e. between 1, 3, 9, 27) cutting off yet other portions from the mixture and placing them in the intervals, so that in each interval there were two kinds of means, the one exceeding and exceeded by equal parts of its extremes (as for example 1, 4/3, 2, in which the mean 4/3 is one-third of 1 more than 1, and one-third of 2 less than 2), the other being that kind of mean which exceeds and is exceeded by an equal number (e.g.

- over 1, 4/3, 3/2, - over 2, 8/3, 3, - over 4, 16/3, 6, - over 8: and
- over 1, 3/2, 2, - over 3, 9/2, 6, - over 9, 27/2, 18, - over 27.

Where there were intervals of 3/2 and of 4/3 and of 9/8, made by the connecting terms in the former intervals, he filled up all the intervals of 4/3 with the interval of 9/8, leaving a fraction over; and the interval which this fraction expressed was in the ratio of 256 to 243 (e.g.

243:256::81/64:4/3::243/128:2::81/32:8/3::243/64:4::81/16:16/3::242/32:8.

And thus the whole mixture out of which he cut these portions was all exhausted by him. This entire compound he divided lengthways into two parts, which he joined to one another at the centre like the letter X, and bent them into a circular form, connecting them with themselves and each other at the point opposite to their original meeting-point; and, comprehending them in a uniform revolution upon the same axis, he made the one the outer and the other the inner circle. Now the motion of the outer circle he called the motion of the same, and the motion of the inner circle the motion of the other or diverse. The motion of the same he carried round by the side (i.e. of the rectangular figure supposed to be inscribed in the circle of the Same) to the right, and the motion of the diverse diagonally (i.e. across the rectangular figure from corner to corner) to the left. And he gave dominion to the motion of the same and like, for that he left single and undivided; but the inner motion he divided in six places and made seven unequal circles having their intervals in ratios of two and three, three of each, and bade the orbits proceed in a direction opposite to one another; and three (Sun, Mercury, Venus) he made to move with equal swiftness, and the remaining four (Moon, Saturn, Mars, Jupiter) to move with unequal swiftness to the three and to one another, but in due proportion.

Now when the Creator had framed the soul according to his will, he formed within her the corporeal universe, and brought the two together, and united them centre to centre. The soul, interfused everywhere from the centre to the circumference of heaven, of which also she is the external envelopment, herself turning in herself, began a divine beginning of never-ceasing and rational life enduring throughout all time. The body of heaven is visible, but the soul is invisible, and partakes of reason and harmony, and being made by the best of intellectual and everlasting natures, is the best of things created. And because she is composed of the same and of the other and of the essence, these three, and is divided and united in due proportion, and in her revolutions returns upon herself, the soul, when touching anything which has essence, whether dispersed in parts or undivided, is stirred through all her powers, to declare the sameness or difference of that thing and some other; and to what individuals are related, and by what affected, and in what way and how and when, both in the world of generation and in the world of immutable being. And when reason, which works with equal truth, whether she be in the circle of the diverse or of the same—in voiceless silence holding her onward course in the sphere of the self-moved—when reason, I say, is hovering around the sensible world and when the circle of the diverse also moving truly imparts the intimations of sense to the whole soul, then arise opinions and beliefs sure and certain. But when reason is concerned with the rational, and the circle of the same moving smoothly declares it, then intelligence and knowledge are necessarily perfected. And if any one affirms that in which these two are found to be other than the soul, he will say the very opposite of the truth.

When the father and creator saw the creature which he had made moving and living, the created image of the eternal gods, he rejoiced, and in his joy determined to make the copy still more like the original; and as this was eternal, he sought to make the universe eternal, so far as might be. Now the nature of the ideal being was everlasting, but to bestow this attribute in its fulness upon a creature was impossible. Wherefore he resolved to have a moving image of eternity, and when he set in order the heaven, he made this image eternal but moving according to number, while eternity itself rests in unity; and this image we call time. For there were no days and nights and months and years before the heaven was created, but when he constructed the heaven he created them also. They are all parts of time, and the past and future are created species of time, which we unconsciously but wrongly transfer to the eternal essence; for we say that he 'was,' he 'is,' he 'will be,' but the truth is that 'is' alone is properly attributed to him, and that 'was' and 'will be' are only to be spoken of becoming in time, for they are motions, but that which is immovably the same cannot become older or younger by time, nor ever did or has become, or hereafter will be, older or younger, nor is subject at all to any of those states which affect moving and sensible things and of which generation is the cause. These are the forms of time, which imitates eternity and revolves according to a law of number. Moreover, when we say that what has become IS become and what becomes IS becoming, and that what will become IS about to become and that the non-existent IS non-existent—all these are inaccurate modes of expression (compare Parmen.). But perhaps this whole subject will be more suitably discussed on some other occasion.

Time, then, and the heaven came into being at the same instant in order that, having been created together, if ever there was to be a dissolution of them, they might be dissolved together. It was framed after the pattern of the eternal nature, that it might resemble this as far as was possible; for the pattern exists from eternity, and the created heaven has been, and is, and will be, in all time. Such was the mind and thought of God in the creation of time. The sun and moon and five other stars, which are called the planets, were created by him in order to distinguish and preserve the numbers of time; and when he had made their several bodies, he placed them in the orbits in which the circle of the other was revolving,—in seven orbits seven stars. First, there was the moon in the orbit nearest the earth, and next the sun, in the second orbit above the earth; then came the morning star and the star sacred to Hermes, moving in orbits which have an equal swiftness with the sun, but in an opposite direction; and this is the reason why the sun and Hermes and Lucifer overtake and are overtaken by each other. To enumerate the places which he assigned to the other stars, and to give all the reasons why he assigned them, although a secondary matter, would give more trouble than the primary. These things at some future time, when we are at leisure, may have the consideration which they deserve, but not at present.

Now, when all the stars which were necessary to the creation of time had attained a motion suitable to them, and had become living creatures having bodies fastened by vital chains, and learnt their appointed task, moving in the motion of the diverse, which is diagonal, and passes through and is governed by the motion of the same, they revolved, some in a larger and some in a lesser orbit—those which had the lesser orbit revolving faster, and those which had the larger more slowly. Now by reason of the motion of the same, those which revolved fastest appeared to be overtaken by those which moved slower although they really overtook them; for the motion of the same made them all turn in a spiral, and, because some went one way and some another, that which receded most slowly from the sphere of the same, which was the swiftest, appeared to follow it most nearly. That there might be some visible measure of their relative swiftness and slowness as they proceeded in their eight courses, God lighted a fire, which we now call the sun, in the second from the earth of these orbits, that it might give light to the whole of heaven, and that the animals, as many as nature intended, might participate in number, learning arithmetic from the revolution of the same and the like. Thus then, and for this reason the night and the day were created, being the period of the one most intelligent revolution. And the month is accomplished when the moon has completed her orbit and overtaken the sun, and the year when the sun has completed his own orbit. Mankind, with hardly an exception, have not remarked the periods of the other stars, and they have no name for them, and do not measure them against one another by the help of number, and hence they can scarcely be said to know that their wanderings, being infinite in number and admirable for their variety, make up time. And yet there is no difficulty in seeing that the perfect number of time fulfils the perfect year when all the eight revolutions, having their relative degrees of swiftness, are accomplished together and attain their completion at the same time, measured by the rotation of the same and equally moving. After this manner, and for these reasons, came into being such of the stars as in their heavenly progress received reversals of motion, to the end that the created heaven might imitate the eternal nature, and be as like as possible to the perfect and intelligible animal.

Thus far and until the birth of time the created universe was made in the likeness of the original, but inasmuch as all animals were not yet comprehended therein, it was still unlike. What remained, the creator then proceeded to fashion after the nature of the pattern. Now as in the ideal animal the mind perceives ideas or species of a certain nature and number, he thought that this created animal ought to have species of a like nature and number. There are four such; one of them is the heavenly race of the gods; another, the race of birds whose way is in the air; the third, the watery species; and the fourth, the pedestrian and land creatures. Of the heavenly and divine, he created the greater part out of fire, that they might be the brightest of all things and fairest to behold, and he fashioned them after the likeness of the universe in the figure of a circle, and made them follow the intelligent motion of the supreme, distributing them over the whole circumference of heaven, which was to be a true cosmos or glorious world spangled with them all over. And he gave to each of them two movements: the first, a movement on the same spot after the same manner, whereby they ever continue to think consistently the same thoughts about the same things; the second, a forward movement, in which they are controlled by the revolution of the same and the like; but by the other five motions they were unaffected, in order that each of them might attain the highest perfection. And for this reason the fixed stars were created, to be divine and eternal animals, ever-abiding and revolving after the same manner and on the same spot; and the other stars which reverse their motion and are subject to deviations of this kind, were created in the manner already described. The earth, which is our nurse, clinging (or 'circling') around the pole which is extended through the universe, he framed to be the guardian and artificer of night and day, first and eldest of gods that are in the interior of heaven. Vain would be the attempt to tell all the figures of them circling as in dance, and their juxtapositions, and the return of them in their revolutions upon themselves, and their approximations, and to say which of these deities in their conjunctions meet, and which of them are in opposition, and in what order they get behind and before one another, and when they are severally eclipsed to our sight and again reappear, sending terrors and intimations of the future to those who cannot calculate their movements—to attempt to tell of all this without a visible representation of the heavenly system would be labour in vain. Enough on this head; and now let what we have said about the nature of the created and visible gods have an end.

To know or tell the origin of the other divinities is beyond us, and we must accept the traditions of the men of old time who affirm themselves to be the offspring of the gods—that is what they say—and they must surely have known their own ancestors. How can we doubt the word of the children of the gods? Although they give no probable or certain proofs, still, as they declare that they are speaking of what took place in their own family, we must conform to custom and believe them. In this manner, then, according to them, the genealogy of these gods is to be received and set forth.

Oceanus and Tethys were the children of Earth and Heaven, and from these sprang Phorcys and Cronos and Rhea, and all that generation; and from Cronos and Rhea sprang Zeus and Here, and all those who are said to be their brethren, and others who were the children of these.

Now, when all of them, both those who visibly appear in their revolutions as well as those other gods who are of a more retiring nature, had come into being, the creator of the universe addressed them in these words: 'Gods, children of gods, who are my works, and of whom I am the artificer and father, my creations are indissoluble, if so I will. All that is bound may be undone, but only an evil being would wish to undo that which is harmonious and happy. Wherefore, since ye are but creatures, ye are not altogether immortal and indissoluble, but ye shall certainly not be dissolved, nor be liable to the fate of death, having in my will a greater and mightier bond than those with which ye were bound at the time of your birth. And now listen to my instructions:— Three tribes of mortal beings remain to be created—without them the universe will be incomplete, for it will not contain every kind of animal which it ought to contain, if it is to be perfect. On the other hand, if they were created by me and received life at my hands, they would be on an equality with the gods. In order then that they may be mortal, and that this universe may be truly universal, do ye, according to your natures, betake yourselves to the formation of animals, imitating the power which was shown by me in creating you. The part of them worthy of the name immortal, which is called divine and is the guiding principle of those who are willing to follow justice and you—of that divine part I will myself sow the seed, and having made a beginning, I will hand the work over to you. And do ye then interweave the mortal with the immortal, and make and beget living creatures, and give them food, and make them to grow, and receive them again in death.'

Thus he spake, and once more into the cup in which he had previously mingled the soul of the universe he poured the remains of the elements, and mingled them in much the same manner; they were not, however, pure as before, but diluted to the second and third degree. And having made it he divided the whole mixture into souls equal in number to the stars, and assigned each soul to a star; and having there placed them as in a chariot, he showed them the nature of the universe, and declared to them the laws of destiny, according to which their first birth would be one and the same for all,—no one should suffer a disadvantage at his hands; they were to be sown in the instruments of time severally adapted to them, and to come forth the most religious of animals; and as human nature was of two kinds, the superior race would hereafter be called man. Now, when they should be implanted in bodies by necessity, and be always gaining or losing some part of their bodily substance, then in the first place it would be necessary that they should all have in them one and the same faculty of sensation, arising out of irresistible impressions; in the second place, they must have love, in which pleasure and pain mingle; also fear and anger, and the feelings which are akin or opposite to them; if they conquered these they would live righteously, and if they were conquered by them, unrighteously. He who lived well during his appointed time was to return and dwell in his native star, and there he would have a blessed and congenial existence. But if he failed in attaining this, at the second birth he would pass into a woman, and if, when in that state of being, he did not desist from evil, he would continually be changed into some brute who resembled him in the evil nature which he had acquired, and would not cease from his toils and transformations until he followed the revolution of the same and the like within him, and overcame by the help of reason the turbulent and irrational mob of later accretions, made up of fire and air and water and earth, and returned to the form of his first and better state. Having given all these laws to his creatures, that he might be guiltless of future evil in any of them, the creator sowed some of them in the earth, and some in the moon, and some in the other instruments of time; and when he had sown them he committed to the younger gods the fashioning of their mortal bodies, and desired them to furnish what was still lacking to the human soul, and having made all the suitable additions, to rule over them, and to pilot the mortal animal in the best and wisest manner which they could, and avert from him all but self-inflicted evils.

When the creator had made all these ordinances he remained in his own accustomed nature, and his children heard and were obedient to their father's word, and receiving from him the immortal principle of a mortal creature, in imitation of their own creator they borrowed portions of fire, and earth, and water, and air from the world, which were hereafter to be restored—these they took and welded them together, not with the indissoluble chains by which they were themselves bound, but with little pegs too small to be visible, making up out of all the four elements each separate body, and fastening the courses of the immortal soul in a body which was in a state of perpetual influx and efflux. Now these courses, detained as in a vast river, neither overcame nor were overcome; but were hurrying and hurried to and fro, so that the whole animal was moved and progressed, irregularly however and irrationally and anyhow, in all the six directions of motion, wandering backwards and forwards, and right and left, and up and down, and in all the six directions. For great as was the advancing and retiring flood which provided nourishment, the affections produced by external contact caused still greater tumult—when the body of any one met and came into collision with some external fire, or with the solid earth or the gliding waters, or was caught in the tempest borne on the air, and the motions produced by any of these impulses were carried through the body to the soul. All such motions have consequently received the general name of 'sensations,' which they still retain. And they did in fact at that time create a very great and mighty movement; uniting with the ever-flowing stream in stirring up and violently shaking the courses of the soul, they completely stopped the revolution of the same by their opposing current, and hindered it from predominating and advancing; and they so disturbed the nature of the other or diverse, that the three double intervals (i.e. between 1, 2, 4, 8), and the three triple intervals (i.e. between 1, 3, 9, 27), together with the mean terms and connecting links which are expressed by the ratios of 3:2, and 4:3, and of 9:8—these, although they cannot be wholly undone except by him who united them, were twisted by them in all sorts of ways, and the circles were broken and disordered in every possible manner, so that when they moved they were tumbling to pieces, and moved irrationally, at one time in a reverse direction, and then again obliquely, and then upside down, as you might imagine a person who is upside down and has his head leaning upon the ground and his feet up against something in the air; and when he is in such a position, both he and the spectator fancy that the right of either is his left, and the left right. If, when powerfully experiencing these and similar effects, the revolutions of the soul come in contact with some external thing, either of the class of the same or of the other, they speak of the same or of the other in a manner the very opposite of the truth; and they become false and foolish, and there is no course or revolution in them which has a guiding or directing power; and if again any sensations enter in violently from without and drag after them the whole vessel of the soul, then the courses of the soul, though they seem to conquer, are really conquered.

And by reason of all these affections, the soul, when encased in a mortal body, now, as in the beginning, is at first without intelligence; but when the flood of growth and nutriment abates, and the courses of the soul, calming down, go their own way and become steadier as time goes on, then the several circles return to their natural form, and their revolutions are corrected, and they call the same and the other by their right names, and make the possessor of them to become a rational being. And if these combine in him with any true nurture or education, he attains the fulness and health of the perfect man, and escapes the worst disease of all; but if he neglects education he walks lame to the end of his life, and returns imperfect and good for nothing to the world below. This, however, is a later stage; at present we must treat more exactly the subject before us, which involves a preliminary enquiry into the generation of the body and its members, and as to how the soul was created—for what reason and by what providence of the gods; and holding fast to probability, we must pursue our way.

First, then, the gods, imitating the spherical shape of the universe, enclosed the two divine courses in a spherical body, that, namely, which we now term the head, being the most divine part of us and the lord of all that is in us: to this the gods, when they put together the body, gave all the other members to be servants, considering that it partook of every sort of motion. In order then that it might not tumble about among the high and deep places of the earth, but might be able to get over the one and out of the other, they provided the body to be its vehicle and means of locomotion; which consequently had length and was furnished with four limbs extended and flexible; these God contrived to be instruments of locomotion with which it might take hold and find support, and so be able to pass through all places, carrying on high the dwelling-place of the most sacred and divine part of us. Such was the origin of legs and hands, which for this reason were attached to every man; and the gods, deeming the front part of man to be more honourable and more fit to command than the hinder part, made us to move mostly in a forward direction. Wherefore man must needs have his front part unlike and distinguished from the rest of his body.

And so in the vessel of the head, they first of all put a face in which they inserted organs to minister in all things to the providence of the soul, and they appointed this part, which has authority, to be by nature the part which is in front. And of the organs they first contrived the eyes to give light, and the principle according to which they were inserted was as follows: So much of fire as would not burn, but gave a gentle light, they formed into a substance akin to the light of every-day life; and the pure fire which is within us and related thereto they made to flow through the eyes in a stream smooth and dense, compressing the whole eye, and especially the centre part, so that it kept out everything of a coarser nature, and allowed to pass only this pure element. When the light of day surrounds the stream of vision, then like falls upon like, and they coalesce, and one body is formed by natural affinity in the line of vision, wherever the light that falls from within meets with an external object. And the whole stream of vision, being similarly affected in virtue of similarity, diffuses the motions of what it touches or what touches it over the whole body, until they reach the soul, causing that perception which we call sight. But when night comes on and the external and kindred fire departs, then the stream of vision is cut off; for going forth to an unlike element it is changed and extinguished, being no longer of one nature with the surrounding atmosphere which is now deprived of fire: and so the eye no longer sees, and we feel disposed to sleep. For when the eyelids, which the gods invented for the preservation of sight, are closed, they keep in the internal fire; and the power of the fire diffuses and equalizes the inward motions; when they are equalized, there is rest, and when the rest is profound, sleep comes over us scarce disturbed by dreams; but where the greater motions still remain, of whatever nature and in whatever locality, they engender corresponding visions in dreams, which are remembered by us when we are awake and in the external world. And now there is no longer any difficulty in understanding the creation of images in mirrors and all smooth and bright surfaces. For from the communion of the internal and external fires, and again from the union of them and their numerous transformations when they meet in the mirror, all these appearances of necessity arise, when the fire from the face coalesces with the fire from the eye on the bright and smooth surface. And right appears left and left right, because the visual rays come into contact with the rays emitted by the object in a manner contrary to the usual mode of meeting; but the right appears right, and the left left, when the position of one of the two concurring lights is reversed; and this happens when the mirror is concave and its smooth surface repels the right stream of vision to the left side, and the left to the right (He is speaking of two kinds of mirrors, first the plane, secondly the concave; and the latter is supposed to be placed, first horizontally, and then vertically.). Or if the mirror be turned vertically, then the concavity makes the countenance appear to be all upside down, and the lower rays are driven upwards and the upper downwards.

All these are to be reckoned among the second and co-operative causes which God, carrying into execution the idea of the best as far as possible, uses as his ministers. They are thought by most men not to be the second, but the prime causes of all things, because they freeze and heat, and contract and dilate, and the like. But they are not so, for they are incapable of reason or intellect; the only being which can properly have mind is the invisible soul, whereas fire and water, and earth and air, are all of them visible bodies. The lover of intellect and knowledge ought to explore causes of intelligent nature first of all, and, secondly, of those things which, being moved by others, are compelled to move others. And this is what we too must do. Both kinds of causes should be acknowledged by us, but a distinction should be made between those which are endowed with mind and are the workers of things fair and good, and those which are deprived of intelligence and always produce chance effects without order or design. Of the second or co-operative causes of sight, which help to give to the eyes the power which they now possess, enough has been said. I will therefore now proceed to speak of the higher use and purpose for which God has given them to us. The sight in my opinion is the source of the greatest benefit to us, for had we never seen the stars, and the sun, and the heaven, none of the words which we have spoken about the universe would ever have been uttered. But now the sight of day and night, and the months and the revolutions of the years, have created number, and have given us a conception of time, and the power of enquiring about the nature of the universe; and from this source we have derived philosophy, than which no greater good ever was or will be given by the gods to mortal man. This is the greatest boon of sight: and of the lesser benefits why should I speak? even the ordinary man if he were deprived of them would bewail his loss, but in vain. Thus much let me say however: God invented and gave us sight to the end that we might behold the courses of intelligence in the heaven, and apply them to the courses of our own intelligence which are akin to them, the unperturbed to the perturbed; and that we, learning them and partaking of the natural truth of reason, might imitate the absolutely unerring courses of God and regulate our own vagaries. The same may be affirmed of speech and hearing: they have been given by the gods to the same end and for a like reason. For this is the principal end of speech, whereto it most contributes. Moreover, so much of music as is adapted to the sound of the voice and to the sense of hearing is granted to us for the sake of harmony; and harmony, which has motions akin to the revolutions of our souls, is not regarded by the intelligent votary of the Muses as given by them with a view to irrational pleasure, which is deemed to be the purpose of it in our day, but as meant to correct any discord which may have arisen in the courses of the soul, and to be our ally in bringing her into harmony and agreement with herself; and rhythm too was given by them for the same reason, on account of the irregular and graceless ways which prevail among mankind generally, and to help us against them.

Thus far in what we have been saying, with small exception, the works of intelligence have been set forth; and now we must place by the side of them in our discourse the things which come into being through necessity — for the creation is mixed, being made up of necessity and mind. Mind, the ruling power, persuaded necessity to bring the greater part of created things to perfection, and thus and after this manner in the beginning, when the influence of reason got the better of necessity, the universe was created. But if a person will truly tell of the way in which the work was accomplished, he must include the other influence of the variable cause as well. Wherefore, we must return again and find another suitable beginning, as about the former matters, so also about these. To which end we must consider the nature of fire, and water, and air, and earth, such as they were prior to the creation of the heaven, and what was happening to them in this previous state; for no one has as yet explained the manner of their generation, but we speak of fire and the rest of them, whatever they mean, as though men knew their natures, and we maintain them to be the first principles and letters or elements of the whole, when they cannot reasonably be compared by a man of any sense even to syllables or first compounds. And let me say thus much: I will not now speak of the first principle or principles of all things, or by whatever name they are to be called, for this reason — because it is difficult to set forth my opinion according to the method of discussion which we are at present employing. Do not imagine, any more than I can bring myself to imagine, that I should be right in undertaking so great and difficult a task. Remembering what I said at first about probability, I will do my best to give as probable an explanation as any other — or rather, more probable; and I will first go back to the beginning and try to speak of each thing and of all. Once more, then, at the commencement of my discourse, I call upon God, and beg him to be our saviour out of a strange and unwonted enquiry, and to bring us to the haven of probability. So now let us begin again.

This new beginning of our discussion of the universe requires a fuller division than the former; for then we made two classes, now a third must be revealed. The two sufficed for the former discussion: one, which we assumed, was a pattern intelligible and always the same; and the second was only the imitation of the pattern, generated and visible. There is also a third kind which we did not distinguish at the time, conceiving that the two would be enough. But now the argument seems to require that we should set forth in words another kind, which is difficult of explanation and dimly seen. What nature are we to attribute to this new kind of being? We reply, that it is the receptacle, and in a manner the nurse, of all generation. I have spoken the truth; but I must express myself in clearer language, and this will be an arduous task for many reasons, and in particular because I must first raise questions concerning fire and the other elements, and determine what each of them is; for to say, with any probability or certitude, which of them should be called water rather than fire, and which should be called any of them rather than all or some one of them, is a difficult matter. How, then, shall we settle this point, and what questions about the elements may be fairly raised?

In the first place, we see that what we just now called water, by condensation, I suppose, becomes stone and earth; and this same element, when melted and dispersed, passes into vapour and air. Air, again, when inflamed, becomes fire; and again fire, when condensed and extinguished, passes once more into the form of air; and once more, air, when collected and condensed, produces cloud and mist; and from these, when still more compressed, comes flowing water, and from water comes earth and stones once more; and thus generation appears to be transmitted from one to the other in a circle. Thus, then, as the several elements never present themselves in the same form, how can any one have the assurance to assert positively that any of them, whatever it may be, is one thing rather than another? No one can. But much the safest plan is to speak of them as follows:—Anything which we see to be continually changing, as, for example, fire, we must not call 'this' or 'that,' but rather say that it is 'of such a nature'; nor let us speak of water as 'this'; but always as 'such'; nor must we imply that there is any stability in any of those things which we indicate by the use of the words 'this' and 'that,' supposing ourselves to signify something thereby; for they are too volatile to be detained in any such expressions as 'this,' or 'that,' or 'relative to this,' or any other mode of speaking which represents them as permanent. We ought not to apply 'this' to any of them, but rather the word 'such'; which expresses the similar principle circulating in each and all of them; for example, that should be called 'fire' which is of such a nature always, and so of everything that has generation. That in which the elements severally grow up, and appear, and decay, is alone to be called by the name 'this' or 'that'; but that which is of a certain nature, hot or white, or anything which admits of opposite qualities, and all things that are compounded of them, ought not to be so denominated. Let me make another attempt to explain my meaning more clearly. Suppose a person to make all kinds of figures of gold and to be

23

always transmuting one form into all the rest;—somebody points to one of them and asks what it is. By far the safest and truest answer is, That is gold; and not to call the triangle or any other figures which are formed in the gold 'these,' as though they had existence, since they are in process of change while he is making the assertion; but if the questioner be willing to take the safe and indefinite expression, 'such,' we should be satisfied. And the same argument applies to the universal nature which receives all bodies—that must be always called the same; for, while receiving all things, she never departs at all from her own nature, and never in any way, or at any time, assumes a form like that of any of the things which enter into her; she is the natural recipient of all impressions, and is stirred and informed by them, and appears different from time to time by reason of them. But the forms which enter into and go out of her are the likenesses of real existences modelled after their patterns in a wonderful and inexplicable manner, which we will hereafter investigate. For the present we have only to conceive of three natures: first, that which is in process of generation; secondly, that in which the generation takes place; and thirdly, that of which the thing generated is a resemblance. And we may liken the receiving principle to a mother, and the source or spring to a father, and the intermediate nature to a child; and may remark further, that if the model is to take every variety of form, then the matter in which the model is fashioned will not be duly prepared, unless it is formless, and free from the impress of any of those shapes which it is hereafter to receive from without. For if the matter were like any of the supervening forms, then whenever any opposite or entirely different nature was stamped upon its surface, it would take the impression badly, because it would intrude its own shape. Wherefore, that which is to receive all forms should have no form; as in making perfumes they first contrive that the liquid substance which is to receive the scent shall be as inodorous as possible; or as those who wish to impress figures on soft substances do not allow any previous impression to remain, but begin by making the surface as even and smooth as possible. In the same way that which is to receive perpetually and through its whole extent the resemblances of all eternal beings ought to be devoid of any particular form. Wherefore, the mother and receptacle of all created and visible and in any way sensible things, is not to be termed earth, or air, or fire, or water, or any of their compounds or any of the elements from which these are derived, but is an invisible and formless being which receives all things and in some mysterious way partakes of the intelligible, and is most incomprehensible. In saying this we shall not be far wrong; as far, however, as we can attain to a knowledge of her from the previous considerations, we may truly say that fire is that part of her nature which from time to time is inflamed, and water that which is moistened, and that the mother substance becomes earth and air, in so far as she receives the impressions of them.

Let us consider this question more precisely. Is there any self-existent fire? and do all those things which we call self-existent exist? or are only those things which we see, or in some way perceive through the bodily organs, truly existent, and nothing whatever besides them? And is all that which we call an intelligible essence nothing at all, and only a name? Here is a question which we must not leave unexamined or undetermined, nor must we affirm too confidently that there can be no decision; neither must we interpolate in our present long discourse a digression equally long, but if it is possible to set forth a great principle in a few words, that is just what we want.

Thus I state my view:—If mind and true opinion are two distinct classes, then I say that there certainly are these self-existent ideas unperceived by sense, and apprehended only by the mind; if, however, as some say, true opinion differs in no respect from mind, then everything that we perceive through the body is to be regarded as most real and certain. But we must affirm them to be distinct, for they have a distinct origin and are of a different nature; the one is implanted in us by instruction, the other by persuasion; the one is always accompanied by true reason, the other is without reason; the one cannot be overcome by persuasion, but the other can: and lastly, every man may be said to share in true opinion, but mind is the attribute of the gods and of very few men. Wherefore also we must acknowledge that there is one kind of being which is always the same, uncreated and indestructible, never receiving anything into itself from without, nor itself going out to any other, but invisible and imperceptible by any sense, and of which the contemplation is granted to intelligence only. And there is another nature of the same name with it, and like to it, perceived by sense, created, always in motion, becoming in place and again vanishing out of place, which is apprehended by opinion and sense. And there is a third nature, which is space, and is eternal, and admits not of destruction and provides a home for all created things, and is apprehended without the help of sense, by a kind of spurious reason, and is hardly real; which we beholding as in a dream, say of all existence that it must of necessity be in some place and occupy a space, but that what is neither in heaven nor in earth has no existence. Of these and other things of the same kind, relating to the true and waking reality of nature, we have only this dreamlike sense, and we are unable to cast off sleep and determine the truth about them. For an image, since the reality, after which it is modelled, does not belong to it, and it exists ever as the fleeting shadow of some other, must be inferred to be in another (i.e. in space), grasping existence in some way or other, or it could not be at all. But true and exact reason, vindicating the nature of true being, maintains that while two things (i.e. the image and space) are different they cannot exist one of them in the other and so be one and also two at the same time.

Thus have I concisely given the result of my thoughts; and my verdict is that being and space and generation, these three, existed in their three ways before the heaven; and that the nurse of generation, moistened by water and inflamed by fire, and receiving the forms of earth and air, and experiencing all the affections which accompany these, presented a strange variety of appearances; and being full of powers which were neither similar nor equally balanced, was never in any part in a state of equipoise, but swaying unevenly hither and thither, was shaken by them, and by its motion again shook them; and the elements when moved were separated and carried continually, some one way, some another; as, when grain is shaken and winnowed by fans and other instruments used in the threshing of corn, the close and heavy particles are borne away and settle in one direction, and the loose and light particles in another. In this manner, the four kinds or elements were then shaken by the receiving vessel, which, moving like a winnowing machine, scattered far away from one another the elements most unlike, and forced the most similar elements into close contact. Wherefore also the various elements had different places before they were arranged so as to form the universe. At first, they were all without reason and measure. But when the world began to get into order, fire and water and earth and air had only certain faint traces of themselves, and were altogether such as everything might be expected to be in the absence of God; this, I say, was their nature at that time, and God fashioned them by form and number. Let it be consistently maintained by us in all that we say that God made them as far as possible the fairest and best, out of things which were not fair and good. And now I will endeavour to show you the disposition and generation of them by an unaccustomed argument, which I am compelled to use; but I believe that you will be able to follow me, for your education has made you familiar with the methods of science.

In the first place, then, as is evident to all, fire and earth and water and air are bodies. And every sort of body possesses solidity, and every solid must necessarily be contained in planes; and every plane rectilinear figure is composed of triangles; and all triangles are originally of two kinds, both of which are made up of one right and two acute angles; one of them has at either end of the base the half of a divided right angle, having equal sides, while in the other the right angle is divided into unequal parts, having unequal sides. These, then, proceeding by a combination of probability with demonstration, we assume to be the original elements of fire and the other bodies; but the principles which are prior to these God only knows, and he of men who is the friend of God. And next we have to determine what are the four most beautiful bodies which are unlike one another, and of which some are capable of resolution into one another; for having discovered thus much, we shall know the true origin of earth and fire and of the proportionate and intermediate elements. And then we shall not be willing to allow that there are any distinct kinds of visible bodies fairer than these. Wherefore we must endeavour to construct the four forms of bodies which excel in beauty, and then we shall be able to say that we have sufficiently apprehended their nature. Now of the two triangles, the isosceles has one form only; the scalene or unequal-sided has an infinite number. Of the infinite forms we must select the most beautiful, if we are to proceed in due order, and any one who can point out a more beautiful form than ours for the construction of these bodies, shall carry off the palm, not as an enemy, but as a friend. Now, the one which we maintain to be the most beautiful of all the many triangles (and we need not speak of the others) is that of which the double forms a third triangle which is equilateral; the reason of this would be long to tell; he who disproves what we are saying, and shows that we are mistaken, may claim a friendly victory. Then let us choose two triangles, out of which fire and the other elements have been constructed, one isosceles, the other having the square of the longer side equal to three times the square of the lesser side.

Now is the time to explain what was before obscurely said: there was an error in imagining that all the four elements might be generated by and into one another; this, I say, was an erroneous supposition, for there are generated from the triangles which we have selected four kinds—three from the one which has the sides unequal; the fourth alone is framed out of the isosceles triangle. Hence they cannot all be resolved into one another, a great number of small bodies being combined into a few large ones, or the converse. But three of them can be thus resolved and compounded, for they all spring from one, and when the greater bodies are broken up, many small bodies will spring up out of them and take their own proper figures; or, again, when many small bodies are dissolved into their triangles, if they become one, they will form one large mass of another kind. So much for their passage into one another. I have now to speak of their several kinds, and show out of what combinations of numbers each of them was formed. The first will be the simplest and smallest construction, and its element is that triangle which has its hypotenuse twice the lesser side. When two such triangles are joined at the diagonal, and this is repeated three times, and the triangles rest their diagonals and shorter sides on the same point as a centre, a single equilateral triangle is formed out of six triangles; and four equilateral triangles, if put together, make out of every three plane angles one solid angle, being that which is nearest to the most obtuse of plane angles; and out of the combination of these four angles arises the first solid form which distributes into equal and similar parts the whole circle in which it is inscribed. The second species of solid is formed out of the same triangles, which unite as eight equilateral triangles and form one solid angle out of four plane angles, and out of six such angles the second body is completed. And the third body is made up of 120 triangular elements, forming twelve solid angles, each of them included in five plane equilateral triangles, having altogether twenty bases, each of which is an equilateral triangle. The one element (that is, the triangle which has its hypotenuse twice the lesser side) having generated these figures, generated no more; but the isosceles triangle produced the fourth elementary figure, which is compounded of four such triangles, joining their right angles in a centre, and forming one equilateral quadrangle. Six of these united form eight solid angles, each of which is made by the combination of three plane right angles; the figure of the body thus composed is a cube, having six plane quadrangular equilateral bases. There was yet a fifth combination which God used in the delineation of the universe.

Now, he who, duly reflecting on all this, enquires whether the worlds are to be regarded as indefinite or definite in number, will be of opinion that the notion of their indefiniteness is characteristic of a sadly indefinite and ignorant mind. He, however, who raises the question whether they are to be truly regarded as one or five, takes up a more reasonable position. Arguing from probabilities, I am of opinion that they are one; another, regarding the question from another point of view, will be of another mind. But, leaving this enquiry, let us proceed to distribute the elementary forms, which have now been created in idea, among the four elements.

To earth, then, let us assign the cubical form; for earth is the most immoveable of the four and the most plastic of all bodies, and that which has the most stable bases must of necessity be of such a nature. Now, of the triangles which we assumed at first, that which has two equal sides is by nature more firmly based than that which has unequal sides; and of the compound figures which are formed out of either, the plane equilateral quadrangle has necessarily a more stable basis than the equilateral triangle, both in the whole and in the parts. Wherefore, in assigning this figure to earth, we adhere to probability; and to water we assign that one of the remaining forms which is the least moveable; and the most moveable of them to fire; and to air that which is intermediate. Also we assign the smallest body to fire, and the greatest to water, and the intermediate in size to air; and, again, the acutest body to fire, and the next in acuteness to air, and the third to water. Of all these elements, that which has the fewest bases must necessarily be the most moveable, for it must be the acutest and most penetrating in every way, and also the lightest as being composed of the smallest number of similar particles: and the second body has similar properties in a second degree, and the third body in the third degree. Let it be agreed, then, both according to strict reason and according to probability, that the pyramid is the solid which is the original element and seed of fire; and let us assign the element which was next in the order of generation to air, and the third to water. We must imagine all these to be so small that no single particle of any of the four kinds is seen by us on account of their smallness: but when many of them are collected together their aggregates are seen. And the ratios of their numbers, motions, and other properties, everywhere God, as far as necessity allowed or gave consent, has exactly perfected, and harmonized in due proportion.

From all that we have just been saying about the elements or kinds, the most probable conclusion is as follows:—earth, when meeting with fire and dissolved by its sharpness, whether the dissolution take place in the fire itself or perhaps in some mass of air or water, is borne hither and thither, until its parts, meeting together and mutually harmonising, again become earth; for they can never take any other form. But water, when divided by fire or by air, on re-forming, may become one part fire and two parts air; and a single volume of air divided becomes two of fire. Again, when a small body of fire is contained in a larger body of air or water or earth, and both are moving, and the fire struggling is overcome and broken up, then two volumes of fire form one volume of air; and when air is overcome and cut up into small pieces, two and a half parts of air are condensed into one part of water. Let us consider the matter in another way. When one of the other elements is fastened upon by fire, and is cut by the sharpness of its angles and sides, it coalesces with the fire, and then ceases to be cut by them any longer. For no element which is one and the same with itself can be changed by or change another of the same kind and in the same state. But so long as in the process of transition the weaker is fighting against the stronger, the dissolution continues. Again, when a few small particles, enclosed in many larger ones, are in process of decomposition and extinction, they only cease from their tendency to extinction when they consent to pass into the conquering nature, and fire becomes air and air water. But if bodies of another kind go and attack them (i.e. the small particles), the latter continue to be dissolved until, being completely forced back and dispersed, they make their escape to their own kindred, or else, being overcome and assimilated to the conquering power, they remain where they are and dwell with their victors, and from being many become one. And owing to these affections, all things are changing their place, for by the motion of the receiving vessel the bulk of each class is distributed into its proper place; but those things which become unlike themselves and like other things, are hurried by the shaking into the place of the things to which they grow like.

Now all unmixed and primary bodies are produced by such causes as these. As to the subordinate species which are included in the greater kinds, they are to be attributed to the varieties in the structure of the two original triangles. For either structure did not originally produce the triangle of one size only, but some larger and some smaller, and there are as many sizes as there are species of the four elements. Hence when they are mingled with themselves and with one another there is an endless variety of them, which those who would arrive at the probable truth of nature ought duly to consider.

Unless a person comes to an understanding about the nature and conditions of rest and motion, he will meet with many difficulties in the discussion which follows. Something has been said of this matter already, and something more remains to be said, which is, that motion never exists in what is uniform. For to conceive that anything can be moved without a mover is hard or indeed impossible, and equally impossible to conceive that there can be a mover unless there be something which can be moved—motion cannot exist where either of these are wanting, and for these to be uniform is impossible; wherefore we must assign rest to uniformity and motion to the want of uniformity. Now inequality is the cause of the nature which is wanting in uniformity; and of this we have already described the origin. But there still remains the further point—why things when divided after their kinds do not cease to pass through one another and to change their place — which we will now proceed to explain. In the revolution of the universe are comprehended all the four elements, and this being circular and having a tendency to come together, compresses everything and will not allow any place to be left void. Wherefore, also, fire above all things penetrates everywhere, and air next, as being next in rarity of the elements; and the two other elements in like manner penetrate according to their degrees of rarity. For those things which are composed of the largest particles have the largest void left in their compositions, and those which are composed of the smallest particles have the least. And the contraction caused by the compression thrusts the smaller particles into the interstices of the larger. And thus, when the small parts are placed side by side with the larger, and the lesser divide the greater and the greater unite the lesser, all the elements are borne up and down and hither and thither towards their own places; for the change in the size of each changes its position in space. And these causes generate an inequality which is always maintained, and is continually creating a perpetual motion of the elements in all time.

# From *Metaphysics*
By Aristotle
Tr. W. D. Ross

## Book I

## Part 1

"ALL men by nature desire to know. An indication of this is the delight we take in our senses; for even apart from their usefulness they are loved for themselves; and above all others the sense of sight. For not only with a view to action, but even when we are not going to do anything, we prefer seeing (one might say) to everything else. The reason is that this, most of all the senses, makes us know and brings to light many differences between things.

"By nature animals are born with the faculty of sensation, and from sensation memory is produced in some of them, though not in others. And therefore the former are more intelligent and apt at learning than those which cannot remember; those which are incapable of hearing sounds are intelligent though they cannot be taught, e.g. the bee, and any other race of animals that may be like it; and those which besides memory have this sense of hearing can be taught.

"The animals other than man live by appearances and memories, and have but little of connected experience; but the human race lives also by art and reasonings. Now from memory experience is produced in men; for the several memories of the same thing produce finally the capacity for a single experience. And experience seems pretty much like science and art, but really science and art come to men through experience; for 'experience made art', as Polus says, 'but inexperience luck.' Now art arises when from many notions gained by experience one universal judgement about a class of objects is produced. For to have a judgement that when Callias was ill of this disease this did him good, and similarly in the case of Socrates and in many individual cases, is a matter of experience; but to judge that it has done good to all persons of a certain constitution, marked off in one class, when they were ill of this disease, e.g. to phlegmatic or bilious people when burning with fevers-this is a matter of art.

"With a view to action experience seems in no respect inferior to art, and men of experience succeed even better than those who have theory without experience. (The reason is that experience is knowledge of individuals, art of universals, and actions and productions are all concerned with the individual; for the physician does not cure man, except in an incidental way, but Callias or Socrates or some other called by some such individual name, who happens to be a man. If, then, a man has the theory without the experience, and recognizes the universal but does not know the individual included in this, he will often fail to cure; for it is the individual that is to be cured.) But yet we think that knowledge and understanding belong to art rather than to experience, and we suppose artists to be wiser than men of experience (which implies that Wisdom depends in all cases rather on knowledge); and this because the former know the cause, but the latter do not. For men of experience know that the thing is so, but do not know why, while the others know the 'why' and the cause. Hence we think also that the masterworkers in each craft are more honourable and know in a truer sense and are wiser than the manual workers, because they know the causes of the things that are done (we think the manual workers are like certain lifeless things which act indeed, but act without knowing what they do, as fire burns,-but while the lifeless things perform each of their functions by a natural tendency, the labourers perform them through habit); thus we view them as being wiser not in virtue of being able to act, but of having the theory for themselves and knowing the causes. And in general it is a sign of the man who knows and of the man who does not know, that the former can teach, and therefore we think art more truly knowledge than experience is; for artists can teach, and men of mere experience cannot.

"Again, we do not regard any of the senses as Wisdom; yet surely these give the most authoritative knowledge of particulars. But they do not tell us the 'why' of anything-e.g. why fire is hot; they only say that it is hot.

"At first he who invented any art whatever that went beyond the common perceptions of man was naturally admired by men, not only because there was something useful in the inventions, but because he was thought wise and superior to the rest. But as more arts were invented, and some were directed to the necessities of life, others to recreation, the inventors of the latter were naturally always regarded as wiser than the inventors of the former, because their branches of knowledge did not aim at utility. Hence when all such inventions were already established, the sciences which do not aim at giving pleasure or at the necessities of life were discovered, and first in the places where men first began to have leisure. This is why the mathematical arts were founded in Egypt; for there the priestly caste was allowed to be at leisure.

"We have said in the Ethics what the difference is between art and science and the other kindred faculties; but the point of our present discussion is this, that all men suppose what is called Wisdom to deal with the first causes and the principles of things; so that, as has been said before, the man of experience is thought to be wiser than the possessors of any sense-perception whatever, the artist wiser than the men of experience, the masterworker than the mechanic, and the theoretical kinds of knowledge to be more of the nature of Wisdom than the productive. Clearly then Wisdom is knowledge about certain principles and causes.

## Part 2

"Since we are seeking this knowledge, we must inquire of what kind are the causes and the principles, the knowledge of which is Wisdom. If one were to take the notions we have about the wise man, this might perhaps make the answer more evident. We suppose first, then, that the wise man knows all things, as far as possible, although he has not knowledge of each of them in detail; secondly, that he who can learn things that are difficult, and not easy for man to know, is wise (sense-perception is common to all, and therefore easy and no mark of Wisdom); again, that he who is more exact and more capable of teaching the causes is wiser, in every branch of knowledge; and that of the sciences, also, that which is desirable on its own account and for the sake of knowing it is more of the nature of Wisdom than that which is desirable on account of its results, and the superior science is more of the nature of Wisdom than the ancillary; for the wise man must not be ordered but must order, and he must not obey another, but the less wise must obey him.

"Such and so many are the notions, then, which we have about Wisdom and the wise. Now of these characteristics that of knowing all things must belong to him who has in the highest degree universal knowledge; for he knows in a sense all the instances that fall under the universal. And these things, the most universal, are on the whole the hardest for men to know; for they are farthest from the senses. And the most exact of the sciences are those which deal most with first principles; for those which involve fewer principles are more exact than those which involve additional principles, e.g. arithmetic than geometry. But the science which investigates causes is also instructive, in a higher degree, for the people who instruct us are those who tell the causes of each thing. And understanding and knowledge pursued for their own sake are found most in the knowledge of that which is most knowable (for he who chooses to know for the sake of knowing will choose most readily that which is most truly knowledge, and such is the knowledge of that which is most knowable); and the first principles and the causes are most knowable; for by reason of these, and from these, all other things come to be known, and not these by means of the things subordinate to them. And the science which knows to what end each thing must be done is the most authoritative of the sciences, and more authoritative than any ancillary science; and this end is the good of that thing, and in general the supreme good in the whole of nature. Judged by all the tests we have mentioned, then, the name in question falls to the same science; this must be a science that investigates the first principles and causes; for the good, i.e. the end, is one of the causes.

"That it is not a science of production is clear even from the history of the earliest philosophers. For it is owing to their wonder that men both now begin and at first began to philosophize; they wondered originally at the obvious difficulties, then advanced little by little and stated difficulties about the greater matters, e.g. about the phenomena of the moon and those of the sun and of the stars, and about the genesis of the universe. And a man who is puzzled and wonders thinks himself ignorant (whence even the lover of myth is in a sense a lover of Wisdom, for the myth is composed of wonders); therefore since they philosophized order to escape from ignorance, evidently they were pursuing science in order to know, and not for any utilitarian end. And this is confirmed by the facts; for it was when almost all the necessities of life and the things that make for comfort and recreation had been secured, that such knowledge began to be sought. Evidently then we do not seek it for the sake of any other advantage; but as the man is free, we say, who exists for his own sake and not for another's, so we pursue this as the only free science, for it alone exists for its own sake.

"Hence also the possession of it might be justly regarded as beyond human power; for in many ways human nature is in bondage, so that according to Simonides 'God alone can have this privilege', and it is unfitting that man should not be content to seek the knowledge that is suited to him. If, then, there is something in what the poets say, and jealousy is natural to the divine power, it would probably occur in this case above all, and all who excelled in this knowledge would be unfortunate. But the divine power cannot be jealous (nay, according to the proverb, 'bards tell a lie'), nor should any other science be thought more honourable than one of this sort. For the most divine science is also most honourable; and this science alone must be, in two ways, most divine. For the science which it would be most meet for God to have is a divine science, and so is any science that deals with divine objects; and this science alone has both these qualities; for (1) God is thought to be among the causes of all things and to be a first principle, and (2) such a science either God alone can have, or God above all others. All the sciences, indeed, are more necessary than this, but none is better.

"Yet the acquisition of it must in a sense end in something which is the opposite of our original inquiries. For all men begin, as we said, by wondering that things are as they are, as they do about self-moving marionettes, or about the solstices or the incommensurability of the diagonal of a square with the side; for it seems wonderful to all who have not yet seen the reason, that there is a thing which cannot be measured even by the smallest unit. But we must end in the contrary and, according to the proverb, the better state, as is the case in these instances too when men learn the cause; for there is nothing which would surprise a geometer so much as if the diagonal turned out to be commensurable.

"We have stated, then, what is the nature of the science we are searching for, and what is the mark which our search and our whole investigation must reach.

Part 3

"Evidently we have to acquire knowledge of the original causes (for we say we know each thing only when we think we recognize its first cause), and causes are spoken of in four senses. In one of these we mean the substance, i.e. the essence (for the 'why' is reducible finally to the definition, and the ultimate 'why' is a cause and principle); in another the matter or substratum, in a third the source of the change, and in a fourth the cause opposed to this, the purpose and the good (for this is the end of all generation and change). We have studied these causes sufficiently in our work on nature, but yet let us call to our aid those who have attacked the investigation of being and philosophized about reality before us. For obviously they too speak of certain principles and causes; to go over their views, then, will be of profit to the present inquiry, for we shall either find another kind of cause, or be more convinced of the correctness of those which we now maintain.

"Of the first philosophers, then, most thought the principles which were of the nature of matter were the only principles of all things. That of which all things that are consist, the first from which they come to be, the last into which they are resolved (the substance remaining, but changing in its modifications), this they say is the element and this the principle of things, and therefore they think nothing is either generated or destroyed, since this sort of entity is always conserved, as we say Socrates neither comes to be absolutely when he comes to be beautiful or musical, nor ceases to be when loses these characteristics, because the substratum, Socrates himself remains. just so they say nothing else comes to be or ceases to be; for there must be some entity-either one or more than one-from which all other things come to be, it being conserved.

"Yet they do not all agree as to the number and the nature of these principles. Thales, the founder of this type of philosophy, says the principle is water (for which reason he declared that the earth rests on water), getting the notion perhaps from seeing that the nutriment of all things is moist, and that heat itself is generated from the moist and kept alive by it (and that from which they come to be is a principle of all things). He got his notion from this fact, and from the fact that the seeds of all things have a moist nature, and that water is the origin of the nature of moist things.

"Some think that even the ancients who lived long before the present generation, and first framed accounts of the gods, had a similar view of nature; for they made Ocean and Tethys the parents of creation, and described the oath of the gods as being by water, to which they give the name of Styx; for what is oldest is most honourable, and the most honourable thing is that by which one swears. It may perhaps be uncertain whether this opinion about nature is primitive and ancient, but Thales at any rate is said to have declared himself thus about the first cause. Hippo no one would think fit to include among these thinkers, because of the paltriness of his thought.

"Anaximenes and Diogenes make air prior to water, and the most primary of the simple bodies, while Hippasus of Metapontium and Heraclitus of Ephesus say this of fire, and Empedocles says it of the four elements (adding a fourth-earth-to those which have been named); for these, he says, always remain and do not come to be, except that they come to be more or fewer, being aggregated into one and segregated out of one.

"Anaxagoras of Clazomenae, who, though older than Empedocles, was later in his philosophical activity, says the principles are infinite in number; for he says almost all the things that are made of parts like themselves, in the manner of water or fire, are generated and destroyed in this way, only by aggregation and segregation, and are not in any other sense generated or destroyed, but remain eternally.

"From these facts one might think that the only cause is the so-called material cause; but as men thus advanced, the very facts opened the way for them and joined in forcing them to investigate the subject. However true it may be that all generation and destruction proceed from some one or (for that matter) from more elements, why does this happen and what is the cause? For at least the substratum itself does not make itself change; e.g. neither the wood nor the bronze causes the change of either of them, nor does the wood manufacture a bed and the bronze a statue, but something else is the cause of the change. And to seek this is to seek the second cause, as we should say,-that from which comes the beginning of the movement. Now those who at the very beginning set themselves to this kind of inquiry, and said the substratum was one, were not at all dissatisfied with themselves; but some at least of those who maintain it to be one-as though defeated by this search for the second cause-say the one and nature as a whole is unchangeable not only in respect of generation and destruction (for this is a primitive belief, and all agreed in it), but also of all other change; and this view is peculiar to them. Of those who said the universe was one, then none succeeded in discovering a cause of this sort, except perhaps Parmenides, and he only inasmuch as he supposes that there is not only one but also in some sense two causes. But for those who make more elements it is more possible to state the second cause, e.g. for those who make hot and cold, or fire and earth, the elements; for they treat fire as having a nature which fits it to move things, and water and earth and such things they treat in the contrary way.

"When these men and the principles of this kind had had their day, as the latter were found inadequate to generate the nature of things men were again forced by the truth itself, as we said, to inquire into the next kind of cause. For it is not likely either that fire or earth or any such element should be the reason why things manifest goodness and, beauty both in their being and in their coming to be, or that those thinkers should have supposed it was;

nor again could it be right to entrust so great a matter to spontaneity and chance. When one man said, then, that reason was present-as in animals, so throughout nature-as the cause of order and of all arrangement, he seemed like a sober man in contrast with the random talk of his predecessors. We know that Anaxagoras certainly adopted these views, but Hermotimus of Clazomenae is credited with expressing them earlier. Those who thought thus stated that there is a principle of things which is at the same time the cause of beauty, and that sort of cause from which things acquire movement.

Part 4

"One might suspect that Hesiod was the first to look for such a thing-or some one else who put love or desire among existing things as a principle, as Parmenides, too, does; for he, in constructing the genesis of the universe, says:- "
"Love first of all the Gods she planned. "
"And Hesiod says:- "
"First of all things was chaos made, and then
"Broad-breasted earth...
"And love, 'mid all the gods pre-eminent, "
which implies that among existing things there must be from the first a cause which will move things and bring them together. How these thinkers should be arranged with regard to priority of discovery let us be allowed to decide later; but since the contraries of the various forms of good were also perceived to be present in nature-not only order and the beautiful, but also disorder and the ugly, and bad things in greater number than good, and ignoble things than beautiful-therefore another thinker introduced friendship and strife, each of the two the cause of one of these two sets of qualities. For if we were to follow out the view of Empedocles, and interpret it according to its meaning and not to its lisping expression, we should find that friendship is the cause of good things, and strife of bad. Therefore, if we said that Empedocles in a sense both mentions, and is the first to mention,

the bad and the good as principles, we should perhaps be right, since the cause of all goods is the good itself.

"These thinkers, as we say, evidently grasped, and to this extent, two of the causes which we distinguished in our work on nature-the matter and the source of the movement-vaguely, however, and with no clearness, but as untrained men behave in fights; for they go round their opponents and often strike fine blows, but they do not fight on scientific principles, and so too these thinkers do not seem to know what they say; for it is evident that, as a rule, they make no use of their causes except to a small extent. For Anaxagoras uses reason as a deus ex machina for the making of the world, and when he is at a loss to tell from what cause something necessarily is, then he drags reason in, but in all other cases ascribes events to anything rather than to reason. And Empedocles, though he uses the causes to a greater extent than this, neither does so sufficiently nor attains consistency in their use. At least, in many cases he makes love segregate things, and strife aggregate them. For whenever the universe is dissolved into its elements by strife, fire is aggregated into one, and so is each of the other elements; but whenever again under the influence of love they come together into one, the parts must again be segregated out of each element.

"Empedocles, then, in contrast with his precessors, was the first to introduce the dividing of this cause, not positing one source of movement, but different and contrary sources. Again, he was the first to speak of four material elements; yet he does not use four, but treats them as two only; he treats fire by itself, and its opposite-earth, air, and water-as one kind of thing. We may learn this by study of his verses.

"This philosopher then, as we say, has spoken of the principles in this way, and made them of this number. Leucippus and his associate Democritus say that the full and the empty are the elements, calling the one being and the other non-being-the full and solid being being, the empty non-being (whence they say being no more is than non-being, because the solid no more is than the empty); and they make these the material causes of things. And as those who make the underlying substance one generate all other things by its modifications, supposing the rare and the dense to be the sources of the modifications, in the same way these philosophers say the differences in the elements are the causes of all other qualities. These differences, they say, are three-shape and order and position. For they say the real is differentiated only by 'rhythm and 'inter-contact' and 'turning'; and of these rhythm is shape, inter-contact is order, and turning is position; for A differs from N in shape, AN from NA in order, M from W in position. The question of movement-whence or how it is to belong to things-these thinkers, like the others, lazily neglected.

"Regarding the two causes, then, as we say, the inquiry seems to have been pushed thus far by the early philosophers.

Part 5

"Contemporaneously with these philosophers and before them, the so-called Pythagoreans, who were the first to take up mathematics, not only advanced this study, but also having been brought up in it they thought its principles were the principles of all things. Since of these principles numbers are by nature the first, and in numbers they seemed to see many resemblances to the things that exist and come into being-more than in fire and earth and water (such and such a modification of numbers being justice, another being soul and reason, another being opportunity-and similarly almost all other things being numerically expressible); since, again, they saw that the modifications and the ratios of the musical scales were expressible in numbers;-since, then, all other things seemed in their whole nature to be modelled on numbers, and numbers seemed to be the first things in the whole of nature, they supposed the elements of numbers to be the elements of all things, and the whole heaven to be a musical scale and a number. And all the properties of numbers and scales which they could show to agree with the attributes and parts and the whole arrangement of the heavens, they collected and fitted into their scheme; and if there was a gap anywhere, they readily made additions so as to make their whole theory coherent. E.g. as the number 10 is thought to be perfect and to comprise the whole nature of numbers, they say that the bodies which move through the heavens are ten, but as the visible bodies are only nine, to meet this they invent a tenth--the 'counter-earth'. We have discussed these matters more exactly elsewhere.

"But the object of our review is that we may learn from these philosophers also what they suppose to be the principles and how these fall under the causes we have named. Evidently, then, these thinkers also consider that number is the principle both as matter for things and as forming both their modifications and their permanent states, and hold that the elements of number are the even and the odd, and that of these the latter is limited, and the former unlimited; and that the One proceeds from both of these (for it is both even and odd), and number from the One; and that the whole heaven, as has been said, is numbers.

"Other members of this same school say there are ten principles, which they arrange in two columns of cognates-limit and unlimited, odd and even, one and plurality, right and left, male and female, resting and moving, straight and curved, light and darkness, good and bad, square and oblong. In this way Alcmaeon of Croton seems also to have conceived the matter, and either he got this view from them or they got it from him; for he expressed himself similarly to them. For he says most human affairs go in pairs, meaning not definite contrarieties such as the Pythagoreans speak of, but any chance contrarieties, e.g. white and black, sweet and bitter, good and bad, great and small. He threw out indefinite suggestions about the other contrarieties, but the Pythagoreans declared both how many and which their contrarieties are.

"From both these schools, then, we can learn this much, that the contraries are the principles of things; and how many these principles are and which they are, we can learn from one of the two schools. But how these principles can be brought together under the causes we have named has not been clearly and articulately stated by them; they seem, however, to range the elements under the head of matter; for out of these as immanent parts they say substance is composed and moulded.

"From these facts we may sufficiently perceive the meaning of the ancients who said the elements of nature were more than one; but there are some who spoke of the universe as if it were one entity, though they were not all alike either in the excellence of their statement or in its conformity to the facts of nature. The discussion of them is in no way appropriate to our present investigation of causes, for. they do not, like some of the natural philosophers, assume being to be one and yet generate it out of the one as out of matter, but they speak in another way; those others add change, since they generate the universe, but these thinkers say the universe is unchangeable. Yet this much is germane to the present inquiry: Parmenides seems to fasten on that which is one in definition, Melissus on that which is one in matter, for which reason the former says that it is limited, the latter that it is unlimited; while Xenophanes, the first of these partisans of the One (for Parmenides is said to have been his pupil), gave no clear statement, nor does he seem to have grasped the nature of either of these causes, but with reference to the whole material universe he says the One is God. Now these thinkers, as we said, must be neglected for the purposes of the present inquiry-two of them entirely, as being a little too naive, viz. Xenophanes and Melissus; but Parmenides seems in places to speak with more insight. For, claiming that, besides the existent, nothing non-existent exists, he thinks that of necessity one thing exists, viz. the existent and nothing else (on this we have spoken more clearly in our work on nature), but being forced to follow the observed facts, and supposing the existence of that which is one in definition, but more than one according to our sensations, he now posits two causes and two principles, calling them hot and cold, i.e. fire and earth; and of these he ranges the hot with the existent, and the other with the non-existent.

"From what has been said, then, and from the wise men who have now sat in council with us, we have got thus much-on the one hand from the earliest philosophers, who regard the first principle as corporeal (for water and fire and such things are bodies), and of whom some suppose that there is one corporeal principle, others that there are more than one, but both put these under the head of matter; and on the other hand from some who posit both this cause and besides this the source of movement, which we have got from some as single and from others as twofold.

"Down to the Italian school, then, and apart from it, philosophers have treated these subjects rather obscurely, except that, as we said, they have in fact used two kinds of cause, and one of these-the source of movement-some treat as one and others as two. But the Pythagoreans have said in the same way that there are two principles, but added this much, which is peculiar to them, that they thought that finitude and infinity were not attributes of certain other things, e.g. of fire or earth or anything else of this kind, but that infinity itself and unity itself were the substance of the things of which they are predicated. This is why number was the substance of all things. On this subject, then, they expressed themselves thus; and regarding the question of essence they began to make statements and definitions, but treated the matter too simply. For they both defined superficially and thought that the first subject of which a given definition was predicable was the substance of the thing defined, as if one supposed that 'double' and '2' were the same, because 2 is the first thing of which 'double' is predicable. But surely to be double and to be 2 are not the same;

if they are, one thing will be many-a consequence which they actually drew. From the earlier philosophers, then, and from their successors we can learn thus much.

Part 6

"After the systems we have named came the philosophy of Plato, which in most respects followed these thinkers, but had pecullarities that distinguished it from the philosophy of the Italians. For, having in his youth first become familiar with Cratylus and with the Heraclitean doctrines (that all sensible things are ever in a state of flux and there is no knowledge about them), these views he held even in later years. Socrates, however, was busying himself about ethical matters and neglecting the world of nature as a whole but seeking the universal in these ethical matters, and fixed thought for the first time on definitions; Plato accepted his teaching, but held that the problem applied not to sensible things but to entities of another kind-for this reason, that the common definition could not be a definition of any sensible thing, as they were always changing. Things of this other sort, then, he called Ideas, and sensible things, he said, were all named after these, and in virtue of a relation to these; for the many existed by participation in the Ideas that have the same name as they. Only the name 'participation' was new; for the Pythagoreans say that things exist by 'imitation' of numbers, and Plato says they exist by participation, changing the name. But what the participation or the imitation of the Forms could be they left an open question.

"Further, besides sensible things and Forms he says there are the objects of mathematics, which occupy an intermediate position, differing from sensible things in being eternal and unchangeable, from Forms in that there are many alike, while the Form itself is in each case unique.

"Since the Forms were the causes of all other things, he thought their elements were the elements of all things. As matter, the great and the small were principles; as essential reality, the One; for from the great and the small, by participation in the One, come the Numbers.

"But he agreed with the Pythagoreans in saying that the One is substance and not a predicate of something else; and in saying that the Numbers are the causes of the reality of other things he agreed with them; but positing a dyad and constructing the infinite out of great and small, instead of treating the infinite as one, is peculiar to him; and so is his view that the Numbers exist apart from sensible things, while they say that the things themselves are Numbers, and do not place the objects of mathematics between Forms and sensible things. His divergence from the Pythagoreans in making the One and the Numbers separate from things, and his introduction of the Forms, were due to his inquiries in the region of definitions (for the earlier thinkers had no tincture of dialectic), and his making the other entity besides the One a dyad was due to the belief that the numbers, except those which were prime, could be neatly produced out of the dyad as out of some plastic material. Yet what happens is the contrary; the theory is not a reasonable one. For they make many things out of the matter, and the form generates only once, but what we observe is that one table is made from one matter, while the man who applies the form, though he is one, makes many tables. And the relation of the male to the female is similar; for the latter is impregnated by one copulation, but the male impregnates many females; yet these are analogues of those first principles.

"Plato, then, declared himself thus on the points in question; it is evident from what has been said that he has used only two causes, that of the essence and the material cause (for the Forms are the causes of the essence of all other things, and the One is the cause of the essence of the Forms); and it is evident what the underlying matter is, of which the Forms are predicated in the case of sensible things, and the One in the case of Forms, viz. that this is a dyad, the great and the small. Further, he has assigned the cause of good and that of evil to the elements, one to each of the two, as we say some of his predecessors sought to do, e.g. Empedocles and Anaxagoras.

## Part 7

"Our review of those who have spoken about first principles and reality and of the way in which they have spoken, has been concise and summary; but yet we have learnt this much from them, that of those who speak about 'principle' and 'cause' no one has mentioned any principle except those which have been distinguished in our work on nature, but all evidently have some inkling of them, though only vaguely. For some speak of the first principle as matter, whether they suppose one or more first principles, and whether they suppose this to be a body or to be incorporeal; e.g. Plato spoke of the great and the small, the Italians of the infinite, Empedocles of fire, earth, water, and air, Anaxagoras of the infinity of things composed of similar parts. These, then, have all had a notion of this kind of cause, and so have all who speak of air or fire or water, or something denser than fire and rarer than air; for some have said the prime element is of this kind.

"These thinkers grasped this cause only; but certain others have mentioned the source of movement, e.g. those who make friendship and strife, or reason, or love, a principle.

"The essence, i.e. the substantial reality, no one has expressed distinctly. It is hinted at chiefly by those who believe in the Forms; for they do not suppose either that the Forms are the matter of sensible things, and the One the matter of the Forms, or that they are the source of movement (for they say these are causes rather of immobility and of being at rest), but they furnish the Forms as the essence of every other thing, and the One as the essence of the Forms.

"That for whose sake actions and changes and movements take place, they assert to be a cause in a way, but not in this way, i.e. not in the way in which it is its nature to be a cause. For those who speak of reason or friendship class these causes as goods; they do not speak, however, as if anything that exists either existed or came into being for the sake of these, but as if movements started from these. In the same way those who say the One or the existent is the good, say that it is the cause of substance, but not that substance either is or comes to be for the sake of this. Therefore it turns out that in a sense they both say and do not say the good is a cause; for they do not call it a cause qua good but only incidentally.

"All these thinkers then, as they cannot pitch on another cause, seem to testify that we have determined rightly both how many and of what sort the causes are. Besides this it is plain that when the causes are being looked for, either all four must be sought thus or they must be sought in one of these four ways. Let us next discuss the possible difficulties with regard to the way in which each of these thinkers has spoken, and with regard to his situation relatively to the first principles.

Part 8

"Those, then, who say the universe is one and posit one kind of thing as matter, and as corporeal matter which has spatial magnitude, evidently go astray in many ways. For they posit the elements of bodies only, not of incorporeal things, though there are also incorporeal things. And in trying to state the causes of generation and destruction, and in giving a physical account of all things, they do away with the cause of movement. Further, they err in not positing the substance, i.e. the essence, as the cause of anything, and besides this in lightly calling any of the simple bodies except earth the first principle, without inquiring how they are produced out of one anothers-I mean fire, water, earth, and air. For some things are produced out of each other by combination, others by separation, and this makes the greatest difference to their priority and posteriority. For (1) in a way the property of being most elementary of all would seem to belong to the first thing from which they are produced by combination, and this property would belong to the most fine-grained and subtle of bodies. For this reason those who make fire the principle would be most in agreement with this argument. But each of the other thinkers agrees that the element of corporeal things is of this sort. At least none of those who named one element claimed that earth was the element, evidently because of the coarseness of its grain. (Of the other three elements each has found some judge on its side; for some maintain that fire, others that water, others that air is the element. Yet why, after all, do they not name earth also, as most men do? For people say all things are earth Hesiod says earth was produced first of corporeal things; so primitive and popular has the opinion been.) According to this argument, then, no one would be right who either says the first principle is any of the elements other than fire, or supposes it to be denser than air but rarer than water. But (2) if that which is later in generation is prior in nature, and that which is concocted and compounded is later in generation, the contrary of what we have been saying must be true,-water must be prior to air, and earth to water.

"So much, then, for those who posit one cause such as we mentioned; but the same is true if one supposes more of these, as Empedocles says matter of things is four bodies. For he too is confronted by consequences some of which are the same as have been mentioned, while others are peculiar to him. For we see these bodies produced from one another, which implies that the same body does not always remain fire or earth (we have spoken about this in our works on nature); and regarding the cause of movement and the question whether we must posit one or two, he must be thought to have spoken neither correctly nor altogether plausibly. And in general, change of quality is necessarily done away with for those who speak thus, for on their view cold will not come from hot nor hot from cold. For if it did there would be something that accepted the contraries themselves, and there would be some one entity that became fire and water, which Empedocles denies.

"As regards Anaxagoras, if one were to suppose that he said there were two elements, the supposition would accord thoroughly with an argument which Anaxagoras himself did not state articulately, but which he must have accepted if any one had led him on to it. True, to say that in the beginning all things were mixed is absurd both on other grounds and because it follows that they must have existed before in an unmixed form, and because nature does not allow any chance thing to be mixed with any chance thing, and also because on this view modifications and accidents could be separated from substances (for the same things which are mixed can be separated); yet if one were to follow him up, piecing together what he means, he would perhaps be seen to be somewhat modern in his views. For when nothing was separated out, evidently nothing could be truly asserted of the substance that then existed. I mean, e.g. that it was neither white nor black, nor grey nor any other colour, but of necessity colourless; for if it had been coloured, it would have had one of these colours. And similarly, by this same argument, it was flavourless, nor had it any similar attribute; for it could not be either of any quality or of any size, nor could it be any definite kind of thing. For if it were, one of the particular forms would have belonged to it, and this is impossible, since all were mixed together; for the particular form would necessarily have been already separated out, but he all were mixed except reason, and this alone was unmixed and pure. From this it follows, then, that he must say the principles are the One (for this is simple and unmixed) and the Other, which is of such a nature as we suppose the indefinite to be before it is defined and partakes of some form. Therefore, while expressing himself neither rightly nor clearly, he means something like what the later thinkers say and what is now more clearly seen to be the case.

"But these thinkers are, after all, at home only in arguments about generation and destruction and movement; for it is practically only of this sort of substance that they seek the principles and the causes. But those who extend their vision to all things that exist, and of existing things suppose some to be perceptible and others not perceptible, evidently study both classes, which is all the more reason why one should devote some time to seeing what is good in their views and what bad from the standpoint of the inquiry we have now before us.

"The 'Pythagoreans' treat of principles and elements stranger than those of the physical philosophers (the reason is that they got the principles from non-sensible things, for the objects of mathematics, except those of astronomy, are of the class of things without movement); yet their discussions and investigations are all about nature; for they generate the heavens, and with regard to their parts and attributes and functions they observe the phenomena, and use up the principles and the causes in explaining these, which implies that they agree with the others, the physical philosophers, that the real is just all that which is perceptible and contained by the so-called 'heavens'. But the causes and the principles which they mention are, as we said, sufficient to act as steps even up to the higher realms of reality, and are more suited to these than to theories about nature. They do not tell us at all, however, how there can be movement if limit and unlimited and odd and even are the only things assumed, or how without movement and change there can be generation and destruction, or the bodies that move through the heavens can do what they do.

"Further, if one either granted them that spatial magnitude consists of these elements, or this were proved, still how would some bodies be light and others have weight? To judge from what they assume and maintain they are speaking no more of mathematical bodies than of perceptible; hence they have said nothing whatever about fire or earth or the other bodies of this sort, I suppose because they have nothing to say which applies peculiarly to perceptible things.

"Further, how are we to combine the beliefs that the attributes of number, and number itself, are causes of what exists and happens in the heavens both from the beginning and now, and that there is no other number than this number out of which the world is composed? When in one particular region they place opinion and opportunity, and, a little above or below, injustice and decision or mixture, and allege, as proof, that each of these is a number, and that there happens to be already in this place a plurality of the extended bodies composed of numbers, because these attributes of number attach to the various places,-this being so, is this number, which we must suppose each of these abstractions to be, the same number which is exhibited in the material universe, or is it another than this? Plato says it is different; yet even he thinks that both these bodies and their causes are numbers, but that the intelligible numbers are causes, while the others are sensible.

Part 9

"Let us leave the Pythagoreans for the present; for it is enough to have touched on them as much as we have done. But as for those who posit the Ideas as causes, firstly, in seeking to grasp the causes of the things around us, they introduced others equal in number to these, as if a man who wanted to count things thought he would not be able to do it while they were few, but tried to count them when he had added to their number. For the Forms are practically equal to-or not fewer than-the things, in trying to explain which these thinkers proceeded from them to the Forms. For to each thing there answers an entity which has the same name and exists apart from the substances, and so also in the case of all other groups there is a one over many, whether the many are in this world or are eternal.

"Further, of the ways in which we prove that the Forms exist, none is convincing; for from some no inference necessarily follows, and from some arise Forms even of things of which we think there are no Forms. For according to the arguments from the existence of the sciences there will be Forms of all things of which there are sciences and according to the 'one over many' argument there will be Forms even of negations, and according to the argument that there is an object for thought even when the thing has perished, there will be Forms of perishable things; for we have an image of these. Further, of the more accurate arguments, some lead to Ideas of relations, of which we say there is no independent class, and others introduce the 'third man'.

"And in general the arguments for the Forms destroy the things for whose existence we are more zealous than for the existence of the Ideas; for it follows that not the dyad but number is first, i.e. that the relative is prior to the absolute,-besides all the other points on which certain people by following out the opinions held about the Ideas have come into conflict with the principles of the theory.

"Further, according to the assumption on which our belief in the Ideas rests, there will be Forms not only of substances but also of many other things (for the concept is single not only in the case of substances but also in the other cases, and there are sciences not only of substance but also of other things, and a thousand other such difficulties confront them). But according to the necessities of the case and the opinions held about the Forms, if Forms can be shared in there must be Ideas of substances only. For they are not shared in incidentally, but a thing must share in its Form as in something not predicated of a subject (by 'being shared in incidentally' I mean that e.g. if a thing shares in 'double itself', it shares also in 'eternal', but incidentally; for 'eternal' happens to be predicable of the 'double'). Therefore the Forms will be substance; but the same terms indicate substance in this and in the ideal world (or what will be the meaning of saying that there is something apart from the particulars-the one over many?). And if the Ideas and the particulars that share in them have the same form, there will be something common to these; for why should '2' be one and the same in the perishable 2's or in those which are many but eternal, and not the same in the '2' itself' as in the particular 2? But if they have not the same form, they must have only the name in common, and it is as if one were to call both Callias and a wooden image a 'man', without observing any community between them.

"Above all one might discuss the question what on earth the Forms contribute to sensible things, either to those that are eternal or to those that come into being and cease to be. For they cause neither movement nor any change in them. But again they help in no wise either towards the knowledge of the other things (for they are not even the substance of these, else they would have been in them), or towards their being, if they are not in the particulars which share in them; though if they were, they might be thought to be causes, as white causes whiteness in a white object by entering into its composition. But this argument, which first Anaxagoras and later Eudoxus and certain others used, is very easily upset; for it is not difficult to collect many insuperable objections to such a view.

"But, further, all other things cannot come from the Forms in any of the usual senses of 'from'. And to say that they are patterns and the other things share in them is to use empty words and poetical metaphors. For what is it that works, looking to the Ideas? And anything can either be, or become, like another without being copied from it, so that whether Socrates or not a man Socrates like might come to be; and evidently this might be so even if Socrates were eternal. And there will be several patterns of the same thing, and therefore several Forms; e.g. 'animal' and 'two-footed' and also 'man himself' will be Forms of man. Again, the Forms are patterns not only sensible things, but of Forms themselves also; i.e. the genus, as genus of various species, will be so; therefore the same thing will be pattern and copy.

"Again, it would seem impossible that the substance and that of which it is the substance should exist apart; how, therefore, could the Ideas, being the substances of things, exist apart? In the Phaedo' the case is stated in this way-that the Forms are causes both of being and of becoming; yet when the Forms exist, still the things that share in them do not come into being, unless there is something to originate movement; and many other things come into being (e.g. a house or a ring) of which we say there are no Forms. Clearly, therefore, even the other things can both be and come into being owing to such causes as produce the things just mentioned.

"Again, if the Forms are numbers, how can they be causes? Is it because existing things are other numbers, e.g. one number is man, another is Socrates, another Callias? Why then are the one set of numbers causes of the other set? It will not make any difference even if the former are eternal and the latter are not. But if it is because things in this sensible world (e.g. harmony) are ratios of numbers, evidently the things between which they are ratios are some one class of things. If, then, this--the matter--is some definite thing, evidently the numbers themselves too will be ratios of something to something else. E.g. if Callias is a numerical ratio between fire and earth and water and air, his Idea also will be a number of certain other underlying things; and man himself, whether it is a number in a sense or not, will still be a numerical ratio of certain things and not a number proper, nor will it be a of number merely because it is a numerical ratio.

"Again, from many numbers one number is produced, but how can one Form come from many Forms? And if the number comes not from the many numbers themselves but from the units in them, e.g. in 10,000, how is it with the units? If they are specifically alike, numerous absurdities will follow, and also if they are not alike (neither the units in one number being themselves like one another nor those in other numbers being all like to all); for in what will they differ, as they are without quality? This is not a plausible view, nor is it consistent with our thought on the matter.

"Further, they must set up a second kind of number (with which arithmetic deals), and all the objects which are called 'intermediate' by some thinkers; and how do these exist or from what principles do they proceed? Or why must they be intermediate between the things in this sensible world and the things-themselves?

"Further, the units in must each come from a prior but this is impossible.

"Further, why is a number, when taken all together, one?

"Again, besides what has been said, if the units are diverse the Platonists should have spoken like those who say there are four, or two, elements; for each of these thinkers gives the name of element not to that which is common, e.g. to body, but to fire and earth, whether there is something common to them, viz. body, or not. But in fact the Platonists speak as if the One were homogeneous like fire or water; and if this is so, the numbers will not be substances. Evidently, if there is a One itself and this is a first principle, 'one' is being used in more than one sense; for otherwise the theory is impossible.

"When we wish to reduce substances to their principles, we state that lines come from the short and long (i.e. from a kind of small and great), and the plane from the broad and narrow, and body from the deep and shallow. Yet how then can either the plane contain a line, or the solid a line or a plane? For the broad and narrow is a different class from the deep and shallow. Therefore, just as number is not present in these, because the many and few are different from these, evidently no other of the higher classes will be present in the lower. But again the broad is not a genus which includes the deep, for then the solid would have been a species of plane. Further, from what principle will the presence of the points in the line be derived? Plato even used to object to this class of things as being a geometrical fiction. He gave the name of principle of the line-and this he often posited-to the indivisible lines. Yet these must have a limit; therefore the argument from which the existence of the line follows proves also the existence of the point.

"In general, though philosophy seeks the cause of perceptible things, we have given this up (for we say nothing of the cause from which change takes its start), but while we fancy we are stating the substance of perceptible things, we assert the existence of a second class of substances, while our account of the way in which they are the substances of perceptible things is empty talk; for 'sharing', as we said before, means nothing.

"Nor have the Forms any connexion with what we see to be the cause in the case of the arts, that for whose sake both all mind and the whole of nature are operative,-with this cause which we assert to be one of the first principles; but mathematics has come to be identical with philosophy for modern thinkers, though they say that it should be studied for the sake of other things. Further, one might suppose that the substance which according to them underlies as matter is too mathematical, and is a predicate and differentia of the substance, ie. of the matter, rather than matter itself; i.e. the great and the small are like the rare and the dense which the physical philosophers speak of, calling these the primary differentiae of the substratum; for these are a kind of excess and defect. And regarding movement, if the great and the small are to he movement, evidently the Forms will be moved; but if they are not to be movement, whence did movement come? The whole study of nature has been annihilated.

"And what is thought to be easy-to show that all things are one-is not done; for what is proved by the method of setting out instances is not that all things are one but that there is a One itself,-if we grant all the assumptions. And not even this follows, if we do not grant that the universal is a genus; and this in some cases it cannot be.

"Nor can it be explained either how the lines and planes and solids that come after the numbers exist or can exist, or what significance they have; for these can neither be Forms (for they are not numbers), nor the intermediates (for those are the objects of mathematics), nor the perishable things. This is evidently a distinct fourth class.

"In general, if we search for the elements of existing things without distinguishing the many senses in which things are said to exist, we cannot find them, especially if the search for the elements of which things are made is conducted in this manner. For it is surely impossible to discover what 'acting' or 'being acted on', or 'the straight', is made of, but if elements can be discovered at all, it is only the elements of substances; therefore either to seek the elements of all existing things or to think one has them is incorrect.

"And how could we learn the elements of all things? Evidently we cannot start by knowing anything before. For as he who is learning geometry, though he may know other things before, knows none of the things with which the science deals and about which he is to learn, so is it in all other cases. Therefore if there is a science of all things, such as some assert to exist, he who is learning this will know nothing before. Yet all learning is by means of premises which are (either all or some of them) known before,-whether the learning be by demonstration or by definitions; for the elements of the definition must be known before and be familiar; and learning by induction proceeds similarly. But again, if the science were actually innate, it were strange that we are unaware of our possession of the greatest of sciences.

"Again, how is one to come to know what all things are made of, and how is this to be made evident? This also affords a difficulty; for there might be a conflict of opinion, as there is about certain syllables; some say za is made out of s and d and a, while others say it is a distinct sound and none of those that are familiar.

"Further, how could we know the objects of sense without having the sense in question? Yet we ought to, if the elements of which all things consist, as complex sounds consist of the elements proper to sound, are the same.

Part 10

"It is evident, then, even from what we have said before, that all men seem to seek the causes named in the Physics, and that we cannot name any beyond these; but they seek these vaguely; and though in a sense they have all been described before, in a sense they have not been described at all. For the earliest philosophy is, on all subjects, like one who lisps, since it is young and in its beginnings. For even Empedocles says bone exists by virtue of the ratio in it. Now this is the essence and the substance of the thing. But it is similarly necessary that flesh and each of the other tissues should be the ratio of its elements, or that not one of them should; for it is on account of this that both flesh and bone and everything else will exist, and not on account of the matter, which he names,- fire and earth and water and air. But while he would necessarily have agreed if another had said this, he has not said it clearly.

"On these questions our views have been expressed before; but let us return to enumerate the difficulties that might be raised on these same points; for perhaps we may get from them some help towards our later difficulties.

Book IV

Part 1

"THERE is a science which investigates being as being and the attributes which belong to this in virtue of its own nature. Now this is not the same as any of the so-called special sciences; for none of these others treats universally of being as being. They cut off a part of being and investigate the attribute of this part; this is what the mathematical sciences for instance do. Now since we are seeking the first principles and the highest causes, clearly there must be some thing to which these belong in virtue of its own nature. If then those who sought the elements of existing things were seeking these same principles, it is necessary that the elements must be elements of being not by accident but just because it is being. Therefore it is of being as being that we also must grasp the first causes. "

Part 2

"There are many senses in which a thing may be said to 'be', but all that 'is' is related to one central point, one definite kind of thing, and is not said to 'be' by a mere ambiguity. Everything which is healthy is related to health, one thing in the sense that it preserves health, another in the sense that it produces it, another in the sense that it is a symptom of health, another because it is capable of it. And that which is medical is relative to the medical art, one thing being called medical because it possesses it, another because it is naturally adapted to it, another because it is a function of the medical art. And we shall find other words used similarly to these. So, too, there are many senses in which a thing is said to be, but all refer to one starting-point; some things are said to be because they are substances, others because they are affections of substance, others because they are a process towards substance, or destructions or privations or qualities of substance, or productive or generative of substance, or of things which are relative to substance, or negations of one of these thing of substance itself. It is for this reason that we say even of non-being that it is nonbeing. As, then, there is one science which deals with all healthy things, the same applies in the other cases also. For not only in the case of things which have one common notion does the investigation belong to one science, but also in the case of things which are related to one common nature; for even these in a sense have one common notion. It is clear then that it is the work of one science also to study the things that are, qua being.-But everywhere science deals chiefly with that which is primary, and on which the other things depend, and in virtue of which they get their names. If, then, this is substance, it will be of substances that the philosopher must grasp the principles and the causes.

"Now for each one class of things, as there is one perception, so there is one science, as for instance grammar, being one science, investigates all articulate sounds. Hence to investigate all the species of being qua being is the work of a science which is generically one, and to investigate the several species is the work of the specific parts of the science.

"If, now, being and unity are the same and are one thing in the sense that they are implied in one another as principle and cause are, not in the sense that they are explained by the same definition (though it makes no difference even if we suppose them to be like that-in fact this would even strengthen our case); for 'one man' and 'man' are the same thing, and so are 'existent man' and 'man', and the doubling of the words in 'one man and one existent man' does not express anything different (it is clear that the two things are not separated either in coming to be or in ceasing to be); and similarly 'one existent man' adds nothing to 'existent man', and that it is obvious that the addition in these cases means the same thing, and unity is nothing apart from being; and if, further, the substance of each thing is one in no merely accidental way, and similarly is from its very nature something that is:-all this being so, there must be exactly as many species of being as of unity. And to investigate the essence of these is the work of a science which is generically one-I mean, for instance, the discussion of the same and the similar and the other concepts of this sort; and nearly all contraries may be referred to this origin; let us take them as having been investigated in the 'Selection of Contraries'.

"And there are as many parts of philosophy as there are kinds of substance, so that there must necessarily be among them a first philosophy and one which follows this. For being falls immediately into genera; for which reason the sciences too will correspond to these genera. For the philosopher is like the mathematician, as that word is used; for mathematics also has parts, and there is a first and a second science and other successive ones within the sphere of mathematics.

"Now since it is the work of one science to investigate opposites, and plurality is opposed to unity-and it belongs to one science to investigate the negation and the privation because in both cases we are really investigating the one thing of which the negation or the privation is a negation or privation (for we either say simply that that thing is not present, or that it is not present in some particular class; in the latter case difference is present over and above what is implied in negation; for negation means just the absence of the thing in question, while in privation there is also employed an underlying nature of which the privation is asserted):-in view of all these facts, the contraries of the concepts we named above, the other and the dissimilar and the unequal, and everything else which is derived either from these or from plurality and unity, must fall within the province of the science above named. And contrariety is one of these concepts; for contrariety is a kind of difference, and difference is a kind of otherness. Therefore, since there are many senses in which a thing is said to be one, these terms also will have many senses, but yet it belongs to one science to know them all; for a term belongs to different sciences not if it has different senses, but if it has not one meaning and its definitions cannot be referred to one central meaning. And since all things are referred to that which is primary, as for instance all things which are called one are referred to the primary one, we must say that this holds good also of the same and the other and of contraries in general; so that after distinguishing the various senses of each, we must then explain by reference to what is primary in the case of each of the predicates in question, saying how they are related to it; for some will be called what they are called because they possess it, others because they produce it, and others in other such ways.

"It is evident, then, that it belongs to one science to be able to give an account of these concepts as well as of substance (this was one of the questions in our book of problems), and that it is the function of the philosopher to be able to investigate all things. For if it is not the function of the philosopher, who is it who will inquire whether Socrates and Socrates seated are the same thing, or whether one thing has one contrary, or what contrariety is, or how many meanings it has? And similarly with all other such questions. Since, then, these are essential modifications of unity qua unity and of being qua being, not qua numbers or lines or fire, it is clear that it belongs to this science to investigate both the essence of these concepts and their properties. And those who study these properties err not by leaving the sphere of philosophy, but by forgetting that substance, of which they have no correct idea, is prior to these other things. For number qua number has peculiar attributes, such as oddness and evenness, commensurability and equality, excess and defect, and these belong to numbers either in themselves or in relation to one another. And similarly the solid and the motionless and that which is in motion and the weightless and that which has weight have other peculiar properties. So too there are certain properties peculiar to being as such, and it is about these that the philosopher has to investigate the truth.-An indication of this may be mentioned: dialecticians and sophists assume the same guise as the philosopher, for sophistic is Wisdom which exists only in semblance, and dialecticians embrace all things in their dialectic, and being is common to all things; but evidently their dialectic embraces these subjects because these are proper to philosophy.- For sophistic and dialectic turn on the same class of things as philosophy, but this differs from dialectic in the nature of the faculty required and from sophistic in respect of the purpose of the philosophic life. Dialectic is merely critical where philosophy claims to know, and sophistic is what appears to be philosophy but is not.

"Again, in the list of contraries one of the two columns is privative, and all contraries are reducible to being and non-being, and to unity and plurality, as for instance rest belongs to unity and movement to plurality. And nearly all thinkers agree that being and substance are composed of contraries; at least all name contraries as their first principles-some name odd and even, some hot and cold, some limit and the unlimited, some love and strife. And all the others as well are evidently reducible to unity and plurality (this reduction we must take for granted), and the principles stated by other thinkers fall entirely under these as their genera. It is obvious then from these considerations too that it belongs to one science to examine being qua being. For all things are either contraries or composed of contraries, and unity and plurality are the starting-points of all contraries. And these belong to one science, whether they have or have not one single meaning. Probably the truth is that they have not; yet even if 'one' has several meanings, the other meanings will be related to the primary meaning (and similarly in the case of the contraries), even if being or unity is not a universal and the same in every instance or is not separable from the particular instances (as in fact it probably is not; the unity is in some cases that of common reference, in some cases that of serial succession). And for this reason it does not belong to the geometer to inquire what is contrariety or completeness or unity or being or the same or the other, but only to presuppose these concepts and reason from this starting-point.--Obviously then it is the work of one science to examine being qua being, and the attributes which belong to it qua being, and the same science will examine not only substances but also their attributes, both those above named and the concepts 'prior' and 'posterior', 'genus' and 'species', 'whole' and 'part', and the others of this sort.

Book VI

Part 1

"WE are seeking the principles and the causes of the things that are, and obviously of them qua being. For, while there is a cause of health and of good condition, and the objects of mathematics have first principles and elements and causes, and in general every science which is ratiocinative or at all involves reasoning deals with causes and principles, more or less precise, all these sciences mark off some particular being-some genus, and inquire into this, but not into being simply nor qua being, nor do they offer any discussion of the essence of the things of which they treat; but starting from the essence-some making it plain to the senses, others assuming it as a hypothesis-they then demonstrate, more or less cogently, the essential attributes of the genus with which they deal. It is obvious, therefore, that such an induction yields no demonstration of substance or of the essence, but some other way of exhibiting it. And similarly the sciences omit the question whether the genus with which they deal exists or does not exist, because it belongs to the same kind of thinking to show what it is and that it is.

"And since natural science, like other sciences, is in fact about one class of being, i.e. to that sort of substance which has the principle of its movement and rest present in itself, evidently it is neither practical nor productive. For in the case of things made the principle is in the maker-it is either reason or art or some faculty, while in the case of things done it is in the doer-viz. will, for that which is done and that which is willed are the same. Therefore, if all thought is either practical or productive or theoretical, physics must be a theoretical science, but it will theorize about such being as admits of being moved, and about substance-as-defined for the most part only as not separable from matter. Now, we must not fail to notice the mode of being of the essence and of its definition, for, without this, inquiry is but idle. Of things defined, i.e. of 'whats', some are like 'snub', and some like 'concave'. And these differ because 'snub' is bound up with matter (for what is snub is a concave nose), while concavity is independent of perceptible matter. If then all natural things are a analogous to the snub in their nature; e.g. nose, eye, face, flesh, bone, and, in general, animal; leaf, root, bark, and, in general, plant (for none of these can be defined without reference to movement-they always have matter), it is clear how we must seek and define the 'what' in the case of natural objects, and also that it belongs to the student of nature to study even soul in a certain sense, i.e. so much of it as is not independent of matter.

"That physics, then, is a theoretical science, is plain from these considerations. Mathematics also, however, is theoretical; but whether its objects are immovable and separable from matter, is not at present clear; still, it is clear that some mathematical theorems consider them qua immovable and qua separable from matter. But if there is something which is eternal and immovable and separable, clearly the knowledge of it belongs to a theoretical science,-not, however, to physics (for physics deals with certain movable things) nor to mathematics, but to a science prior to both. For physics deals with things which exist separately but are not immovable, and some parts of mathematics deal with things which are immovable but presumably do not exist separately, but as embodied in matter; while the first science deals with things which both exist separately and are immovable. Now all causes must be eternal, but especially these; for they are the causes that operate on so much of the divine as appears to us. There must, then, be three theoretical philosophies, mathematics, physics, and what we may call theology, since it is obvious that if the divine is present anywhere, it is present in things of this sort. And the highest science must deal with the highest genus. Thus, while the theoretical sciences are more to be desired than the other sciences, this is more to be desired than the other theoretical sciences. For one might raise the question whether first philosophy is universal, or deals with one genus, i.e. some one kind of being; for not even the mathematical sciences are all alike in this respect,-geometry and astronomy deal with a certain particular kind of thing, while universal mathematics applies alike to all. We answer that if there is no substance other than those which are formed by nature, natural science will be the first science; but if there is an immovable substance, the science of this must be prior and must be first philosophy, and universal in this way, because it is first. And it will belong to this to consider being qua being-both what it is and the attributes which belong to it qua being.

## Book VII

## Part 1

"THERE are several senses in which a thing may be said to 'be', as we pointed out previously in our book on the various senses of words;' for in one sense the 'being' meant is 'what a thing is' or a 'this', and in another sense it means a quality or quantity or one of the other things that are predicated as these are. While 'being' has all these senses, obviously that which 'is' primarily is the 'what', which indicates the substance of the thing. For when we say of what quality a thing is, we say that it is good or bad, not that it is three cubits long or that it is a man; but when we say what it is, we do not say 'white' or 'hot' or 'three cubits long', but 'a man' or 'a 'god'. And all other things are said to be because they are, some of them, quantities of that which is in this primary sense, others qualities of it, others affections of it, and others some other determination of it. And so one might even raise the question whether the words 'to walk', 'to be healthy', 'to sit' imply that each of these things is existent, and similarly in any other case of this sort; for none of them is either self-subsistent or capable of being separated from substance, but rather, if anything, it is that which walks or sits or is healthy that is an existent thing. Now these are seen to be more real because there is something definite which underlies them (i.e. the substance or individual), which is implied in such a predicate; for we never use the word 'good' or 'sitting' without implying this. Clearly then it is in virtue of this category that each of the others also is. Therefore that which is primarily, i.e. not in a qualified sense but without qualification, must be substance.

"Now there are several senses in which a thing is said to be first; yet substance is first in every sense-(1) in definition, (2) in order of knowledge, (3) in time. For (3) of the other categories none can exist independently, but only substance. And (1) in definition also this is first; for in the definition of each term the definition of its substance must be present. And (2) we think we know each thing most fully, when we know what it is, e.g. what man is or what fire is, rather than when we know its quality, its quantity, or its place; since we know each of these predicates also, only when we know what the quantity or the quality is.

"And indeed the question which was raised of old and is raised now and always, and is always the subject of doubt, viz. what being is, is just the question, what is substance? For it is this that some assert to be one, others more than one, and that some assert to be limited in number, others unlimited. And so we also must consider chiefly and primarily and almost exclusively what that is which is in this sense.

Part 2

"Substance is thought to belong most obviously to bodies; and so we say that not only animals and plants and their parts are substances, but also natural bodies such as fire and water and earth and everything of the sort, and all things that are either parts of these or composed of these (either of parts or of the whole bodies), e.g. the physical universe and its parts, stars and moon and sun. But whether these alone are substances, or there are also others, or only some of these, or others as well, or none of these but only some other things, are substances, must be considered. Some think the limits of body, i.e. surface, line, point, and unit, are substances, and more so than body or the solid.

"Further, some do not think there is anything substantial besides sensible things, but others think there are eternal substances which are more in number and more real; e.g. Plato posited two kinds of substance-the Forms and objects of mathematics-as well as a third kind, viz. the substance of sensible bodies. And Speusippus made still more kinds of substance, beginning with the One, and assuming principles for each kind of substance, one for numbers, another for spatial magnitudes, and then another for the soul; and by going on in this way he multiplies the kinds of substance. And some say Forms and numbers have the same nature, and the other things come after them-lines and planes-until we come to the substance of the material universe and to sensible bodies.

"Regarding these matters, then, we must inquire which of the common statements are right and which are not right, and what substances there are, and whether there are or are not any besides sensible substances, and how sensible substances exist, and whether there is a substance capable of separate existence (and if so why and how) or no such substance, apart from sensible substances; and we must first sketch the nature of substance.

Part 3

"The word 'substance' is applied, if not in more senses, still at least to four main objects; for both the essence and the universal and the genus, are thought to be the substance of each thing, and fourthly the substratum. Now the substratum is that of which everything else is predicated, while it is itself not predicated of anything else. And so we must first determine the nature of this; for that which underlies a thing primarily is thought to be in the truest sense its substance. And in one sense matter is said to be of the nature of substratum, in another, shape, and in a third, the compound of these. (By the matter I mean, for instance, the bronze, by the shape the pattern of its form, and by the compound of these the statue, the concrete whole.) Therefore if the form is prior to the matter and more real, it will be prior also to the compound of both, for the same reason.

"We have now outlined the nature of substance, showing that it is that which is not predicated of a stratum, but of which all else is predicated. But we must not merely state the matter thus; for this is not enough. The statement itself is obscure, and further, on this view, matter becomes substance. For if this is not substance, it baffles us to say what else is. When all else is stripped off evidently nothing but matter remains. For while the rest are affections, products, and potencies of bodies, length, breadth, and depth are quantities and not substances (for a quantity is not a substance), but the substance is rather that to which these belong primarily. But when length and breadth and depth are taken away we see nothing left unless there is something that is bounded by these; so that to those who consider the question thus matter alone must seem to be substance. By matter I mean that which in itself is neither a particular thing nor of a certain quantity nor assigned to any other of the categories by which being is determined. For there is something of which each of these is predicated, whose being is different from that of each of the predicates (for the predicates other than substance are predicated of substance, while substance is predicated of matter). Therefore the ultimate substratum is of itself neither a particular thing nor of a particular quantity nor otherwise positively characterized; nor yet is it the negations of these, for negations also will belong to it only by accident.

"If we adopt this point of view, then, it follows that matter is substance. But this is impossible; for both separability and 'thisness' are thought to belong chiefly to substance. And so form and the compound of form and matter would be thought to be substance, rather than matter. The substance compounded of both, i.e. of matter and shape, may be dismissed; for it is posterior and its nature is obvious. And matter also is in a sense manifest. But we must inquire into the third kind of substance; for this is the most perplexing.

"Some of the sensible substances are generally admitted to be substances, so that we must look first among these. For it is an advantage to advance to that which is more knowable. For learning proceeds for all in this way-through that which is less knowable by nature to that which is more knowable; and just as in conduct our task is to start from what is good for each and make what is without qualification good good for each, so it is our task to start from what is more knowable to oneself and make what is knowable by nature knowable to oneself. Now what is knowable and primary for particular sets of people is often knowable to a very small extent, and has little or nothing of reality. But yet one must start from that which is barely knowable but knowable to oneself, and try to know what is knowable without qualification, passing, as has been said, by way of those very things which one does know.

Part 4

"Since at the start we distinguished the various marks by which we determine substance, and one of these was thought to be the essence, we must investigate this. And first let us make some linguistic remarks about it. The essence of each thing is what it is said to be propter se. For being you is not being musical, since you are not by your very nature musical. What, then, you are by your very nature is your essence.

"Nor yet is the whole of this the essence of a thing; not that which is propter se as white is to a surface, because being a surface is not identical with being white. But again the combination of both-'being a white surface'-is not the essence of surface, because 'surface' itself is added. The formula, therefore, in which the term itself is not present but its meaning is expressed, this is the formula of the essence of each thing. Therefore if to be a white surface is to be a smooth surface, to be white and to be smooth are one and the same.

"But since there are also compounds answering to the other categories (for there is a substratum for each category, e.g. for quality, quantity, time, place, and motion), we must inquire whether there is a formula of the essence of each of them, i.e. whether to these compounds also there belongs an essence, e.g. 'white man'. Let the compound be denoted by 'cloak'. What is the essence of cloak? But, it may be said, this also is not a propter se expression. We reply that there are just two ways in which a predicate may fail to be true of a subject propter se, and one of these results from the addition, and the other from the omission, of a determinant. One kind of predicate is not propter se because the term that is being defined is combined with another determinant, e.g. if in defining the essence of white one were to state the formula of white man; the other because in the subject another determinant is combined with that which is expressed in the formula, e.g. if 'cloak' meant 'white man', and one were to define cloak as white; white man is white indeed, but its essence is not to be white.

"But is being-a-cloak an essence at all? Probably not. For the essence is precisely what something is; but when an attribute is asserted of a subject other than itself, the complex is not precisely what some 'this' is, e.g. white man is not precisely what some 'this' is, since thisness belongs only to substances. Therefore there is an essence only of those things whose formula is a definition. But we have a definition not where we have a word and a formula identical in meaning (for in that case all formulae or sets of words would be definitions; for there will be some name for any set of words whatever, so that even the Iliad will be a definition), but where there is a formula of something primary; and primary things are those which do not imply the predication of one element in them of another element. Nothing, then, which is not a species of a genus will have an essence-only species will have it, for these are thought to imply not merely that the subject participates in the attribute and has it as an affection, or has it by accident; but for ever thing else as well, if it has a name, there be a formula of its meaning-viz. that this attribute belongs to this subject; or instead of a simple formula we shall be able to give a more accurate one; but there will be no definition nor essence.

"Or has 'definition', like 'what a thing is', several meanings? 'What a thing is' in one sense means substance and the 'this', in another one or other of the predicates, quantity, quality, and the like. For as 'is' belongs to all things, not however in the same sense, but to one sort of thing primarily and to others in a secondary way, so too 'what a thing is' belongs in the simple sense to substance, but in a limited sense to the other categories. For even of a quality we might ask what it is, so that quality also is a 'what a thing is',-not in the simple sense, however, but just as, in the case of that which is not, some say, emphasizing the linguistic form, that that is which is not is-not is simply, but is non-existent; so too with quality.

"We must no doubt inquire how we should express ourselves on each point, but certainly not more than how the facts actually stand. And so now also, since it is evident what language we use, essence will belong, just as 'what a thing is' does, primarily and in the simple sense to substance, and in a secondary way to the other categories also,-not essence in the simple sense, but the essence of a quality or of a quantity. For it must be either by an equivocation that we say these are, or by adding to and taking from the meaning of 'are' (in the way in which that which is not known may be said to be known),-the truth being that we use the word neither ambiguously nor in the same sense, but just as we apply the word 'medical' by virtue of a reference to one and the same thing, not meaning one and the same thing, nor yet speaking ambiguously; for a patient and an operation and an instrument are called medical neither by an ambiguity nor with a single meaning, but with reference to a common end. But it does not matter at all in which of the two ways one likes to describe the facts; this is evident, that definition and essence in the primary and simple sense belong to substances. Still they belong to other things as well, only not in the primary sense. For if we suppose this it does not follow that there is a definition of every word which means the same as any formula; it must mean the same as a particular kind of formula; and this condition is satisfied if it is a formula of something which is one, not by continuity like the Iliad or the things that are one by being bound together, but in one of the main senses of 'one', which answer to the senses of 'is'; now 'that which is' in one sense denotes a 'this', in another a quantity, in another a quality. And so there can be a formula or definition even of white man, but not in the sense in which there is a definition either of white or of a substance.

## Part 5

"It is a difficult question, if one denies that a formula with an added determinant is a definition, whether any of the terms that are not simple but coupled will be definable. For we must explain them by adding a determinant. E.g. there is the nose, and concavity, and snubness, which is compounded out of the two by the presence of the one in the other, and it is not by accident that the nose has the attribute either of concavity or of snubness, but in virtue of its nature; nor do they attach to it as whiteness does to Callias, or to man (because Callias, who happens to be a man, is white), but as 'male' attaches to animal and 'equal' to quantity, and as all so-called 'attributes propter se' attach to their subjects. And such attributes are those in which is involved either the formula or the name of the subject of the particular attribute, and which cannot be explained without this; e.g. white can be explained apart from man, but not female apart from animal. Therefore there is either no essence and definition of any of these things, or if there is, it is in another sense, as we have said.

"But there is also a second difficulty about them. For if snub nose and concave nose are the same thing, snub and concave will be the thing; but if snub and concave are not the same (because it is impossible to speak of snubness apart from the thing of which it is an attribute propter se, for snubness is concavity-in-a-nose), either it is impossible to say 'snub nose' or the same thing will have been said twice, concave-nose nose; for snub nose will be concave-nose nose. And so it is absurd that such things should have an essence; if they have, there will be an infinite regress; for in snub-nose nose yet another 'nose' will be involved.

"Clearly, then, only substance is definable. For if the other categories also are definable, it must be by addition of a determinant, e.g. the qualitative is defined thus, and so is the odd, for it cannot be defined apart from number; nor can female be defined apart from animal. (When I say 'by addition' I mean the expressions in which it turns out that we are saying the same thing twice, as in these instances.) And if this is true, coupled terms also, like 'odd number', will not be definable (but this escapes our notice because our formulae are not accurate.). But if these also are definable, either it is in some other way or, as we definition and essence must be said to have more than one sense. Therefore in one sense nothing will have a definition and nothing will have an essence, except substances, but in another sense other things will have them. Clearly, then, definition is the formula of the essence, and essence belongs to substances either alone or chiefly and primarily and in the unqualified sense.

Part 6

"We must inquire whether each thing and its essence are the same or different. This is of some use for the inquiry concerning substance; for each thing is thought to be not different from its substance, and the essence is said to be the substance of each thing.

"Now in the case of accidental unities the two would be generally thought to be different, e.g. white man would be thought to be different from the essence of white man. For if they are the same, the essence of man and that of white man are also the same; for a man and a white man are the same thing, as people say, so that the essence of white man and that of man would be also the same. But perhaps it does not follow that the essence of accidental unities should be the same as that of the simple terms. For the extreme terms are not in the same way identical with the middle term. But perhaps this might be thought to follow, that the extreme terms, the accidents, should turn out to be the same, e.g. the essence of white and that of musical; but this is not actually thought to be the case.

"But in the case of so-called self-subsistent things, is a thing necessarily the same as its essence? E.g. if there are some substances which have no other substances nor entities prior to them-substances such as some assert the Ideas to be?-If the essence of good is to be different from good-itself, and the essence of animal from animal-itself, and the essence of being from being-itself, there will, firstly, be other substances and entities and Ideas besides those which are asserted, and, secondly, these others will be prior substances, if essence is substance. And if the posterior substances and the prior are severed from each other, (a) there will be no knowledge of the former, and (b) the latter will have no being. (By 'severed' I mean, if the good-itself has not the essence of good, and the latter has not the property of being good.) For (a) there is knowledge of each thing only when we know its essence. And (b) the case is the same for other things as for the good; so that if the essence of good is not good, neither is the essence of reality real, nor the essence of unity one. And all essences alike exist or none of them does; so that if the essence of reality is not real, neither is any of the others. Again, that to which the essence of good does not belong is not good.-The good, then, must be one with the essence of good, and the beautiful with the essence of beauty, and so with all things which do not depend on something else but are self-subsistent and primary. For it is enough if they are this, even if they are not Forms; or rather, perhaps, even if they are Forms. (At the same time it is clear that if there are Ideas such as some people say there are, it will not be substratum that is substance; for these must be substances, but not predicable of a substratum; for if they were they would exist only by being participated in.)

"Each thing itself, then, and its essence are one and the same in no merely accidental way, as is evident both from the preceding arguments and because to know each thing, at least, is just to know its essence, so that even by the exhibition of instances it becomes clear that both must be one.

"(But of an accidental term, e.g.'the musical' or 'the white', since it has two meanings, it is not true to say that it itself is identical with its essence; for both that to which the accidental quality belongs, and the accidental quality, are white, so that in a sense the accident and its essence are the same, and in a sense they are not; for the essence of white is not the same as the man or the white man, but it is the same as the attribute white.)

"The absurdity of the separation would appear also if one were to assign a name to each of the essences; for there would be yet another essence besides the original one, e.g. to the essence of horse there will belong a second essence. Yet why should not some things be their essences from the start, since essence is substance? But indeed not only are a thing and its essence one, but the formula of them is also the same, as is clear even from what has been said; for it is not by accident that the essence of one, and the one, are one. Further, if they are to be different, the process will go on to infinity; for we shall have (1) the essence of one, and (2) the one, so that to terms of the former kind the same argument will be applicable.

"Clearly, then, each primary and self-subsistent thing is one and the same as its essence. The sophistical objections to this position, and the question whether Socrates and to be Socrates are the same thing, are obviously answered by the same solution; for there is no difference either in the standpoint from which the question would be asked, or in that from which one could answer it successfully. We have explained, then, in what sense each thing is the same as its essence and in what sense it is not.
Part 7

"Of things that come to be, some come to be by nature, some by art, some spontaneously. Now everything that comes to be comes to be by the agency of something and from something and comes to be something. And the something which I say it comes to be may be found in any category; it may come to be either a 'this' or of some size or of some quality or somewhere.

"Now natural comings to be are the comings to be of those things which come to be by nature; and that out of which they come to be is what we call matter; and that by which they come to be is something which exists naturally; and the something which they come to be is a man or a plant or one of the things of this kind, which we say are substances if anything is-all things produced either by nature or by art have matter; for each of them is capable both of being and of not being, and this capacity is the matter in each-and, in general, both that from which they are produced is nature, and the type according to which they are produced is nature (for that which is produced, e.g. a plant or an animal, has a nature), and so is that by which they are produced--the so-called 'formal' nature, which is specifically the same (though this is in another individual); for man begets man.

"Thus, then, are natural products produced; all other productions are called 'makings'. And all makings proceed either from art or from a faculty or from thought. Some of them happen also spontaneously or by luck just as natural products sometimes do; for there also the same things sometimes are produced without seed as well as from seed. Concerning these cases, then, we must inquire later, but from art proceed the things of which the form is in the soul of the artist. (By form I mean the essence of each thing and its primary substance.) For even contraries have in a sense the same form; for the substance of a privation is the opposite substance, e.g. health is the substance of disease (for disease is the absence of health); and health is the formula in the soul or the knowledge of it. The healthy subject is produced as the result of the following train of thought:-since this is health, if the subject is to be healthy this must first be present, e.g. a uniform state of body, and if this is to be present, there must be heat; and the physician goes on thinking thus until he reduces the matter to a final something which he himself can produce. Then the process from this point onward, i.e. the process towards health, is called a 'making'. Therefore it follows that in a sense health comes from health and house from house, that with matter from that without matter; for the medical art and the building art are the form of health and of the house, and when I speak of substance without matter I mean the essence.

"Of the productions or processes one part is called thinking and the other making,-that which proceeds from the starting-point and the form is thinking, and that which proceeds from the final step of the thinking is making. And each of the other, intermediate, things is produced in the same way. I mean, for instance, if the subject is to be healthy his bodily state must be made uniform. What then does being made uniform imply? This or that. And this depends on his being made warm. What does this imply?

Something else. And this something is present potentially; and what is present potentially is already in the physician's power.

"The active principle then and the starting point for the process of becoming healthy is, if it happens by art, the form in the soul, and if spontaneously, it is that, whatever it is, which starts the making, for the man who makes by art, as in healing the starting-point is perhaps the production of warmth (and this the physician produces by rubbing). Warmth in the body, then, is either a part of health or is followed (either directly or through several intermediate steps) by something similar which is a part of health; and this, viz. that which produces the part of health, is the limiting-point--and so too with a house (the stones are the limiting-point here) and in all other cases. Therefore, as the saying goes, it is impossible that anything should be produced if there were nothing existing before. Obviously then some part of the result will pre-exist of necessity; for the matter is a part; for this is present in the process and it is this that becomes something. But is the matter an element even in the formula? We certainly describe in both ways what brazen circles are; we describe both the matter by saying it is brass, and the form by saying that it is such and such a figure; and figure is the proximate genus in which it is placed. The brazen circle, then, has its matter in its formula.

"As for that out of which as matter they are produced, some things are said, when they have been produced, to be not that but 'thaten'; e.g. the statue is not gold but golden. And a healthy man is not said to be that from which he has come. The reason is that though a thing comes both from its privation and from its substratum, which we call its matter (e.g. what becomes healthy is both a man and an invalid), it is said to come rather from its privation (e.g. it is from an invalid rather than from a man that a healthy subject is produced). And so the healthy subject is not said to he an invalid, but to be a man, and the man is said to be healthy. But as for the things whose privation is obscure and nameless, e.g. in brass the privation of a particular shape or in bricks and timber the privation of arrangement as a house, the thing is thought to be produced from these materials, as in the former case the healthy man is produced from an invalid. And so, as there also a thing is not said to be that from which it comes, here the statue is not said to be wood but is said by a verbal change to be wooden, not brass but brazen, not gold but golden, and the house is said to be not bricks but bricken (though we should not say without qualification, if we looked at the matter carefully, even that a statue is produced from wood or a house from bricks, because coming to be implies change in that from which a thing comes to be, and not permanence). It is for this reason, then, that we use this way of speaking.

Part 8

"Since anything which is produced is produced by something (and this I call the starting-point of the production), and from something (and let this be taken to be not the privation but the matter; for the meaning we attach to this has already been explained), and since something is produced (and this is either a sphere or a circle or whatever else it may chance to be), just as we do not make the substratum (the brass), so we do not make the sphere, except incidentally, because the brazen sphere is a sphere and we make the forme. For to make a 'this' is to make a 'this' out of the substratum in the full sense of the word. (I mean that to make the brass round is not to make the round or the sphere, but something else, i.e. to produce this form in something different from itself. For if we make the form, we must make it out of something else; for this was assumed. E.g. we make a brazen sphere; and that in the sense that out of this, which is brass, we make this other, which is a sphere.) If, then, we also make the substratum itself, clearly we shall make it in the same way, and the processes of making will regress to infinity. Obviously then the form also, or whatever we ought to call the shape present in the sensible thing, is not produced, nor is there any production of it, nor is the essence produced; for this is that which is made to be in something else either by art or by nature or by some faculty. But that there is a brazen sphere, this we make. For we make it out of brass and the sphere; we bring the form into this particular matter, and the result is a brazen sphere. But if the essence of sphere in general is to be produced, something must be produced out of something. For the product will always have to be divisible, and one part must be this and another that; I mean the one must be matter and the other form. If, then, a sphere is 'the figure whose circumference is at all points equidistant from the centre', part of this will be the medium in which the thing made will be, and part will be in that medium, and the whole will be the thing produced, which corresponds to the brazen sphere. It is obvious, then, from what has been said, that that which is spoken of as form or substance is not produced, but the concrete thing which gets its name from this is produced, and that in everything which is generated matter is present, and one part of the thing is matter and the other form.

"Is there, then, a sphere apart from the individual spheres or a house apart from the bricks? Rather we may say that no 'this' would ever have been coming to be, if this had been so, but that the 'form' means the 'such', and is not a 'this'-a definite thing; but the artist makes, or the father begets, a 'such' out of a 'this'; and when it has been begotten, it is a 'this such'. And the whole 'this', Callias or Socrates, is analogous to 'this brazen sphere', but man and animal to 'brazen sphere' in general. Obviously, then, the cause which consists of the Forms (taken in the sense in which some maintain the existence of the Forms, i.e. if they are something apart from the individuals) is useless, at least with regard to comings-to-be and to substances; and the Forms need not, for this reason at least, be self-subsistent substances. In some cases indeed it is even obvious that the begetter is of the same kind as the begotten (not, however, the same nor one in number, but in form), i.e. in the case of natural products (for man begets man), unless something happens contrary to nature, e.g. the production of a mule by a horse. (And even these cases are similar; for that which would be found to be common to horse and ass, the genus next above them, has not received a name, but it would doubtless be both in fact something like a mule.) Obviously, therefore, it is quite unnecessary to set up a Form as a pattern (for we should have looked for Forms in these cases if in any; for these are substances if anything is so); the begetter is adequate to the making of the product and to the causing of the form in the matter. And when we have the whole, such and such a form in this flesh and in these bones, this is Callias or Socrates; and they are different in virtue of their matter (for that is different), but the same in form; for their form is indivisible.

## Part 9

"The question might be raised, why some things are produced spontaneously as well as by art, e.g. health, while others are not, e.g. a house. The reason is that in some cases the matter which governs the production in the making and producing of any work of art, and in which a part of the product is present,-some matter is such as to be set in motion by itself and some is not of this nature, and of the former kind some can move itself in the particular way required, while other matter is incapable of this; for many things can be set in motion by themselves but not in some particular way, e.g. that of dancing. The things, then, whose matter is of this sort, e.g. stones, cannot be moved in the particular way required, except by something else, but in another way they can move themselves-and so it is with fire. Therefore some things will not exist apart from some one who has the art of making them, while others will; for motion will be started by these things which have not the art but can themselves be moved by other things which have not the art or with a motion starting from a part of the product.

"And it is clear also from what has been said that in a sense every product of art is produced from a thing which shares its name (as natural products are produced), or from a part of itself which shares its name (e.g. the house is produced from a house, qua produced by reason; for the art of building is the form of the house), or from something which contains a art of it,-if we exclude things produced by accident; for the cause of the thing's producing the product directly per se is a part of the product. The heat in the movement caused heat in the body, and this is either health, or a part of health, or is followed by a part of health or by health itself. And so it is said to cause health, because it causes that to which health attaches as a consequence.

"Therefore, as in syllogisms, substance is the starting-point of everything. It is from 'what a thing is' that syllogisms start; and from it also we now find processes of production to start.

"Things which are formed by nature are in the same case as these products of art. For the seed is productive in the same way as the things that work by art; for it has the form potentially, and that from which the seed comes has in a sense the same name as the offspring only in a sense, for we must not expect parent and offspring always to have exactly the same name, as in the production of 'human being' from 'human' for a 'woman' also can be produced by a 'man'-unless the offspring be an imperfect form; which is the reason why the parent of a mule is not a mule. The natural things which (like the artificial objects previously considered) can be produced spontaneously are those whose matter can be moved even by itself in the way in which the seed usually moves it; those things which have not such matter cannot be produced except from the parent animals themselves.

"But not only regarding substance does our argument prove that its form does not come to be, but the argument applies to all the primary classes alike, i.e. quantity, quality, and the other categories. For as the brazen sphere comes to be, but not the sphere nor the brass, and so too in the case of brass itself, if it comes to be, it is its concrete unity that comes to be (for the matter and the form must always exist before), so is it both in the case of substance and in that of quality and quantity and the other categories likewise; for the quality does not come to be, but the wood of that quality, and the quantity does not come to be, but the wood or the animal of that size. But we may learn from these instances a peculiarity of substance, that there must exist beforehand in complete reality another substance which produces it, e.g. an animal if an animal is produced; but it is not necessary that a quality or quantity should pre-exist otherwise than potentially.

Part 10

"Since a definition is a formula, and every formula has parts, and as the formula is to the thing, so is the part of the formula to the part of the thing, the question is already being asked whether the formula of the parts must be present in the formula of the whole or not. For in some cases the formulae of the parts are seen to be present, and in some not. The formula of the circle does not include that of the segments, but that of the syllable includes that of the letters; yet the circle is divided into segments as the syllable is into letters.-And further if the parts are prior to the whole, and the acute angle is a part of the right angle and the finger a part of the animal, the acute angle will be prior to the right angle and finger to the man. But the latter are thought to be prior; for in formula the parts are explained by reference to them, and in respect also of the power of existing apart from each other the wholes are prior to the parts.

"Perhaps we should rather say that 'part' is used in several senses. One of these is 'that which measures another thing in respect of quantity'. But let this sense be set aside; let us inquire about the parts of which substance consists. If then matter is one thing, form another, the compound of these a third, and both the matter and the form and the compound are substance even the matter is in a sense called part of a thing, while in a sense it is not, but only the elements of which the formula of the form consists. E.g. of concavity flesh (for this is the matter in which it is produced) is not a part, but of snubness it is a part; and the bronze is a part of the concrete statue, but not of the statue when this is spoken of in the sense of the form. (For the form, or the thing as having form, should be said to be the thing, but the material element by itself must never be said to be so.) And so the formula of the circle does not include that of the segments, but the formula of the syllable includes that of the letters; for the letters are parts of the formula of the form, and not matter, but the segments are parts in the sense of matter on which the form supervenes; yet they are nearer the form than the bronze is when roundness is produced in bronze. But in a sense not even every kind of letter will be present in the formula of the syllable, e.g. particular waxen letters or the letters as movements in the air; for in these also we have already something that is part of the syllable only in the sense that it is its perceptible matter. For even if the line when divided passes away into its halves, or the man into bones and muscles and flesh, it does not follow that they are composed of these as parts of their essence, but rather as matter; and these are parts of the concrete thing, but not also of the form, i.e. of that to which the formula refers; wherefore also they are not present in the formulae. In one kind of formula, then, the formula of such parts will be present, but in another it must not be present, where the formula does not refer to the concrete object. For it is for this reason that some things have as their constituent principles parts into which they pass away, while some have not. Those things which are the form and the matter taken together, e.g. the snub, or the bronze circle, pass away into these materials, and the matter is a part of them; but those things which do not involve matter but are without matter, and whose formulae are formulae of the form only, do not pass away,-either not at all or at any rate not in this way. Therefore these materials are principles and parts of the concrete things, while of the form they are neither parts nor principles. And therefore the clay statue is resolved into clay and the ball into bronze and Callias into flesh and bones, and again the circle into its segments; for there is a sense of 'circle' in which involves matter. For 'circle' is used ambiguously, meaning both the circle, unqualified, and the individual circle, because there is no name peculiar to the individuals.

"The truth has indeed now been stated, but still let us state it yet more clearly, taking up the question again. The parts of the formula, into which the formula is divided, are prior to it, either all or some of them. The formula of the right angle, however, does not include the formula of the acute, but the formula of the acute includes that of the right angle; for he who defines the acute uses the right angle; for the acute is 'less than a right angle'. The circle and the semicircle also are in a like relation; for the semicircle is defined by the circle; and so is the finger by the whole body, for a finger is 'such and such a part of a man'. Therefore the parts which are of the nature of matter, and into which as its matter a thing is divided, are posterior; but those which are of the nature of parts of the formula, and of the substance according to its formula, are prior, either all or some of them. And since the soul of animals (for this is the substance of a living being) is their substance according to the formula, i.e. the form and the essence of a body of a certain kind (at least we shall define each part, if we define it well, not without reference to its function, and this cannot belong to it without perception), so that the parts of soul are prior, either all or some of them, to the concrete 'animal', and so too with each individual animal; and the body and parts are posterior to this, the essential substance, and it is not the substance but the concrete thing that is divided into these parts as its matter:-this being so, to the concrete thing these are in a sense prior, but in a sense they are not. For they cannot even exist if severed from the whole; for it is not a finger in any and every state that is the finger of a living thing, but a dead finger is a finger only in name. Some parts are neither prior nor posterior to the whole, i.e. those which are dominant and in which the formula, i.e. the essential substance, is immediately present, e.g. perhaps the heart or the brain; for it does not matter in the least which of the two has this quality. But man and horse and terms which are thus applied to individuals, but universally, are not substance but something composed of this particular formula and this particular matter treated as universal; and as regards the individual, Socrates already includes in him ultimate individual matter; and similarly in all other cases. 'A part' may be a part either of the form (i.e. of the essence), or of the compound of the form and the matter, or of the matter itself. But only the parts of the form are parts of the formula, and the formula is of the universal; for 'being a circle' is the same as the circle, and 'being a soul' the same as the soul. But when we come to the concrete thing, e.g. this circle, i.e. one of the individual circles, whether perceptible or intelligible (I mean by intelligible circles the mathematical, and by perceptible circles those of bronze and of wood),-of these there is no definition, but they are known by the aid of intuitive thinking or of perception; and when they pass out of this complete realization it is not clear whether they exist or not; but they are always stated and recognized by means of the universal formula. But matter is unknowable in itself. And some matter is perceptible and some intelligible, perceptible matter being for instance bronze and wood and all matter that is changeable, and intelligible matter being that which is present in perceptible things not qua perceptible, i.e. the objects of mathematics.

"We have stated, then, how matters stand with regard to whole and part, and their priority and posteriority. But when any one asks whether the right angle and the circle and the animal are prior, or the things into which they are divided and of which they consist, i.e. the parts, we must meet the inquiry by saying that the question cannot be answered simply. For if even bare soul is the animal or the living thing, or the soul of each individual is the individual itself, and 'being a circle' is the circle, and 'being a right angle' and the essence of the right angle is the right angle, then the whole in one sense must be called posterior to the art in one sense, i.e. to the parts included in the formula and to the parts of the individual right angle (for both the material right angle which is made of bronze, and that which is formed by individual lines, are posterior to their parts); while the immaterial right angle is posterior to the parts included in the formula, but prior to those included in the particular instance, and the question must not be answered simply. If, however, the soul is something different and is not identical with the animal, even so some parts must, as we have maintained, be called prior and others must not.

Part 11

"Another question is naturally raised, viz. what sort of parts belong to the form and what sort not to the form, but to the concrete thing. Yet if this is not plain it is not possible to define any thing; for definition is of the universal and of the form. If then it is not evident what sort of parts are of the nature of matter and what sort are not, neither will the formula of the thing be evident. In the case of things which are found to occur in specifically different materials, as a circle may exist in bronze or stone or wood, it seems plain that these, the bronze or the stone, are no part of the essence of the circle, since it is found apart from them. Of things which are not seen to exist apart, there is no reason why the same may not be true, just as if all circles that had ever been seen were of bronze; for none the less the bronze would be no part of the form; but it is hard to eliminate it in thought. E.g. the form of man is always found in flesh and bones and parts of this kind; are these then also parts of the form and the formula? No, they are matter; but because man is not found also in other matters we are unable to perform the abstraction.

"Since this is thought to be possible, but it is not clear when it is the case, some people already raise the question even in the case of the circle and the triangle, thinking that it is not right to define these by reference to lines and to the continuous, but that all these are to the circle or the triangle as flesh and bones are to man, and bronze or stone to the statue; and they reduce all things to numbers, and they say the formula of 'line' is that of 'two'. And of those who assert the Ideas some make 'two' the line-itself, and others make it the Form of the line; for in some cases they say the

Form and that of which it is the Form are the same, e.g. 'two' and the Form of two; but in the case of 'line' they say this is no longer so.

"It follows then that there is one Form for many things whose form is evidently different (a conclusion which confronted the Pythagoreans also); and it is possible to make one thing the Form-itself of all, and to hold that the others are not Forms; but thus all things will be one.

"We have pointed out, then, that the question of definitions contains some difficulty, and why this is so. And so to reduce all things thus to Forms and to eliminate the matter is useless labour; for some things surely are a particular form in a particular matter, or particular things in a particular state. And the comparison which Socrates the younger used to make in the case of 'animal' is not sound; for it leads away from the truth, and makes one suppose that man can possibly exist without his parts, as the circle can without the bronze. But the case is not similar; for an animal is something perceptible, and it is not possible to define it without reference to movement-nor, therefore, without reference to the parts' being in a certain state. For it is not a hand in any and every state that is a part of man, but only when it can fulfil its work, and therefore only when it is alive; if it is not alive it is not a part.

"Regarding the objects of mathematics, why are the formulae of the parts not parts of the formulae of the wholes; e.g. why are not the semicircles included in the formula of the circle? It cannot be said, 'because these parts are perceptible things'; for they are not. But perhaps this makes no difference; for even some things which are not perceptible must have matter; indeed there is some matter in everything which is not an essence and a bare form but a 'this'. The semicircles, then, will not be parts of the universal circle, but will be parts of the individual circles, as has been said before; for while one kind of matter is perceptible, there is another which is intelligible.

"It is clear also that the soul is the primary substance and the body is matter, and man or animal is the compound of both taken universally; and 'Socrates' or 'Coriscus', if even the soul of Socrates may be called Socrates, has two meanings (for some mean by such a term the soul, and others mean the concrete thing), but if 'Socrates' or 'Coriscus' means simply this particular soul and this particular body, the individual is analogous to the universal in its composition.

"Whether there is, apart from the matter of such substances, another kind of matter, and one should look for some substance other than these, e.g. numbers or something of the sort, must be considered later. For it is for the sake of this that we are trying to determine the nature of perceptible substances as well, since in a sense the inquiry about perceptible substances is the work of physics, i.e. of second philosophy; for the physicist must come to know not only about the matter, but also about the substance expressed in the formula, and even more than about the other. And in the case of definitions, how the elements in the formula are parts of the definition, and why the definition is one formula (for clearly the thing is one, but in virtue of what is the thing one, although it has parts?),-this must be considered later.

"What the essence is and in what sense it is independent, has been stated universally in a way which is true of every case, and also why the formula of the essence of some things contains the parts of the thing defined, while that of others does not. And we have stated that in the formula of the substance the material parts will not be present (for they are not even parts of the substance in that sense, but of the concrete substance; but of this there is in a sense a formula, and in a sense there is not; for there is no formula of it with its matter, for this is indefinite, but there is a formula of it with reference to its primary substance-e.g. in the case of man the formula of the soul-, for the substance is the indwelling form, from which and the matter the so-called concrete substance is derived; e.g. concavity is a form of this sort, for from this and the nose arise 'snub nose' and 'snubness'); but in the concrete substance, e.g. a snub nose or Callias, the matter also will be present. And we have stated that the essence and the thing itself are in some cases the same; ie. in the case of primary substances, e.g. curvature and the essence of curvature if this is primary. (By a 'primary' substance I mean one which does not imply the presence of something in something else, i.e. in something that underlies it which acts as matter.) But things which are of the nature of matter, or of wholes that include matter, are not the same as their essences, nor are accidental unities like that of 'Socrates' and 'musical'; for these are the same only by accident.

## Part 12

"Now let us treat first of definition, in so far as we have not treated of it in the Analytics; for the problem stated in them is useful for our inquiries concerning substance. I mean this problem:-wherein can consist the unity of that, the formula of which we call a definition, as for instance, in the case of man, 'two-footed animal'; for let this be the formula of man. Why, then, is this one, and not many, viz. 'animal' and 'two-footed'? For in the case of 'man' and 'pale' there is a plurality when one term does not belong to the other, but a unity when it does belong and the subject, man, has a certain attribute; for then a unity is produced and we have 'the pale man'. In the present case, on the other hand, one does not share in the other; the genus is not thought to share in its differentiae (for then the same thing would share in contraries; for the differentiae by which the genus is divided are contrary). And even if the genus does share in them, the same argument applies, since the differentiae present in man are many, e.g. endowed with feet, two-footed, featherless. Why are these one and not many? Not because they are present in one thing; for on this principle a unity can be made out of all the attributes of a thing. But surely all the attributes in the definition must be one; for the definition is a single formula and a formula of substance, so that it must be a formula of some one thing; for substance means a 'one' and a 'this', as we maintain.

"We must first inquire about definitions reached by the method of divisions. There is nothing in the definition except the first-named and the differentiae. The other genera are the first genus and along with this the differentiae that are taken with it, e.g. the first may be 'animal', the next 'animal which is two-footed', and again 'animal which is two-footed and featherless', and similarly if the definition includes more terms. And in general it makes no difference whether it includes many or few terms,-nor, therefore, whether it includes few or simply two; and of the two the one is differentia and the other genus; e.g. in 'two-footed animal' 'animal' is genus, and the other is differentia.

"If then the genus absolutely does not exist apart from the species-of-a-genus, or if it exists but exists as matter (for the voice is genus and matter, but its differentiae make the species, i.e. the letters, out of it), clearly the definition is the formula which comprises the differentiae.

"But it is also necessary that the division be by the differentia of the diferentia; e.g. 'endowed with feet' is a differentia of 'animal'; again the differentia of 'animal endowed with feet' must be of it qua endowed with feet. Therefore we must not say, if we are to speak rightly, that of that which is endowed with feet one part has feathers and one is featherless (if we do this we do it through incapacity); we must divide it only into cloven-footed and not cloven; for these are differentiae in the foot; cloven-footedness is a form of footedness. And the process wants always to go on so till it reaches the species that contain no differences. And then there will be as many kinds of foot as there are differentiae, and the kinds of animals endowed with feet will be equal in number to the differentiae. If then this is so, clearly the last differentia will be the substance of the thing and its definition, since it is not right to state the same things more than once in our definitions; for it is superfluous. And this does happen; for when we say 'animal endowed with feet and two-footed' we have said nothing other than 'animal having feet, having two feet'; and if we divide this by the proper division, we shall be saying the same thing more than once-as many times as there are differentiae.

"If then a differentia of a differentia be taken at each step, one differentia-the last-will be the form and the substance; but if we divide according to accidental qualities, e.g. if we were to divide that which is endowed with feet into the white and the black, there will be as many differentiae as there are cuts. Therefore it is plain that the definition is the formula which contains the differentiae, or, according to the right method, the last of these. This would be evident, if we were to change the order of such definitions, e.g. of that of man, saying 'animal which is two-footed and endowed with feet'; for 'endowed with feet' is superfluous when 'two-footed' has been said. But there is no order in the substance; for how are we to think the one element posterior and the other prior? Regarding the definitions, then, which are reached by the method of divisions, let this suffice as our first attempt at stating their nature.

Part 13

"Let us return to the subject of our inquiry, which is substance. As the substratum and the essence and the compound of these are called substance, so also is the universal. About two of these we have spoken; both about the essence and about the substratum, of which we have said that it underlies in two senses, either being a 'this'-which is the way in which an animal underlies its attributes-or as the matter underlies the complete reality. The universal also is thought by some to be in the fullest sense a cause, and a principle; therefore let us attack the discussion of this point also. For it seems impossible that any universal term should be the name of a substance. For firstly the substance of each thing is that which is peculiar to it, which does not belong to anything else; but the universal is common, since that is called universal which is such as to belong to more than one thing. Of which individual then will this be the substance? Either of all or of none; but it cannot be the substance of all. And if it is to be the substance of one, this one will be the others also; for things whose substance is one and whose essence is one are themselves also one.

"Further, substance means that which is not predicable of a subject, but the universal is predicable of some subject always.

"But perhaps the universal, while it cannot be substance in the way in which the essence is so, can be present in this; e.g. 'animal' can be present in 'man' and 'horse'. Then clearly it is a formula of the essence. And it makes no difference even if it is not a formula of everything that is in the substance; for none the less the universal will be the substance of something, as 'man' is the substance of the individual man in whom it is present, so that the same result will follow once more; for the universal, e.g. 'animal', will be the substance of that in which it is present as something peculiar to it. And further it is impossible and absurd that the 'this', i.e. the substance, if it consists of parts, should not consist of substances nor of what is a 'this', but of quality; for that which is not substance, i.e. the quality, will then be prior to substance and to the 'this'. Which is impossible; for neither in formula nor in time nor in coming to be can the modifications be prior to the substance; for then they will also be separable from it. Further, Socrates will contain a substance present in a substance, so that this will be the substance of two things. And in general it follows, if man and such things are substance, that none of the elements in their formulae is the substance of anything, nor does it exist apart from the species or in anything else; I mean, for instance, that no 'animal' exists apart from the particular kinds of animal, nor does any other of the elements present in formulae exist apart.

"If, then, we view the matter from these standpoints, it is plain that no universal attribute is a substance, and this is plain also from the fact that no common predicate indicates a 'this', but rather a 'such'. If not, many difficulties follow and especially the 'third man'.

"The conclusion is evident also from the following consideration. A substance cannot consist of substances present in it in complete reality; for things that are thus in complete reality two are never in complete reality one, though if they are potentially two, they can be one (e.g. the double line consists of two halves-potentially; for the complete realization of the halves divides them from one another); therefore if the substance is one, it will not consist of substances present in it and present in this way, which Democritus describes rightly; he says one thing cannot be made out of two nor two out of one; for he identifies substances with his indivisible magnitudes. It is clear therefore that the same will hold good of number, if number is a synthesis of units, as is said by some; for two is either not one, or there is no unit present in it in complete reality. But our result involves a difficulty. If no substance can consist of universals because a universal indicates a 'such', not a 'this', and if no substance can be composed of substances existing in complete reality, every substance would be incomposite, so that there would not even be a formula of any substance. But it is thought by all and was stated long ago that it is either only, or primarily, substance that can defined; yet now it seems that not even substance can. There cannot, then, be a definition of anything; or in a sense there can be, and in a sense there cannot. And what we are saying will be plainer from what follows.

Part 14

"It is clear also from these very facts what consequence confronts those who say the Ideas are substances capable of separate existence, and at the same time make the Form consist of the genus and the differentiae. For if the Forms exist and 'animal' is present in 'man' and 'horse', it is either one and the same in number, or different. (In formula it is clearly one; for he who states the formula will go through the formula in either case.) If then there is a 'man-in-himself' who is a 'this' and exists apart, the parts also of which he consists, e.g. 'animal' and 'two-footed', must indicate 'thises', and be capable of separate existence, and substances; therefore 'animal', as well as 'man', must be of this sort.

"Now (1) if the 'animal' in 'the horse' and in 'man' is one and the same, as you are with yourself, (a) how will the one in things that exist apart be one, and how will this 'animal' escape being divided even from itself?

"Further, (b) if it is to share in 'two-footed' and 'many-footed', an impossible conclusion follows; for contrary attributes will belong at the same time to it although it is one and a 'this'. If it is not to share in them, what is the relation implied when one says the animal is two-footed or possessed of feet? But perhaps the two things are 'put together' and are 'in contact', or are 'mixed'. Yet all these expressions are absurd.

"But (2) suppose the Form to be different in each species. Then there will be practically an infinite number of things whose substance is animal'; for it is not by accident that 'man' has 'animal' for one of its elements. Further, many things will be 'animal-itself'. For (i) the 'animal' in each species will be the substance of the species; for it is after nothing else that the species is called; if it were, that other would be an element in 'man', i.e. would be the genus of man. And further, (ii) all the elements of which 'man' is composed will be Ideas. None of them, then, will be the Idea of one thing and the substance of another; this is impossible. The 'animal', then, present in each species of animals will be animal-itself. Further, from what is this 'animal' in each species derived, and how will it be derived from animal-itself? Or how can this 'animal', whose essence is simply animality, exist apart from animal-itself?

"Further, (3)in the case of sensible things both these consequences and others still more absurd follow. If, then, these consequences are impossible, clearly there are not Forms of sensible things in the sense in which some maintain their existence.

## Part 15

"Since substance is of two kinds, the concrete thing and the formula (I mean that one kind of substance is the formula taken with the matter, while another kind is the formula in its generality), substances in the former sense are capable of destruction (for they are capable also of generation), but there is no destruction of the formula in the sense that it is ever in course of being destroyed (for there is no generation of it either; the being of house is not generated, but only the being of this house), but without generation and destruction formulae are and are not; for it has been shown that no one begets nor makes these. For this reason, also, there is neither definition of nor demonstration about sensible individual substances, because they have matter whose nature is such that they are capable both of being and of not being; for which reason all the individual instances of them are destructible. If then demonstration is of necessary truths and definition is a scientific process, and if, just as knowledge cannot be sometimes knowledge and sometimes ignorance, but the state which varies thus is opinion, so too demonstration and definition cannot vary thus, but it is opinion that deals with that which can be otherwise than as it is, clearly there can neither be definition of nor demonstration about sensible individuals. For perishing things are obscure to those who have the relevant knowledge, when they have passed from our perception; and though the formulae remain in the soul unchanged, there will no longer be either definition or demonstration. And so when one of the definition-mongers defines any individual, he must recognize that his definition may always be overthrown; for it is not possible to define such things.

"Nor is it possible to define any Idea. For the Idea is, as its supporters say, an individual, and can exist apart; and the formula must consist of words; and he who defines must not invent a word (for it would be unknown), but the established words are common to all the members of a class; these then must apply to something besides the thing defined; e.g. if one were defining you, he would say 'an animal which is lean' or 'pale', or something else which will apply also to some one other than you. If any one were to say that perhaps all the attributes taken apart may belong to many subjects, but together they belong only to this one, we must reply first that they belong also to both the elements; e.g. 'two-footed animal' belongs to animal and to the two-footed. (And in the case of eternal entities this is even necessary, since the elements are prior to and parts of the compound; nay more, they can also exist apart, if 'man' can exist apart. For either neither or both can. If, then, neither can, the genus will not exist apart from the various species; but if it does, the differentia will also.) Secondly, we must reply that 'animal' and 'two-footed' are prior in being to 'two-footed animal'; and things which are prior to others are not destroyed when the others are.

"Again, if the Ideas consist of Ideas (as they must, since elements are simpler than the compound), it will be further necessary that the elements also of which the Idea consists, e.g. 'animal' and 'two-footed', should be predicated of many subjects. If not, how will they come to be known? For there will then be an Idea which cannot be predicated of more subjects than one. But this is not thought possible-every Idea is thought to be capable of being shared.

"As has been said, then, the impossibility of defining individuals escapes notice in the case of eternal things, especially those which are unique, like the sun or the moon. For people err not only by adding attributes whose removal the sun would survive, e.g. 'going round the earth' or 'night-hidden' (for from their view it follows that if it stands still or is visible, it will no longer be the sun; but it is strange if this is so; for 'the sun' means a certain substance); but also by the mention of attributes which can belong to another subject; e.g. if another thing with the stated attributes comes into existence, clearly it will be a sun; the formula therefore is general. But the sun was supposed to be an individual, like Cleon or Socrates. After all, why does not one of the supporters of the Ideas produce a definition of an Idea? It would become clear, if they tried, that what has now been said is true.

Part 16

"Evidently even of the things that are thought to be substances, most are only potencies,-both the parts of animals (for none of them exists separately; and when they are separated, then too they exist, all of them, merely as matter) and earth and fire and air; for none of them is a unity, but as it were a mere heap, till they are worked up and some unity is made out of them. One might most readily suppose the parts of living things and the parts of the soul nearly related to them to turn out to be both, i.e. existent in complete reality as well as in potency, because they have sources of movement in something in their joints; for which reason some animals live when divided. Yet all the parts must exist only potentially, when they are one and continuous by nature,-not by force or by growing into one, for such a phenomenon is an abnormality.

"Since the term 'unity' is used like the term 'being', and the substance of that which is one is one, and things whose substance is numerically one are numerically one, evidently neither unity nor being can be the substance of things, just as being an element or a principle cannot be the substance, but we ask what, then, the principle is, that we may reduce the thing to something more knowable. Now of these concepts 'being' and 'unity' are more substantial than 'principle' or 'element' or 'cause', but not even the former are substance, since in general nothing that is common is substance; for substance does not belong to anything but to itself and to that which has it, of which it is the substance. Further, that which is one cannot be in many places at the same time, but that which is common is present in many places at the same time; so that clearly no universal exists apart from its individuals.

"But those who say the Forms exist, in one respect are right, in giving the Forms separate existence, if they are substances; but in another respect they are not right, because they say the one over many is a Form. The reason for their doing this is that they cannot declare what are the substances of this sort, the imperishable substances which exist apart from the individual and sensible substances. They make them, then, the same in kind as the perishable things (for this kind of substance we know)--'man-himself' and 'horse-itself', adding to the sensible things the word 'itself'. Yet even if we had not seen the stars, none the less, I suppose, would they have been eternal substances apart from those which we knew; so that now also if we do not know what non-sensible substances there are, yet it is doubtless necessary that there should he some.-Clearly, then, no universal term is the name of a substance, and no substance is composed of substances.

Part 17

"Let us state what, i.e. what kind of thing, substance should be said to be, taking once more another starting-point; for perhaps from this we shall get a clear view also of that substance which exists apart from sensible substances. Since, then, substance is a principle and a cause, let us pursue it from this starting-point. The 'why' is always sought in this form--'why does one thing attach to some other?' For to inquire why the musical man is a musical man, is either to inquire--as we have said why the man is musical, or it is something else. Now 'why a thing is itself' is a meaningless inquiry (for (to give meaning to the question 'why') the fact or the existence of the thing must already be evident-e.g. that the moon is eclipsed-but the fact that a thing is itself is the single reason and the single cause to be given in answer to all such questions as why the man is man, or the musician musical', unless one were to answer 'because each thing is inseparable from itself, and its being one just meant this'; this, however, is common to all things and is a short and easy way with the question). But we can inquire why man is an animal of such and such a nature. This, then, is plain, that we are not inquiring why he who is a man is a man. We are inquiring, then, why something is predicable of something (that it is predicable must be clear; for if not, the inquiry is an inquiry into nothing). E.g. why does it thunder? This is the same as 'why is sound produced in the clouds?' Thus the inquiry is about the predication of one thing of another. And why are these things, i.e. bricks and stones, a house? Plainly we are seeking the cause. And this is the essence (to speak abstractly), which in some cases is the end, e.g. perhaps in the case of a house or a bed, and in some cases is the first mover; for this also is a cause. But while the efficient cause is sought in the case of genesis and destruction, the final cause is sought in the case of being also.

"The object of the inquiry is most easily overlooked where one term is not expressly predicated of another (e.g. when we inquire 'what man is'), because we do not distinguish and do not say definitely that certain elements make up a certain whole. But we must articulate our meaning before we begin to inquire; if not, the inquiry is on the border-line between being a search for something and a search for nothing. Since we must have the existence of the thing as something given, clearly the question is why the matter is some definite thing; e.g. why are these materials a house? Because that which was the essence of a house is present. And why is this individual thing, or this body having this form, a man? Therefore what we seek is the cause, i.e. the form, by reason of which the matter is some definite thing; and this is the substance of the thing. Evidently, then, in the case of simple terms no inquiry nor teaching is possible; our attitude towards such things is other than that of inquiry.

"Since that which is compounded out of something so that the whole is one, not like a heap but like a syllable-now the syllable is not its elements, ba is not the same as b and a, nor is flesh fire and earth (for when these are separated the wholes, i.e. the flesh and the syllable, no longer exist, but the elements of the syllable exist, and so do fire and earth); the syllable, then, is something-not only its elements (the vowel and the consonant) but also something else, and the flesh is not only fire and earth or the hot and the cold, but also something else:-if, then, that something must itself be either an element or composed of elements, (1) if it is an element the same argument will again apply; for flesh will consist of this and fire and earth and something still further, so that the process will go on to infinity. But (2) if it is a compound, clearly it will be a compound not of one but of more than one (or else that one will be the thing itself), so that again in this case we can use the same argument as in the case of flesh or of the syllable. But it would seem that this 'other' is something, and not an element, and that it is the cause which makes this thing flesh and that a syllable. And similarly in all other cases. And this is the substance of each thing (for this is the primary cause of its being); and since, while some things are not substances, as many as are substances are formed in accordance with a nature of their own and by a process of nature, their substance would seem to be this kind of 'nature', which is not an element but a principle. An element, on the other hand, is that into which a thing is divided and which is present in it as matter; e.g. a and b are the elements of the syllable.

Book XII

Part 1

"The subject of our inquiry is substance; for the principles and the causes we are seeking are those of substances. For if the universe is of the nature of a whole, substance is its first part; and if it coheres merely by virtue of serial succession, on this view also substance is first, and is succeeded by quality, and then by quantity. At the same time these latter are not even being in the full sense, but are qualities and movements of it,-or else even the not-white and the not-straight would be being; at least we say even these are, e.g. 'there is a not-white'. Further, none of the categories other than substance can exist apart. And the early philosophers also in practice testify to the primacy of substance; for it was of substance that they sought the principles and elements and causes. The thinkers of the present day tend to rank universals as substances (for genera are universals, and these they tend to describe as principles and substances, owing to the abstract nature of their inquiry); but the thinkers of old ranked particular things as substances, e.g. fire and earth, not what is common to both, body.

"There are three kinds of substance-one that is sensible (of which one subdivision is eternal and another is perishable; the latter is recognized by all men, and includes e.g. plants and animals), of which we must grasp the elements, whether one or many; and another that is immovable, and this certain thinkers assert to be capable of existing apart, some dividing it into two, others identifying the Forms and the objects of mathematics, and others positing, of these two, only the objects of mathematics. The former two kinds of substance are the subject of physics (for they imply movement); but the third kind belongs to another science, if there is no principle common to it and to the other kinds.

Part 2

"Sensible substance is changeable. Now if change proceeds from opposites or from intermediates, and not from all opposites (for the voice is not-white, (but it does not therefore change to white)), but from the contrary, there must be something underlying which changes into the contrary state; for the contraries do not change. Further, something persists, but the contrary does not persist; there is, then, some third thing besides the contraries, viz. the matter. Now since changes are of four kinds-either in respect of the 'what' or of the quality or of the quantity or of the place, and change in respect of 'thisness' is simple generation and destruction, and change in quantity is increase and diminution, and change in respect of an affection is alteration, and change of place is motion, changes will be from given states into those contrary to them in these several respects. The matter, then, which changes must be capable of both states. And since that which 'is' has two senses, we must say that everything changes from that which is potentially to that which is actually, e.g. from potentially white to actually white, and similarly in the case of increase and diminution. Therefore not only can a thing come to be, incidentally, out of that which is not, but also all things come to be out of that which is, but is potentially, and is not actually. And this is the 'One' of Anaxagoras; for instead of 'all things were together'-and the 'Mixture' of Empedocles and Anaximander and the account given by Democritus-it is better to say 'all things were together potentially but not actually'. Therefore these thinkers seem to have had some notion of matter. Now all things that change have matter, but different matter; and of eternal things those which are not generable but are movable in space have matter-not matter for generation, however, but for motion from one place to another.

"One might raise the question from what sort of non-being generation proceeds; for 'non-being' has three senses. If, then, one form of non-being exists potentially, still it is not by virtue of a potentiality for any and every thing, but different things come from different things; nor is it satisfactory to say that 'all things were together'; for they differ in their matter, since otherwise why did an infinity of things come to be, and not one thing? For 'reason' is one, so that if matter also were one, that must have come to be in actuality which the matter was in potency. The causes and the principles, then, are three, two being the pair of contraries of which one is definition and form and the other is privation, and the third being the matter.

Part 3

"Note, next, that neither the matter nor the form comes to be-and I mean the last matter and form. For everything that changes is something and is changed by something and into something. That by which it is changed is the immediate mover; that which is changed, the matter; that into which it is changed, the form. The process, then, will go on to infinity, if not only the bronze comes to be round but also the round or the bronze comes to be; therefore there must be a stop.

"Note, next, that each substance comes into being out of something that shares its name. (Natural objects and other things both rank as substances.) For things come into being either by art or by nature or by luck or by spontaneity. Now art is a principle of movement in something other than the thing moved, nature is a principle in the thing itself (for man begets man), and the other causes are privations of these two.

"There are three kinds of substance-the matter, which is a 'this' in appearance (for all things that are characterized by contact and not, by organic unity are matter and substratum, e.g. fire, flesh, head; for these are all matter, and the last matter is the matter of that which is in the full sense substance); the nature, which is a 'this' or positive state towards which movement takes place; and again, thirdly, the particular substance which is composed of these two, e.g. Socrates or Callias. Now in some cases the 'this' does not exist apart from the composite substance, e.g. the form of house does not so exist, unless the art of building exists apart (nor is there generation and destruction of these forms, but it is in another way that the house apart from its matter, and health, and all ideals of art, exist and do not exist); but if the 'this' exists apart from the concrete thing, it is only in the case of natural objects. And so Plato was not far wrong when he said that there are as many Forms as there are kinds of natural object (if there are Forms distinct from the things of this earth). The moving causes exist as things preceding the effects, but causes in the sense of definitions are simultaneous with their effects. For when a man is healthy, then health also exists; and the shape of a bronze sphere exists at the same time as the bronze sphere. (But we must examine whether any form also survives afterwards. For in some cases there is nothing to prevent this; e.g. the soul may be of this sort-not all soul but the reason; for presumably it is impossible that all soul should survive.) Evidently then there is no necessity, on this ground at least, for the existence of the Ideas. For man is begotten by man, a given man by an individual father; and similarly in the arts; for the medical art is the formal cause of health.

Part 4

"The causes and the principles of different things are in a sense different, but in a sense, if one speaks universally and analogically, they are the same for all. For one might raise the question whether the principles and elements are different or the same for substances and for relative terms, and similarly in the case of each of the categories. But it would be paradoxical if they were the same for all. For then from the same elements will proceed relative terms and substances. What then will this common element be? For (1) (a) there is nothing common to and distinct from substance and the other categories, viz. those which are predicated; but an element is prior to the things of which it is an element. But again (b) substance is not an element in relative terms, nor is any of these an element in substance. Further, (2) how can all things have the same elements? For none of the elements can be the same as that which is composed of elements, e.g. b or a cannot be the same as ba. (None, therefore, of the intelligibles, e.g. being or unity, is an element; for these are predicable of each of the compounds as well.) None of the elements, then, will be either a substance or a relative term; but it must be one or other. All things, then, have not the same elements. "Or, as we are wont to put it, in a sense they have and in a sense they have not; e.g. perhaps the elements of perceptible bodies are, as form, the hot, and in another sense the cold, which is the privation; and, as matter, that which directly and of itself potentially has these attributes; and substances comprise both these and the things composed of these, of which these are the principles, or any unity which is produced out of the hot and the cold, e.g. flesh or bone; for the product must be different from the elements. These things then have the same elements and principles (though specifically different things have specifically different elements); but all things have not the same elements in this sense, but only analogically; i.e. one might say that there are three principles-the form, the privation, and the matter. But each of these is different for each class; e.g. in colour they are white, black, and surface, and in day and night they are light, darkness, and air.

"Since not only the elements present in a thing are causes, but also something external, i.e. the moving cause, clearly while 'principle' and 'element' are different both are causes, and 'principle' is divided into these two kinds; and that which acts as producing movement or rest is a principle and a substance. Therefore analogically there are three elements, and four causes and principles; but the elements are different in different things, and the proximate moving cause is different for different things. Health, disease, body; the moving cause is the medical art. Form, disorder of a particular kind, bricks; the moving cause is the building art. And since the moving cause in the case of natural things is-for man, for instance, man, and in the products of thought the form or its contrary, there will be in a sense three causes, while in a sense there are four. For the medical art is in some sense health, and the building art is the form of the house, and man begets man; further, besides these there is that which as first of all things moves all things.

Part 5

"Some things can exist apart and some cannot, and it is the former that are substances. And therefore all things have the same causes, because, without substances, modifications and movements do not exist. Further, these causes will probably be soul and body, or reason and desire and body.

"And in yet another way, analogically identical things are principles, i.e. actuality and potency; but these also are not only different for different things but also apply in different ways to them. For in some cases the same thing exists at one time actually and at another potentially, e.g. wine or flesh or man does so. (And these too fall under the above-named causes. For the form exists actually, if it can exist apart, and so does the complex of form and matter, and the privation, e.g. darkness or disease; but the matter exists potentially; for this is that which can become qualified either by the form or by the privation.) But the distinction of actuality and potentiality applies in another way to cases where the matter of cause and of effect is not the same, in some of which cases the form is not the same but different; e.g. the cause of man is (1) the elements in man (viz. fire and earth as matter, and the peculiar form), and further (2) something else outside, i.e. the father, and (3) besides these the sun and its oblique course, which are neither matter nor form nor privation of man nor of the same species with him, but moving causes.

"Further, one must observe that some causes can be expressed in universal terms, and some cannot. The proximate principles of all things are the 'this' which is proximate in actuality, and another which is proximate in potentiality. The universal causes, then, of which we spoke do not exist. For it is the individual that is the originative principle of the individuals. For while man is the originative principle of man universally, there is no universal man, but Peleus is the originative principle of Achilles, and your father of you, and this particular b of this particular ba, though b in general is the originative principle of ba taken without qualification.

"Further, if the causes of substances are the causes of all things, yet different things have different causes and elements, as was said; the causes of things that are not in the same class, e.g. of colours and sounds, of substances and quantities, are different except in an analogical sense; and those of things in the same species are different, not in species, but in the sense that the causes of different individuals are different, your matter and form and moving cause being different from mine, while in their universal definition they are the same. And if we inquire what are the principles or elements of substances and relations and qualities-whether they are the same or different-clearly when the names of the causes are used in several senses the causes of each are the same, but when the senses are distinguished the causes are not the same but different, except that in the following senses the causes of all are the same. They are (1) the same or analogous in this sense, that matter, form, privation, and the moving cause are common to all things; and (2) the causes of substances may be treated as causes of all things in this sense, that when substances are removed all things are removed; further, (3) that which is first in respect of complete reality is the cause of all things. But in another sense there are different first causes, viz. all the contraries which are neither generic nor ambiguous terms; and, further, the matters of different things are different. We have stated, then, what are the principles of sensible things and how many they are, and in what sense they are the same and in what sense different.

Part 6

"Since there were three kinds of substance, two of them physical and one unmovable, regarding the latter we must assert that it is necessary that there should be an eternal unmovable substance. For substances are the first of existing things, and if they are all destructible, all things are destructible. But it is impossible that movement should either have come into being or cease to be (for it must always have existed), or that time should. For there could not be a before and an after if time did not exist. Movement also is continuous, then, in the sense in which time is; for time is either the same thing as movement or an attribute of movement. And there is no continuous movement except movement in place, and of this only that which is circular is continuous.

"But if there is something which is capable of moving things or acting on them, but is not actually doing so, there will not necessarily be movement; for that which has a potency need not exercise it. Nothing, then, is gained even if we suppose eternal substances, as the believers in the Forms do, unless there is to be in them some principle which can cause change; nay, even this is not enough, nor is another substance besides the Forms enough; for if it is not to act, there will be no movement. Further even if it acts, this will not be enough, if its essence is potency; for there will not be eternal movement, since that which is potentially may possibly not be. There must, then, be such a principle, whose very essence is actuality. Further, then, these substances must be without matter; for they must be eternal, if anything is eternal. Therefore they must be actuality.

"Yet there is a difficulty; for it is thought that everything that acts is able to act, but that not everything that is able to act acts, so that the potency is prior. But if this is so, nothing that is need be; for it is possible for all things to be capable of existing but not yet to exist.

"Yet if we follow the theologians who generate the world from night, or the natural philosophers who say that 'all things were together', the same impossible result ensues. For how will there be movement, if there is no actually existing cause? Wood will surely not move itself-the carpenter's art must act on it; nor will the menstrual blood nor the earth set themselves in motion, but the seeds must act on the earth and the semen on the menstrual blood.

"This is why some suppose eternal actuality-e.g. Leucippus and Plato; for they say there is always movement. But why and what this movement is they do say, nor, if the world moves in this way or that, do they tell us the cause of its doing so. Now nothing is moved at random, but there must always be something present to move it; e.g. as a matter of fact a thing moves in one way by nature, and in another by force or through the influence of reason or something else. (Further, what sort of movement is primary? This makes a vast difference.) But again for Plato, at least, it is not permissible to name here that which he sometimes supposes to be the source of movement-that which moves itself; for the soul is later, and coeval with the heavens, according to his account. To suppose potency prior to actuality, then, is in a sense right, and in a sense not; and we have specified these senses. That actuality is prior is testified by Anaxagoras (for his 'reason' is actuality) and by Empedocles in his doctrine of love and strife, and by those who say that there is always movement, e.g. Leucippus. Therefore chaos or night did not exist for an infinite time, but the same things have always existed (either passing through a cycle of changes or obeying some other law), since actuality is prior to potency. If, then, there is a constant cycle, something must always remain, acting in the same way. And if there is to be generation and destruction, there must be something else which is always acting in different ways. This must, then, act in one way in virtue of itself, and in another in virtue of something else-either of a third agent, therefore, or of the first. Now it must be in virtue of the first. For otherwise this again causes the motion both of the second agent and of the third. Therefore it is better to say 'the first'. For it was the cause of eternal uniformity; and something else is the cause of variety, and evidently both together are the cause of eternal variety. This, accordingly, is the character which the motions actually exhibit. What need then is there to seek for other principles?

Part 7

"Since (1) this is a possible account of the matter, and (2) if it were not true, the world would have proceeded out of night and 'all things together' and out of non-being, these difficulties may be taken as solved. There is, then, something which is always moved with an unceasing motion, which is motion in a circle; and this is plain not in theory only but in fact. Therefore the first heaven must be eternal. There is therefore also something which moves it. And since that which moves and is moved is intermediate, there is something which moves without being moved, being eternal, substance, and actuality. And the object of desire and the object of thought move in this way; they move without being moved. The primary objects of desire and of thought are the same. For the apparent good is the object of appetite, and the real good is the primary object of rational wish. But desire is consequent on opinion rather than opinion on desire; for the thinking is the starting-point. And thought is moved by the object of thought, and one of the two columns of opposites is in itself the object of thought; and in this, substance is first, and in substance, that which is simple and exists actually. (The one and the simple are not the same; for 'one' means a measure, but 'simple' means that the thing itself has a certain nature.) But the beautiful, also, and that which is in itself desirable are in the same column; and the first in any class is always best, or analogous to the best.

"That a final cause may exist among unchangeable entities is shown by the distinction of its meanings. For the final cause is (a) some being for whose good an action is done, and (b) something at which the action aims; and of these the latter exists among unchangeable entities though the former does not. The final cause, then, produces motion as being loved, but all other things move by being moved. Now if something is moved it is capable of being otherwise than as it is. Therefore if its actuality is the primary form of spatial motion, then in so far as it is subject to change, in this respect it is capable of being otherwise,-in place, even if not in substance. But since there is something which moves while itself unmoved, existing actually, this can in no way be otherwise than as it is. For motion in space is the first of the kinds of change, and motion in a circle the first kind of spatial motion; and this the first mover produces. The first mover, then, exists of necessity; and in so far as it exists by necessity, its mode of being is good, and it is in this sense a first principle. For the necessary has all these senses-that which is necessary perforce because it is contrary to the natural impulse, that without which the good is impossible, and that which cannot be otherwise but can exist only in a single way.

"On such a principle, then, depend the heavens and the world of nature. And it is a life such as the best which we enjoy, and enjoy for but a short time (for it is ever in this state, which we cannot be), since its actuality is also pleasure. (And for this reason are waking, perception, and thinking most pleasant, and hopes and memories are so on account of these.) And thinking in itself deals with that which is best in itself, and that which is thinking in the fullest sense with that which is best in the fullest sense. And thought thinks on itself because it shares the nature of the object of thought; for it becomes an object of thought in coming into contact with and thinking its objects, so that thought and object of thought are the same. For that which is capable of receiving the object of thought, i.e. the essence, is thought. But it is active when it possesses this object. Therefore the possession rather than the receptivity is the divine element which thought seems to contain, and the act of contemplation is what is most pleasant and best. If, then, God is always in that good state in which we sometimes are, this compels our wonder; and if in a better this compels it yet more. And God is in a better state. And life also belongs to God; for the actuality of thought is life, and God is that actuality; and God's self-dependent actuality is life most good and eternal. We say therefore that God is a living being, eternal, most good, so that life and duration continuous and eternal belong to God; for this is God.

"Those who suppose, as the Pythagoreans and Speusippus do, that supreme beauty and goodness are not present in the beginning, because the beginnings both of plants and of animals are causes, but beauty and completeness are in the effects of these, are wrong in their opinion. For the seed comes from other individuals which are prior and complete, and the first thing is not seed but the complete being; e.g. we must say that before the seed there is a man,-not the man produced from the seed, but another from whom the seed comes.

"It is clear then from what has been said that there is a substance which is eternal and unmovable and separate from sensible things. It has been shown also that this substance cannot have any magnitude, but is without parts and indivisible (for it produces movement through infinite time, but nothing finite has infinite power; and, while every magnitude is either infinite or finite, it cannot, for the above reason, have finite magnitude, and it cannot have infinite magnitude because there is no infinite magnitude at all). But it has also been shown that it is impassive and unalterable; for all the other changes are posterior to change of place.

Part 8

"It is clear, then, why these things are as they are. But we must not ignore the question whether we have to suppose one such substance or more than one, and if the latter, how many; we must also mention, regarding the opinions expressed by others, that they have said nothing about the number of the substances that can even be clearly stated. For the theory of Ideas has no special discussion of the subject; for those who speak of Ideas say the Ideas are numbers, and they speak of numbers now as unlimited, now as limited by the number 10; but as for the reason why there should be just so many numbers, nothing is said with any demonstrative exactness. We however must discuss the subject, starting from the presuppositions and distinctions we have mentioned. The first principle or primary being is not movable either in itself or accidentally, but produces the primary eternal and single movement. But since that which is moved must be moved by something, and the first mover must be in itself unmovable, and eternal movement must be produced by something eternal and a single movement by a single thing, and since we see that besides the simple spatial movement of the universe, which we say the first and unmovable substance produces, there are other spatial movements-those of the planets-which are eternal (for a body which moves in a circle is eternal and unresting; we have proved these points in the physical treatises), each of these movements also must be caused by a substance both unmovable in itself and eternal. For the nature of the stars is eternal just because it is a certain kind of substance, and the mover is eternal and prior to the moved, and that which is prior to a substance must be a substance. Evidently, then, there must be substances which are of the same number as the movements of the stars, and in their nature eternal, and in themselves unmovable, and without magnitude, for the reason before mentioned. That the movers are substances, then, and that one of these is first and another second according to the same order as the movements of the stars, is evident. But in the number of the movements we reach a problem which must be treated from the standpoint of that one of the mathematical sciences which is most akin to philosophy-viz. of astronomy; for this science speculates about substance which is perceptible but eternal, but the other mathematical sciences, i.e. arithmetic and geometry, treat of no substance. That the movements are more numerous than the bodies that are moved is evident to those who have given even moderate attention to the matter; for each of the planets has more than one movement. But as to the actual number of these movements, we now-to give some notion of the subject-quote what some of the mathematicians say, that our thought may have some definite number to grasp; but, for the rest, we must partly investigate for ourselves, Partly learn from other investigators, and if those who study this subject form an opinion contrary to what we have now stated, we must esteem both parties indeed, but follow the more accurate.

"Eudoxus supposed that the motion of the sun or of the moon involves, in either case, three spheres, of which the first is the sphere of the fixed stars, and the second moves in the circle which runs along the middle of the zodiac, and the third in the circle which is inclined across the breadth of the zodiac; but the circle in which the moon moves is inclined at a greater angle than that in which the sun moves. And the motion of the planets involves, in each case, four spheres, and of these also the first and second are the same as the first two mentioned above (for the sphere of the fixed stars is that which moves all the other spheres, and that which is placed beneath this and has its movement in the circle which bisects the zodiac is common to all), but the poles of the third sphere of each planet are in the circle which bisects the zodiac, and the motion of the fourth sphere is in the circle which is inclined at an angle to the equator of the third sphere; and the poles of the third sphere are different for each of the other planets, but those of Venus and Mercury are the same.

"Callippus made the position of the spheres the same as Eudoxus did, but while he assigned the same number as Eudoxus did to Jupiter and to Saturn, he thought two more spheres should be added to the sun and two to the moon, if one is to explain the observed facts; and one more to each of the other planets.

"But it is necessary, if all the spheres combined are to explain the observed facts, that for each of the planets there should be other spheres (one fewer than those hitherto assigned) which counteract those already mentioned and bring back to the same position the outermost sphere of the star which in each case is situated below the star in question; for only thus can all the forces at work produce the observed motion of the planets. Since, then, the spheres involved in the movement of the planets themselves are-- eight for Saturn and Jupiter and twenty-five for the others, and of these only those involved in the movement of the lowest-situated planet need not be counteracted the spheres which counteract those of the outermost two planets will be six in number, and the spheres which counteract those of the next four planets will be sixteen; therefore the number of all the spheres--both those which move the planets and those which counteract these--will be fifty-five. And if one were not to add to the moon and to the sun the movements we mentioned, the whole set of spheres will be forty-seven in number.

"Let this, then, be taken as the number of the spheres, so that the unmovable substances and principles also may probably be taken as just so many; the assertion of necessity must be left to more powerful thinkers. But if there can be no spatial movement which does not conduce to the moving of a star, and if further every being and every substance which is immune from change and in virtue of itself has attained to the best must be considered an end, there can be no other being apart from these we have named, but this must be the number of the substances. For if there are others, they will cause change as being a final cause of movement; but there cannot he other movements besides those mentioned. And it is reasonable to infer this from a consideration of the bodies that are moved; for if everything that moves is for the sake of that which is moved, and every movement belongs to something that is moved, no movement can be for the sake of itself or of another movement, but all the movements must be for the sake of the stars. For if there is to be a movement for the sake of a movement, this latter also will have to be for the sake of something else; so that since there cannot be an infinite regress, the end of every movement will be one of the divine bodies which move through the heaven.

"(Evidently there is but one heaven. For if there are many heavens as there are many men, the moving principles, of which each heaven will have one, will be one in form but in number many. But all things that are many in number have matter; for one and the same definition, e.g. that of man, applies to many things, while Socrates is one. But the primary essence has not matter; for it is complete reality. So the unmovable first mover is one both in definition and in number; so too, therefore, is that which is moved always and continuously; therefore there is one heaven alone.) Our forefathers in the most remote ages have handed down to their posterity a tradition, in the form of a myth, that these bodies are gods, and that the divine encloses the whole of nature. The rest of the tradition has been added later in mythical form with a view to the persuasion of the multitude and to its legal and utilitarian expediency; they say these gods are in the form of men or like some of the other animals, and they say other things consequent on and similar to these which we have mentioned. But if one were to separate the first point from these additions and take it alone-that they thought the first substances to be gods, one must regard this as an inspired utterance, and reflect that, while probably each art and each science has often been developed as far as possible and has again perished, these opinions, with others, have been preserved until the present like relics of the ancient treasure. Only thus far, then, is the opinion of our ancestors and of our earliest predecessors clear to us.

Part 9

"The nature of the divine thought involves certain problems; for while thought is held to be the most divine of things observed by us, the question how it must be situated in order to have that character involves difficulties. For if it thinks of nothing, what is there here of dignity? It is just like one who sleeps. And if it thinks, but this depends on something else, then (since that which is its substance is not the act of thinking, but a potency) it cannot be the best substance; for it is through thinking that its value belongs to it. Further, whether its substance is the faculty of thought or the act of thinking, what does it think of? Either of itself or of something else; and if of something else, either of the same thing always or of something different. Does it matter, then, or not, whether it thinks of the good or of any chance thing? Are there not some things about which it is incredible that it should think? Evidently, then, it thinks of that which is most divine and precious, and it does not change; for change would be change for the worse, and this would be already a movement. First, then, if 'thought' is not the act of thinking but a potency, it would be reasonable to suppose that the continuity of its thinking is wearisome to it. Secondly, there would evidently be something else more precious than thought, viz. that which is thought of. For both thinking and the act of thought will belong even to one who thinks of the worst thing in the world, so that if this ought to be avoided (and it ought, for there are even some things which it is better not to see than to see), the act of thinking cannot be the best of things. Therefore it must be of itself that the divine thought thinks (since it is the most excellent of things), and its thinking is a thinking on thinking.

"But evidently knowledge and perception and opinion and understanding have always something else as their object, and themselves only by the way. Further, if thinking and being thought of are different, in respect of which does goodness belong to thought? For to he an act of thinking and to he an object of thought are not the same thing. We answer that in some cases the knowledge is the object. In the productive sciences it is the substance or essence of the object, matter omitted, and in the theoretical sciences the definition or the act of thinking is the object. Since, then, thought and the object of thought are not different in the case of things that have not matter, the divine thought and its object will be the same, i.e. the thinking will be one with the object of its thought.

"A further question is left-whether the object of the divine thought is composite; for if it were, thought would change in passing from part to part of the whole. We answer that everything which has not matter is indivisible-as human thought, or rather the thought of composite beings, is in a certain period of time (for it does not possess the good at this moment or at that, but its best, being something different from it, is attained only in a whole period of time), so throughout eternity is the thought which has itself for its object.

Part 10

"We must consider also in which of two ways the nature of the universe contains the good, and the highest good, whether as something separate and by itself, or as the order of the parts. Probably in both ways, as an army does; for its good is found both in its order and in its leader, and more in the latter; for he does not depend on the order but it depends on him. And all things are ordered together somehow, but not all alike,-both fishes and fowls and plants; and the world is not such that one thing has nothing to do with another, but they are connected. For all are ordered together to one end, but it is as in a house, where the freemen are least at liberty to act at random, but all things or most things are already ordained for them, while the slaves and the animals do little for the common good, and for the most part live at random; for this is the sort of principle that constitutes the nature of each. I mean, for instance, that all must at least come to be dissolved into their elements, and there are other functions similarly in which all share for the good of the whole.

"We must not fail to observe how many impossible or paradoxical results confront those who hold different views from our own, and what are the views of the subtler thinkers, and which views are attended by fewest difficulties. All make all things out of contraries. But neither 'all things' nor 'out of contraries' is right; nor do these thinkers tell us how all the things in which the contraries are present can be made out of the contraries; for contraries are not affected by one another. Now for us this difficulty is solved naturally by the fact that there is a third element. These thinkers however make one of the two contraries matter; this is done for instance by those who make the unequal matter for the equal, or the many matter for the one. But this also is refuted in the same way; for the one matter which underlies any pair of contraries is contrary to nothing. Further, all things, except the one, will, on the view we are criticizing, partake of evil; for the bad itself is one of the two elements. But the other school does not treat the good and the bad even as principles; yet in all things the good is in the highest degree a principle. The school we first mentioned is right in saying that it is a principle, but how the good is a principle they do not say-whether as end or as mover or as form.

"Empedocles also has a paradoxical view; for he identifies the good with love, but this is a principle both as mover (for it brings things together) and as matter (for it is part of the mixture). Now even if it happens that the same thing is a principle both as matter and as mover, still the being, at least, of the two is not the same. In which respect then is love a principle? It is paradoxical also that strife should be imperishable; the nature of his 'evil' is just strife.

"Anaxagoras makes the good a motive principle; for his 'reason' moves things. But it moves them for an end, which must be something other than it, except according to our way of stating the case; for, on our view, the medical art is in a sense health. It is paradoxical also not to suppose a contrary to the good, i.e. to reason. But all who speak of the contraries make no use of the contraries, unless we bring their views into shape. And why some things are perishable and others imperishable, no one tells us; for they make all existing things out of the same principles. Further, some make existing things out of the nonexistent; and others to avoid the necessity of this make all things one.

"Further, why should there always be becoming, and what is the cause of becoming?-this no one tells us. And those who suppose two principles must suppose another, a superior principle, and so must those who believe in the Forms; for why did things come to participate, or why do they participate, in the Forms? And all other thinkers are confronted by the necessary consequence that there is something contrary to Wisdom, i.e. to the highest knowledge; but we are not. For there is nothing contrary to that which is primary; for all contraries have matter, and things that have matter exist only potentially; and the ignorance which is contrary to any knowledge leads to an object contrary to the object of the knowledge; but what is primary has no contrary.

"Again, if besides sensible things no others exist, there will be no first principle, no order, no becoming, no heavenly bodies, but each principle will have a principle before it, as in the accounts of the theologians and all the natural philosophers. But if the Forms or the numbers are to exist, they will be causes of nothing; or if not that, at least not of movement. Further, how is extension, i.e. a continuum, to be produced out of unextended parts? For number will not, either as mover or as form, produce a continuum. But again there cannot be any contrary that is also essentially a productive or moving principle; for it would be possible for it not to be. Or at least its action would be posterior to its potency. The world, then, would not be eternal. But it is; one of these premises, then, must be denied. And we have said how this must be done. Further, in virtue of what the numbers, or the soul and the body, or in general the form and the thing, are one-of this no one tells us anything; nor can any one tell, unless he says, as we do, that the mover makes them one. And those who say mathematical number is first and go on to generate one kind of substance after another and give different principles for each, make the substance of the universe a mere series of episodes (for one substance has no

127

influence on another by its existence or nonexistence), and they give us many governing principles; but the world refuses to be governed badly. "

'"The rule of many is not good; one ruler let there be.'

## *On Being and Essence*
### By St. Thomas Aquinas

1. A small mistake in the beginning is a big one in the end, according to the Philosopher in the first book of On the Heavens and the Earth. And as Ibn-Sînâ says in the beginning of his Metaphysics, being and essence are what is first conceived by the intellect.

2. Thus, to avoid making mistakes out of ignorance of them, and to become familiar with the difficulties they entail, we must point out what is signified by the words "being" and "essence," and how they are found in diverse things, and how they are related to the logical intentions, genus, species, and difference.

3. Since we ought to acquire knowledge of what is simple from what is composed, and come to what is prior from what is posterior, so that, beginning with what is easier, we may progress more suitably in learning; we ought proceed from the meaning of the word "being" to that of the word "essence."

4. We should notice, therefore, that the word "being," taken without qualifiers, has two uses, as the Philosopher says in the fifth book of the Metaphysics. (1) In one way, it is used apropos of what is divided into the ten genera; (2) in another way, it is used to signify the truth of propositions. The difference between the two is that in the second way everything about which we can form an affirmative proposition can be called a being, even though it posits nothing in reality. It is in this way that privations and negations are called beings; for we say that affirmation is opposed to negation, and that blindness is in the eye. In the first way, however, only what posits something in reality can be called a being. In the first way, therefore, blindness and the like are not beings.

5. So, the word "essence" is not taken from the word "being" used in the second way; for some things which do not have an essence are called beings in this way as is clear in the case of privations. Rather, the word "essence" is taken from the word "being" used in the first way. It is for this reason that the Commentator says in the same place that the word "being" used in the first way is what signifies the essence of a real thing.

6. And because the word "being" used in this way is used apropos of what is divided into the ten genera, as we have said, the word "essence" must signify something common to all natures, by means of which (nature) diverse beings are placed into diverse genera and species; as, for example, humanity is the essence of man, and so with other things.

7. And because that by which a real thing is constituted in its proper genus or species is what is signified by the definition expressing what the real thing is, philosophers sometimes use the word "quiddity" for the word "essence." This is what the Philosopher often calls what something was to be, i.e., that by which it belongs to something to be what it is.

8. It is also called form, in the sense in which the word "form" signifies the full determination of each real thing, as Ibn-Sînâ says in the second book of his Metaphysics.

9. Further, it is given another name, nature, taking the word "nature" in the first of the four ways given by Boethius in his book On the Two Natures. In this way, whatever can in any way be grasped by the intellect is called a nature. For a real thing is not intelligible except through its definition and essence.

10. The Philosopher, too, says in the fifth book of the Metaphysics that every substance is a nature. But the word "nature" taken in this way appears to signify the essence of a real thing according as

it has an ordering to the thing's proper operation; and no real thing lacks a proper operation.

11. The name "quiddity," however, is taken from the fact that what is signified by the definition is the essence. But it is called essence from the fact that through it and in it a real being has existence.

12. Because the word "being" is used absolutely and with priority of substances, and only posteriorly and with qualification of accidents, essence is in substances truly and properly, in accidents only in some way with qualification.

13. Further, some substances are simple and some are composed, and essence is in each. But essence is in simple substances in a truer and more noble way, according to which they also have a more noble existence; for they — at least that simple substance which is first, and which is God — are the cause of those which are composed. But because the essences of the simple substances are more hidden from us, we ought to begin with the essences of composed substances, so that we may progress more suitably in learning from what is easier.

14. In composed substances there are form and matter, for example, in man soul and body.

15. But we cannot say that either one of them alone may be said to be the essence. That matter alone is not the essence of a real thing is clear, since through its essence a real thing is knowable and assigned to a species or to a genus. But matter alone is neither a principle of knowledge, nor is it that by which something is assigned to a genus or to a species; rather a thing is so assigned by reason of its being something actual.

16. Neither can the form alone of a composed substance be said to be its essence, although some try to assert this. For it is evident

from what has been said that essence is what is signified by the definition of a real thing. And the definition of natural substances contains not only form, but matter as well; otherwise natural definitions and mathematical ones would not differ.

17. Neither can it be said that matter is placed in the definition of a natural substance as something added to its essence or as something outside its essence, because this mode of definition is proper to accidents, which do not have a perfect essence. This is why accidents must include in their definition a subject which is outside their genus. It is clear therefore that essence includes matter and form.

18. Further, neither can it be said that essence signifies some relation between matter and form or something added to them, because this would of necessity be an accident or something extraneous to the real thing, and the real thing would not be known through it. And these are traits of essence. For through the form, which is the actuality of matter, matter becomes something actual and something individual. Whence what supervenes does not confer on matter actual existence simply, but such an actual existence; as accidents in fact do. Whiteness, for example, makes something actually white. Whence the acquisition of such a form is not called generation simply, but generation in a certain respect. It remains, therefore, that the word "essence" in composed substances signifies that which is composed of matter and form.

19. Boethius is in agreement with this in his commentary on the Predicaments, where he says that ousia signifies the composite. For ousia in Greek is the same as essentia in Latin, as he himself says in his book On the Two Natures. Ibn-Sînâ, too, says that the quiddity of composed substances is the composition itself of form and matter. And the Commentator, likewise, in his considerations on the seventh book of the Metaphysics says: "The nature which species have in generable things is something in between, i.e., composed of matter and form."

20. Reason, too, is in accord with this, because the existence of a composed substance is not the existence of the form alone nor of the matter alone, but of the composite itself; and essence is that according to which a real thing is said to be. Whence it is necessary that the essence, whereby a real thing is denominated a being, be neither the form alone nor the matter alone, but both, although the form alone in its own way is the cause of such existence.

21. We see the same in other things which are constituted of a plurality of principles, namely, that the real thing is not denominated from one of these principles alone, but from what includes both, as is evident in the case of tastes. Sweetness, for example, is caused by the action of what is hot dispersing what is moist; and although heat in this way is the cause of sweetness, a body is not denominated sweet from heat, but from the taste which includes what is hot and what is moist.

22. But matter is the principle of individuation. From this it might perhaps appear to follow that an essence which includes in itself matter along with form is only particular and not universal. And from this it would follow that universals would not have a definition, if essence is that which is signified by a definition.

23. We should notice, therefore, that the principle of individuation is not matter taken in just any way whatever, but only designated matter. And I call that matter designated which is considered under determined dimensions. Such matter is not placed in the definition of man as man, but it would be placed in the definition of Socrates, if Socrates had a definition. Rather, it is non-designated matter which. is placed in the definition of man; for this bone and this flesh are not placed in the definition of man, but bone and flesh absolutely. These latter are man's non-designated matter.

24. It is clear, therefore, that the essence of man and the essence of Socrates do not differ, except as the non-designated from the designated. Whence the Commentator says in his considerations on the seventh book of the Metaphysics that "Socrates is nothing other than animality and rationality, which are his quiddity."

25. The essence of the genus and that of the species also differ in this way, i.e., as the non-designated from the designated, although the mode of the designation differs in each case. Whereas the designation of the individual with respect to the species is through matter determined by dimensions, the designation of the species with respect to the genus is through the constitutive difference which is taken from the form of the thing.

26. This designation which is in the species with respect to the genus is not through something in the essence of the species which is in no way in the essence of the genus; rather, whatever is in the species is also in the genus, but as undetermined. For, if animal were not the whole that man is, but a part of man, it would not be predicated of man, since no integral part may be predicated of its whole.

27. We can see how this comes about if we examine how body taken as part of animal differs from body taken as genus; for body cannot be a genus in the same way in which body is an integral part.

28. The word "body" can be taken in many ways. Body according as it is in the genus substance is so called from the fact that it has a nature such that three dimensions can be designated in it; but the three designated dimensions themselves are a body according as body is in the genus quantity. Now, it happens in things that what has one perfection may also attain to further perfection. This is clear, for example, in man who has a sensitive nature, and further an intellectual nature. Similarly, another perfection, such as life or some other such perfection, can be added to the perfection of

having a form such that three dimensions can be designated in it. The word "body," therefore can signify some real thing which has a form from which follows the possibility of designating in it three dimensions, and signify this in an excluding way, i.e., in such a way such that no further perfection may follow from that form; in a way such that if anything be added, it is outside the signification of body. Taken in this way, body will be an integral and material part of animal because soul will be outside what is signified by the word "body"; the soul will be something over and above the body, in a way such that animal is constituted out of these two as out of parts, i.e., out of soul and body.

29. The word "body" can also be taken in another way, namely, to signify a thing which has a form such that three dimensions can be designated in it, no matter what sort of form it is, whether some further perfection can come from it or not. And taken in this way, body will be a genus of animal, because there is nothing in animal which is not implicitly contained in body. Soul is not a form other than the form through which three dimensions could be designated in that thing; thus, when we said that body is that which has a form such that because of it three dimensions can be designated in the body, form meant any form, whether animality or stoneness, or any other form. And so the form of animal is implicitly contained in the form of body, when body is its genus.

30. And such likewise is the relation of animal to man. For, if animal were to name only that thing which has a perfection such that it can sense and be moved by a principle within itself, and name this thing as excluding other perfection, then any further perfection would be related to animal as a part, and not as implicitly contained in the notion of animal; and so, animal would not be a genus. Animal is a genus according as it signifies a thing from whose form the senses and movement can come forth, no matter what sort of form it is, whether a sensible soul only or a soul which is both sensible and rational.

31. The genus, thus, signifies indeterminately everything that is in the species; it does not signify the matter alone. Similarly, the difference, too, signifies everything in the species, and not the form alone; the definition, too, signifies the whole, and so does the species, but in diverse ways.

32. The genus signifies the whole as a name determining what is material in the real thing without the determination of the proper form. Whence the genus is taken from the matter, although it is not the matter. And from this it is clear that a body is called a body from the fact that it has a perfection such that three dimensions can be designated in the body, and that this perfection is related materially to further perfection.

33. The difference, on the contrary, is a name taken from a determinate form, and taken in a determinate way, i.e. as not including a determinate matter in its meaning. This is clear, for example, when we say animated, i.e., that which has a soul; for what it is, whether a body or something other, is not expressed. Whence Ibn-Sînâ says that the genus is not understood in the difference as a part of its essence, but only as something outside its essence, as the subject also is understood in its properties. And this is why the genus is not predicated essentially of the difference, as the Philosopher says in the third book of the Metaphysics and in the fourth book of the Topics, but only in the way in which a subject is predicated of its property.

34. The definition, lastly, and the species include both, namely the determinate matter which the name of the genus designates, and the determinate form which the name of the difference designates.

35. From this it is clear why the genus, the difference, and the species are related proportionately to the matter, to the form, and to the composite in the real world, although they are not identical with them.

36. The genus is not the matter, but taken from the matter as signifying the whole; nor is the difference the form, but taken from the form as signifying the whole.

37. Whence we say that man is a rational animal, and not that man is made up of animal and rational as we say that man is made up of soul and body. Man is said to be composed of soul and body as some third thing constituted of two other things, and which is neither of them. For man is neither soul nor body. But if man may be said in some way to be composed of animal and rational, it will not be as a third thing out of two other things, but as a third concept out of two other concepts. For the concept "animal" is without the determination of the form of the species, and it expresses the nature of a thing from that which is material in relation to the ultimate perfection. But the concept of the difference "rational" consists in the determination of the form of the species. And from these two concepts the concept of the species or of the definition is constituted. And thus just as the constituents of a real thing are not predicated of that real thing, so too the concepts which are constituents of another concept are not predicated of that concept; for we do not say that the definition is the genus or the difference.

38. Although the genus signifies the whole essence of the species, it is not necessary that the diverse species in a same genus have one essence.

39. For the oneness of the genus proceeds from its very indetermination or indifference; not however in such a way that what is signified by the genus is some numerically one nature found in diverse species, and to which another thing supervenes, namely the difference, determining the genus as form determines matter which is numerically one. It is rather because the genus signifies some form, not determinately this form or that form, which the difference expresses determinately, but which is not

other than the form which was indeterminately signified by the genus.

40. This is why the Commentator says in his considerations on the eleventh book of the Metaphysics that prime matter is said to be one by reason of the removal of all forms, whereas the genus is said to be one by reason of the commonness of the designated form.

41. Whence, it is clear that when one adds the difference and removes that indetermination which was the cause of the oneness of the genus, there remain species which are diverse in essence.

42. The nature of the species, as we have said, is indeterminate in relation to the individual, as the nature of the genus is indeterminate in relation to the species.

43. Because of this, just as that which is a genus, as predicated of the species, implies in its signification, though indistinctly, everything that is determinately in the species; so too that which is a species, according as it is predicated of the individual, must signify, though indistinctly, everything which is essentially in the individual.

44. And it is in this way that the essence of the species is signified by the word "man"; whence man is predicated of Socrates. But if the nature of the species is signified as excluding designated matter, which is the principle of individuation, it will be as a part; and in this way it is signified by the word "humanity," for humanity signifies that by which man is man; and it is not the case that man is man by reason of designated matter. And so designated matter is in no way included among the things by which man is man. Since, therefore, humanity includes in its concept only those things by which man is man, it is clear that designated matter is excluded from or is cut out of its

signification. And because a part is not predicated of its whole, humanity is not predicated of man, nor is it predicated of Socrates.

45. Whence Ibn-Sînâ says that the quiddity of a composite is not the composite itself whose quiddity it is, even though the quiddity too is composed. Humanity, for example, though composed, is not man; it must be received into something which is designated matter.

46. As we have said, the designation of the species with respect to the genus is through forms, whereas the designation of the individual with respect to the species is through matter. This is why the word which signifies that from which the nature of the genus is taken, and signifies it as excluding the determinate form which perfects the species, must signify a material part of the whole, as, for example, body is a material part of man. But the word which signifies that from which the nature of the species is taken, and signifies it as excluding designated matter, signifies a formal part.

47. And thus humanity is signified as a certain form, and it is said to be the form of the whole, not indeed as something added to the essential parts, namely to form and matter, as the form of a house is added to its integral parts; rather, it is a form which is a whole, that is, a form which includes both form and matter, but which excludes those things by reason of which matter can be designated.

48. It is clear, therefore, that the word "man" and the word "humanity" signify the essence of man, but diversely, as we have said; the word "man" signifies it as a whole, inasmuch as it does not exclude designation by matter, but contains it implicitly and indistinctly, as we have said before that the genus contains the difference. And this is why the word "man" is predicated of individuals. But the word "humanity" signifies it as a part, because it contains in its signification only what belongs to man as

man, and it excludes all designation by matter. Whence it is not predicated of individual men.

49. And this is why the word "essence" is sometimes found predicated of a real thing, for we say that Socrates is a certain essence; and sometimes it is denied, as when we say that the essence of Socrates is not Socrates.

50. Having seen what is signified by the word "essence" in composed substances, we must see how a composed essence is related to the notion of the genus, of the species, and of the difference.

51. Because that to which the notion of the genus, or of the species, or of the difference, belongs is predicated of this designated singular, it is impossible that the notion of a universal — e.g., of the genus or of the species — belong to an essence according as it is signified a part, as by the word "humanity" or "animality." And this is why Ibn-Sînâ says that rationality is not a difference, but the principle of a difference. And for the same reason humanity is not a species, and animality not a genus.

52. Similarly, it cannot be said that the notion of the genus, or of the species, belongs to an essence as to some real thing existing outside singular things, as the Platonists held, because in this way the genus and the species would not be predicated of this individual; for it cannot be said that Socrates is what is separated from him. Nor, further, would this separated something be of any use in knowing this singular.

53. Whence it remains that the notion of the genus, or of the species, belongs to an essence according as it is signified as a whole, as by the word "man" or "animal" according as it contains implicitly and indistinctly everything that is in the individual.

54. Now, a nature or essence signified as a whole can be considered in two ways. In one way it can be considered according to its proper content, and this is an absolute consideration of it. And in this way nothing is true of it except what belongs to it as such; whence if anything else is attributed to it, the attribution is false. For example, to man as man belong rational and animal, and whatever else falls in his definition. But white or black, or anything of this sort, which is not of the content of humanity, does not belong to man as man. Whence, if one should ask whether the nature so considered can be said to be one or many, neither should be allowed, because each is outside the content of humanity and either can be added to it. For if plurality were of its content, it could never be one, as it is in Socrates. Similarly, if oneness were of its content, then the nature of Socrates and Plato would be one and the same, and it could not be plurified into many individuals.

55. In the other way an essence is considered according to the existence it has in this or that. When the essence is so considered, something is predicated of it accidentally, by reason of that in which it is; for example, it is said that man is white because Socrates is white, although to be white does not belong to man as man.

56. This nature has a twofold existence, one in singular things, the other in the soul; and accidents follow upon the nature according to either existence. In singular things it has a multiple existence in accord with the diversity of these singular things; yet the existence of none of these things belongs to the nature considered in itself, i.e., absolutely. For it is false to say that the nature of man, as such, has existence in this singular thing; because if existence in this singular thing belonged to man as man, man would never exist outside this singular thing. Similarly, if it belonged to man as man not to exist in this singular thing, man would never exist in it. But it is true to say that it does not belong to man as man to exist in this or that singular thing, or in the soul. It is clear, therefore, that

the nature of man, absolutely considered, abstracts from any of these existences, but in a way such that it excludes no one of them.

57. And it is the nature so considered which is predicated of all individuals. Yet it cannot be said that the notion of a universal belongs to the nature so considered, because oneness and commonness are of the notion of a universal. Neither of these belongs to human nature considered absolutely, for if commonness were of the content of man, commonness would be found in whatever thing humanity is found. And this is false, because in Socrates there is no commonness, but whatever is in him is individuated.

58. Similarly, it cannot be said that the notion of the genus or of the species attaches to human nature according as it has existence in individuals, because human nature is not found in individuals with a oneness such that it would be some one thing belonging to all, which the notion of a universal requires.

59. It remains, therefore, that the notion of the species attaches to human nature according to the existence it has in the intellect.

60. For human nature exists in the intellect in abstraction from all that individuates; and this is why it has a content which is the same in relation to all individual men outside the soul; it is equally the likeness of all of them, and leads to a knowledge of all insofar as they are men. And it is from the fact that the nature has such a relation to all individuals that the intellect discovers and attributes the notion of the species to it. Whence the Commentator says in his considerations on the first book of On the Soul that "it is the intellect which causes universality in things." Ibn-Sînâ, too, says this in his Metaphysics.

61. And although the intellectually grasped nature has the character of a universal according as it is compared to things outside the soul, because it is one likeness of all of them; still

according as it exists in this intellect or in that one, it is something particular — a particular species grasped by a particular intellect. From this one can see the weakness of what the Commentator says in his considerations of the third book of On the Soul; from the universality of the intellectually grasped form he wanted to conclude that there is one intellect in all men. This falls short of the truth because the intellectually grasped form has its universality not according to the existence which it has in an intellect, but according as it is related to real things as a likeness of them.

62. What is true here is like what would be true of a corporeal statue representing many men: the image or form of the statue would have its own and individual existence according as it exists in this matter, and it would have the character of commonness according as it is the common representation of many.

63. Further, because it belongs to human nature absolutely considered to be predicated of Socrates, and because the notion of the species does not belong to it absolutely considered but is among the accidents which follow upon it according to the existence it has in the intellect, one can see why the word "species" is not predicated of Socrates, i.e., why it is not said that "Socrates is a species." This would of necessity be said if the notion of the species belonged to man according to the existence which man has in Socrates; or, if the notion of the species belonged to man absolutely considered, i.e., to man as man, for whatever belongs to man as man is predicated of Socrates.

64. Still, to be predicated belongs to the genus in virtue of what it is, since this is placed in its definition. For predication is something which is achieved by the combining and dividing activity of the intellect, and which has for its foundation in the real thing the union of those things, one of which is said of another. Whence the notion of predicability can be included in the notion of that intention which is the genus, which (intention) is similarly

achieved by the activity of the intellect. Nonetheless, that to which the intellect, combining one thing with another, attributes the intention of predicability is not the intention of the genus itself; rather it is that to which the intellect attributes the intention of the genus, for example, that which is signified by the word "animal."

65. It is clear, therefore, how an essence or nature is related to the notion of the species. The notion of the species is not among the things which belong to the nature absolutely considered, nor is it among the accidents which follow upon the nature according to the existence it has outside the soul, as whiteness or blackness. Rather the notion of the species is among the accidents which follow upon the nature according to the existence it has in the intellect; and it is in this way, too, that the notion of the genus and of the difference belong to it.

66. It remains, now, for us to see in what way essence is in separated substances, namely, in the soul, in the intelligences, and in the First Cause.

67. Although everyone admits the simplicity of the First Cause, some try to introduce a composition of matter and form in the intelligences and in souls. The originator of this position appears to have been Ibn-Gabirol, author of the book Fountain of Life.

68. But this is not in agreement with what philosophers commonly say, because they call them substances separated from matter, and prove them to be without all matter. The strongest demonstration of this is from the power of understanding which is in them. For we see that forms are not actually intelligible except according as they are separated from matter and from its conditions; nor are they made actually intelligible except by the power of a substance understanding them, according as they are received into, and are affected by, that substance.

69. Whence it is necessary that there be in any intelligent substance a total freedom from matter, such that the substance does not have matter as a part of itself, such too that the substance is not a form impressed on matter, as is the case with material forms.

70. Nor can it be said that it is only corporeal matter that impedes intelligibility, and not any matter whatsoever. For if this were so by reason of corporeal matter alone, then it would have to be that matter impedes intelligibility by reason of the corporeal form, since matter is called corporeal only according as it is found under the corporeal form. But this cannot be — namely, that matter impedes intelligibility by reason of the corporeal form — because the corporeal form itself, just as other forms, is actually intelligible according as it is abstracted from matter. Whence there is in no way a composition of matter and form in the soul or in an intelligence if matter in them is taken in the sense in which matter is taken in corporeal substances.

71. But there is in them a composition of form and existence. Whence it is said, in the commentary on the ninth proposition of the Book on Causes, that "an intelligence is something having form and existence," and form is taken there for the simple quiddity or nature itself.

72. It is easy to see how this may be so. Whatever things are so related to one another that one is a cause of the other's existence, the one which is the cause can have existence without the other, but not conversely. Now the relation of matter and form is such that form gives existence to matter. It is impossible, therefore, that matter exist without some form. But it is not impossible that some form exist without matter, for form, to the extent that it is form, does not depend on matter. But if some forms are found which cannot exist except in matter, this happens to them because of their distance from the first principle, which is first and pure act. Whence those forms which are nearest to the first principle are

forms subsisting of themselves, that is without matter. For not every sort of form needs matter, as has been said; and the intelligences are forms of this sort. And therefore it is not necessary that the essences or quiddities of these substances be other than form itself.

73. Thus the essence of a composed substance and that of a simple substance differ in this: the essence of a composed substance is not form alone, but includes form and matter; the essence of a simple substance is form alone.

74. And from this follow two other differences. One difference is that the essence of a composed substance can be signified as a whole or as a part. This happens on account of the designation of matter, as has been said. And therefore the essence of a composed thing is not predicated of the composed thing itself in just any way, for it cannot be said that man is his quiddity. But the essence of a simple thing, which (essence) is its form, cannot be signified except as a whole, since nothing is there besides the form as receiving the form. Thus, no matter what way the essence of a simple substance is taken, it is predicated of the simple substance. Whence Ibn-Sînâ says that the quiddity of a simple thing is the simple thing itself, because there is nothing other receiving the quiddity.

75; The second difference is that the essences of composed things, because they are received into designated matter, are multiplied according to its division. And this is why it happens that certain things are the same in species and diverse in number. But since the essence of a simple thing is not received into matter, such a multiplication is impossible here. And this is why, of necessity, many individuals of a same species are not found among these substances; rather, as Ibn-Sînâ expressly says, there are among them as many species as there are individuals.

76. Although substances of this sort are forms alone without matter, they are not utterly simple so as to be pure act. They have

an admixture of potency, which becomes clear in the following consideration.

77. Whatever is not of the understood content of an essence or quality is something which comes from without and makes a composition with the essence, because no essence can be understood without the things which are parts of it. Now, every essence or quiddity can be understood without anything being understood about its existence. For I can understand what a man is, or what a phoenix is, and yet not know whether they have existence in the real world. It is clear, therefore, that existence is other than essence or quiddity, unless perhaps there exists a thing whose quiddity is its existence.

78. And there can be but one such thing, the First Thing, because it is impossible to plurify a thing except: (1) by the addition of some difference, as the nature of the genus is multiplied in its species, or (2) by the reception of a form into diverse matters, as the nature of the species is multiplied in diverse individuals, or (3) by this: that one is absolute and the other is received into something; for example, if there were a separated heat, it would by virtue of its very separation be other than heat which is not separated. Now, if we posit a thing which is existence alone, such that this existence is subsistent, this existence will not receive the addition of a difference because it would no longer be existence alone, but existence plus some form. And much less will it receive the addition of matter because it would no longer be a subsistent existence, but a material existence. Whence it remains that such a thing, which is its own existence, cannot be but one.

79. Whence it is necessary, that in every thing other than this one its existence be other than its quiddity, or its nature, or its form. Whence it is necessary that existence in the intelligences be something besides the form, and this is why it was said that an intelligence is form and existence.

80. Now, whatever belongs to a thing is either caused by the principles of its nature, as the ability to laugh in man, or comes to it from some extrinsic principle, as light in the air from the influence of the sun. But it cannot be that the existence of a thing is caused by the form or quiddity of that thing — I say caused as by an efficient cause — because then something would be its own cause, and would bring itself into existence, which is impossible. It is therefore necessary that every such thing, the existence of which is other than its nature, have its existence from some other thing. And because every thing which exists by virtue of another is led back, as to its first cause, to that which exists by virtue of itself, it is necessary that there be some thing which is the cause of the existence of all things because it is existence alone. Otherwise, there would be an infinite regress among causes, since every thing which is not existence alone has a cause of its existence, as has been said. It is clear, therefore, that an intelligence is form and existence, and that it has existence from the First Being, which is existence alone. And this is the First Cause, which is God.

81. Now everything which receives something from another is in potency with respect to what it receives, and what is received into it is its act. It is necessary therefore that the quiddity itself or the form, which is the intelligence, be in potency with respect to the existence which it receives from God; and this existence is received as an act. It is in this way that potency and act are found in the intelligences, but not form and matter, unless equivocally.

82. Whence, to suffer, and to receive, and to be a subject, and all things of this sort, which are observed to belong to things by reason of matter, also belong equivocally to intellectual and to corporeal substances, as the Commentator says in his considerations on the third book of On The Soul.

83. And because the quiddity of an intelligence is, as has been said, the intelligence itself, its quiddity or essence is identically that which it itself is; and its existence received from God is that

whereby it subsists in reality. And this is why substances of this sort are said by some to be composed of "that by which it is" and "that which is," or as Boethius says, of "that which is" and "existence."

84. And because there is potency in the intelligences as well as act, it will not be difficult to find a multitude of intelligences, which would be impossible if there were no potency in them. Whence the Commentator says, in his considerations on the third book of On The Soul, that if the nature of the possible intellect were not known, we would not be able to find multitude among the separated substances. The separated substances, therefore, are distinct from one another according to their grade of potency and act, in such a way that a superior intelligence which is nearer to the First Being has more act and less potency, and so with the others.

85. This grading has its termination in the human soul, which holds the lowest grade among intellectual substances. Whence its possible intellect is related to intelligible forms in the way in which prime matter, which holds the lowest grade in sensible existence, is related to sensible forms, as the Commentator remarks in his considerations on the third book of On The Soul. And this is why the Philosopher compares it to a blank tablet on which nothing has been written.

86. And because it has more potency than other intelligible substances, the human soul is so close to material things that a material thing is drawn to it to share its existence, but in such a way that from soul and body results one existence in one composed thing; and yet this existence is not dependent on the body inasmuch as it is the soul's existence.

87. And posterior to this form which is the soul are found other forms which have more potency, and which are still closer to matter, so close that they do not exist without matter. Among

these forms, too, is found an order and a grading, down to the first forms of the elements, which are the closest to matter. These last are so close to matter that they operate only according to the active and passive qualities, and the other sorts of things, which are required as the means by which matter is disposed for the receiving of form.

88. From the preceding it is clear how essence is found in diverse substances. For we find that they have essence in three different ways.

89. There is a thing, God, whose essence is his existence itself. And this is why we find some philosophers who say that Cod does not have a quiddity or essence, because his essence is not other than his existence. And from this it follows that he is not in a genus, because everything which is in a genus must have a quiddity which is other than its existence. And this is so since the quiddity or nature of a genus or species, in the case of those things which have a genus or species, is not multiplied according to the intelligible content of the nature; rather, it is the existence in these diverse things which is diverse.

90. Nor is it necessary, if we say that God is existence alone, for us to fall into the error of those who say that God is universal existence whereby each and every thing formally exists. For the existence which God is, is such that no addition can be made to it. Whence by virtue of its purity it is an existence distinct from every existence. This is why, in the commentary on the ninth proposition of the Book on Causes, it is said that the individuation of the First Cause, which is existence alone, is through its pure goodness. But as regards that universal existence, just as it does not include in its intelligible content any addition, so too neither does it include in its intelligible content any exclusion of addition, because if this were the case, nothing in which something is added over and above its existence could be understood to be.

91. Similarly, although God is existence alone, it is not necessary that the other perfections or excellences be wanting in him. Rather he has all the perfections which are in every genus. This is why he is called simply perfect, as the Philosopher and the Commentator say in book five of the Metaphysics. But he has these perfections in a more excellent way than all things because in him they are one, whereas in other things they have diversity. And this is so because all these perfections belong to him according to his simple existence. If some one could perform the operations of all the qualities through some one quality, he would have every quality in that one quality; so too God has all these perfections in his existence itself.

92. Essence is found in a second way in created intellectual substances. Existence in them is other than their essence, although essence is without matter. Whence their existence is not absolute, but received, and therefore limited and confined to the capacity of the recipient nature. But their nature or quiddity is absolute, not received in any matter. And this is why it is said in the Book on Causes that the intelligences are unlimited from below and limited from above, for they are limited as regards their existence, which they receive from above; but they are not limited from below because their forms are not limited to the capacity of a matter receiving them.

93. And this is why, as has been said, there is not found among such substances a multitude of individuals in one species, with the exception of the human soul on account of the body to which it is united. And although its individuation depends on the body as upon the occasion for its beginning because it does not acquire its individuated existence except in the body of which it is the actuality, it is not necessary that its individuation be lost when the body is taken away because that existence, since it is absolute, always remains individuated once the soul acquires it by being made the form of this individual body. And this is why Ibn-Sînâ says that the individuation and multiplication of souls depends on

the body as regards its beginning, but not as regards its termination.

94. And because quiddity in these substances is not the same as existence, they are orderable within a predicament. And this is why they have a genus, a species, and a difference, although their proper differences are hidden from us. For even in the case of sensible things, the essential differences themselves are not known; whence they are signified through accidental differences which rise out of the essential ones, as a cause is signified through its effect; this is what is done when biped, for example, is given as the difference of man. But the proper accidents of immaterial substances are unknown to us; whence their differences cannot be signified by us either through themselves or through accidental differences.

95. But we must notice that the genus and the difference of these substances are not taken in the same way in which the genus and the difference of sensible substances are taken. In the case of sensible substances the genus is taken from that which is material in the thing, whereas the difference is taken from that which is formal in it. Whence Ibn-Sînâ says at the beginning of his book On the Soul that form in things composed of matter and form is the simple difference of that which is constituted by it; but not in such a way that the form is the difference, but because the form is the principle of the difference, as the same writer says in his Metaphysics. And this sort of difference is called a simple difference because it is taken from what is part of the quiddity of the thing, namely, from the form. But since immaterial substances are simple quiddities, their difference cannot be taken from what is part of the quiddity, but from the whole quiddity. This is why Ibn-Sînâ says, at the beginning of On the Soul, that only those species have a simple difference whose essences are composed of matter and form.

96. Similarly, their genus too is taken from the whole essence, but in a different way, for separated substances agree with each other in immateriality, and differ from each other in grade of perfection, according as they withdraw from potentiality and approach pure actuality. The genus is taken from that in them which follows upon their being immaterial; for example, intellectuality or something of this sort. But the difference, which is unknown to us, is taken from that in them which follows upon their grade of perfection.

97. And it is not necessary that these differences be accidental because they are determined by greater and lesser perfection which does not diversify a species. For grades of perfection in the reception of a same form do not diversify a species, as whiter and less white in participating whiteness which is of the same nature. But a diverse grade in the forms or natures themselves which are participated does diversify a species. For example, nature proceeds by grades from plants to animals by way of certain things which are midway between animals and plants, according to the Philosopher in book seven of On Animals. Nor, similarly, is it necessary that intellectual substances be divided always by two true differences, because this cannot come about in the case of all things, as the Philosopher says in book eleven of On Animals.

98. Essence is found in a third way in substances composed of matter and form. Here it is both the case that existence is received and limited because they have existence from another; and that their nature or quiddity is received in designated matter. And so, they are limited both from above and from below. And because of the division of designated matter, the multiplication of individuals in one species is here possible. As regards the question how the essence of these substances is related to the logical intentions, we have explained that above.

99. What remains now is to see how essence is in accidents; how it is in all substances has been discussed.

100. And because essence, as has been said, is that which is signified by the definition, it is necessary that accidents have essence in the way in which they have definition. They have an incomplete definition because they cannot be defined unless a subject is placed in their definition. And this is so because they do not have existence in themselves free of a subject.

101. But just as a substantial existence results from matter and form when they are composed, so from an accident and a subject results an accidental existence when the accident comes to the subject. And this is also why neither substantial form nor matter have a complete essence because it is necessary to place in the definition of substantial form that of which it is the form; and so its definition is formulated by the addition of something which is outside its genus, just like the definition of an accidental form. Whence, also, the body is placed in the definition of the soul by the natural philosopher, who considers the soul only insofar as it is the form of a physical body.

102. But there is this difference between substantial and accidental forms. Just as substantial form does not have existence in itself, separately from that to which it comes, neither does that to which it comes, namely, matter. And thus from the conjunction of the two results that existence in which a thing subsists in itself, and from them is produced something essentially one; and because of this an essence is the result of their conjunction. Whence, although the form considered in itself does not have the complete nature of an essence, it is nonetheless part of a complete essence. But that to which an accident comes is a being complete in itself and subsisting in its own existence. And this existence naturally precedes the accident which supervenes. And this is why the supervening accident does not, by its conjunction with that to which it comes, cause that existence in which a thing subsists, and through which the thing is a being in itself. It causes, rather, a certain second existence, without which the subsisting thing can be understood to be, just as what is first can be understood

without what is second. Whence something essentially one is not produced from an accident and a subject, but something accidentally one. And this is why an essence does not result from their conjunction, as from the conjunction of form and matter. And this is why an accident neither has the nature of a complete essence, nor is it part of a complete essence. But just as it is a being in a qualified way, so too does it have essence in a qualified way.

103. Now, whatever is said to be most fully and most truly in any genus is the cause of the things which are posterior in that genus; for example, fire, which is unsurpassed in heat, is the cause of heat in hot things, as it is said in the second book of the Metaphysics. This is why substance, which has first place in the genus of being, having essence most truly and most fully, must be the cause of accidents, which participate in the nature of being secondarily and in a qualified way.

104. But this happens in diverse ways. For, since the parts of substance are matter and form, certain accidents follow principally on form, certain others follow principally on matter. There are forms whose existence does not depend on matter, for example, intellectual souls; but matter does not have existence except through form. Whence some of the accidents which follow on form are such that they share nothing with matter; for example, to understand, which does not take place through a bodily organ, as the Philosopher proves in the third book of On the Soul. But some other of the accidents following on form are such that they do share something with matter; for example, to sense. But no accident follows on matter which shares nothing with form.

105. Among those accidents which follow on matter we find a certain diversity. For some accidents follow on matter according to the ordering which it has to a special form; for example, male and female among animals, the diversity of which derives from matter, as is said in the tenth book of the Metaphysics. Whence these accidents do not remain on the removal of the form of

animal, except equivocally. Other accidents follow on matter according to the ordering which lt has to a general form. Thus, on the removal of the special form they still remain in the matter; for example, the blackness of an Ethiopian's skin is from the mixture of the elements and not from his soul; and this is why it remains in him after death. And because each and every thing is individuated by matter and placed in a genus or species by its form, accidents which follow on matter are accidents of the individual, and it is according to these that individuals of a same species differ from one another.

106. But accidents following on form are the proper attributes of the genus or of the species. Whence they are found in every thing which participates in the nature of the genus or of the species. For example, man's ability to laugh follows on the form because laughter takes place by reason of the fact that a man's soul has grasped something.

107. It should also be noticed that sometimes the essential principles cause accidents in a state of perfect actuality, as heat in the case of fire which is always actually hot. But sometimes they cause accidents which are only aptitudes, their completion being received from an exterior agent; for example, transparency in the air, which is completed by some exterior light-emitting body. And in such things the aptitude is an inseparable accident, but the completion, which comes from some principle which is outside the essence of the thing, or which does not enter the constitution of the thing, is separable; for example, being moved and things of this sort.

108. It should be noticed, further, that the genus, the species, and the difference of accidents are taken in a way which differs from the way in which those of substances are taken.

109. In substances something essentially one results from the substantial form and matter, a certain nature results from their

conjunction, a nature which is properly placed in the predicament of substance. This is why concrete names of substances which signify the composite are properly said to be in a genus, as species or genera; for example, man or animal. But the form, or the matter, is not in a predicament in this way, though each is in a predicament by reduction, as principles are said to be in a genus. Something essentially one does not, on the contrary, result from an accident and its subject. Whence the result of their conjunction is not a certain nature, to which the intention of genus or species may be attributed. Whence names of accidents expressed concretely are not placed in a predicament as species or genera; for example, white or musical, except by reduction. They are placed in a predicament only according as they are signified in the abstract; for example, whiteness and music.

110. And because accidents are not composed of matter and form, their genus cannot be taken from matter and their difference from form, as in the case of composed substances. Rather, their first genus must be taken from their way of existing itself, according to which the word "being" is diversely predicated of the ten genera according to a priority and posteriority; for example, an accident is called quantity from the fact that it is the measure of substance, and quality according as it is the disposition of substance, and so with the other accidents, according to the Philosopher in the fourth book of the Metaphysics. But their differences are taken from the diversity of the principles by which they are caused. And because proper attributes are caused by the proper principles of the subject, the subject is placed in their definition to function as the difference if they are defined in the abstract, which is the way in which they are properly in a genus; as when it is said that snubnosedness is the turned-up-ness of the nose. But the converse would be the case if their definition were taken according as they are said concretely. For in this way the subject is placed in their definition as a genus because they are then being defined after the manner of composed substance, in which the genus is taken from matter; as when we say that a snub nose is a turned up nose.

111. We have a similar case if one accident is the principle of another, as action and passion and quantity are principles of relation. And this is why the Philosopher divides relation according to these in book five of the Metaphysics.

112. But because the proper principles of accidents are not always manifest, we sometimes take the difference of accidents from their effects; as when concentrating and diffusing are called the differences of color. These effects are caused by the abundance and the scarcity of light, which cause the diverse species of color.

113. And so it is clear how essence is in substances and in accidents, and how it is in composed substances in simple ones, and how the universal intentions of logic are found in all of these, with the exception of the First Principle, which is infinitely simple, and to which, because of its simplicity, belongs the notion neither of the genus nor of the species, nor consequently definition. With this, let the discussion, its tasks achieve brought to a close.

# On Truth
by St. Thomas Aquinas
tr. Robert W. Mulligan, S.J.

Question I, ARTICLE I

The problem under discussion is truth, and in the first article we ask: What is truth?
[Cf. S.T., I. 16, aa. 1, 3; I Sent., 19, 5, 1; C.G., I, 60; I Perih., lect. 3, nn. 3-10; VI Metaph., lect. 4, nn. 1230-44.]

Difficulties

It seems that the true is exactly the same as being, for

1. Augustine says: "The true is that which is." But that which is, is simply being. The true, therefore, means exactly the same as being.

2. It was said in reply that the true and being are the same materially but differ formally.—On the contrary the nature of a thing is signified by its definition; and the definition of the true, according to Augustine, is that which is." He rejects all other definitions. Now, since the true and being are materially the same, it seems that they are also formally the same.

3. Things which differ conceptually are so related to each other that one of them can be understood without the other. For this reason, Boethius says that the existence of God can be understood if for a moment we mentally separate His goodness from His existence. Being, however can in no way be understood apart from the true, for being is known only in so far as it is true. Therefore, the true and being do differ conceptually.

4. If the true is not the same as being, it must be a state of being. But it cannot be a state of being. It is not a state that entirely corrupts—otherwise, this would follow: "It is true. Therefore, it is non-being"—as it follows when we say: "This man is dead. Therefore, this is not a man."

Similarly, the true is not a state that limits. If it were, one could not say: "It is true. Therefore it is." For one cannot say that a thing is white simply because it has white teeth. Finally, the true is not a state which contracts or specifies being, for it is convertible with being. It follows, therefore, that the true and being are entirely the same.

5. Things in the same state are the same. But the true and being are in the same state. Therefore, they are the same. For Aristotle writes: "The state of a thing in its act of existence is the same as its state in truth." Therefore, the true and being are entirely the same.

6. Thing not the same differ in some respect. But the true and being differ in no respect. They do not differ essentially, for every being is true by its very essence. And they do not differ in any other ways, for they must belong to some common genus. Therefore, they are entirely the same.

7. If they were not entirely the same, the true would add something to being. But the true adds nothing to being, even though it has greater extension than being. This is borne out by the statement of the Philosopher that we define the true as: "That which affirms the existence of what is, and denies the existence of what is not." Consequently, the true includes both being and non-being; since it does not add anything to being, it seems to be entirely the same as being.

To the Contrary

1. Useless repetition of the same thing is meaningless; so, if the true were the same as being, it would be meaningless to say: "Being is true." This, however, is hardly correct. Therefore, they are not the same.

2. Being and the good are convertible. The true and the good, however, are not interchangeable, for some things, such as fornication, are true but not good. The true, therefore, and being are not interchangeable. And so they are not the same.

3. In all creatures, as Boethius has pointed out, "to be is other than that which is." Now, the true signifies the existence of things.

Consequently, in creatures it is different from that which is. But that which is, is the same as being. Therefore, in creatures the true is different from being.

4. Things related as before and after must differ. But the true and being are related in the aforesaid manner; for, as is said in The Causes: "The first of all created things is the act of existence." In a study of this work, a commentator writes as follows: "Everything else is predicated as a specification of being." Consequently, everything else comes after being. Therefore, the true and being are not the same.

5. What are predicated of a cause and of the effects of the cause are more united in the cause than in its effects—and more so in God than in creatures. But in God four predicates—being, the one, the true—are appropriated as follows: being, to the essence; the one, to the Father; the true, to the Son; and the good, to the Holy Spirit.

Since the divine Persons are really and not merely conceptually distinct, these notions cannot be predicated of each other; if really distinct when verified of the divine Persons, the four notions in question are much more so when verified of creatures.

REPLY

When investigating the nature of anything, one should make the same kind of analysis as he makes when he reduces a proposition to certain self-evident principles. Otherwise, both types of knowledge will become involved in an infinite regress, and science and our knowledge of things will perish.

Now, as Avicenna says, that which the intellect first conceives as, in a way, the most evident, and to which it reduces all its concepts, is being. Consequently, all the other conceptions of the intellect are had by additions to being. But nothing can be added to being as though it were something not included in being—in the way that a difference is added to a genus or an accident to a subject—for every reality is essentially a being. The Philosopher has shown this by proving that being cannot be a genus. Yet, in this sense, some predicates may be said to add to being inasmuch as they express a mode of being not expressed by the term being. This happens in two ways.

First, the mode expressed is a certain special manner of being; for there are different grades of being according to which we speak when we speak of different levels of existence, and according to these grades different things are classified. Consequently, substance does not add a difference to being by signifying some reality added to it, but substance simply expresses a special manner of existing, namely, as a being in itself. The same is true of the other classes of existents.

Second. some are said to add to being because the mode they express is one that is common, and consequent upon every being. This mode can be taken in two ways: first, in so far as it follows upon every being considered absolutely; second, in so far as it follows upon every being considered in relation to another. In the first, the term is used in two ways, because it expresses something in the being either affirmatively or negatively. We can, however, find nothing that can be predicated of every being affirmatively and, at the same time, absolutely, with the exception of its essence by which the being is said to be. To express this, the term thing is used; for, according to Avicenna," thing differs from being because being gets its name from to-be, but thing expresses the quiddity or essence of the being. There is, however, a negation consequent upon every being considered absolutely: its undividedness, and this is expressed by one. For the one is simply undivided being.

If the mode of being is taken in the second way—according to the relation of one being to another—we find a twofold use. The first is based on the distinction of one being from another, and this distinctness is expressed by the word something, which implies, as it were, some other thing. For, just as a being is said to be one in so far as it is without division in itself, so it is said to be something in so far as it is divided from others. The second division is based on the correspondence one being has with another. This is possible only if there is something which is such that it agrees with every being. Such a being is the soul, which, as is said in The Soul, "in some way is all things." The soul, however, has both knowing and appetitive powers. Good expresses the correspondence of being to the appetitive power, for, and so we note in the Ethics, the good is "that which all desire." True expresses the correspondence of being to the knowing power, for all knowing is produced by an assimilation of the knower to the thing known, so that assimilation is said to be the cause of knowledge. Similarly, the sense of sight knows a color by being informed with a species of the color.

The first reference of being to the intellect, therefore, consists in its agreement with the intellect. This agreement is called "the conformity of thing and intellect." In this conformity is fulfilled the formal constituent of the true, and this is what the true adds to being, namely, the conformity or equation of thing and intellect. As we said, the knowledge of a thing is a consequence of this conformity; therefore, it is an effect of truth, even though the fact that the thing is a being is prior to its truth.

Consequently, truth or the true has been defined in three ways. First of all, it is defined according to that which precedes truth and is the basis of truth. This is why Augustine writes: "The true is that which is"; and Avicenna: "The truth of each thing is a property of the act of being which has been established for it." Still others say: "The true is the undividedness of the act of existence from that which is." Truth is also defined in another way — according to that in which its intelligible determination is formally completed. Thus, Isaac writes: "Truth is the conformity of thing and intellect"; and Anselm: "Truth is a rectitude perceptible only by the mind." This rectitude, of course, is said to be based on some conformity. The Philosopher says that in defining truth we say that truth is had when one affirms that "to be which is, and that not to be which is not."

The third way of defining truth is according to the effect following upon it. Thus, Hilary says that the true is that which manifests and proclaims existence. And Augustine says: "Truth is that by which that which is, is shown"; and also: "Truth is that according to which we, judge about inferior things."

Answers to Difficulties

1. That definition of Augustine is given for the true as it has its foundation in reality and not as its formal nature is given complete expression by conformity of thing and intellect. An alternative answer would be that in the statement, "The true is that which is," the word is is not here understood as referring to the act of existing, but rather as the mark of the intellectual act of judging, signifying, that is, the affirmation of a proposition. The meaning would then be this: "The true is that which is—it is had when the existence of what is, is affirmed." If this is its meaning, then Augustine's definition agrees with that of the Philosopher mentioned above.

2. The answer is clear from what has been said.

3. "Something can be understood without another" can be taken in two ways. It can mean that something can be known while another remains unknown. Taken in this way, it is true that things which differ conceptually are such that one can be understood without the other. But there is another way that a thing can be understood without another: when it is known even though the other does not exist. Taken in this sense, being cannot be known without the true, for it cannot be known unless it agrees with or conforms to intellect, It is not necessary, however, that everyone who understands the formal notion of being should also understand the formal notion of the true—just as not everyone

who understands being understands the agent intellect, even though nothing can be known without the agent intellect.

4. The true is a state of being even though it does not add any reality to being or express any special mode of existence. It is rather something that is generally found in every being, although it is not expressed by the word being. Consequently, it is not a state that corrupts, limits, or contracts.

5. In this objection, condition should not be understood as belonging to the genus of quality. It implies, rather, a certain order; for those which are the cause of the existence of other things are themselves beings most completely, and those which are the cause of the truth of other things are themselves true most completely. It is for this reason that the Philosopher concludes that the rank of a thing in its existence corresponds to its rank in truth, so that when one finds that which is most fully being, he finds there also that which is most fully true. But this does not mean that being and the true are the same in concept. It means simply that in the degree in which a thing has being, in that degree it is capable of being proportioned to intellect. Consequently, the true is dependent upon the formal character of being.

6. There is a conceptual difference between the true and being since there is something in the notion of the true that is not in the concept of the existing—not in such a way, however, that there is something in the concept of being which is not in the concept of the true. They do not differ essentially nor are they distinguished from one another by opposing differences.

7. The true does not have a wider extension than being. Being is, in some way, predicated of non-being in so far as non-being is apprehended by the intellect. For, as the Philosopher says, the negation or the privation of being may, in a sense, be called being. Avicenna supports this by pointing out that one can form propositions only of beings, for that about which a proposition is

formed must be apprehended by the intellect. Consequently, it is clear that everything true is being in some way.

## Answers to Contrary Difficulties

1. The reason why it is not tautological to call a being true is that something is expressed by the word true that is not expressed by the word being, and not that the two differ in reality.

2. Although fornication is evil, it possesses some being and can conform to intellect. Accordingly, the formal character of the true is found here. So it is clear that true is coextensive with being.

3. In the statement, "To be is other than that which is," the act of being is distinguished from that to which that act belongs. But the name of being is taken from the act of existence, not from that whose act it is. Hence, the argument does not follow.

4. The true comes after being in this respect, that the notion of the true differs from that of being in the manner we have described. This argument has three flaws. First, although the Persons are really distinct, the things appropriated to each Person are only conceptually, and not really, distinct. Secondly, although the Persons are really distinct from each other, they are not really distinct from the essence; so, truth appropriated to the Person of the Son is not distinct from the act of existence He possesses through the divine essence. Thirdly, although being, the true, the one, and the good are more united in God than they are in created things, it does not follow from the fact that they are conceptually distinct in God that they are really distinct in created beings. This line of argument is valid only when it is applied to things which are not by their very nature one in reality, as wisdom and power, which, although one in God, are distinct in creatures. But being, the true, the one, and the good are such that by their very nature they are one in reality. Therefore, no matter where they are found, they are really one. Their unity in God, however, is more perfect than their unity in creatures.

## *Summa Theologica* I.16.3-4
### St. Thomas Aquinas

Article 3. Whether the true and being are convertible terms?

Objection 1. It seems that the true and being are not convertible terms. For the true resides properly in the intellect, as stated (1); but being is properly in things. Therefore they are not convertible.

Objection 2. Further, that which extends to being and not-being is not convertible with being. But the true extends to being and not-being; for it is true that what is, is; and that what is not, is not. Therefore the true and being are not convertible.

Objection 3. Further, things which stand to each other in order of priority and posteriority seem not to be convertible. But the true appears to be prior to being; for being is not understood except under the aspect of the true. Therefore it seems they are not convertible.

On the contrary, the Philosopher says (Metaph. ii) that there is the same disposition of things in being and in truth.

I answer that, As good has the nature of what is desirable, so truth is related to knowledge. Now everything, in as far as it has being, so far is it knowable. Wherefore it is said in De Anima iii that "the soul is in some manner all things," through the senses and the intellect. And therefore, as good is convertible with being, so is the true. But as good adds to being the notion of desirable, so the true adds relation to the intellect.

Reply to Objection 1. The true resides in things and in the intellect, as said before (1). But the true that is in things is convertible with being as to substance; while the true that is in the intellect is convertible with being, as the manifestation with the manifested; for this belongs to the nature of truth, as has been said already (1). It may, however, be said that being also is in the things and in the intellect, as is the true; although truth is primarily in things; and this is so because truth and being differ in idea.

Reply to Objection 2. Not-being has nothing in itself whereby it can be known; yet it is known in so far as the intellect renders it knowable. Hence the true is based on being, inasmuch as not-being is a kind of logical being, apprehended, that is, by reason.

Reply to Objection 3. When it is said that being cannot be apprehended except under the notion of the true, this can be understood in two ways. In the one way so as to mean that being is not apprehended, unless the idea of the true follows apprehension of being; and this is true. In the other way, so as to mean that being cannot be apprehended unless the idea of the true be apprehended also; and this is false. But the true cannot be apprehended unless the idea of being be apprehended also; since being is included in the idea of the true. The case is the same if we compare the intelligible object with being. For being cannot be understood, unless being is intelligible. Yet being can be understood while its intelligibility is not understood. Similarly, being when understood is true, yet the true is not understood by understanding being.

Article 4. Whether good is logically prior to the true?

Objection 1. It seems that good is logically prior to the true. For what is more universal is logically prior, as is evident from Phys. i. But the good is more universal than the true, since the true is a kind of good, namely, of the intellect. Therefore the good is logically prior to the true.

Objection 2. Further, good is in things, but the true in the intellect composing and dividing as said above (Article 2). But that which is in things is prior to that which is in the intellect. Therefore good is logically prior to the true.

Objection 3. Further, truth is a species of virtue, as is clear from Ethic. iv. But virtue is included under good; since, as Augustine says (De Lib. Arbit. ii, 19), it is a good quality of the mind. Therefore the good is prior to the true.

On the contrary, What is in more things is prior logically. But the true is in some things wherein good is not, as, for instance, in mathematics. Therefore the true is prior to good.

I answer that, Although the good and the true are convertible with being, as to suppositum, yet they differ logically. And in this manner the true, speaking absolutely, is prior to good, as appears from two reasons.

First, because the true is more closely related to being than is good. For the true regards being itself simply and immediately; while the nature of good follows being in so far as being is in some way perfect; for thus it is desirable.

Secondly, it is evident from the fact that knowledge naturally precedes appetite. Hence, since the true regards knowledge, but the good regards the appetite, the true must be prior in idea to the good.

Reply to Objection 1. The will and the intellect mutually include one another: for the intellect understands the will, and the will wills the intellect to understand. So then, among things directed to the object of the will, are comprised also those that belong to the intellect; and conversely. Whence in the order of things desirable, good stands as the universal, and the true as the particular; whereas in the order of intelligible things the converse of the case. From the fact, then, that the true is a kind of good, it follows that the good is prior in the order of things desirable; but not that it is prior absolutely.

Reply to Objection 2. A thing is prior logically in so far as it is prior to the intellect. Now the intellect apprehends primarily being itself; secondly, it apprehends that it understands being; and thirdly, it apprehends that it desires being. Hence the idea of being is first, that of truth second, and the idea of good third, though good is in things.

Reply to Objection 3. The virtue which is called "truth" is not truth in general, but a certain kind of truth according to which man shows himself in deed and word as he really is. But truth as applied to "life" is used in a particular sense, inasmuch as a man fulfills in his life that to which he is ordained by the divine intellect, as it has been said that truth exists in other things (1). Whereas the truth of "justice" is found in man as he fulfills his duty to his neighbor, as ordained by law. Hence we cannot argue from these particular truths to truth in general.

*Summa Theologica* I-II.27.1

Article 1. Whether good is the only cause of love?

Objection 1. It would seem that good is not the only cause of love. For good does not cause love, except because it is loved. But it happens that evil also is loved, according to Psalm 10:6: "He that loveth iniquity, hateth his own soul": else, every love would be good. Therefore good is not the only cause of love.

Objection 2. Further, the Philosopher says (Rhet. ii, 4) that "we love those who acknowledge their evils." Therefore it seems that evil is the cause of love.

Objection 3. Further, Dionysius says (Div. Nom. iv) that not "the good" only but also "the beautiful is beloved by all."

On the contrary, Augustine says (De Trin. viii, 3): "Assuredly the good alone is beloved." Therefore good alone is the cause of love.

I answer that, As stated above (Question 26, Article 1), Love belongs to the appetitive power which is a passive faculty. Wherefore its object stands in relation to it as the cause of its movement or act. Therefore the cause of love must needs be love's object. Now the proper object of love is the good; because, as stated above (26, 1,2), love implies a certain connaturalness or complacency of the lover for the thing beloved, and to everything, that thing is a good, which is akin and proportionate to it. It follows, therefore, that good is the proper cause of love.

Reply to Objection 1. Evil is never loved except under the aspect of good, that is to say, in so far as it is good in some respect, and is considered as being good simply. And thus a certain love is evil, in so far as it tends to that which is not simply a true good. It is in this way that man "loves iniquity," inasmuch as, by means of iniquity, some good is gained; pleasure, for instance, or money, or such like.

Reply to Objection 2. Those who acknowledge their evils, are beloved, not for their evils, but because they acknowledge them, for it is a good thing to acknowledge one's faults, in so far as it excludes insincerity or hypocrisy.

Reply to Objection 3. The beautiful is the same as the good, and they differ in aspect only. For since good is what all seek, the notion of good is that which calms the desire; while the notion of the beautiful is that which calms the desire, by being seen or known. Consequently those senses chiefly regard the beautiful, which are the most cognitive, viz. sight and hearing, as ministering to reason; for we speak of beautiful sights and beautiful sounds. But in reference to the other objects of the other senses, we do not use the expression "beautiful," for we do not speak of beautiful tastes, and beautiful odors. Thus it is evident that beauty adds to goodness a relation to the cognitive faculty: so that "good" means that which simply pleases the appetite; while the "beautiful" is something pleasant to apprehend.

*Summa Theologica* I.39.8

Article 8. Whether the essential attributes are appropriated to the persons in a fitting manner by the holy doctors?

Objection 1. It would seem that the essential attributes are appropriated to the persons unfittingly by the holy doctors. For Hilary says (De Trin. ii): "Eternity is in the Father, the species in the Image; and use is in the Gift." In which words he designates three names proper to the persons: the name of the "Father," the name "Image" proper to the Son (35, 2), and the name "Bounty" or "Gift," which is proper to the Holy Ghost (38, 2). He also designates three appropriated terms. For he appropriates "eternity" to the Father, "species" to the Son, and "use" to the Holy Ghost. This he does apparently without reason. For "eternity" imports duration of existence; "species," the principle of existence; and 'use' belongs to the operation. But essence and operation are not found to be appropriated to any person. Therefore the above terms are not fittingly appropriated to the persons.

Objection 2. Further, Augustine says (De Doctr. Christ. i, 5): "Unity is in the Father, equality in the Son, and in the Holy Ghost is the concord of equality and unity." This does not, however, seem fitting; because one person does not receive formal denomination from what is appropriated to another. For the Father is not wise by the wisdom begotten, as above explained (37, 2, ad 1). But, as he subjoins, "All these three are one by the Father; all are equal by the Son, and all united by the Holy Ghost." The above, therefore, are not fittingly appropriated to the Persons.

Objection 3. Further, according to Augustine, to the Father is attributed "power," to the Son "wisdom," to the Holy Ghost "goodness." Nor does this seem fitting; for "strength" is part of power, whereas strength is found to be appropriated to the Son, according to the text, "Christ the strength [Douay: power] of God" (1 Corinthians 1:24). So it is likewise appropriated to the Holy Ghost, according to the words, "strength [Douay: virtue] came out from Him and healed all" (Luke 6:19). Therefore power should not be appropriated to the Father.

Objection 4. Likewise Augustine says (De Trin. vi, 10): "What the Apostle says, "From Him, and by Him, and in Him," is not to be taken in a confused sense." And (Contra Maxim. ii) "'from Him' refers to the Father, 'by Him' to the Son, 'in Him' to the Holy Ghost.'" This, however, seems to be incorrectly said; for the words "in Him" seem to imply the relation of final cause, which is first among the causes. Therefore this relation of cause should be appropriated to the Father, Who is "the principle from no principle."

Objection 5. Likewise, Truth is appropriated to the Son, according to John 14:6, "I am the Way, the Truth, and the Life"; and likewise "the book of life," according to Psalm 39:9, "In the beginning of the book it is written of Me," where a gloss observes, "that is, with the Father Who is My head," also this word "Who is"; because on the text of Isaiah 65:1, "Behold I go to the Gentiles," a gloss adds, "The Son speaks Who said to Moses, I am Who am." These appear to belong to the Son, and are not appropriated. For "truth," according to Augustine (De Vera Relig. 36), "is the supreme similitude of the principle without any dissimilitude." So it seems that it properly belongs to the Son, Who has a principle. Also the "book of life" seems proper to the Son, as signifying "a thing from another"; for every book is written by someone. This also, "Who is," appears to be proper to the Son; because if when it was said to Moses, "I am Who am," the Trinity spoke, then Moses could have said, "He Who is Father, Son, and Holy Ghost, and the Holy Ghost sent me to you," so also he could have said further, "He Who is the Father, and the Son, and the Holy Ghost sent me to you," pointing out a certain person. This, however, is false; because no person is Father, Son and Holy Ghost. Therefore it cannot be common to the Trinity, but is proper to the Son.

I answer that, Our intellect, which is led to the knowledge of God from creatures, must consider God according to the mode derived from creatures. In considering any creature four points present themselves to us in due order. Firstly, the thing itself taken absolutely is considered as a being. Secondly, it is considered as one. Thirdly, its intrinsic power of operation and causality is considered. The fourth point of consideration embraces its relation to its effects. Hence this fourfold consideration comes to our mind in reference to God.

According to the first point of consideration, whereby we consider God absolutely in His being, the appropriation mentioned by Hilary applies, according to which "eternity" is appropriated to the Father, "species" to the Son, "use" to the Holy Ghost. For "eternity" as meaning a "being" without a principle, has a likeness to the property of the Father, Who is "a principle without a principle." Species or beauty has a likeness to the property of the Son. For beauty includes three conditions, "integrity" or "perfection," since those things which are impaired are by the very fact ugly; due "proportion" or "harmony"; and lastly, "brightness" or "clarity," whence things are called beautiful which have a bright color.

The first of these has a likeness to the property of the Son, inasmuch as He as Son has in Himself truly and perfectly the nature of the Father. To insinuate this, Augustine says in his explanation (De Trin. vi, 10): "Where--that is, in the Son--there is supreme and primal life," etc.

The second agrees with the Son's property, inasmuch as He is the express Image of the Father. Hence we see that an image is said to be beautiful, if it perfectly represents even an ugly thing. This is indicated by Augustine when he says (De Trin. vi, 10), "Where there exists wondrous proportion and primal equality," etc.

The third agrees with the property of the Son, as the Word, which is the light and splendor of the intellect, as Damascene says (De Fide Orth. iii, 3). Augustine alludes to the same when he says (De Trin. vi, 10): "As the perfect Word, not wanting in anything, and, so to speak, the art of the omnipotent God," etc.

"Use" has a likeness to the property of the Holy Ghost; provided the "use" be taken in a wide sense, as including also the sense of "to enjoy"; according as "to use" is to employ something at the beck of the will, and "to enjoy" means to use joyfully, as Augustine says (De Trin. x, 11). So "use," whereby the Father and the Son enjoy each other, agrees with the property of the Holy Ghost, as Love. This is what Augustine says (De Trin. vi, 10): "That love, that delectation, that felicity or beatitude, is called use by him" (Hilary). But the "use" by which we enjoy God, is likened to the property of the Holy Ghost as the Gift; and Augustine points to this when he says (De Trin. vi, 10): "In the Trinity, the Holy Ghost, the sweetness of the Begettor and the Begotten, pours out upon us mere creatures His immense bounty and wealth." Thus it is clear how "eternity," "species," and "use" are attributed or appropriated to the persons, but not essence or operation; because, being common, there is nothing in their concept to liken them to the properties of the Persons.

The second consideration of God regards Him as "one." In that view Augustine (De Doctr. Christ. i, 5) appropriates "unity" to the Father, "equality" to the Son, "concord" or "union" to the Holy Ghost. It is manifest that these three imply unity, but in different ways. For "unity" is said absolutely, as it does not presuppose anything else; and for this reason it is appropriated to the Father, to Whom any other person is not presupposed since He is the "principle without principle." "Equality" implies unity as regards another; for that is equal which has the same quantity as another. So equality is appropriated to the Son, Who is the "principle from a principle." "Union" implies the unity of two; and is therefore appropriated to the Holy Ghost, inasmuch as He proceeds from two. And from this we can understand what Augustine means when he says (De Doctr. Christ. i, 5) that "The Three are one, by reason of the Father; They are equal by reason of the Son; and are united by reason of the Holy Ghost." For it is clear that we trace a thing back to that in which we find it first: just as in this lower world we attribute life to the vegetative soul, because therein we find the first trace of life. Now "unity" is perceived at once in the person of the Father, even if by an impossible hypothesis, the other persons were removed. So the other persons derive their unity from the Father. But if the other persons be removed, we do not find equality in the Father, but we find it as soon as we suppose the Son. So, all are equal by reason of the Son, not as if the Son were the principle of equality in the Father, but that, without the Son equal to the Father, the Father could not be called equal; because His equality is considered firstly in regard to the Son: for that the Holy Ghost is equal to the Father, is also from the Son. Likewise, if the Holy Ghost, Who is the union of the two, be excluded, we cannot understand the oneness of the union between the Father and the Son. So all are connected by reason of the Holy Ghost; because given the Holy Ghost, we find whence the Father and the Son are said to be united.

According to the third consideration, which brings before us the adequate power of God in the sphere of causality, there is said to be a third kind of appropriation, of "power," "wisdom," and "goodness." This kind of appropriation is made both by reason of similitude as regards what exists in the divine persons, and by reason of dissimilitude if we consider what is in creatures. For "power" has the nature of a principle, and so it has a likeness to the heavenly Father, Who is the principle of the whole Godhead.

But in an earthly father it is wanting sometimes by reason of old age. "Wisdom" has likeness to the heavenly Son, as the Word, for a word is nothing but the concept of wisdom. In an earthly son this is sometimes absent by reason of lack of years. "Goodness," as the nature and object of love, has likeness to the Holy Ghost; but seems repugnant to the earthly spirit, which often implies a certain violent impulse, according to Isaiah 25:4: "The spirit of the strong is as a blast beating on the wall." "Strength" is appropriated to the Son and to the Holy Ghost, not as denoting the power itself of a thing, but as sometimes used to express that which proceeds from power; for instance, we say that the strong work done by an agent is its strength.

According to the fourth consideration, i.e. God's relation to His effects, there arise appropriation of the expression "from Whom, by Whom, and in Whom." For this preposition "from" [ex] sometimes implies a certain relation of the material cause; which has no place in God; and sometimes it expresses the relation of the efficient cause, which can be applied to God by reason of His active power; hence it is appropriated to the Father in the same way as power. The preposition "by" [per] sometimes designates an intermediate cause; thus we may say that a smith works "by" a hammer. Hence the word "by" is not always appropriated to the Son, but belongs to the Son properly and strictly, according to the text, "All things were made by Him" (John 1:3); not that the Son is an instrument, but as "the principle from a principle." Sometimes it designates the habitude of a form "by" which an agent works; thus we say that an artificer works by his art. Hence, as wisdom and art are appropriated to the Son, so also is the expression "by Whom." The preposition "in" strictly denotes the habitude of one containing. Now, God contains things in two ways: in one way by their similitudes; thus things are said to be in God, as existing in His knowledge. In this sense the expression "in Him" should be appropriated to the Son. In another sense things are contained in God forasmuch as He in His goodness preserves and governs them, by guiding them to a fitting end; and in this sense the expression "in Him" is appropriated to the Holy Ghost, as likewise is "goodness." Nor need the habitude of the final cause (though the first of causes) be appropriated to the Father, Who is "the principle without a principle": because the divine persons, of Whom the Father is the principle, do not proceed from Him as towards an end, since each of Them is the last end; but They proceed by a natural procession, which seems more to belong to the nature of a natural power.

Regarding the other points of inquiry, we can say that since "truth" belongs to the intellect, as stated above (Question 16, Article 1), it is appropriated to the Son, without, however, being a property of His. For truth can be considered as existing in the thought or in the thing itself. Hence, as intellect and thing in their essential meaning, are referred to the essence, and not to the persons, so the same is to be said of truth. The definition quoted from Augustine belongs to truth as appropriated to the Son. The "book of life" directly means knowledge but indirectly it means life. For, as above explained (24, 1), it is God's knowledge regarding those who are to possess eternal life. Consequently, it is appropriated to the Son; although life is appropriated to the Holy Ghost, as implying a certain kind of interior movement, agreeing in that sense with the property of the Holy Ghost as Love. To be written by another is not of the essence of a book considered as such; but this belongs to it only as a work produced. So this does not imply origin; nor is it personal, but an appropriation to a person. The expression "Who is" is appropriated to the person of the Son, not by reason of itself, but by reason of an adjunct, inasmuch as, in God's word to Moses, was prefigured the delivery of the human race accomplished by the Son. Yet, forasmuch as the word "Who" is taken in a relative sense, it may sometimes relate to the person of the Son; and in that sense it would be taken personally; as, for instance, were we to say, "The Son is the begotten 'Who is,'" inasmuch as "God begotten is personal." But taken indefinitely, it is an essential term. And although the pronoun "this" [iste] seems grammatically to point to a particular person, nevertheless everything that we can point to can be grammatically treated as a person, although in its own nature it is not a person; as we may say, "this stone," and "this ass." So, speaking in a grammatical sense, so far as the word "God" signifies and stands for the divine essence, the latter may be designated by the pronoun "this," according to Exodus 15:2: "This is my God, and I will glorify Him."

# *Summa Theologica* I.2-4

Question 2. The existence of God

Article 1. Whether the existence of God is self-evident?

Objection 1. It seems that the existence of God is self-evident. Now those things are said to be self-evident to us the knowledge of which is naturally implanted in us, as we can see in regard to first principles. But as Damascene says (De Fide Orth. i, 1,3), "the knowledge of God is naturally implanted in all." Therefore the existence of God is self-evident.

Objection 2. Further, those things are said to be self-evident which are known as soon as the terms are known, which the Philosopher (1 Poster. iii) says is true of the first principles of demonstration. Thus, when the nature of a whole and of a part is known, it is at once recognized that every whole is greater than its part. But as soon as the signification of the word "God" is understood, it is at once seen that God exists. For by this word is signified that thing than which nothing greater can be conceived. But that which exists actually and mentally is greater than that which exists only mentally. Therefore, since as soon as the word "God" is understood it exists mentally, it also follows that it exists actually. Therefore the proposition "God exists" is self-evident.

Objection 3. Further, the existence of truth is self-evident. For whoever denies the existence of truth grants that truth does not exist: and, if truth does not exist, then the proposition "Truth does not exist" is true: and if there is anything true, there must be truth. But God is truth itself: "I am the way, the truth, and the life" (John 14:6) Therefore "God exists" is self-evident.

On the contrary, No one can mentally admit the opposite of what is self-evident; as the Philosopher (Metaph. iv, lect. vi) states concerning the first principles of demonstration. But the opposite of the proposition "God is" can be mentally admitted: "The fool said in his heart, There is no God" (Psalm 52:1). Therefore, that God exists is not self-evident.

I answer that, A thing can be self-evident in either of two ways: on the one hand, self-evident in itself, though not to us; on the other, self-evident in itself, and to us. A proposition is self-evident because the predicate is included in the essence of the subject, as "Man is an animal," for animal is contained in the essence of man. If, therefore the essence of the predicate and subject be known to all, the proposition will be self-evident to all; as is clear with regard to the first principles of demonstration, the terms of which are common things that no one is ignorant of, such as being and non-being, whole and part, and such like. If, however, there are some to whom the essence of the predicate and subject is unknown, the proposition will be self-evident in itself, but not to those who do not know the meaning of the predicate and subject of the proposition. Therefore, it happens, as Boethius says (Hebdom., the title of which is: "Whether all that is, is good"), "that there are some mental concepts self-evident only to the learned, as that incorporeal substances are not in space." Therefore I say that this proposition, "God exists," of itself is self-evident, for the predicate is the same as the subject, because God is His own existence as will be hereafter shown (3, 4). Now because we do not know the essence of God, the proposition is not self-evident to us; but needs to be demonstrated by things that are more known to us, though less known in their nature — namely, by effects.

Reply to Objection 1. To know that God exists in a general and confused way is implanted in us by nature, inasmuch as God is man's beatitude. For man naturally desires happiness, and what is naturally desired by man must be naturally known to him. This, however, is not to know absolutely that God exists; just as to know that someone is approaching is not the same as to know that Peter is approaching, even though it is Peter who is approaching; for many there are who imagine that man's perfect good which is happiness, consists in riches, and others in pleasures, and others in something else.

Reply to Objection 2. Perhaps not everyone who hears this word "God" understands it to signify something than which nothing greater can be thought, seeing that some have believed God to be a body. Yet, granted that everyone understands that by this word "God" is signified something than which nothing greater can be thought, nevertheless, it does not therefore follow that he understands that what the word signifies exists actually, but only that it exists mentally. Nor can it be argued that it actually exists, unless it be admitted that there actually exists something than which nothing greater can be thought; and this precisely is not admitted by those who hold that God does not exist.

Reply to Objection 3. The existence of truth in general is self-evident but the existence of a Primal Truth is not self-evident to us.

Article 2. Whether it can be demonstrated that God exists?

Objection 1. It seems that the existence of God cannot be demonstrated. For it is an article of faith that God exists. But what is of faith cannot be demonstrated, because a demonstration produces scientific knowledge; whereas faith is of the unseen (Hebrews 11:1). Therefore it cannot be demonstrated that God exists.

Objection 2. Further, the essence is the middle term of demonstration. But we cannot know in what God's essence consists, but solely in what it does not consist; as Damascene says (De Fide Orth. i, 4). Therefore we cannot demonstrate that God exists.

Objection 3. Further, if the existence of God were demonstrated, this could only be from His effects. But His effects are not proportionate to Him, since He is infinite and His effects are finite; and between the finite and infinite there is no proportion. Therefore, since a cause cannot be demonstrated by an effect not proportionate to it, it seems that the existence of God cannot be demonstrated.

On the contrary, The Apostle says: "The invisible things of Him are clearly seen, being understood by the things that are made" (Romans 1:20). But this would not be unless the existence of God could be demonstrated through the things that are made; for the first thing we must know of anything is whether it exists.

I answer that, Demonstration can be made in two ways: One is through the cause, and is called "a priori," and this is to argue from what is prior absolutely. The other is through the effect, and is called a demonstration "a posteriori"; this is to argue from what is prior relatively only to us. When an effect is better known to us than its cause, from the effect we proceed to the knowledge of the cause. And from every effect the existence of its proper cause can be demonstrated, so long as its effects are better known to us; because since every effect depends upon its cause, if the effect exists, the cause must pre-exist. Hence the existence of God, in so far as it is not self-evident to us, can be demonstrated from those of His effects which are known to us.

Reply to Objection 1. The existence of God and other like truths about God, which can be known by natural reason, are not articles of faith, but are preambles to the articles; for faith presupposes natural knowledge, even as grace presupposes nature, and perfection supposes something that can be perfected. Nevertheless, there is nothing to prevent a man, who cannot grasp a proof, accepting, as a matter of faith, something which in itself is capable of being scientifically known and demonstrated.

Reply to Objection 2. When the existence of a cause is demonstrated from an effect, this effect takes the place of the definition of the cause in proof of the cause's existence. This is especially the case in regard to God, because, in order to prove the existence of anything, it is necessary to accept as a middle term the meaning of the word, and not its essence, for the question of its essence follows on the question of its existence. Now the names given to God are derived from His effects; consequently, in demonstrating the existence of God from His effects, we may take for the middle term the meaning of the word "God".

Reply to Objection 3. From effects not proportionate to the cause no perfect knowledge of that cause can be obtained. Yet from every effect the existence of the cause can be clearly demonstrated, and so we can demonstrate the existence of God from His effects; though from them we cannot perfectly know God as He is in His essence.

Article 3. Whether God exists?

Objection 1. It seems that God does not exist; because if one of two contraries be infinite, the other would be altogether destroyed. But the word "God" means that He is infinite goodness. If, therefore, God existed, there would be no evil discoverable; but there is evil in the world. Therefore God does not exist.

Objection 2. Further, it is superfluous to suppose that what can be accounted for by a few principles has been produced by many. But it seems that everything we see in the world can be accounted for by other principles, supposing God did not exist. For all natural things can be reduced to one principle which is nature; and all voluntary things can be reduced to one principle which is human reason, or will. Therefore there is no need to suppose God's existence.

On the contrary, It is said in the person of God: "I am Who am." (Exodus 3:14)

I answer that, The existence of God can be proved in five ways.

The first and more manifest way is the argument from motion. It is certain, and evident to our senses, that in the world some things are in motion. Now whatever is in motion is put in motion by another, for nothing can be in motion except it is in potentiality to that towards which it is in motion; whereas a thing moves inasmuch as it is in act. For motion is nothing else than the reduction of something from potentiality to actuality. But nothing can be reduced from potentiality to actuality, except by something in a state of actuality. Thus that which is actually hot, as fire, makes wood, which is potentially hot, to be actually hot, and thereby moves and changes it. Now it is not possible that the same thing should be at once in actuality and potentiality in the same respect, but only in different respects. For what is actually hot cannot simultaneously be potentially hot; but it is simultaneously potentially cold. It is therefore impossible that in the same respect and in the same way a thing should be both mover and moved, i.e. that it should move itself. Therefore, whatever is in motion must be put in motion by another. If that by which it is put in motion be itself put in motion, then this also must needs be put in motion by another, and that by another again. But this cannot go on to infinity, because then there would be no first mover, and, consequently, no other mover; seeing that subsequent movers move only inasmuch as they are put in motion by the first mover; as the staff moves only because it is put in motion by the hand. Therefore it is necessary to arrive at a first mover, put in motion by no other; and this everyone understands to be God.

The second way is from the nature of the efficient cause. In the world of sense we find there is an order of efficient causes. There is no case known (neither is it, indeed, possible) in which a thing is found to be the efficient cause of itself; for so it would be prior to itself, which is impossible. Now in efficient causes it is not possible to go on to infinity, because in all efficient causes following in order, the first is the cause of the intermediate cause, and the intermediate is the cause of the ultimate cause, whether the intermediate cause be several, or only one. Now to take away the cause is to take away the effect. Therefore, if there be no first cause among efficient causes, there will be no ultimate, nor any intermediate cause. But if in efficient causes it is possible to go on to infinity, there will be no first efficient cause, neither will there be an ultimate effect, nor any intermediate efficient causes; all of which is plainly false. Therefore it is necessary to admit a first efficient cause, to which everyone gives the name of God.

The third way is taken from possibility and necessity, and runs thus. We find in nature things that are possible to be and not to be, since they are found to be generated, and to corrupt, and consequently, they are possible to be and not to be. But it is impossible for these always to exist, for that which is possible not to be at some time is not. Therefore, if everything is possible not to be, then at one time there could have been nothing in existence. Now if this were true, even now there would be nothing in existence, because that which does not exist only begins to exist by something already existing. Therefore, if at one time nothing was in existence, it would have been impossible for anything to have begun to exist; and thus even now nothing would be in existence — which is absurd. Therefore, not all beings are merely possible, but there must exist something the existence of which is necessary. But every necessary thing either has its necessity caused by another, or not. Now it is impossible to go on to infinity in necessary things which have their necessity caused by another, as has been already proved in regard to efficient causes. Therefore we cannot but postulate the existence of some being having of itself its own necessity, and not receiving it from another, but rather causing in others their necessity. This all men speak of as God.

The fourth way is taken from the gradation to be found in things. Among beings there are some more and some less good, true, noble and the like. But "more" and "less" are predicated of different things, according as they resemble in their different ways something which is the maximum, as a thing is said to be hotter according as it more nearly resembles that which is hottest; so that there is something which is truest, something best, something noblest and, consequently, something which is uttermost being; for those things that are greatest in truth are greatest in being, as it is written in Metaph. ii. Now the maximum in any genus is the cause of all in that genus; as fire, which is the maximum heat, is the cause of all hot things. Therefore there must also be something which is to all beings the cause of their being, goodness, and every other perfection; and this we call God.

The fifth way is taken from the governance of the world. We see that things which lack intelligence, such as natural bodies, act for an end, and this is evident from their acting always, or nearly always, in the same way, so as to obtain the best result. Hence it is plain that not fortuitously, but designedly, do they achieve their end. Now whatever lacks intelligence cannot move towards an end, unless it be directed by some being endowed with knowledge and intelligence; as the arrow is shot to its mark by the archer. Therefore some intelligent being exists by whom all natural things are directed to their end; and this being we call God.

Reply to Objection 1. As Augustine says (Enchiridion xi): "Since God is the highest good, He would not allow any evil to exist in His works, unless His omnipotence and goodness were such as to bring good even out of evil." This is part of the infinite goodness of God, that He should allow evil to exist, and out of it produce good.

Reply to Objection 2. Since nature works for a determinate end under the direction of a higher agent, whatever is done by nature must needs be traced back to God, as to its first cause. So also whatever is done voluntarily must also be traced back to some higher cause other than human reason or will, since these can change or fail; for all things that are changeable and capable of defect must be traced back to an immovable and self-necessary first principle, as was shown in the body of the Article.

## Question 3. The simplicity of God

### Article 1. Whether God is a body?

Objection 1. It seems that God is a body. For a body is that which has the three dimensions. But Holy Scripture attributes the three dimensions to God, for it is written: "He is higher than Heaven, and what wilt thou do? He is deeper than Hell, and how wilt thou know? The measure of Him is longer than the earth and broader than the sea" (Job 11:8-9). Therefore God is a body.

Objection 2. Further, everything that has figure is a body, since figure is a quality of quantity. But God seems to have figure, for it is written: "Let us make man to our image and likeness" (Genesis 1:26). Now a figure is called an image, according to the text: "Who being the brightness of His glory and the figure," i.e. the image, "of His substance" (Hebrews 1:3). Therefore God is a body.

Objection 3. Further, whatever has corporeal parts is a body. Now Scripture attributes corporeal parts to God. "Hast thou an arm like God?" (Job 40:4); and "The eyes of the Lord are upon the just" (Psalm 33:16); and "The right hand of the Lord hath wrought strength" (Psalm 117:16). Therefore God is a body.

Objection 4. Further, posture belongs only to bodies. But something which supposes posture is said of God in the Scriptures: "I saw the Lord sitting" (Isaiah 6:1), and "He standeth up to judge" (Isaiah 3:13). Therefore God is a body.

Objection 5. Further, only bodies or things corporeal can be a local term "wherefrom" or "whereto." But in the Scriptures God is spoken of as a local term "whereto," according to the words, "Come ye to Him and be enlightened" (Psalm 33:6), and as a term "wherefrom": "All they that depart from Thee shall be written in the earth" (Jeremiah 17:13). Therefore God is a body.

On the contrary, It is written in the Gospel of St. John (John 4:24): "God is a spirit."

I answer that, It is absolutely true that God is not a body; and this can be shown in three ways.

First, because no body is in motion unless it be put in motion, as is evident from induction. Now it has been already proved (2, 3), that God is the First Mover, and is Himself unmoved. Therefore it is clear that God is not a body.

Secondly, because the first being must of necessity be in act, and in no way in potentiality. For although in any single thing that passes from potentiality to actuality, the potentiality is prior in time to the actuality; nevertheless, absolutely speaking, actuality is prior to potentiality; for whatever is in potentiality can be reduced into actuality only by some being in actuality. Now it has been already proved that God is the First Being. It is therefore impossible that in God there should be any potentiality. But every body is in potentiality because the continuous, as such, is divisible to infinity; it is therefore impossible that God should be a body.

Thirdly, because God is the most noble of beings. Now it is impossible for a body to be the most noble of beings; for a body must be either animate or inanimate; and an animate body is manifestly nobler than any inanimate body. But an animate body is not animate precisely as body; otherwise all bodies would be animate. Therefore its animation depends upon some other thing, as our body depends for its animation on the soul. Hence that by which a body becomes animated must be nobler than the body. Therefore it is impossible that God should be a body.

Reply to Objection 1. As we have said above (Question 1, Article 9), Holy Writ puts before us spiritual and divine things under the comparison of corporeal things. Hence, when it attributes to God the three dimensions under the comparison of corporeal quantity, it implies His virtual quantity; thus, by depth, it signifies His power of knowing hidden things; by height, the transcendence of His excelling power; by length, the duration of His existence; by breadth, His act of love for all. Or, as says Dionysius (Div. Nom. ix), by the depth of God is meant the incomprehensibility of His essence; by length, the procession of His all-pervading power; by breadth, His overspreading all things, inasmuch as all things lie under His protection.

Reply to Objection 2. Man is said to be after the image of God, not as regards his body, but as regards that whereby he excels other animals. Hence, when it is said, "Let us make man to our image and likeness", it is added, "And let him have dominion over the fishes of the sea" (Genesis 1:26). Now man excels all animals by his reason and intelligence; hence it is according to his intelligence and reason, which are incorporeal, that man is said to be according to the image of God.

Reply to Objection 3. Corporeal parts are attributed to God in Scripture on account of His actions, and this is owing to a certain parallel. For instance the act of the eye is to see; hence the eye attributed to God signifies His power of seeing intellectually, not sensibly; and so on with the other parts.

Reply to Objection 4. Whatever pertains to posture, also, is only attributed to God by some sort of parallel. He is spoken of as sitting, on account of His unchangeableness and dominion; and as standing, on account of His power of overcoming whatever withstands Him.

Reply to Objection 5. We draw near to God by no corporeal steps, since He is everywhere, but by the affections of our soul, and by the actions of that same soul do we withdraw from Him; thus, to draw near to or to withdraw signifies merely spiritual actions based on the metaphor of local motion.

Article 2. Whether God is composed of matter and form?

Objection 1. It seems that God is composed of matter and form. For whatever has a soul is composed of matter and form; since the soul is the form of the body. But Scripture attributes a soul to God; for it is mentioned in Hebrews (Hebrews 10:38), where God says: "But My just man liveth by faith; but if he withdraw himself, he shall not please My soul." Therefore God is composed of matter and form.

Objection 2. Further, anger, joy and the like are passions of the composite. But these are attributed to God in Scripture: "The Lord was exceeding angry with His people" (Psalm 105:40). Therefore God is composed of matter and form.

Objection 3. Further, matter is the principle of individualization. But God seems to be individual, for He cannot be predicated of many. Therefore He is composed of matter and form.

On the contrary, Whatever is composed of matter and form is a body; for dimensive quantity is the first property of matter. But God is not a body as proved in the preceding Article; therefore He is not composed of matter and form.

I answer that, It is impossible that matter should exist in God.

First, because matter is in potentiality. But we have shown (I:2:3) that God is pure act, without any potentiality. Hence it is impossible that God should be composed of matter and form.

Secondly, because everything composed of matter and form owes its perfection and goodness to its form; therefore its goodness is participated, inasmuch as matter participates the form. Now the first good and the best--viz. God--is not a participated good, because the essential good is prior to the participated good. Hence it is impossible that God should be composed of matter and form.

Thirdly, because every agent acts by its form; hence the manner in which it has its form is the manner in which it is an agent. Therefore whatever is primarily and essentially an agent must be primarily and essentially form. Now God is the first agent, since He is the first efficient cause. He is therefore of His essence a form; and not composed of matter and form.

Reply to Objection 1. A soul is attributed to God because His acts resemble the acts of a soul; for, that we will anything, is due to our soul. Hence what is pleasing to His will is said to be pleasing to His soul.

Reply to Objection 2. Anger and the like are attributed to God on account of a similitude of effect. Thus, because to punish is properly the act of an angry man, God's punishment is metaphorically spoken of as His anger.

Reply to Objection 3. Forms which can be received in matter are individualized by matter, which cannot be in another as in a subject since it is the first underlying subject; although form of itself, unless something else prevents it, can be received by many. But that form which cannot be received in matter, but is self-subsisting, is individualized precisely because it cannot be received in a subject; and such a form is God. Hence it does not follow that matter exists in God.

Article 3. Whether God is the same as His essence or nature?

Objection 1. It seems that God is not the same as His essence or nature. For nothing can be in itself. But the substance or nature of

God--i.e. the Godhead--is said to be in God. Therefore it seems that God is not the same as His essence or nature.

Objection 2. Further, the effect is assimilated to its cause; for every agent produces its like. But in created things the "suppositum" is not identical with its nature; for a man is not the same as his humanity. Therefore God is not the same as His Godhead.

On the contrary, It is said of God that He is life itself, and not only that He is a living thing: "I am the way, the truth, and the life" (John 14:6). Now the relation between Godhead and God is the same as the relation between life and a living thing. Therefore God is His very Godhead.

I answer that, God is the same as His essence or nature. To understand this, it must be noted that in things composed of matter and form, the nature or essence must differ from the "suppositum," because the essence or nature connotes only what is included in the definition of the species; as, humanity connotes all that is included in the definition of man, for it is by this that man is man, and it is this that humanity signifies, that, namely, whereby man is man. Now individual matter, with all the individualizing accidents, is not included in the definition of the species. For this particular flesh, these bones, this blackness or whiteness, etc., are not included in the definition of a man. Therefore this flesh, these bones, and the accidental qualities distinguishing this particular matter, are not included in humanity; and yet they are included in the thing which is man. Hence the thing which is a man has something more in it than has humanity. Consequently humanity and a man are not wholly identical; but humanity is taken to mean the formal part of a man, because the principles whereby a thing is defined are regarded as the formal constituent in regard to the individualizing matter. On the other hand, in things not composed of matter and form, in which individualization is not due to individual matter--that is to say, to "this" matter--the very forms being individualized of themselves--it is necessary the forms themselves should be subsisting "supposita." Therefore "suppositum" and nature in them are identified. Since God then is not composed of matter and form, He must be His own Godhead, His own Life, and whatever else is thus predicated of Him.

Reply to Objection 1. We can speak of simple things only as though they were like the composite things from which we derive our knowledge. Therefore in speaking of God, we use concrete nouns to signify His subsistence, because with us only those things subsist which are composite; and we use abstract nouns to signify His simplicity. In saying therefore that Godhead, or life, or the like are in God, we indicate the composite way in which our intellect understands, but not that there is any composition in God.

Reply to Objection 2. The effects of God do not imitate Him perfectly, but only as far as they are able; and the imitation is here defective, precisely because what is simple and one, can only be represented by divers things; consequently, composition is accidental to them, and therefore, in them "suppositum" is not the same as nature.

Article 4. Whether essence and existence are the same in God?

Objection 1. It seems that essence and existence are not the same in God. For if it be so, then the divine being has nothing added to it. Now being to which no addition is made is universal being which is predicated of all things. Therefore it follows that God is being in general which can be predicated of everything. But this is false: "For men gave the incommunicable name to stones and wood" (Wisdom 14:21). Therefore God's existence is not His essence.

Objection 2. Further, we can know "whether" God exists as said above (I:2:2); but we cannot know "what" He is. Therefore God's existence is not the same as His essence--that is, as His quiddity or nature.

On the contrary, Hilary says (Trin. vii): "In God existence is not an accidental quality, but subsisting truth." Therefore what subsists in God is His existence.

I answer that, God is not only His own essence, as shown in the preceding article, but also His own existence. This may be shown in several ways.

First, whatever a thing has besides its essence must be caused either by the constituent principles of that essence (like a property that necessarily accompanies the species--as the faculty of laughing is proper to a man--and is caused by the constituent principles of the species), or by some exterior agent--as heat is caused in water by fire. Therefore, if the existence of a thing differs from its essence, this existence must be caused either by some exterior agent or by its essential principles. Now it is impossible for a thing's existence to be caused by its essential constituent principles, for nothing can be the sufficient cause of its own existence, if its existence is caused. Therefore that thing, whose existence differs from its essence, must have its existence caused by another. But this cannot be true of God; because we call God the first efficient cause. Therefore it is impossible that in God His existence should differ from His essence.

Secondly, existence is that which makes every form or nature actual; for goodness and humanity are spoken of as actual, only because they are spoken of as existing. Therefore existence must be compared to essence, if the latter is a distinct reality, as actuality to potentiality. Therefore, since in God there is no potentiality, as shown above (Article 1), it follows that in Him essence does not differ from existence. Therefore His essence is His existence.

Thirdly, because, just as that which has fire, but is not itself fire, is on fire by participation; so that which has existence but is not existence, is a being by participation. But God is His own essence, as shown above (Article 3) if, therefore, He is not His own existence He will be not essential, but participated being. He will not therefore be the first being--which is absurd. Therefore God is His own existence, and not merely His own essence.

Reply to Objection 1. A thing that has nothing added to it can be of two kinds. Either its essence precludes any addition; thus, for example, it is of the essence of an irrational animal to be without reason. Or we may understand a thing to have nothing added to it, inasmuch as its essence does not require that anything should be added to it; thus the genus animal is without reason, because it is not of the essence of animal in general to have reason; but neither is it to lack reason. And so the divine being has nothing added to it in the first sense; whereas universal being has nothing added to it in the second sense.

Reply to Objection 2. "To be" can mean either of two things. It may mean the act of essence, or it may mean the composition of a proposition effected by the mind in joining a predicate to a subject. Taking "to be" in the first sense, we cannot understand God's existence nor His essence; but only in the second sense. We know that this proposition which we form about God when we say "God is," is true; and this we know from His effects (I:2:2).

Article 5. Whether God is contained in a genus?

Objection 1. It seems that God is contained in a genus. For a substance is a being that subsists of itself. But this is especially true of God. Therefore God is in a genus of substance.

Objection 2. Further, nothing can be measured save by something of its own genus; as length is measured by length and numbers by number. But God is the measure of all substances, as the

Commentator shows (Metaph. x). Therefore God is in the genus of substance.

On the contrary, In the mind, genus is prior to what it contains. But nothing is prior to God either really or mentally. Therefore God is not in any genus.

I answer that, A thing can be in a genus in two ways; either absolutely and properly, as a species contained under a genus; or as being reducible to it, as principles and privations. For example, a point and unity are reduced to the genus of quantity, as its principles; while blindness and all other privations are reduced to the genus of habit. But in neither way is God in a genus. That He cannot be a species of any genus may be shown in three ways.

First, because a species is constituted of genus and difference. Now that from which the difference constituting the species is derived, is always related to that from which the genus is derived, as actuality is related to potentiality. For animal is derived from sensitive nature, by concretion as it were, for that is animal, which has a sensitive nature. Rational being, on the other hand, is derived from intellectual nature, because that is rational, which has an intellectual nature, and intelligence is compared to sense, as actuality is to potentiality. The same argument holds good in other things. Hence since in God actuality is not added to potentiality, it is impossible that He should be in any genus as a species.

Secondly, since the existence of God is His essence, if God were in any genus, He would be the genus "being", because, since genus is predicated as an essential it refers to the essence of a thing. But the Philosopher has shown (Metaph. iii) that being cannot be a genus, for every genus has differences distinct from its generic essence. Now no difference can exist distinct from being; for non-being cannot be a difference. It follows then that God is not in a genus.

Thirdly, because all in one genus agree in the quiddity or essence of the genus which is predicated of them as an essential, but they differ in their existence. For the existence of man and of horse is not the same; as also of this man and that man: thus in every member of a genus, existence and quiddity--i.e. essence--must differ. But in God they do not differ, as shown in the preceding article. Therefore it is plain that God is not in a genus as if He were a species. From this it is also plain that He has no genus nor difference, nor can there be any definition of Him; nor, save through His effects, a demonstration of Him: for a definition is from genus and difference; and the mean of a demonstration is a definition. That God is not in a genus, as reducible to it as its principle, is clear from this, that a principle reducible to any genus does not extend beyond that genus; as, a point is the principle of continuous quantity alone; and unity, of discontinuous quantity. But God is the principle of all being. Therefore He is not contained in any genus as its principle.

Reply to Objection 1. The word substance signifies not only what exists of itself--for existence cannot of itself be a genus, as shown in the body of the article; but, it also signifies an essence that has the property of existing in this way--namely, of existing of itself; this existence, however, is not its essence. Thus it is clear that God is not in the genus of substance.

Reply to Objection 2. This objection turns upon proportionate measure which must be homogeneous with what is measured. Now, God is not a measure proportionate to anything. Still, He is called the measure of all things, in the sense that everything has being only according as it resembles Him.

Article 6. Whether in God there are any accidents?

Objection 1. It seems that there are accidents in God. For substance cannot be an accident, as Aristotle says (Phys. i). Therefore that which is an accident in one, cannot, in another, be a substance.

Thus it is proved that heat cannot be the substantial form of fire, because it is an accident in other things. But wisdom, virtue, and the like, which are accidents in us, are attributes of God. Therefore in God there are accidents.

Objection 2. Further, in every genus there is a first principle. But there are many "genera" of accidents. If, therefore, the primal members of these genera are not in God, there will be many primal beings other than God--which is absurd.

On the contrary, Every accident is in a subject. But God cannot be a subject, for "no simple form can be a subject", as Boethius says (De Trin.). Therefore in God there cannot be any accident.

I answer that, From all we have said, it is clear there can be no accident in God.

First, because a subject is compared to its accidents as potentiality to actuality; for a subject is in some sense made actual by its accidents. But there can be no potentiality in God, as was shown (2, 3).

Secondly, because God is His own existence; and as Boethius says (Hebdom.), although every essence may have something superadded to it, this cannot apply to absolute being: thus a heated substance can have something extraneous to heat added to it, as whiteness, nevertheless absolute heat can have nothing else than heat.

Thirdly, because what is essential is prior to what is accidental. Whence as God is absolute primal being, there can be in Him nothing accidental. Neither can He have any essential accidents (as the capability of laughing is an essential accident of man), because such accidents are caused by the constituent principles of the subject. Now there can be nothing caused in God, since He is the first cause. Hence it follows that there is no accident in God.

Reply to Objection 1. Virtue and wisdom are not predicated of God and of us univocally. Hence it does not follow that there are accidents in God as there are in us.

Reply to Objection 2. Since substance is prior to its accidents, the principles of accidents are reducible to the principles of the substance as to that which is prior; although God is not first as if contained in the genus of substance; yet He is first in respect to all being, outside of every genus.

Article 7. Whether God is altogether simple?

Objection 1. It seems that God is not altogether simple. For whatever is from God must imitate Him. Thus from the first being are all beings; and from the first good is all good. But in the things which God has made, nothing is altogether simple. Therefore neither is God altogether simple.

Objection 2. Further, whatever is best must be attributed to God. But with us that which is composite is better than that which is simple; thus, chemical compounds are better than simple elements, and animals than the parts that compose them. Therefore it cannot be said that God is altogether simple.

On the contrary, Augustine says (De Trin. iv, 6,7): "God is truly and absolutely simple."

I answer that, The absolute simplicity of God may be shown in many ways.

First, from the previous articles of this question. For there is neither composition of quantitative parts in God, since He is not a body; nor composition of matter and form; nor does His nature differ from His "suppositum"; nor His essence from His existence; neither is there in Him composition of genus and difference, nor of subject and accident. Therefore, it is clear that God is nowise composite, but is altogether simple.

Secondly, because every composite is posterior to its component parts, and is dependent on them; but God is the first being, as shown above (Question 2, Article 3).

Thirdly, because every composite has a cause, for things in themselves different cannot unite unless something causes them to unite. But God is uncaused, as shown above (Question 2, Article 3), since He is the first efficient cause.

Fourthly, because in every composite there must be potentiality and actuality; but this does not apply to God; for either one of the parts actuates another, or at least all the parts are potential to the whole.

Fifthly, because nothing composite can be predicated of any single one of its parts. And this is evident in a whole made up of dissimilar parts; for no part of a man is a man, nor any of the parts of the foot, a foot. But in wholes made up of similar parts, although something which is predicated of the whole may be predicated of a part (as a part of the air is air, and a part of water, water), nevertheless certain things are predicable of the whole which cannot be predicated of any of the parts; for instance, if the whole volume of water is two cubits, no part of it can be two cubits. Thus in every composite there is something which is not it itself. But, even if this could be said of whatever has a form, viz. that it has something which is not it itself, as in a white object there is something which does not belong to the essence of white; nevertheless in the form itself, there is nothing besides itself. And so, since God is absolute form, or rather absolute being, He can be in no way composite. Hilary implies this argument, when he says (De Trin. vii): "God, Who is strength, is not made up of things that are weak; nor is He Who is light, composed of things that are dim."

Reply to Objection 1. Whatever is from God imitates Him, as caused things imitate the first cause. But it is of the essence of a thing to be in some sort composite; because at least its existence differs from its essence, as will be shown hereafter, (4, 3).

Reply to Objection 2. With us composite things are better than simple things, because the perfections of created goodness cannot be found in one simple thing, but in many things. But the perfection of divine goodness is found in one simple thing (4, 1 and 6, 2).

Article 8. Whether God enters into the composition of other things?

Objection 1. It seems that God enters into the composition of other things, for Dionysius says (Coel. Hier. iv): "The being of all things is that which is above being--the Godhead." But the being of all things enters into the composition of everything. Therefore God enters into the composition of other things.

Objection 2. Further, God is a form; for Augustine says (De Verb. Dom., [Serm. xxxviii) that, "the word of God, which is God, is an uncreated form." But a form is part of a compound. Therefore God is part of some compound.

Objection 3. Further, whatever things exist, in no way differing from each other, are the same. But God and primary matter exist, and in no way differ from each other. Therefore they are absolutely the same. But primary matter enters into the composition things. Therefore also does God. Proof of the minor-- whatever things differ, they differ by some differences, and therefore must be composite. But God and primary matter are altogether simple. Therefore they nowise differ from each other.

On the contrary, Dionysius says (Div. Nom. ii): "There can be no touching Him," i.e. God, "nor any other union with Him by mingling part with part."

Further, the first cause rules all things without commingling with them, as the Philosopher says (De Causis).

I answer that, On this point there have been three errors. Some have affirmed that God is the world-soul, as is clear from Augustine (De Civ. Dei vii, 6). This is practically the same as the opinion of those who assert that God is the soul of the highest heaven. Again, others have said that God is the formal principle of all things; and this was the theory of the Almaricians. The third error is that of David of Dinant, who most absurdly taught that God was primary matter. Now all these contain manifest untruth; since it is not possible for God to enter into the composition of anything, either as a formal or a material principle.

First, because God is the first efficient cause. Now the efficient cause is not identical numerically with the form of the thing caused, but only specifically: for man begets man. But primary matter can be neither numerically nor specifically identical with an efficient cause; for the former is merely potential, while the latter is actual.

Secondly, because, since God is the first efficient cause, to act belongs to Him primarily and essentially. But that which enters into composition with anything does not act primarily and essentially, but rather the composite so acts; for the hand does not act, but the man by his hand; and, fire warms by its heat. Hence God cannot be part of a compound.

Thirdly, because no part of a compound can be absolutely primal among beings--not even matter, nor form, though they are the primal parts of every compound. For matter is merely potential; and potentiality is absolutely posterior to actuality, as is clear from the foregoing (3, 1): while a form which is part of a compound is a participated form; and as that which participates is posterior to that which is essential, so likewise is that which is participated; as fire in ignited objects is posterior to fire that is essentially such. Now it has been proved that God is absolutely primal being (2, 3).

Reply to Objection 1. The Godhead is called the being of all things, as their efficient and exemplar cause, but not as being their essence.

Reply to Objection 2. The Word is an exemplar form; but not a form that is part of a compound.

Reply to Objection 3. Simple things do not differ by added differences--for this is the property of compounds. Thus man and horse differ by their differences, rational and irrational; which differences, however, do not differ from each other by other differences. Hence, to be quite accurate, it is better to say that they are, not different, but diverse. Hence, according to the Philosopher (Metaph. x), "things which are diverse are absolutely distinct, but things which are different differ by something." Therefore, strictly speaking, primary matter and God do not differ, but are by their very being, diverse. Hence it does not follow they are the same.

Question 4. The perfection of God

Article 1. Whether God is perfect?

Objection 1. It seems that perfection does not belong to God. For we say a thing is perfect if it is completely made. But it does not befit God to be made. Therefore He is not perfect.

Objection 2. Further, God is the first beginning of things. But the beginnings of things seem to be imperfect, as seed is the beginning of animal and vegetable life. Therefore God is imperfect.

Objection 3. Further, as shown above (Question 3, Article 4), God's essence is existence. But existence seems most imperfect, since it is most universal and receptive of all modification. Therefore God is imperfect.

On the contrary, It is written: "Be you perfect as also your heavenly Father is perfect" (Matthew 5:48).

I answer that, As the Philosopher relates (Metaph. xii), some ancient philosophers, namely, the Pythagoreans and Leucippus, did not predicate "best" and "most perfect" of the first principle. The reason was that the ancient philosophers considered only a material principle; and a material principle is most imperfect. For since matter as such is merely potential, the first material principle must be simply potential, and thus most imperfect. Now God is the first principle, not material, but in the order of efficient cause, which must be most perfect. For just as matter, as such, is merely potential, an agent, as such, is in the state of actuality. Hence, the first active principle must needs be most actual, and therefore most perfect; for a thing is perfect in proportion to its state of actuality, because we call that perfect which lacks nothing of the mode of its perfection.

Reply to Objection 1. As Gregory says (Moral. v, 26,29): "Though our lips can only stammer, we yet chant the high things of God." For that which is not made is improperly called perfect. Nevertheless because created things are then called perfect, when from potentiality they are brought into actuality, this word "perfect" signifies whatever is not wanting in actuality, whether this be by way of perfection or not.

Reply to Objection 2. The material principle which with us is found to be imperfect, cannot be absolutely primal; but must be preceded by something perfect. For seed, though it be the principle of animal life reproduced through seed, has previous to it, the animal or plant from which is came. Because, previous to that which is potential, must be that which is actual; since a potential being can only be reduced into act by some being already actual.

Reply to Objection 3. Existence is the most perfect of all things, for it is compared to all things as that by which they are made actual; for nothing has actuality except so far as it exists. Hence existence is that which actuates all things, even their forms. Therefore it is not compared to other things as the receiver is to the received; but rather as the received to the receiver. When therefore I speak of the existence of man, or horse, or anything else, existence is considered a formal principle, and as something received; and not as that which exists.

Article 2. Whether the perfections of all things are in God?

Objection 1. It seems that the perfections of all things are not in God. For God is simple, as shown above (Question 3, Article 7); whereas the perfections of things are many and diverse. Therefore the perfections of all things are not in God.

Objection 2. Further, opposites cannot coexist. Now the perfections of things are opposed to each other, for each thing is perfected by its specific difference. But the differences by which "genera" are divided, and "species" constituted, are opposed to each other. Therefore because opposites cannot coexist in the same subject, it seems that the perfections of all things are not in God.

Objection 3. Further, a living thing is more perfect than what merely exists; and an intelligent thing than what merely lives. Therefore life is more perfect than existence; and knowledge than life. But the essence of God is existence itself. Therefore He has not the perfections of life, and knowledge, and other similar perfections.

On the contrary, Dionysius says (Div. Nom. v) that "God in His one existence prepossesses all things."

I answer that, All created perfections are in God. Hence He is spoken of as universally perfect, because He lacks not (says the Commentator, Metaph. v) any excellence which may be found in any genus. This may be seen from two considerations.

First, because whatever perfection exists in an effect must be found in the effective cause: either in the same formality, if it is a univocal agent--as when man reproduces man; or in a more eminent degree, if it is an equivocal agent--thus in the sun is the likeness of whatever is generated by the sun's power. Now it is plain that the effect pre-exists virtually in the efficient cause: and although to pre-exist in the potentiality of a material cause is to pre-exist in a more imperfect way, since matter as such is imperfect, and an agent as such is perfect; still to pre-exist virtually in the efficient cause is to pre-exist not in a more imperfect, but in a more perfect way. Since therefore God is the first effective cause of things, the perfections of all things must pre-exist in God in a more eminent way. Dionysius implies the same line of argument by saying of God (Div. Nom. v): "It is not that He is this and not that, but that He is all, as the cause of all."

Secondly, from what has been already proved, God is existence itself, of itself subsistent (3, 4). Consequently, He must contain within Himself the whole perfection of being. For it is clear that if some hot thing has not the whole perfection of heat, this is because heat is not participated in its full perfection; but if this heat were self-subsisting, nothing of the virtue of heat would be wanting to it. Since therefore God is subsisting being itself, nothing of the perfection of being can be wanting to Him. Now all created perfections are included in the perfection of being; for things are perfect, precisely so far as they have being after some fashion. It follows therefore that the perfection of no one thing is wanting to God. This line of argument, too, is implied by Dionysius (Div. Nom. v), when he says that, "God exists not in any single mode, but embraces all being within Himself, absolutely, without limitation, uniformly;" and afterwards he adds that, "He is the very existence to subsisting things."

Reply to Objection 1. Even as the sun (as Dionysius remarks, (Div. Nom. v), while remaining one and shining uniformly, contains within itself first and uniformly the substances of sensible things, and many and diverse qualities; "a fortiori" should all things in a kind of natural unity pre-exist in the cause of all things; and thus things diverse and in themselves opposed to each other, pre-exist in God as one, without injury to His simplicity. This suffices for the Reply to the Second Objection.

Reply to Objection 3. The same Dionysius says (Div. Nom. v) that, although existence is more perfect than life, and life than wisdom, if they are considered as distinguished in idea; nevertheless, a living thing is more perfect than what merely exists, because living things also exist and intelligent things both exist and live. Although therefore existence does not include life and wisdom, because that which participates in existence need not participate in every mode of existence; nevertheless God's existence includes in itself life and wisdom, because nothing of the perfection of being can be wanting to Him who is subsisting being itself.

Article 3. Whether any creature can be like God?

Objection 1. It seems that no creature can be like God. For it is written (Psalm 85:8): "There is none among the gods like unto Thee, O Lord." But of all creatures the most excellent are those which are called participation gods. Therefore still less can other creatures be said to be like God.

Objection 2. Further, likeness implies comparison. But there can be no comparison between things in a different "genus." Therefore neither can there be any likeness. Thus we do not say that sweetness is like whiteness. But no creature is in the same "genus" as God: since God is no "genus," as shown above (Question 3, Article 5). Therefore no creature is like God.

Objection 3. Further, we speak of those things as like which agree in form. But nothing can agree with God in form; for, save in God alone, essence and existence differ. Therefore no creature can be like to God.

Objection 4. Further, among like things there is mutual likeness; for like is like to like. If therefore any creature is like God, God will be like some creature, which is against what is said by Isaias: "To whom have you likened God?" (Isaiah 40:18).

On the contrary, It is written: "Let us make man to our image and likeness" (Genesis 1:26), and: "When He shall appear we shall be like to Him" (1 John 3:2).

I answer that, Since likeness is based upon agreement or communication in form, it varies according to the many modes of communication in form. Some things are said to be like, which communicate in the same form according to the same formality, and according to the same mode; and these are said to be not merely like, but equal in their likeness; as two things equally white are said to be alike in whiteness; and this is the most perfect likeness. In another way, we speak of things as alike which communicate in form according to the same formality, though not according to the same measure, but according to more or less, as something less white is said to be like another thing more white; and this is imperfect likeness. In a third way some things are said to be alike which communicate in the same form, but not according to the same formality; as we see in non-univocal agents. For since every agent reproduces itself so far as it is an agent, and everything acts according to the manner of its form, the effect must in some way resemble the form of the agent. If therefore the agent is contained in the same species as its effect, there will be a likeness in form between that which makes and that which is made, according to the same formality of the species; as man reproduces man. If, however, the agent and its effect are not contained in the same species, there will be a likeness, but not according to the formality of the same species; as things generated by the sun's heat may be in some sort spoken of as like the sun, not as though they received the form of the sun in its specific likeness, but in its generic likeness. Therefore if there is an agent not contained in any "genus," its effect will still more distantly reproduce the form of the agent, not, that is, so as to participate in the likeness of the agent's form according to the same specific or generic formality, but only according to some sort of analogy; as existence is common to all. In this way all created things, so far as they are beings, are like God as the first and universal principle of all being.

Reply to Objection 1. As Dionysius says (Div. Nom. ix), when Holy Writ declares that nothing is like God, it does not mean to deny all likeness to Him. For, "the same things can be like and unlike to God: like, according as they imitate Him, as far as He, Who is not perfectly imitable, can be imitated; unlike according as they fall short of their cause," not merely in intensity and remission, as that which is less white falls short of that which is more white; but because they are not in agreement, specifically or generically.

Reply to Objection 2. God is not related to creatures as though belonging to a different "genus," but as transcending every "genus," and as the principle of all "genera."

Reply to Objection 3. Likeness of creatures to God is not affirmed on account of agreement in form according to the formality of the same genus or species, but solely according to analogy, inasmuch as God is essential being, whereas other things are beings by participation.

Reply to Objection 4. Although it may be admitted that creatures are in some sort like God, it must nowise be admitted that God is like creatures; because, as Dionysius says (Div. Nom. ix): "A mutual likeness may be found between things of the same order, but not between a cause and that which is caused." For, we say that a statue is like a man, but not conversely; so also a creature can be spoken of as in some sort like God; but not that God is like a creature.

## *Summa Theologica* I.6-11, 13

Question 6. The goodness of God

Article 1. Whether God is good?

Objection 1. It seems that to be good does not belong to God. For goodness consists in mode, species and order. But these do not seem to belong to God; since God is immense and is not ordered to anything else. Therefore to be good does not belong to God.

Objection 2. Further, the good is what all things desire. But all things do not desire God, because all things do not know Him; and nothing is desired unless it is known. Therefore to be good does not belong to God.

On the contrary, It is written (Lamentations 3:25): "The Lord is good to them that hope in Him, to the soul that seeketh Him."

I answer that, To be good belongs pre-eminently to God. For a thing is good according to its desirableness. Now everything seeks after its own perfection; and the perfection and form of an effect consist in a certain likeness to the agent, since every agent makes its like; and hence the agent itself is desirable and has the nature of good. For the very thing which is desirable in it is the participation of its likeness. Therefore, since God is the first effective cause of all things, it is manifest that the aspect of good and of desirableness belong to Him; and hence Dionysius (Div. Nom. iv) attributes good to God as to the first efficient cause, saying that, God is called good "as by Whom all things subsist."

Reply to Objection 1. To have mode, species and order belongs to the essence of caused good; but good is in God as in its cause, and hence it belongs to Him to impose mode, species and order on others; wherefore these three things are in God as in their cause.

Reply to Objection 2. All things, by desiring their own perfection, desire God Himself, inasmuch as the perfections of all things are so many similitudes of the divine being; as appears from what is said above (Question 4, Article 3). And so of those things which desire God, some know Him as He is Himself, and this is proper to the rational creature; others know some participation of His goodness, and this belongs also to sensible knowledge; others have a natural desire without knowledge, as being directed to their ends by a higher intelligence.

Article 2. Whether God is the supreme good?

Objection 1. It seems that God is not the supreme good. For the supreme good adds something to good; otherwise it would belong to every good. But everything which is an addition to anything else is a compound thing: therefore the supreme good is a compound. But God is supremely simple; as was shown above (Question 3, Article 7). Therefore God is not the supreme good.

Objection 2. Further, "Good is what all desire," as the Philosopher says (Ethic. i, 1). Now what all desire is nothing but God, Who is the end of all things: therefore there is no other good but God. This appears also from what is said (Luke 18:19): "None is good but God alone." But we use the word supreme in comparison with others, as e.g. supreme heat is used in comparison with all other heats. Therefore God cannot be called the supreme good.

Objection 3. Further, supreme implies comparison. But things not in the same genus are not comparable; as, sweetness is not properly greater or less than a line. Therefore, since God is not in the same genus as other good things, as appears above (3, 5; 4, 3) it seems that God cannot be called the supreme good in relation to others.

On the contrary, Augustine says (De Trin. ii) that, the Trinity of the divine persons is "the supreme good, discerned by purified minds."

I answer that, God is the supreme good simply, and not only as existing in any genus or order of things. For good is attributed to God, as was said in the preceding article, inasmuch as all desired perfections flow from Him as from the first cause. They do not, however, flow from Him as from a univocal agent, as shown above (Question 4, Article 2); but as from an agent which does not agree with its effects either in species or genus. Now the likeness of an effect in the univocal cause is found uniformly; but in the equivocal cause it is found more excellently, as, heat is in the sun more excellently than it is in fire. Therefore as good is in God as in the first, but not the univocal, cause of all things, it must be in Him in a most excellent way; and therefore He is called the supreme good.

Reply to Objection 1. The supreme good does not add to good any absolute thing, but only a relation. Now a relation of God to creatures, is not a reality in God, but in the creature; for it is in God in our idea only: as, what is knowable is so called with relation to knowledge, not that it depends on knowledge, but because knowledge depends on it. Thus it is not necessary that there should be composition in the supreme good, but only that other things are deficient in comparison with it.

Reply to Objection 2. When we say that good is what all desire, it is not to be understood that every kind of good thing is desired by all; but that whatever is desired has the nature of good. And when it is said, "None is good but God alone," this is to be understood of essential goodness, as will be explained in the next article.

Reply to Objection 3. Things not of the same genus are in no way comparable to each other if indeed they are in different genera. Now we say that God is not in the same genus with other good things; not that He is any other genus, but that He is outside genus, and is the principle of every genus; and thus He is compared to others by excess, and it is this kind of comparison the supreme good implies.

Article 3. Whether to be essentially good belongs to God alone?

Objection 1. It seems that to be essentially good does not belong to God alone. For as "one" is convertible with "being," so is "good"; as we said above (Question 5, Article 1). But every being is one essentially, as appears from the Philosopher (Metaph. iv); therefore every being is good essentially.

Objection 2. Further, if good is what all things desire, since being itself is desired by all, then the being of each thing is its good. But everything is a being essentially; therefore every being is good essentially.

Objection 3. Further, everything is good by its own goodness. Therefore if there is anything which is not good essentially, it is necessary to say that its goodness is not its own essence. Therefore its goodness, since it is a being, must be good; and if it is good by some other goodness, the same question applies to that goodness also; therefore we must either proceed to infinity, or come to some goodness which is not good by any other goodness. Therefore the first supposition holds good. Therefore everything is good essentially.

On the contrary, Boethius says (De Hebdom.), that "all things but God are good by participation." Therefore they are not good essentially.

I answer that, God alone is good essentially. For everything is called good according to its perfection. Now perfection of a thing is threefold: first, according to the constitution of its own being; secondly, in respect of any accidents being added as necessary for

215

its perfect operation; thirdly, perfection consists in the attaining to something else as the end. Thus, for instance, the first perfection of fire consists in its existence, which it has through its own substantial form; its secondary perfection consists in heat, lightness and dryness, and the like; its third perfection is to rest in its own place. This triple perfection belongs to no creature by its own essence; it belongs to God only, in Whom alone essence is existence; in Whom there are no accidents; since whatever belongs to others accidentally belongs to Him essentially; as, to be powerful, wise and the like, as appears from what is stated above (Question 3, Article 6); and He is not directed to anything else as to an end, but is Himself the last end of all things. Hence it is manifest that God alone has every kind of perfection by His own essence; therefore He Himself alone is good essentially.

Reply to Objection 1. "One" does not include the idea of perfection, but only of indivision, which belongs to everything according to its own essence. Now the essences of simple things are undivided both actually and potentially, but the essences of compounds are undivided only actually; and therefore everything must be one essentially, but not good essentially, as was shown above.

Reply to Objection 2. Although everything is good in that it has being, yet the essence of a creature is not very being; and therefore it does not follow that a creature is good essentially.

Reply to Objection 3. The goodness of a creature is not its very essence, but something superadded; it is either its existence, or some added perfection, or the order to its end. Still, the goodness itself thus added is good, just as it is being. But for this reason is it called being because by it something has being, not because it itself has being through something else: hence for this reason is it called good because by it something is good, and not because it itself has some other goodness whereby it is good.

216

Article 4. Whether all things are good by the divine goodness?

Objection 1. It seems that all things are good by the divine goodness. For Augustine says (De Trin. viii), "This and that are good; take away this and that, and see good itself if thou canst; and so thou shalt see God, good not by any other good, but the good of every good." But everything is good by its own good; therefore everything is good by that very good which is God.

Objection 2. Further, as Boethius says (De Hebdom.), all things are called good, accordingly as they are directed to God, and this is by reason of the divine goodness; therefore all things are good by the divine goodness.

On the contrary, All things are good, inasmuch as they have being. But they are not called beings through the divine being, but through their own being; therefore all things are not good by the divine goodness, but by their own goodness.

I answer that, As regards relative things, we must admit extrinsic denomination; as, a thing is denominated "placed" from "place," and "measured" from "measure." But as regards absolute things opinions differ. Plato held the existence of separate ideas (84, 4) of all things, and that individuals were denominated by them as participating in the separate ideas; for instance, that Socrates is called man according to the separate idea of man. Now just as he laid down separate ideas of man and horse which he called absolute man and absolute horse, so likewise he laid down separate ideas of "being" and of "one," and these he called absolute being and absolute oneness; and by participation of these, everything was called "being" or "one"; and what was thus absolute being and absolute one, he said was the supreme good. And because good is convertible with being, as one is also; he called God the absolute good, from whom all things are called good by way of participation.

Although this opinion appears to be unreasonable in affirming separate ideas of natural things as subsisting of themselves--as Aristotle argues in many ways--still, it is absolutely true that there is first something which is essentially being and essentially good, which we call God, as appears from what is shown above (Question 2, Article 3), and Aristotle agrees with this. Hence from the first being, essentially such, and good, everything can be called good and a being, inasmuch as it participates in it by way of a certain assimilation which is far removed and defective; as appears from the above (Question 4, Article 3).

Everything is therefore called good from the divine goodness, as from the first exemplary effective and final principle of all goodness. Nevertheless, everything is called good by reason of the similitude of the divine goodness belonging to it, which is formally its own goodness, whereby it is denominated good. And so of all things there is one goodness, and yet many goodnesses.

This is a sufficient Reply to the Objections.

Question 7. The infinity of God

Article 1. Whether God is infinite?

Objection 1. It seems that God is not infinite. For everything infinite is imperfect, as the Philosopher says; because it has parts and matter, as is said in Phys. iii. But God is most perfect; therefore He is not infinite.

Objection 2. Further, according to the Philosopher (Phys. i), finite and infinite belong to quantity. But there is no quantity in God, for He is not a body, as was shown above (Question 3, Article 1). Therefore it does not belong to Him to be infinite.

Objection 3. Further, what is here in such a way as not to be elsewhere, is finite according to place. Therefore that which is a thing in such a way as not to be another thing, is finite according to substance. But God is this, and not another; for He is not a stone or wood. Therefore God is not infinite in substance.

On the contrary, Damascene says (De Fide Orth. i, 4) that "God is infinite and eternal, and boundless."

I answer that, All the ancient philosophers attribute infinitude to the first principle, as is said (Phys. iii), and with reason; for they considered that things flow forth infinitely from the first principle. But because some erred concerning the nature of the first principle, as a consequence they erred also concerning its infinity; forasmuch as they asserted that matter was the first principle; consequently they attributed to the first principle a material infinity to the effect that some infinite body was the first principle of things.

We must consider therefore that a thing is called infinite because it is not finite. Now matter is in a way made finite by form, and the form by matter. Matter indeed is made finite by form, inasmuch as matter, before it receives its form, is in potentiality to many forms; but on receiving a form, it is terminated by that one. Again, form is made finite by matter, inasmuch as form, considered in itself, is common to many; but when received in matter, the form is determined to this one particular thing. Now matter is perfected by the form by which it is made finite; therefore infinite as attributed to matter, has the nature of something imperfect; for it is as it were formless matter. On the other hand, form is not made perfect by matter, but rather is contracted by matter; and hence the infinite, regarded on the part of the form not determined by matter, has the nature of something perfect. Now being is the most formal of all things, as appears from what is shown above (4, 1, Objection 3). Since therefore the divine being is not a being received in anything, but He is His own subsistent being as was shown above (Question 3, Article 4), it is clear that God Himself is infinite and perfect.

From this appears the Reply to the First Objection.

Reply to Objection 2. Quantity is terminated by its form, which can be seen in the fact that a figure which consists in quantity terminated, is a kind of quantitative form. Hence the infinite of quantity is the infinite of matter; such a kind of infinite cannot be attributed to God; as was said above, in this article.

Reply to Objection 3. The fact that the being of God is self-subsisting, not received in any other, and is thus called infinite, shows Him to be distinguished from all other beings, and all others to be apart from Him. Even so, were there such a thing as a self-subsisting whiteness, the very fact that it did not exist in anything else, would make it distinct from every other whiteness existing in a subject.

Article 2. Whether anything but God can be essentially infinite?

Objection 1. It seems that something else besides God can be essentially infinite. For the power of anything is proportioned to its essence. Now if the essence of God is infinite, His power must also be infinite. Therefore He can produce an infinite effect, since the extent of a power is known by its effect.

Objection 2. Further, whatever has infinite power, has an infinite essence. Now the created intellect has an infinite power; for it apprehends the universal, which can extend itself to an infinitude of singular things. Therefore every created intellectual substance is infinite.

Objection 3. Further, primary matter is something other than God, as was shown above (Question 3, Article 8). But primary matter is infinite. Therefore something besides God can be infinite.

On the contrary, The infinite cannot have a beginning, as said in Phys. iii. But everything outside God is from God as from its first principle. Therefore besides God nothing can be infinite.

I answer that, Things other than God can be relatively infinite, but not absolutely infinite. For with regard to infinite as applied to matter, it is manifest that everything actually existing possesses a form; and thus its matter is determined by form. But because matter, considered as existing under some substantial form, remains in potentiality to many accidental forms, which is absolutely finite can be relatively infinite; as, for example, wood is finite according to its own form, but still it is relatively infinite, inasmuch as it is in potentiality to an infinite number of shapes. But if we speak of the infinite in reference to form, it is manifest that those things, the forms of which are in matter, are absolutely finite, and in no way infinite. If, however, any created forms are not received into matter, but are self-subsisting, as some think is the case with angels, these will be relatively infinite, inasmuch as such kinds of forms are not terminated, nor contracted by any matter. But because a created form thus subsisting has being, and yet is not its own being, it follows that its being is received and contracted to a determinate nature. Hence it cannot be absolutely infinite.

Reply to Objection 1. It is against the nature of a made thing for its essence to be its existence; because subsisting being is not a created being; hence it is against the nature of a made thing to be absolutely infinite. Therefore, as God, although He has infinite power, cannot make a thing to be not made (for this would imply that two contradictories are true at the same time), so likewise He cannot make anything to be absolutely infinite.

Reply to Objection 2. The fact that the power of the intellect extends itself in a way to infinite things, is because the intellect is a form not in matter, but either wholly separated from matter, as is the angelic substance, or at least an intellectual power, which is not the act of any organ, in the intellectual soul joined to a body.

Reply to Objection 3. Primary matter does not exist by itself in nature, since it is not actually being, but potentially only; hence it is something concreated rather than created. Nevertheless, primary matter even as a potentiality is not absolutely infinite, but relatively, because its potentiality extends only to natural forms.

Article 3. Whether an actually infinite magnitude can exist?

Objection 1. It seems that there can be something actually infinite in magnitude. For in mathematics there is no error, since "there is no lie in things abstract," as the Philosopher says (Phys. ii). But mathematics uses the infinite in magnitude; thus, the geometrician in his demonstrations says, "Let this line be infinite." Therefore it is not impossible for a thing to be infinite in magnitude.

Objection 2. Further, what is not against the nature of anything, can agree with it. Now to be infinite is not against the nature of magnitude; but rather both the finite and the infinite seem to be properties of quantity. Therefore it is not impossible for some magnitude to be infinite.

Objection 3. Further, magnitude is infinitely divisible, for the continuous is defined that which is infinitely divisible, as is clear from Phys. iii. But contraries are concerned about one and the same thing. Since therefore addition is opposed to division, and increase opposed to diminution, it appears that magnitude can be increased to infinity. Therefore it is possible for magnitude to be infinite.

Objection 4. Further, movement and time have quantity and continuity derived from the magnitude over which movement passes, as is said in Phys. iv. But it is not against the nature of time and movement to be infinite, since every determinate indivisible in time and circular movement is both a beginning and an end. Therefore neither is it against the nature of magnitude to be infinite.

On the contrary, Every body has a surface. But every body which has a surface is finite; because surface is the term of a finite body. Therefore all bodies are finite. The same applies both to surface and to a line. Therefore nothing is infinite in magnitude.

I answer that, It is one thing to be infinite in essence, and another to be infinite in magnitude. For granted that a body exists infinite in magnitude, as fire or air, yet this could not be infinite in essence, because its essence would be terminated in a species by its form, and confined to individuality by matter. And so assuming from these premises that no creature is infinite in essence, it still remains to inquire whether any creature can be infinite in magnitude.

We must therefore observe that a body, which is a complete magnitude, can be considered in two ways; mathematically, in respect to its quantity only; and naturally, as regards its matter and form.

Now it is manifest that a natural body cannot be actually infinite. For every natural body has some determined substantial form. Since therefore the accidents follow upon the substantial form, it is necessary that determinate accidents should follow upon a determinate form; and among these accidents is quantity. So every natural body has a greater or smaller determinate quantity. Hence it is impossible for a natural body to be infinite. The same appears from movement; because every natural body has some natural movement; whereas an infinite body could not have any natural movement; neither direct, because nothing moves naturally by a direct movement unless it is out of its place; and this could not happen to an infinite body, for it would occupy every place, and thus every place would be indifferently its own place. Neither could it move circularly; forasmuch as circular motion requires that one part of the body is necessarily transferred to a place occupied by another part, and this could not happen as regards an infinite circular body: for if two lines be drawn from the centre, the farther they extend from the centre, the farther they are from each other; therefore, if a body were infinite, the lines would be infinitely distant from each other; and thus one could never occupy the place belonging to any other.

The same applies to a mathematical body. For if we imagine a mathematical body actually existing, we must imagine it under some form, because nothing is actual except by its form; hence, since the form of quantity as such is figure, such a body must have some figure, and so would be finite; for figure is confined by a term or boundary.

Reply to Objection 1. A geometrician does not need to assume a line actually infinite, but takes some actually finite line, from which he subtracts whatever he finds necessary; which line he calls infinite.

Reply to Objection 2. Although the infinite is not against the nature of magnitude in general, still it is against the nature of any species of it; thus, for instance, it is against the nature of a bicubical or tricubical magnitude, whether circular or triangular, and so on. Now what is not possible in any species cannot exist in the genus; hence there cannot be any infinite magnitude, since no species of magnitude is infinite.

Reply to Objection 3. The infinite in quantity, as was shown above, belongs to matter. Now by division of the whole we approach to matter, forasmuch as parts have the aspect of matter; but by addition we approach to the whole which has the aspect of a form. Therefore the infinite is not in the addition of magnitude, but only in division.

Reply to Objection 4. Movement and time are whole, not actually but successively; hence they have potentiality mixed with actuality. But magnitude is an actual whole; therefore the infinite in quantity refers to matter, and does not agree with the totality of magnitude; yet it agrees with the totality of time and movement: for it is proper to matter to be in potentiality.

Article 4. Whether an infinite multitude can exist?

Objection 1. It seems that an actually infinite multitude is possible. For it is not impossible for a potentiality to be made actual. But number can be multiplied to infinity. Therefore it is possible for an infinite multitude actually to exist.

Objection 2. Further, it is possible for any individual of any species to be made actual. But the species of figures are infinite. Therefore an infinite number of actual figures is possible.

Objection 3. Further, things not opposed to each other do not obstruct each other. But supposing a multitude of things to exist, there can still be many others not opposed to them. Therefore it is not impossible for others also to coexist with them, and so on to infinitude; therefore an actual infinite number of things is possible.

On the contrary, It is written, "Thou hast ordered all things in measure, and number, and weight" (Wisdom 11:21).

I answer that, A twofold opinion exists on this subject. Some, as Avicenna and Algazel, said that it was impossible for an actually infinite multitude to exist absolutely; but that an accidentally infinite multitude was not impossible. A multitude is said to be infinite absolutely, when an infinite multitude is necessary that something may exist. Now this is impossible; because it would entail something dependent on an infinity for its existence; and hence its generation could never come to be, because it is impossible to pass through an infinite medium.

A multitude is said to be accidentally infinite when its existence as such is not necessary, but accidental. This can be shown, for example, in the work of a carpenter requiring a certain absolute multitude; namely, art in the soul, the movement of the hand, and a hammer; and supposing that such things were infinitely multiplied, the carpentering work would never be finished, forasmuch as it would depend on an infinite number of causes. But the multitude of hammers, inasmuch as one may be broken and another used, is an accidental multitude; for it happens by accident that many hammers are used, and it matters little whether one or two, or many are used, or an infinite number, if the work is carried on for an infinite time. In this way they said that there can be an accidentally infinite multitude.

This, however, is impossible; since every kind of multitude must belong to a species of multitude. Now the species of multitude are to be reckoned by the species of numbers. But no species of number is infinite; for every number is multitude measured by one. Hence it is impossible for there to be an actually infinite multitude, either absolute or accidental. Likewise multitude in nature is created; and everything created is comprehended under some clear intention of the Creator; for no agent acts aimlessly. Hence everything created must be comprehended in a certain number. Therefore it is impossible for an actually infinite multitude to exist, even accidentally. But a potentially infinite multitude is possible; because the increase of multitude follows upon the division of magnitude; since the more a thing is divided, the greater number of things result. Hence, as the infinite is to be found potentially in the division of the continuous, because we thus approach matter, as was shown in the preceding article, by the same rule, the infinite can be also found potentially in the addition of multitude.

Reply to Objection 1. Every potentiality is made actual according to its mode of being; for instance, a day is reduced to act successively, and not all at once. Likewise the infinite in multitude is reduced to act successively, and not all at once; because every multitude can be succeeded by another multitude to infinity.

Reply to Objection 2. Species of figures are infinite by infinitude of number. Now there are various species of figures, such as trilateral, quadrilateral and so on; and as an infinitely numerable multitude is not all at once reduced to act, so neither is the multitude of figures.

Reply to Objection 3. Although the supposition of some things does not preclude the supposition of others, still the supposition of an infinite number is opposed to any single species of multitude. Hence it is not possible for an actually infinite multitude to exist.

Question 8. The existence of God in things

Article 1. Whether God is in all things?

Objection 1. It seems that God is not in all things. For what is above all things is not in all things. But God is above all, according to the Psalm (Psalm 112:4), "The Lord is high above all nations," etc. Therefore God is not in all things.

Objection 2. Further, what is in anything is thereby contained. Now God is not contained by things, but rather does He contain them. Therefore God is not in things but things are rather in Him. Hence Augustine says (Octog. Tri. Quaest. qu. 20), that "in Him things are, rather than He is in any place."

Objection 3. Further, the more powerful an agent is, the more extended is its action. But God is the most powerful of all agents.

Therefore His action can extend to things which are far removed from Him; nor is it necessary that He should be in all things.

Objection 4. Further, the demons are beings. But God is not in the demons; for there is no fellowship between light and darkness (2 Corinthians 6:14). Therefore God is not in all things.

On the contrary, A thing is wherever it operates. But God operates in all things, according to Isaiah 26:12, "Lord . . . Thou hast wrought all our works in [Vulgate: 'for'] us." Therefore God is in all things.

I answer that, God is in all things; not, indeed, as part of their essence, nor as an accident, but as an agent is present to that upon which it works. For an agent must be joined to that wherein it acts immediately and touch it by its power; hence it is proved in Phys. vii that the thing moved and the mover must be joined together. Now since God is very being by His own essence, created being must be His proper effect; as to ignite is the proper effect of fire. Now God causes this effect in things not only when they first begin to be, but as long as they are preserved in being; as light is caused in the air by the sun as long as the air remains illuminated. Therefore as long as a thing has being, God must be present to it, according to its mode of being. But being is innermost in each thing and most fundamentally inherent in all things since it is formal in respect of everything found in a thing, as was shown above (Question 7, Article 1). Hence it must be that God is in all things, and innermostly.

Reply to Objection 1. God is above all things by the excellence of His nature; nevertheless, He is in all things as the cause of the being of all things; as was shown above in this article.

Reply to Objection 2. Although corporeal things are said to be in another as in that which contains them, nevertheless, spiritual things contain those things in which they are; as the soul contains the body. Hence also God is in things containing them; nevertheless, by a certain similitude to corporeal things, it is said that all things are in God; inasmuch as they are contained by Him.

Reply to Objection 3. No action of an agent, however powerful it may be, acts at a distance, except through a medium. But it belongs to the great power of God that He acts immediately in all things. Hence nothing is distant from Him, as if it could be without God in itself. But things are said to be distant from God by the unlikeness to Him in nature or grace; as also He is above all by the excellence of His own nature.

Reply to Objection 4. In the demons there is their nature which is from God, and also the deformity of sin which is not from Him; therefore, it is not to be absolutely conceded that God is in the demons, except with the addition, "inasmuch as they are beings." But in things not deformed in their nature, we must say absolutely that God is.

Article 2. Whether God is everywhere?

Objection 1. It seems that God is not everywhere. For to be everywhere means to be in every place. But to be in every place does not belong to God, to Whom it does not belong to be in place at all; for "incorporeal things," as Boethius says (De Hebdom.), "are not in a place." Therefore God is not everywhere.

Objection 2. Further, the relation of time to succession is the same as the relation of place to permanence. But one indivisible part of action or movement cannot exist in different times; therefore neither can one indivisible part in the genus of permanent things be in every place. Now the divine being is not successive but permanent. Therefore God is not in many places; and thus He is not everywhere.

Objection 3. Further, what is wholly in any one place is not in part elsewhere. But if God is in any one place He is all there; for He has no parts. No part of Him then is elsewhere; and therefore God is not everywhere.

On the contrary, It is written, "I fill heaven and earth." (Jeremiah 23:24).

I answer that, Since place is a thing, to be in place can be understood in a twofold sense; either by way of other things--i.e. as one thing is said to be in another no matter how; and thus the accidents of a place are in place; or by a way proper to place; and thus things placed are in a place. Now in both these senses, in some way God is in every place; and this is to be everywhere.

First, as He is in all things giving them being, power and operation; so He is in every place as giving it existence and locative power. Again, things placed are in place, inasmuch as they fill place; and God fills every place; not, indeed, like a body, for a body is said to fill place inasmuch as it excludes the co-presence of another body; whereas by God being in a place, others are not thereby excluded from it; indeed, by the very fact that He gives being to the things that fill every place, He Himself fills every place.

Reply to Objection 1. Incorporeal things are in place not by contact of dimensive quantity, as bodies are but by contact of power.

Reply to Objection 2. The indivisible is twofold. One is the term of the continuous; as a point in permanent things, and as a moment in succession; and this kind of the indivisible in permanent things, forasmuch as it has a determinate site, cannot be in many parts of place, or in many places; likewise the indivisible of action or movement, forasmuch as it has a determinate order in movement or action, cannot be in many parts of time. Another kind of the indivisible is outside of the whole genus of the continuous; and in this way incorporeal substances, like God, angel and soul, are called indivisible. Such a kind of indivisible does not belong to the continuous, as a part of it, but as touching it by its power; hence, according as its power can extend itself to one or to many, to a small thing, or to a great one, in this way it is in one or in many places, and in a small or large place.

Reply to Objection 3. A whole is so called with reference to its parts. Now part is twofold: viz. a part of the essence, as the form and the matter are called parts of the composite, while genus and difference are called parts of species. There is also part of quantity into which any quantity is divided. What therefore is whole in any place by totality of quantity, cannot be outside of that place, because the quantity of anything placed is commensurate to the quantity of the place; and hence there is no totality of quantity without totality of place. But totality of essence is not commensurate to the totality of place. Hence it is not necessary for that which is whole by totality of essence in a thing, not to be at all outside of it. This appears also in accidental forms which have accidental quantity; as an example, whiteness is whole in each part of the surface if we speak of its totality of essence; because according to the perfect idea of its species it is found to exist in every part of the surface. But if its totality be considered according to quantity which it has accidentally, then it is not whole in every part of the surface. On the other hand, incorporeal substances have no totality either of themselves or accidentally, except in reference to the perfect idea of their essence. Hence, as the soul is whole in every part of the body, so is God whole in all things and in each one.

Article 3. Whether God is everywhere by essence, presence and power?

Objection 1. It seems that the mode of God's existence in all things is not properly described by way of essence, presence and power. For what is by essence in anything, is in it essentially. But God is not essentially in things; for He does not belong to the essence of anything. Therefore it ought not to be said that God is in things by essence, presence and power.

Objection 2. Further, to be present in anything means not to be absent from it. Now this is the meaning of God being in things by His essence, that He is not absent from anything. Therefore the presence of God in all things by essence and presence means the same thing. Therefore it is superfluous to say that God is present in things by His essence, presence and power.

Objection 3. Further, as God by His power is the principle of all things, so He is the same likewise by His knowledge and will. But it is not said that He is in things by knowledge and will. Therefore neither is He present by His power.

Objection 4. Further, as grace is a perfection added to the substance of a thing, so many other perfections are likewise added. Therefore if God is said to be in certain persons in a special way by grace, it seems that according to every perfection there ought to be a special mode of God's existence in things.

On the contrary, A gloss on the Canticle of Canticles (5) says that, "God by a common mode is in all things by His presence, power and substance; still He is said to be present more familiarly in some by grace" [The quotation is from St. Gregory, (Hom. viii in Ezech.)].

I answer that, God is said to be in a thing in two ways; in one way after the manner of an efficient cause; and thus He is in all things created by Him; in another way he is in things as the object of operation is in the operator; and this is proper to the operations of the soul, according as the thing known is in the one who knows; and the thing desired in the one desiring. In this second way God is especially in the rational creature which knows and loves Him actually or habitually. And because the rational creature possesses this prerogative by grace, as will be shown later (12). He is said to be thus in the saints by grace.

But how He is in other things created by Him, may be considered from human affairs. A king, for example, is said to be in the whole kingdom by his power, although he is not everywhere present. Again a thing is said to be by its presence in other things which are subject to its inspection; as things in a house are said to be present to anyone, who nevertheless may not be in substance in every part of the house. Lastly, a thing is said to be by way of substance or essence in that place in which its substance may be. Now there were some (the Manichees) who said that spiritual and incorporeal things were subject to the divine power; but that visible and corporeal things were subject to the power of a contrary principle. Therefore against these it is necessary to say that God is in all things by His power.

But others, though they believed that all things were subject to the divine power, still did not allow that divine providence extended to these inferior bodies, and in the person of these it is said, "He walketh about the poles of the heavens; and He doth not consider our things [Vulgate: 'He doth not consider . . . and He walketh,' etc.]" (Job 22:14). Against these it is necessary to say that God is in all things by His presence.

Further, others said that, although all things are subject to God's providence, still all things are not immediately created by God; but that He immediately created the first creatures, and these created the others. Against these it is necessary to say that He is in all things by His essence.

Therefore, God is in all things by His power, inasmuch as all things are subject to His power; He is by His presence in all things, as all things are bare and open to His eyes; He is in all things by His essence, inasmuch as He is present to all as the cause of their being.

Reply to Objection 1. God is said to be in all things by essence, not indeed by the essence of the things themselves, as if He were of their essence; but by His own essence; because His substance is present to all things as the cause of their being.

Reply to Objection 2. A thing can be said to be present to another, when in its sight, though the thing may be distant in substance, as was shown in this article; and therefore two modes of presence are necessary; viz. by essence and by presence.

Reply to Objection 3. Knowledge and will require that the thing known should be in the one who knows, and the thing willed in the one who wills. Hence by knowledge and will things are more truly in God than God in things. But power is the principle of acting on another; hence by power the agent is related and applied to an external thing; thus by power an agent may be said to be present to another.

Reply to Objection 4. No other perfection, except grace, added to substance, renders God present in anything as the object known and loved; therefore only grace constitutes a special mode of God's existence in things. There is, however, another special mode of God's existence in man by union, which will be treated of in its own place (III).

Article 4. Whether to be everywhere belongs to God alone?

Objection 1. It seems that to be everywhere does not belong to God alone. For the universal, according to the Philosopher (Poster. i), is everywhere, and always; primary matter also, since it is in all bodies, is everywhere. But neither of these is God, as appears from what is said above (Article 3). Therefore to be everywhere does not belong to God alone.

Objection 2. Further, number is in things numbered. But the whole universe is constituted in number, as appears from the Book of

Wisdom (Wisdom 11:21). Therefore there is some number which is in the whole universe, and is thus everywhere.

Objection 3. Further, the universe is a kind of "whole perfect body" (Coel. et Mund. i). But the whole universe is everywhere, because there is no place outside it. Therefore to be everywhere does not belong to God alone.

Objection 4. Further, if any body were infinite, no place would exist outside of it, and so it would be everywhere. Therefore to be everywhere does not appear to belong to God alone.

Objection 5. Further, the soul, as Augustine says (De Trin. vi, 6), is "whole in the whole body, and whole in every one of its parts." Therefore if there was only one animal in the world, its soul would be everywhere; and thus to be everywhere does not belong to God alone.

Objection 6. Further, as Augustine says (Ep. 137), "The soul feels where it sees, and lives where it feels, and is where it lives." But the soul sees as it were everywhere: for in a succession of glances it comprehends the entire space of the heavens in its sight. Therefore the soul is everywhere.

On the contrary, Ambrose says (De Spir. Sanct. i, 7): "Who dares to call the Holy Ghost a creature, Who in all things, and everywhere, and always is, which assuredly belongs to the divinity alone?"

I answer that, To be everywhere primarily and absolutely, is proper to God. Now to be everywhere primarily is said of that which in its whole self is everywhere; for if a thing were everywhere according to its parts in different places, it would not be primarily everywhere, forasmuch as what belongs to anything according to part does not belong to it primarily; thus if a man has white teeth, whiteness belongs primarily not to the man but to his teeth. But a thing is everywhere absolutely when it does not belong to it to be everywhere accidentally, that is, merely on some supposition; as a grain of millet would be everywhere, supposing that no other body existed. It belongs therefore to a thing to be everywhere absolutely when, on any supposition, it must be everywhere; and this properly belongs to God alone. For whatever number of places be supposed, even if an infinite number be supposed besides what already exist, it would be necessary that God should be in all of them; for nothing can exist except by Him. Therefore to be everywhere primarily and absolutely belongs to God and is proper to Him: because whatever number of places be supposed to exist, God must be in all of them, not as to a part of Him, but as to His very self.

Reply to Objection 1. The universal, and also primary matter are indeed everywhere; but not according to the same mode of existence.

Reply to Objection 2. Number, since it is an accident, does not, of itself, exist in place, but accidentally; neither is the whole but only part of it in each of the things numbered; hence it does not follow that it is primarily and absolutely everywhere.

Reply to Objection 3. The whole body of the universe is everywhere, but not primarily; forasmuch as it is not wholly in each place, but according to its parts; nor again is it everywhere absolutely, because, supposing that other places existed besides itself, it would not be in them.

Reply to Objection 4. If an infinite body existed, it would be everywhere; but according to its parts.

Reply to Objection 5. Were there one animal only, its soul would be everywhere primarily indeed, but only accidentally.

Reply to Objection 6. When it is said that the soul sees anywhere, this can be taken in two senses. In one sense the adverb "anywhere" determines the act of seeing on the part of the object; and in this sense it is true that while it sees the heavens, it sees in the heavens; and in the same way it feels in the heavens; but it does not follow that it lives or exists in the heavens, because to live and to exist do not import an act passing to an exterior object. In another sense it can be understood according as the adverb determines the act of the seer, as proceeding from the seer; and thus it is true that where the soul feels and sees, there it is, and there it lives according to this mode of speaking; and thus it does not follow that it is everywhere.

Question 9. The immutability of God

Article 1. Whether God is altogether immutable?

Objection 1. It seems that God is not altogether immutable. For whatever moves itself is in some way mutable. But, as Augustine says (Gen. ad lit viii, 20), "The Creator Spirit moves Himself neither by time, nor by place." Therefore God is in some way mutable.

Objection 2. Further, it is said of Wisdom, that "it is more mobile than all things active [Vulgate 'mobilior']" (Wisdom 7:24). But God is wisdom itself; therefore God is movable.

Objection 3. Further, to approach and to recede signify movement. But these are said of God in Scripture, "Draw nigh to God and He will draw nigh to you" (James 4:8). Therefore God is mutable.

On the contrary, It is written, "I am the Lord, and I change not" (Malachi 3:6).

I answer that, From what precedes, it is shown that God is altogether immutable.

First, because it was shown above that there is some first being, whom we call God; and that this first being must be pure act, without the admixture of any potentiality, for the reason that, absolutely, potentiality is posterior to act. Now everything which is in any way changed, is in some way in potentiality. Hence it is evident that it is impossible for God to be in any way changeable.

Secondly, because everything which is moved, remains as it was in part, and passes away in part; as what is moved from whiteness to blackness, remains the same as to substance; thus in everything which is moved, there is some kind of composition to be found. But it has been shown above (Question 3, Article 7) that in God there is no composition, for He is altogether simple. Hence it is manifest that God cannot be moved.

Thirdly, because everything which is moved acquires something by its movement, and attains to what it had not attained previously. But since God is infinite, comprehending in Himself all the plenitude of perfection of all being, He cannot acquire anything new, nor extend Himself to anything whereto He was not extended previously. Hence movement in no way belongs to Him. So, some of the ancients, constrained, as it were, by the truth, decided that the first principle was immovable.

Reply to Objection 1. Augustine there speaks in a similar way to Plato, who said that the first mover moves Himself; calling every operation a movement, even as the acts of understanding, and willing, and loving, are called movements. Therefore because God understands and loves Himself, in that respect they said that God moves Himself, not, however, as movement and change belong to a thing existing in potentiality, as we now speak of change and movement.

Reply to Objection 2. Wisdom is called mobile by way of similitude, according as it diffuses its likeness even to the outermost of things; for nothing can exist which does not proceed from the divine wisdom by way of some kind of imitation, as from the first effective and formal principle; as also works of art proceed from the wisdom of the artist. And so in the same way, inasmuch as the similitude of the divine wisdom proceeds in degrees from the highest things, which participate more fully of its likeness, to the lowest things which participate of it in a lesser degree, there is said to be a kind of procession and movement of the divine wisdom to things; as when we say that the sun proceeds to the earth, inasmuch as the ray of light touches the earth. In this way Dionysius (Coel. Hier. i) expounds the matter, that every procession of the divine manifestation comes to us from the movement of the Father of light.

Reply to Objection 3. These things are said of God in Scripture metaphorically. For as the sun is said to enter a house, or to go out, according as its rays reach the house, so God is said to approach to us, or to recede from us, when we receive the influx of His goodness, or decline from Him.

Article 2. Whether to be immutable belongs to God alone?

Objection 1. It seems that to be immutable does not belong to God alone. For the Philosopher says (Metaph. ii) that "matter is in everything which is moved." But, according to some, certain created substances, as angels and souls, have not matter. Therefore to be immutable does not belong to God alone.

Objection 2. Further, everything in motion moves to some end. What therefore has already attained its ultimate end, is not in motion. But some creatures have already attained to their ultimate end; as all the blessed in heaven. Therefore some creatures are immovable.

Objection 3. Further, everything which is mutable is variable. But forms are invariable; for it is said (Sex Princip. i) that "form is essence consisting of the simple and invariable." Therefore it does not belong to God alone to be immutable.

On the contrary, Augustine says (De Nat. Boni. i), "God alone is immutable; and whatever things He has made, being from nothing, are mutable."

I answer that, God alone is altogether immutable; whereas every creature is in some way mutable. Be it known therefore that a mutable thing can be called so in two ways: by a power in itself; and by a power possessed by another. For all creatures before they existed, were possible, not by any created power, since no creature is eternal, but by the divine power alone, inasmuch as God could produce them into existence. Thus, as the production of a thing into existence depends on the will of God, so likewise it depends on His will that things should be preserved; for He does not preserve them otherwise than by ever giving them existence; hence if He took away His action from them, all things would be reduced to nothing, as appears from Augustine (Gen. ad lit. iv, 12). Therefore as it was in the Creator's power to produce them before they existed in themselves, so likewise it is in the Creator's power when they exist in themselves to bring them to nothing. In this way therefore, by the power of another--namely, of God--they are mutable, inasmuch as they are producible from nothing by Him, and are by Him reducible from existence to non-existence.

If, however, a thing is called mutable by a power in itself, thus also in some manner every creature is mutable. For every creature has a twofold power, active and passive; and I call that power passive which enables anything to attain its perfection either in being, or in attaining to its end. Now if the mutability of a thing be considered according to its power for being, in that way all creatures are not mutable, but those only in which what is potential in them is consistent with non-being. Hence, in the inferior bodies there is mutability both as regards substantial being, inasmuch as their matter can exist with privation of their substantial form, and also as regards their accidental being, supposing the subject to coexist with privation of accident; as, for example, this subject "man" can exist with "not-whiteness" and can therefore be changed from white to not-white. But supposing the accident to be such as to follow on the essential principles of the subject, then the privation of such an accident cannot coexist with the subject. Hence the subject cannot be changed as regards that kind of accident; as, for example, snow cannot be made black. Now in the celestial bodies matter is not consistent with privation of form, because the form perfects the whole potentiality of the matter; therefore these bodies are not mutable as to substantial being, but only as to locality, because the subject is consistent with privation of this or that place. On the other hand incorporeal substances, being subsistent forms which, although with respect to their own existence are as potentiality to act, are not consistent with the privation of this act; forasmuch as existence is consequent upon form, and nothing corrupts except it lose its form. Hence in the form itself there is no power to non-existence; and so these kinds of substances are immutable and invariable as regards their existence. Wherefore Dionysius says (Div. Nom. iv) that "intellectual created substances are pure from generation and from every variation, as also are incorporeal and immaterial substances." Still, there remains in them a twofold mutability: one as regards their potentiality to their end; and in that way there is in them a mutability according to choice from good to evil, as Damascene says (De Fide ii, 3,4); the other as regards place, inasmuch as by their finite power they attain to certain fresh places--which cannot be said of God, who by His infinity fills all places, as was shown above (Question 8, Article 2).

Thus in every creature there is a potentiality to change either as regards substantial being as in the case of things corruptible; or as regards locality only, as in the case of the celestial bodies; or as regards the order to their end, and the application of their powers to divers objects, as in the case with the angels; and universally all creatures generally are mutable by the power of the Creator, in

Whose power is their existence and non-existence. Hence since God is in none of these ways mutable, it belongs to Him alone to be altogether immutable.

Reply to Objection 1. This objection proceeds from mutability as regards substantial or accidental being; for philosophers treated of such movement.

Reply to Objection 2. The good angels, besides their natural endowment of immutability of being, have also immutability of election by divine power; nevertheless there remains in them mutability as regards place.

Reply to Objection 3. Forms are called invariable, forasmuch as they cannot be subjects of variation; but they are subject to variation because by them their subject is variable. Hence it is clear that they vary in so far as they are; for they are not called beings as though they were the subject of being, but because through them something has being.

Question 10. The eternity of God

Article 1. Whether this is a good definition of eternity, "The simultaneously-whole and perfect possession of interminable life"?

Objection 1. It seems that the definition of eternity given by Boethius (De Consol. v) is not a good one: "Eternity is the simultaneously-whole and perfect possession of interminable life." For the word "interminable" is a negative one. But negation only belongs to what is defective, and this does not belong to eternity. Therefore in the definition of eternity the word "interminable" ought not to be found.

Objection 2. Further, eternity signifies a certain kind of duration. But duration regards existence rather than life. Therefore the word "life" ought not to come into the definition of eternity; but rather the word "existence."

Objection 3. Further, a whole is what has parts. But this is alien to eternity which is simple. Therefore it is improperly said to be "whole."

Objection 4. Many days cannot occur together, nor can many times exist all at once. But in eternity, days and times are in the plural, for it is said, "His going forth is from the beginning, from the days of eternity" (Micah 5:2); and also it is said, "According to the revelation of the mystery hidden from eternity" (Romans 16:25). Therefore eternity is not omni-simultaneous.

Objection 5. Further, the whole and the perfect are the same thing. Supposing, therefore, that it is "whole," it is superfluously described as "perfect."

Objection 6. Further, duration does not imply "possession." But eternity is a kind of duration. Therefore eternity is not possession.

I answer that, As we attain to the knowledge of simple things by way of compound things, so must we reach to the knowledge of eternity by means of time, which is nothing but the numbering of movement by "before" and "after." For since succession occurs in every movement, and one part comes after another, the fact that we reckon before and after in movement, makes us apprehend time, which is nothing else but the measure of before and after in movement. Now in a thing bereft of movement, which is always the same, there is no before or after. As therefore the idea of time consists in the numbering of before and after in movement; so likewise in the apprehension of the uniformity of what is outside of movement, consists the idea of eternity.

Further, those things are said to be measured by time which have a beginning and an end in time, because in everything which is moved there is a beginning, and there is an end. But as whatever is wholly immutable can have no succession, so it has no beginning, and no end.

Thus eternity is known from two sources: first, because what is eternal is interminable--that is, has no beginning nor end (that is, no term either way); secondly, because eternity has no succession, being simultaneously whole.

Reply to Objection 1. Simple things are usually defined by way of negation; as "a point is that which has no parts." Yet this is not to be taken as if the negation belonged to their essence, but because our intellect which first apprehends compound things, cannot attain to the knowledge of simple things except by removing the opposite.

Reply to Objection 2. What is truly eternal, is not only being, but also living; and life extends to operation, which is not true of being. Now the protraction of duration seems to belong to operation rather than to being; hence time is the numbering of movement.

Reply to Objection 3. Eternity is called whole, not because it has parts, but because it is wanting in nothing.

Reply to Objection 4. As God, although incorporeal, is named in Scripture metaphorically by corporeal names, so eternity though simultaneously whole, is called by names implying time and succession.

Reply to Objection 5. Two things are to be considered in time: time itself, which is successive; and the "now" of time, which is imperfect. Hence the expression "simultaneously-whole" is used to remove the idea of time, and the word "perfect" is used to exclude the "now" of time.

Reply to Objection 6. Whatever is possessed, is held firmly and quietly; therefore to designate the immutability and permanence of eternity, we use the word "possession."

Article 2. Whether God is eternal?

Objection 1. It seems that God is not eternal. For nothing made can be predicated of God; for Boethius says (De Trin. iv) that, "The now that flows away makes time, the now that stands still makes eternity;" and Augustine says (Octog. Tri. Quaest. qu. 28) "that God is the author of eternity." Therefore God is not eternal.

Objection 2. Further, what is before eternity, and after eternity, is not measured by eternity. But, as Aristotle says (De Causis), "God is before eternity and He is after eternity": for it is written that "the Lord shall reign for eternity, and beyond [Douay: 'for ever and ever']" (Exodus 15:18). Therefore to be eternal does not belong to God.

Objection 3. Further, eternity is a kind of measure. But to be measured belongs not to God. Therefore it does not belong to Him to be eternal.

Objection 4. Further, in eternity, there is no present, past or future, since it is simultaneously whole; as was said in the preceding article. But words denoting present, past and future time are applied to God in Scripture. Therefore God is not eternal.

On the contrary, Athanasius says in his Creed: "The Father is eternal, the Son is eternal, the Holy Ghost is eternal."

I answer that, The idea of eternity follows immutability, as the idea of time follows movement, as appears from the preceding article. Hence, as God is supremely immutable, it supremely belongs to Him to be eternal. Nor is He eternal only; but He is His own eternity; whereas, no other being is its own duration, as no other is its own being. Now God is His own uniform being; and hence as He is His own essence, so He is His own eternity.

Reply to Objection 1. The "now" that stands still, is said to make eternity according to our apprehension. As the apprehension of time is caused in us by the fact that we apprehend the flow of the "now," so the apprehension of eternity is caused in us by our apprehending the "now" standing still. When Augustine says that "God is the author of eternity," this is to be understood of participated eternity. For God communicates His eternity to some in the same way as He communicates His immutability.

Reply to Objection 2. From this appears the answer to the Second Objection. For God is said to be before eternity, according as it is shared by immaterial substances. Hence, also, in the same book, it is said that "intelligence is equal to eternity." In the words of Exodus, "The Lord shall reign for eternity, and beyond," eternity stands for age, as another rendering has it. Thus it is said that the Lord will reign beyond eternity, inasmuch as He endures beyond every age, i.e. beyond every kind of duration. For age is nothing more than the period of each thing, as is said in the book De Coelo i. Or to reign beyond eternity can be taken to mean that if any other thing were conceived to exist for ever, as the movement of the heavens according to some philosophers, then God would still reign beyond, inasmuch as His reign is simultaneously whole.

Reply to Objection 3. Eternity is nothing else but God Himself. Hence God is not called eternal, as if He were in any way measured; but the idea of measurement is there taken according to the apprehension of our mind alone.

Reply to Objection 4. Words denoting different times are applied to God, because His eternity includes all times; not as if He Himself were altered through present, past and future.

Article 3. Whether to be eternal belongs to God alone?

Objection 1. It seems that it does not belong to God alone to be eternal. For it is written that "those who instruct many to justice," shall be "as stars unto perpetual eternities [Douay: 'for all eternity']" (Daniel 12:3). Now if God alone were eternal, there could not be many eternities. Therefore God alone is not the only eternal.

Objection 2. Further, it is written "Depart, ye cursed into eternal [Douay: 'everlasting'] fire" (Matthew 25:41). Therefore God is not the only eternal.

Objection 3. Further, every necessary thing is eternal. But there are many necessary things; as, for instance, all principles of demonstration and all demonstrative propositions. Therefore God is not the only eternal.

On the contrary, Jerome says (Ep. ad Damasum. xv) that "God is the only one who has no beginning." Now whatever has a beginning, is not eternal. Therefore God is the only one eternal.

I answer that, Eternity truly and properly so called is in God alone, because eternity follows on immutability; as appears from the first article. But God alone is altogether immutable, as was shown above (Question 9, Article 1). Accordingly, however, as some receive immutability from Him, they share in His eternity. Thus some receive immutability from God in the way of never ceasing to exist; in that sense it is said of the earth, "it standeth for ever" (Ecclesiastes 1:4). Again, some things are called eternal in Scripture because of the length of their duration, although they are in nature corruptible; thus (Psalm 75:5) the hills are called "eternal" and we read "of the fruits of the eternal hills." (Deuteronomy 33:15). Some again, share more fully than others in the nature of eternity, inasmuch as they possess unchangeableness either in being or further still in operation; like the angels, and the blessed, who enjoy the Word, because "as regards that vision of the Word, no changing thoughts exist in the Saints," as Augustine says (De Trin. xv). Hence those who see God are said to have eternal life; according to that text, "This is eternal life, that they may know Thee the only true God," etc. (John 17:3).

Reply to Objection 1. There are said to be many eternities, accordingly as many share in eternity, by the contemplation of God.

Reply to Objection 2. The fire of hell is called eternal, only because it never ends. Still, there is change in the pains of the lost, according to the words "To extreme heat they will pass from snowy waters" (Job 24:19). Hence in hell true eternity does not exist, but rather time; according to the text of the Psalm "Their time will be for ever" (Psalm 80:16).

Reply to Objection 3. Necessary means a certain mode of truth; and truth, according to the Philosopher (Metaph. vi), is in the mind. Therefore in this sense the true and necessary are eternal, because they are in the eternal mind, which is the divine intellect alone; hence it does not follow that anything beside God is eternal.

Article 4. Whether eternity differs from time?

Objection 1. It seems that eternity does not differ from time. For two measures of duration cannot exist together, unless one is part of the other; for instance two days or two hours cannot be together; nevertheless, we may say that a day or an hour are together, considering hour as part of a day. But eternity and time occur together, each of which imports a certain measure of duration. Since therefore eternity is not a part of time, forasmuch as eternity exceeds time, and includes it, it seems that time is a part of eternity, and is not a different thing from eternity.

Objection 2. Further, according to the Philosopher (Phys. iv), the "now" of time remains the same in the whole of time. But the nature of eternity seems to be that it is the same indivisible thing in the whole space of time. Therefore eternity is the "now" of time. But the "now" of time is not substantially different from time. Therefore eternity is not substantially different from time.

Objection 3. Further, as the measure of the first movement is the measure of every movement, as said in Phys. iv, it thus appears that the measure of the first being is that of every being. But eternity is the measure of the first being--that is, of the divine being. Therefore eternity is the measure of every being. But the being of things corruptible is measured by time. Time therefore is either eternity or is a part of eternity.

On the contrary, Eternity is simultaneously whole. But time has a "before" and an "after." Therefore time and eternity are not the same thing.

I answer that, It is manifest that time and eternity are not the same. Some have founded this difference on the fact that eternity has neither beginning nor an end; whereas time has a beginning and an end. This, however, makes a merely accidental, and not an absolute difference because, granted that time always was and always will be, according to the idea of those who think the movement of the heavens goes on for ever, there would yet remain a difference between eternity and time, as Boethius says (De Consol. v), arising from the fact that eternity is simultaneously whole; which cannot be applied to time: for eternity is the measure of a permanent being; while time is a measure of movement. Supposing, however, that the aforesaid difference be considered on the part of the things measured, and not as regards the measures, then there is some reason for it, inasmuch as that alone is measured by time which has beginning and end in time. Hence, if the movement of the heavens lasted always, time would not be of its measure as regards the whole of its duration, since the infinite is not measurable; but it would be the measure of that part of its revolution which has beginning and end in time.

Another reason for the same can be taken from these measures in themselves, if we consider the end and the beginning as potentialities; because, granted also that time always goes on, yet it is possible to note in time both the beginning and the end, by considering its parts: thus we speak of the beginning and the end of a day or of a year; which cannot be applied to eternity. Still these differences follow upon the essential and primary differences, that eternity is simultaneously whole, but that time is not so.

Reply to Objection 1. Such a reason would be a valid one if time and eternity were the same kind of measure; but this is seen not to be the case when we consider those things of which the respective measures are time and eternity.

Reply to Objection 2. The "now" of time is the same as regards its subject in the whole course of time, but it differs in aspect; for inasmuch as time corresponds to movement, its "now" corresponds to what is movable; and the thing movable has the same one subject in all time, but differs in aspect a being here and there; and such alteration is movement. Likewise the flow of the "now" as alternating in aspect is time. But eternity remains the same according to both subject and aspect; and hence eternity is not the same as the "now" of time.

Reply to Objection 3. As eternity is the proper measure of permanent being, so time is the proper measure of movement; and hence, according as any being recedes from permanence of being, and is subject to change, it recedes from eternity, and is subject to time. Therefore the being of things corruptible, because it is changeable, is not measured by eternity, but by time; for time measures not only things actually changed, but also things changeable; hence it not only measures movement but it also measures repose, which belongs to whatever is naturally movable, but is not actually in motion.

Article 5. The difference of aeviternity and time

Objection 1. It seems that aeviternity is the same as time. For Augustine says (Gen. ad lit. viii, 20,22,23), that "God moves the spiritual through time." But aeviternity is said to be the measure of spiritual substances. Therefore time is the same as aeviternity.

Objection 2. Further, it is essential to time to have "before" and "after"; but it is essential to eternity to be simultaneously whole, as was shown above in the first article. Now aeviternity is not eternity; for it is written (Sirach 1:1) that eternal "Wisdom is before age." Therefore it is not simultaneously whole but has "before" and "after"; and thus it is the same as time.

Objection 3. Further, if there is no "before" and "after" in aeviternity, it follows that in aeviternal things there is no difference between being, having been, or going to be. Since then it is impossible for aeviternal things not to have been, it follows that it is impossible for them not to be in the future; which is false, since God can reduce them to nothing.

Objection 4. Further, since the duration of aeviternal things is infinite as to subsequent duration, if aeviternity is simultaneously whole, it follows that some creature is actually infinite; which is impossible. Therefore aeviternity does not differ from time.

On the contrary, Boethius says (De Consol. iii) "Who commandest time to be separate from aeviternity."

I answer that, Aeviternity differs from time, and from eternity, as the mean between them both. This difference is explained by some to consist in the fact that eternity has neither beginning nor end, aeviternity, a beginning but no end, and time both beginning and end. This difference, however, is but an accidental one, as was shown above, in the preceding article; because even if aeviternal things had always been, and would always be, as some think, and even if they might sometimes fail to be, which is possible to God to allow; even granted this, aeviternity would still be distinguished from eternity, and from time.

Others assign the difference between these three to consist in the fact that eternity has no "before" and "after"; but that time has both, together with innovation and veteration; and that aeviternity has "before" and "after" without innovation and veteration. This theory, however, involves a contradiction; which manifestly appears if innovation and veteration be referred to the measure itself. For since "before" and "after" of duration cannot exist together, if aeviternity has "before" and "after," it must follow that with the receding of the first part of aeviternity, the after part of aeviternity must newly appear; and thus innovation would occur in aeviternity itself, as it does in time. And if they be referred to the things measured, even then an incongruity would follow. For a thing which exists in time grows old with time, because it has a changeable existence, and from the changeableness of a thing measured, there follows "before" and "after" in the measure, as is clear from Phys. iv. Therefore the fact that an aeviternal thing is neither inveterate, nor subject to innovation, comes from its changelessness; and consequently its measure does not contain "before" and "after." We say then that since eternity is the measure of a permanent being, in so far as anything recedes from permanence of being, it recedes from eternity. Now some things recede from permanence of being, so that their being is subject to change, or consists in change; and these things are measured by time, as are all movements, and also the being of all things corruptible. But others recede less from permanence of being, forasmuch as their being neither consists in change, nor is the subject of change; nevertheless they have change annexed to them either actually or potentially. This appears in the heavenly bodies, the substantial being of which is unchangeable; and yet with unchangeable being they have changeableness of place. The same applies to the angels, who have an unchangeable being as regards their nature with changeableness as regards choice; moreover they have changeableness of intelligence, of affections and of places in their own degree. Therefore these are measured by aeviternity which is a mean between eternity and time. But the being that is measured by eternity is not changeable, nor is it annexed to change. In this way time has "before" and "after"; aeviternity in itself has no "before" and "after," which can, however, be annexed to it; while eternity has neither "before" nor "after," nor is it compatible with such at all.

Reply to Objection 1. Spiritual creatures as regards successive affections and intelligences are measured by time. Hence also Augustine says (Gen. ad lit. viii, 20,22,23) that to be moved through time, is to be moved by affections. But as regards their nature they are measured by aeviternity; whereas as regards the vision of glory, they have a share of eternity.

Reply to Objection 2. Aeviternity is simultaneously whole; yet it is not eternity, because "before" and "after" are compatible with it.

Reply to Objection 3. In the very being of an angel considered absolutely, there is no difference of past and future, but only as regards accidental change. Now to say that an angel was, or is, or will be, is to be taken in a different sense according to the acceptation of our intellect, which apprehends the angelic existence by comparison with different parts of time. But when we say that an angel is, or was, we suppose something, which being supposed, its opposite is not subject to the divine power. Whereas when we say he will be, we do not as yet suppose anything. Hence, since the existence and non-existence of an angel considered absolutely is subject to the divine power, God can make the existence of an angel not future; but He cannot cause him not to be while he is, or not to have been, after he has been.

Reply to Objection 4. The duration of aeviternity is infinite, forasmuch as it is not finished by time. Hence, there is no incongruity in saying that a creature is infinite, inasmuch as it is not ended by any other creature.

Article 6. Whether there is only one aeviternity?

Objection 1. It seems that there is not only one aeviternity; for it is written in the apocryphal books of Esdras: "Majesty and power of ages are with Thee, O Lord."

Objection 2. Further, different genera have different measures. But some aeviternal things belong to the corporeal genus, as the heavenly bodies; and others are spiritual substances, as are the angels. Therefore there is not only one aeviternity.

Objection 3. Further, since aeviternity is a term of duration, where there is one aeviternity, there is also one duration. But not all aeviternal things have one duration, for some begin to exist after others; as appears in the case especially of human souls. Therefore there is not only one aeviternity.

Objection 4. Further, things not dependent on each other do not seem to have one measure of duration; for there appears to be one time for all temporal things; since the first movement, measured by time, is in some way the cause of all movement. But aeviternal things do not depend on each other, for one angel is not the cause of another angel. Therefore there is not only one aeviternity.

On the contrary, Aeviternity is a more simple thing than time, and is nearer to eternity. But time is one only. Therefore much more is aeviternity one only.

I answer that, A twofold opinion exists on this subject. Some say there is only one aeviternity; others that there are many aeviternities. Which of these is true, may be considered from the cause why time is one; for we can rise from corporeal things to the knowledge of spiritual things.

Now some say that there is only one time for temporal things, forasmuch as one number exists for all things numbered; as time is a number, according to the Philosopher (Phys. iv). This, however, is not a sufficient reason; because time is not a number abstracted from the thing numbered, but existing in the thing numbered; otherwise it would not be continuous; for ten ells of cloth are continuous not by reason of the number, but by reason of the thing numbered. Now number as it exists in the thing numbered, is not the same for all; but it is different for different things. Hence, others assert that the unity of eternity as the principle of all duration is the cause of the unity of time. Thus all durations are one in that view, in the light of their principle, but are many in the light of the diversity of things receiving duration from the influx of the first principle. On the other hand others assign primary matter as the cause why time is one; as it is the first subject of movement, the measure of which is time. Neither of these reasons, however, is sufficient; forasmuch as things which are one in principle, or in subject, especially if distant, are not one absolutely, but accidentally. Therefore the true reason why time is one, is to be found in the oneness of the first movement by which, since it is most simple, all other movements are measured. Therefore time is referred to that movement, not only as a measure is to the thing measured, but also as accident is to subject; and thus receives unity from it. Whereas to other movements it is compared only as the measure is to the thing measured. Hence it is not multiplied by their multitude, because by one separate measure many things can be measured.

This being established, we must observe that a twofold opinion existed concerning spiritual substances. Some said that all proceeded from God in a certain equality, as Origen said (Peri Archon. i); or at least many of them, as some others thought. Others said that all spiritual substances proceeded from God in a certain degree and order; and Dionysius (Coel. Hier. x) seems to have thought so, when he said that among spiritual substances there are the first, the middle and the last; even in one order of angels. Now according to the first opinion, it must be said that there are many aeviternities as there are many aeviternal things of first degree. But according to the second opinion, it would be necessary to say that there is one aeviternity only; because since each thing is measured by the most simple element of its genus, it must be that the existence of all aeviternal things should be measured by the existence of the first aeviternal thing, which is all the more simple the nearer it is to the first. Wherefore because the second opinion is truer, as will be shown later (47, 2); we concede at present that there is only one aeviternity.

Reply to Objection 1. Aeviternity is sometimes taken for age, that is, a space of a thing's duration; and thus we say many aeviternities when we mean ages.

Reply to Objection 2. Although the heavenly bodies and spiritual things differ in the genus of their nature, still they agree in having a changeless being, and are thus measured by aeviternity.

Reply to Objection 3. All temporal things did not begin together; nevertheless there is one time for all of them, by reason of the first measured by time; and thus all aeviternal things have one aeviternity by reason of the first, though all did not begin together.

Reply to Objection 4. For things to be measured by one, it is not necessary that the one should be the cause of all, but that it be more simple than the rest.

Question 11. The unity of God

Article 1. Whether "one" adds anything to "being"?

Objection 1. It seems that "one" adds something to "being." For everything is in a determinate genus by addition to being, which penetrates all "genera." But "one" is a determinate genus, for it is the principle of number, which is a species of quantity. Therefore "one" adds something to "being."

Objection 2. Further, what divides a thing common to all, is an addition to it. But "being" is divided by "one" and by "many." Therefore "one" is an addition to "being."

Objection 3. Further, if "one" is not an addition to "being," "one" and "being" must have the same meaning. But it would be nugatory to call "being" by the name of "being"; therefore it would be equally so to call being "one." Now this is false. Therefore "one" is an addition to "being."

On the contrary, Dionysius says (Div. Nom. 5, ult.): "Nothing which exists is not in some way one," which would be false if "one" were an addition to "being," in the sense of limiting it. Therefore "one" is not an addition to "being."

I answer that, "One" does not add any reality to "being"; but is only a negation of division; for "one" means undivided "being." This is the very reason why "one" is the same as "being." Now every being is either simple or compound. But what is simple is undivided, both actually and potentially. Whereas what is compound, has not being whilst its parts are divided, but after they make up and compose it. Hence it is manifest that the being of anything consists in undivision; and hence it is that everything guards its unity as it guards its being.

Reply to Objection 1. Some, thinking that the "one" convertible with "being" is the same as the "one" which is the principle of number, were divided into contrary opinions. Pythagoras and Plato, seeing that the "one" convertible with "being" did not add any reality to "being," but signified the substance of "being" as undivided, thought that the same applied to the "one" which is the principle of number. And because number is composed of unities, they thought that numbers were the substances of all things. Avicenna, however, on the contrary, considering that "one" which is the principle of number, added a reality to the substance of "being" (otherwise number made of unities would not be a species of quantity), thought that the "one" convertible with "being" added a reality to the substance of beings; as "white" to "man." This, however, is manifestly false, inasmuch as each thing is "one" by its substance. For if a thing were "one" by anything else but by its substance, since this again would be "one," supposing it were again "one" by another thing, we should be driven on to infinity. Hence we must adhere to the former statement; therefore we must say that the "one" which is convertible with "being," does not add a reality to being; but that the "one" which is the principle of number, does add a reality to "being," belonging to the genus of quantity.

Reply to Objection 2. There is nothing to prevent a thing which in one way is divided, from being another way undivided; as what is divided in number, may be undivided in species; thus it may be that a thing is in one way "one," and in another way "many." Still, if it is absolutely undivided, either because it is so according to what belongs to its essence, though it may be divided as regards what is outside its essence, as what is one in subject may have many accidents; or because it is undivided actually, and divided potentially, as what is "one" in the whole, and is "many" in parts; in such a case a thing will be "one" absolutely and "many" accidentally. On the other hand, if it be undivided accidentally, and divided absolutely, as if it were divided in essence and undivided in idea or in principle or cause, it will be "many" absolutely and "one" accidentally; as what are "many" in number and "one" in species or "one" in principle. Hence in that way, being is divided by "one" and by "many"; as it were by "one" absolutely and by "many" accidentally. For multitude itself would not be contained under "being," unless it were in some way contained under "one." Thus Dionysius says (Div. Nom. cap. ult.) that "there is no kind of multitude that is not in a way one. But what are many in their parts, are one in their whole; and what are many in accidents, are one in subject; and what are many in number, are one in species; and what are many in species, are one in genus; and what are many in processions, are one in principle."

Reply to Objection 3. It does not follow that it is nugatory to say "being" is "one"; forasmuch as "one" adds an idea to "being."

Article 2. Whether "one" and "many" are opposed to each other?

Objection 1. It seems that "one" and "many" are not mutually opposed. For no opposite thing is predicated of its opposite. But every "multitude" is in a certain way "one," as appears from the preceding article. Therefore "one" is not opposed to "multitude."

Objection 2. Further, no opposite thing is constituted by its opposite. But "multitude" is constituted by "one." Therefore it is not opposed to "multitude."

Objection 3. Further, "one" is opposed to "one." But the idea of "few" is opposed to "many." Therefore "one" is not opposed to "many."

Objection 4. Further, if "one" is opposed to "multitude," it is opposed as the undivided is to the divided; and is thus opposed to it as privation is to habit. But this appears to be incongruous; because it would follow that "one" comes after "multitude," and is defined by it; whereas, on the contrary, "multitude" is defined by "one." Hence there would be a vicious circle in the definition;

which is inadmissible. Therefore "one" and "many" are not opposed.

On the contrary, Things which are opposed in idea, are themselves opposed to each other. But the idea of "one" consists in indivisibility; and the idea of "multitude" contains division. Therefore "one" and "many" are opposed to each other.

I answer that, "One" is opposed to "many," but in various ways. The "one" which is the principle of number is opposed to "multitude" which is number, as the measure is to the thing measured. For "one" implies the idea of a primary measure; and number is "multitude" measured by "one," as is clear from Metaph. x. But the "one" which convertible with "being" is opposed to "multitude" by way of privation; as the undivided is to the thing divided.

Reply to Objection 1. No privation entirely takes away the being of a thing, inasmuch as privation means "negation in the subject," according to the Philosopher (Categor. viii). Nevertheless every privation takes away some being; and so in being, by reason of its universality, the privation of being has its foundation in being; which is not the case in privations of special forms, as of sight, or of whiteness and the like. And what applies to being applies also to one and to good, which are convertible with being, for the privation of good is founded in some good; likewise the removal of unity is founded in some one thing. Hence it happens that multitude is some one thing; and evil is some good thing, and non-being is some kind of being. Nevertheless, opposite is not predicated of opposite; forasmuch as one is absolute, and the other is relative; for what is relative being (as a potentiality) is non-being absolutely, i.e. actually; or what is absolute being in the genus of substance is non-being relatively as regards some accidental being. In the same way, what is relatively good is absolutely bad, or vice versa; likewise what is absolutely "one" is relatively "many," and vice versa.

Reply to Objection 2. A "whole" is twofold. In one sense it is homogeneous, composed of like parts; in another sense it is heterogeneous, composed of dissimilar parts. Now in every homogeneous whole, the whole is made up of parts having the form of the whole; as, for instance, every part of water is water; and such is the constitution of a continuous thing made up of its parts. In every heterogeneous whole, however, every part is wanting in the form belonging to the whole; as, for instance, no part of a house is a house, nor is any part of a man a man. Now multitude is such a kind of a whole. Therefore inasmuch as its part has not the form of the multitude, the latter is composed of unities, as a house is composed of not houses; not, indeed, as if unities constituted multitude so far as they are undivided, in which way they are opposed to multitude; but so far as they have being, as also the parts of a house make up the house by the fact that they are beings, not by the fact that they are not houses.

Reply to Objection 3. "Many" is taken in two ways: absolutely, and in that sense it is opposed to "one"; in another way as importing some kind of excess, in which sense it is opposed to "few"; hence in the first sense two are many but not in the second sense.

Reply to Objection 4. "One" is opposed to "many" privatively, inasmuch as the idea of "many" involves division. Hence division must be prior to unity, not absolutely in itself, but according to our way of apprehension. For we apprehend simple things by compound things; and hence we define a point to be, "what has no part," or "the beginning of a line." "Multitude" also, in idea, follows on "one"; because we do not understand divided things to convey the idea of multitude except by the fact that we attribute unity to every part. Hence "one" is placed in the definition of "multitude"; but "multitude" is not placed in the definition of "one." But division comes to be understood from the very negation of being: so what first comes to mind is being; secondly, that this being is not that being, and thus we apprehend division as a consequence; thirdly, comes the notion of one; fourthly, the notion of multitude.

Article 3. Whether God is one?

Objection 1. It seems that God is not one. For it is written "For there be many gods and many lords" (1 Corinthians 8:5).

Objection 2. Further, "One," as the principle of number, cannot be predicated of God, since quantity is not predicated of God; likewise, neither can "one" which is convertible with "being" be predicated of God, because it imports privation, and every privation is an imperfection, which cannot apply to God. Therefore God is not one.

On the contrary, It is written "Hear, O Israel, the Lord our God is one Lord" (Deuteronomy 6:4).

I answer that, It can be shown from these three sources that God is one.

First from His simplicity. For it is manifest that the reason why any singular thing is "this particular thing" is because it cannot be communicated to many: since that whereby Socrates is a man, can be communicated to many; whereas, what makes him this particular man, is only communicable to one. Therefore, if Socrates were a man by what makes him to be this particular man, as there cannot be many Socrates, so there could not in that way be many men. Now this belongs to God alone; for God Himself is His own nature, as was shown above (Question 3, Article 3). Therefore, in the very same way God is God, and He is this God. Impossible is it therefore that many Gods should exist.

Secondly, this is proved from the infinity of His perfection. For it was shown above (Question 4, Article 2) that God comprehends in Himself the whole perfection of being. If then many gods existed, they would necessarily differ from each other. Something therefore would belong to one which did not belong to another. And if this were a privation, one of them would not be absolutely perfect; but if a perfection, one of them would be without it. So it is impossible for many gods to exist. Hence also the ancient philosophers, constrained as it were by truth, when they asserted an infinite principle, asserted likewise that there was only one such principle.

Thirdly, this is shown from the unity of the world. For all things that exist are seen to be ordered to each other since some serve others. But things that are diverse do not harmonize in the same order, unless they are ordered thereto by one. For many are reduced into one order by one better than by many: because one is the "per se" cause of one, and many are only the accidental cause of one, inasmuch as they are in some way one. Since therefore what is first is most perfect, and is so "per se" and not accidentally, it must be that the first which reduces all into one order should be only one. And this one is God.

Reply to Objection 1. Gods are called many by the error of some who worshipped many deities, thinking as they did that the planets and other stars were gods, and also the separate parts of the world. Hence the Apostle adds: "Our God is one," etc.

Reply to Objection 2. "One" which is the principle of number is not predicated of God, but only of material things. For "one" the principle of number belongs to the "genus" of mathematics, which are material in being, and abstracted from matter only in idea. But "one" which is convertible with being is a metaphysical entity and does not depend on matter in its being. And although in God there is no privation, still, according to the mode of our apprehension, He is known to us by way only of privation and remotion. Thus there is no reason why a certain kind of privation should not be predicated of God; for instance, that He is incorporeal and infinite; and in the same way it is said of God that He is one.

Article 4. Whether God is supremely one?

Objection 1. It seems that God is not supremely "one." For "one" is so called from the privation of division. But privation cannot be greater or less. Therefore God is not more "one" than other things which are called "one."

Objection 2. Further, nothing seems to be more indivisible than what is actually and potentially indivisible; such as a point and unity. But a thing is said to be more "one" according as it is indivisible. Therefore God is not more "one" than unity is "one" and a point is "one."

Objection 3. Further, what is essentially good is supremely good. Therefore what is essentially "one" is supremely "one." But every being is essentially "one," as the Philosopher says (Metaph. iv). Therefore every being is supremely "one"; and therefore God is not "one" more than any other being is "one."

On the contrary, Bernard says (De Consid. v): "Among all things called one, the unity of the Divine Trinity holds the first place."

I answer that, Since "one" is an undivided being, if anything is supremely "one" it must be supremely being, and supremely undivided. Now both of these belong to God. For He is supremely being, inasmuch as His being is not determined by any nature to which it is adjoined; since He is being itself, subsistent, absolutely undetermined. But He is supremely undivided inasmuch as He is divided neither actually nor potentially, by any mode of division; since He is altogether simple, as was shown above (Question 3, Article 7). Hence it is manifest that God is "one" in the supreme degree.

Reply to Objection 1. Although privation considered in itself is not susceptive of more or less, still according as its opposite is subject to more or less, privation also can be considered itself in the light of more and less. Therefore according as a thing is more divided, or is divisible, either less or not at all, in the degree it is called more, or less, or supremely, "one."

Reply to Objection 2. A point and unity which is the principle of number, are not supremely being, inasmuch as they have being only in some subject. Hence neither of them can be supremely "one." For as a subject cannot be supremely "one," because of the difference within it of accident and subject, so neither can an accident.

Reply to Objection 3. Although every being is "one" by its substance, still every such substance is not equally the cause of unity; for the substance of some things is compound and of others simple.

Question 13. The names of God

Article 1. Whether a name can be given to God?

Objection 1. It seems that no name can be given to God. For Dionysius says (Div. Nom. i) that, "Of Him there is neither name, nor can one be found of Him;" and it is written: "What is His name, and what is the name of His Son, if thou knowest?" (Proverbs 30:4).

Objection 2. Further, every name is either abstract or concrete. But concrete names do not belong to God, since He is simple, nor do abstract names belong to Him, forasmuch as they do not signify any perfect subsisting thing. Therefore no name can be said of God.

Objection 3. Further, nouns are taken to signify substance with quality; verbs and participles signify substance with time; pronouns the same with demonstration or relation. But none of these can be applied to God, for He has no quality, nor accident, nor time; moreover, He cannot be felt, so as to be pointed out; nor can He be described by relation, inasmuch as relations serve to recall a thing mentioned before by nouns, participles, or demonstrative pronouns. Therefore God cannot in any way be named by us.

On the contrary, It is written (Exodus 15:3): "The Lord is a man of war, Almighty is His name."

I answer that, Since according to the Philosopher (Peri Herm. i), words are signs of ideas, and ideas the similitude of things, it is evident that words relate to the meaning of things signified through the medium of the intellectual conception. It follows therefore that we can give a name to anything in as far as we can understand it. Now it was shown above (12, 11, 12) that in this life we cannot see the essence of God; but we know God from creatures as their principle, and also by way of excellence and remotion. In this way therefore He can be named by us from creatures, yet not so that the name which signifies Him expresses the divine essence in itself. Thus the name "man" expresses the essence of man in himself, since it signifies the definition of man by manifesting his essence; for the idea expressed by the name is the definition.

Reply to Objection 1. The reason why God has no name, or is said to be above being named, is because His essence is above all that we understand about God, and signify in word.

Reply to Objection 2. Because we know and name God from creatures, the names we attribute to God signify what belongs to material creatures, of which the knowledge is natural to us. And because in creatures of this kind what is perfect and subsistent is compound; whereas their form is not a complete subsisting thing, but rather is that whereby a thing is; hence it follows that all names used by us to signify a complete subsisting thing must have a concrete meaning as applicable to compound things; whereas names given to signify simple forms, signify a thing not as subsisting, but as that whereby a thing is; as, for instance, whiteness signifies that whereby a thing is white. And as God is simple, and subsisting, we attribute to Him abstract names to signify His simplicity, and concrete names to signify His substance and perfection, although both these kinds of names fail to express His mode of being, forasmuch as our intellect does not know Him in this life as He is.

Reply to Objection 3. To signify substance with quality is to signify the "suppositum" with a nature or determined form in which it subsists. Hence, as some things are said of God in a concrete sense, to signify His subsistence and perfection, so likewise nouns are applied to God signifying substance with quality. Further, verbs and participles which signify time, are applied to Him because His eternity includes all time. For as we can apprehend and signify simple subsistences only by way of compound things, so we can understand and express simple eternity only by way of temporal things, because our intellect has a natural affinity to compound and temporal things. But demonstrative pronouns are applied to God as describing what is understood, not what is sensed. For we can only describe Him as far as we understand Him. Thus, according as nouns, participles and demonstrative pronouns are applicable to God, so far can He be signified by relative pronouns.

Article 2. Whether any name can be applied to God substantially?

Objection 1. It seems that no name can be applied to God substantially. For Damascene says (De Fide Orth. i, 9): "Everything said of God signifies not His substance, but rather shows forth what He is not; or expresses some relation, or something following from His nature or operation."

Objection 2. Further, Dionysius says (Div. Nom. i): "You will find a chorus of holy doctors addressed to the end of distinguishing clearly and praiseworthily the divine processions in the denomination of God." Thus the names applied by the holy doctors in praising God are distinguished according to the divine processions themselves. But what expresses the procession of anything, does not signify its essence. Therefore the names applied to God are not said of Him substantially.

Objection 3. Further, a thing is named by us according as we understand it. But God is not understood by us in this life in His substance. Therefore neither is any name we can use applied substantially to God.

On the contrary, Augustine says (De Trin. vi): "The being of God is the being strong, or the being wise, or whatever else we may say of that simplicity whereby His substance is signified." Therefore all names of this kind signify the divine substance.

I answer that, Negative names applied to God, or signifying His relation to creatures manifestly do not at all signify His substance, but rather express the distance of the creature from Him, or His relation to something else, or rather, the relation of creatures to Himself.

But as regards absolute and affirmative names of God, as "good," "wise," and the like, various and many opinions have been given. For some have said that all such names, although they are applied to God affirmatively, nevertheless have been brought into use more to express some remotion from God, rather than to express anything that exists positively in Him. Hence they assert that when we say that God lives, we mean that God is not like an inanimate thing; and the same in like manner applies to other names; and this was taught by Rabbi Moses. Others say that these names applied to God signify His relationship towards creatures: thus in the words, "God is good," we mean, God is the cause of goodness in things; and the same rule applies to other names.

Both of these opinions, however, seem to be untrue for three reasons.

First because in neither of them can a reason be assigned why some names more than others are applied to God. For He is assuredly the cause of bodies in the same way as He is the cause of good things; therefore if the words "God is good," signified no more than, "God is the cause of good things," it might in like manner be said that God is a body, inasmuch as He is the cause of bodies. So also to say that He is a body implies that He is not a mere potentiality, as is primary matter.

Secondly, because it would follow that all names applied to God would be said of Him by way of being taken in a secondary sense, as healthy is secondarily said of medicine, forasmuch as it signifies only the cause of the health in the animal which primarily is called healthy.

Thirdly, because this is against the intention of those who speak of God. For in saying that God lives, they assuredly mean more than to say the He is the cause of our life, or that He differs from inanimate bodies.

Therefore we must hold a different doctrine--viz. that these names signify the divine substance, and are predicated substantially of God, although they fall short of a full representation of Him. Which is proved thus. For these names express God, so far as our intellects know Him. Now since our intellect knows God from creatures, it knows Him as far as creatures represent Him. Now it is shown above (Question 4, Article 2) that God prepossesses in Himself all the perfections of creatures, being Himself simply and universally perfect. Hence every creature represents Him, and is like Him so far as it possesses some perfection; yet it represents Him not as something of the same species or genus, but as the excelling principle of whose form the effects fall short, although they derive some kind of likeness thereto, even as the forms of inferior bodies represent the power of the sun. This was explained above (Question 4, Article 3), in treating of the divine perfection. Therefore the aforesaid names signify the divine substance, but in an imperfect manner, even as creatures represent it imperfectly. So when we say, "God is good," the meaning is not, "God is the cause of goodness," or "God is not evil"; but the meaning is, "Whatever good we attribute to creatures, pre-exists in God," and in a more excellent and higher way. Hence it does not follow that God is good, because He causes goodness; but rather, on the contrary, He causes goodness in things because He is good; according to what Augustine says (De Doctr. Christ. i, 32), "Because He is good, we are."

Reply to Objection 1. Damascene says that these names do not signify what God is, forasmuch as by none of these names is perfectly expressed what He is; but each one signifies Him in an imperfect manner, even as creatures represent Him imperfectly.

Reply to Objection 2. In the significance of names, that from which the name is derived is different sometimes from what it is intended to signify, as for instance, this name "stone" [lapis] is imposed from the fact that it hurts the foot [loedit pedem], but it is not imposed to signify that which hurts the foot, but rather to signify a certain kind of body; otherwise everything that hurts the foot would be a stone [This refers to the Latin etymology of the word "lapis" which has no place in English]. So we must say that these kinds of divine names are imposed from the divine processions; for as according to the diverse processions of their perfections, creatures are the representations of God, although in an imperfect manner; so likewise our intellect knows and names God according to each kind of procession; but nevertheless these names are not imposed to signify the procession themselves, as if when we say "God lives," the sense were, "life proceeds from Him"; but to signify the principle itself of things, in so far as life pre-exists in Him, although it pre-exists in Him in a more eminent way than can be understood or signified.

Reply to Objection 3. We cannot know the essence of God in this life, as He really is in Himself; but we know Him accordingly as He is represented in the perfections of creatures; and thus the names imposed by us signify Him in that manner only.

Article 3. Whether any name can be applied to God in its literal sense?

Objection 1. It seems that no name is applied literally to God. For all names which we apply to God are taken from creatures; as was explained above (Article 1). But the names of creatures are applied to God metaphorically, as when we say, God is a stone, or a lion, or the like. Therefore names are applied to God in a metaphorical sense.

Objection 2. Further, no name can be applied literally to anything if it should be withheld from it rather than given to it. But all such names as "good," "wise," and the like are more truly withheld from God than given to Him; as appears from Dionysius says (Coel. Hier. ii). Therefore none of these names belong to God in their literal sense.

Objection 3. Further, corporeal names are applied to God in a metaphorical sense only; since He is incorporeal. But all such names imply some kind of corporeal condition; for their meaning is bound up with time and composition and like corporeal conditions. Therefore all these names are applied to God in a metaphorical sense.

On the contrary, Ambrose says (De Fide ii), "Some names there are which express evidently the property of the divinity, and some which express the clear truth of the divine majesty, but others there are which are applied to God metaphorically by way of similitude." Therefore not all names are applied to God in a metaphorical sense, but there are some which are said of Him in their literal sense.

I answer that, According to the preceding article, our knowledge of God is derived from the perfections which flow from Him to creatures, which perfections are in God in a more eminent way than in creatures. Now our intellect apprehends them as they are in creatures, and as it apprehends them it signifies them by names. Therefore as to the names applied to God--viz. the perfections which they signify, such as goodness, life and the like, and their mode of signification. As regards what is signified by these names, they belong properly to God, and more properly than they belong to creatures, and are applied primarily to Him. But as regards their mode of signification, they do not properly and strictly apply to God; for their mode of signification applies to creatures.

Reply to Objection 1. There are some names which signify these perfections flowing from God to creatures in such a way that the imperfect way in which creatures receive the divine perfection is part of the very signification of the name itself as "stone" signifies a material being, and names of this kind can be applied to God only in a metaphorical sense. Other names, however, express these perfections absolutely, without any such mode of participation being part of their signification as the words "being," "good," "living," and the like, and such names can be literally applied to God.

Reply to Objection 2. Such names as these, as Dionysius shows, are denied of God for the reason that what the name signifies does not belong to Him in the ordinary sense of its signification, but in a more eminent way. Hence Dionysius says also that God is above all substance and all life.

Reply to Objection 3. These names which are applied to God literally imply corporeal conditions not in the thing signified, but as regards their mode of signification; whereas those which are applied to God metaphorically imply and mean a corporeal condition in the thing signified.

Article 4. Whether names applied to God are synonymous?

Objection 1. It seems that these names applied to God are synonymous names. For synonymous names are those which mean exactly the same. But these names applied to God mean entirely the same thing in God; for the goodness of God is His essence, and likewise it is His wisdom. Therefore these names are entirely synonymous.

Objection 2. Further, if it be said these names signify one and the same thing in reality, but differ in idea, it can be objected that an idea to which no reality corresponds is a vain notion. Therefore if these ideas are many, and the thing is one, it seems also that all these ideas are vain notions.

Objection 3. Further, a thing which is one in reality and in idea, is more one than what is one in reality and many in idea. But God is supremely one. Therefore it seems that He is not one in reality and many in idea; and thus the names applied to God do not signify different ideas; and thus they are synonymous.

On the contrary, All synonyms united with each other are redundant, as when we say, "vesture clothing." Therefore if all names applied to God are synonymous, we cannot properly say "good God" or the like, and yet it is written, "O most mighty, great and powerful, the Lord of hosts is Thy name" (Jeremiah 32:18).

I answer that, These names spoken of God are not synonymous. This would be easy to understand, if we said that these names are used to remove, or to express the relation of cause to creatures; for thus it would follow that there are different ideas as regards the diverse things denied of God, or as regards diverse effects connoted. But even according to what was said above (Article 2), that these names signify the divine substance, although in an imperfect manner, it is also clear from what has been said (1,2) that they have diverse meanings. For the idea signified by the name is the conception in the intellect of the thing signified by the name. But our intellect, since it knows God from creatures, in order to understand God, forms conceptions proportional to the perfections flowing from God to creatures, which perfections pre-exist in God unitedly and simply, whereas in creatures they are received and divided and multiplied. As therefore, to the different perfections of creatures, there corresponds one simple principle represented by different perfections of creatures in a various and manifold manner, so also to the various and multiplied conceptions of our intellect, there corresponds one altogether simple principle, according to these conceptions, imperfectly understood. Therefore although the names applied to God signify one thing, still because they signify that under many and different aspects, they are not synonymous.

Thus appears the solution of the First Objection, since synonymous terms signify one thing under one aspect; for words which signify different aspects of one things, do not signify primarily and absolutely one thing; because the term only signifies the thing through the medium of the intellectual conception, as was said above.

Reply to Objection 2. The many aspects of these names are not empty and vain, for there corresponds to all of them one simple reality represented by them in a manifold and imperfect manner.

Reply to Objection 3. The perfect unity of God requires that what are manifold and divided in others should exist in Him simply and unitedly. Thus it comes about that He is one in reality, and yet multiple in idea, because our intellect apprehends Him in a manifold manner, as things represent Him.

Article 5. Whether what is said of God and of creatures is univocally predicated of them?

Objection 1. It seems that the things attributed to God and creatures are univocal. For every equivocal term is reduced to the univocal, as many are reduced to one; for if the name "dog" be said equivocally of the barking dog, and of the dogfish, it must be said of some univocally--viz. of all barking dogs; otherwise we proceed to infinitude. Now there are some univocal agents which agree with their effects in name and definition, as man generates man; and there are some agents which are equivocal, as the sun which causes heat, although the sun is hot only in an equivocal sense. Therefore it seems that the first agent to which all other agents are reduced, is an univocal agent: and thus what is said of God and creatures, is predicated univocally.

Objection 2. Further, there is no similitude among equivocal things. Therefore as creatures have a certain likeness to God, according to the word of Genesis (Genesis 1:26), "Let us make man to our image and likeness," it seems that something can be said of God and creatures univocally.

Objection 3. Further, measure is homogeneous with the thing measured. But God is the first measure of all beings. Therefore God is homogeneous with creatures; and thus a word may be applied univocally to God and to creatures.

On the contrary, whatever is predicated of various things under the same name but not in the same sense, is predicated equivocally. But no name belongs to God in the same sense that it belongs to creatures; for instance, wisdom in creatures is a quality, but not in God. Now a different genus changes an essence, since the genus is part of the definition; and the same applies to other things. Therefore whatever is said of God and of creatures is predicated equivocally.

Further, God is more distant from creatures than any creatures are from each other. But the distance of some creatures makes any univocal predication of them impossible, as in the case of those things which are not in the same genus. Therefore much less can anything be predicated univocally of God and creatures; and so only equivocal predication can be applied to them.

I answer that, Univocal predication is impossible between God and creatures. The reason of this is that every effect which is not an adequate result of the power of the efficient cause, receives the similitude of the agent not in its full degree, but in a measure that falls short, so that what is divided and multiplied in the effects resides in the agent simply, and in the same manner; as for example the sun by exercise of its one power produces manifold and various forms in all inferior things. In the same way, as said in the preceding article, all perfections existing in creatures divided and multiplied, pre-exist in God unitedly. Thus when any term expressing perfection is applied to a creature, it signifies that perfection distinct in idea from other perfections; as, for instance, by the term "wise" applied to man, we signify some perfection distinct from a man's essence, and distinct from his power and existence, and from all similar things; whereas when we apply to it God, we do not mean to signify anything distinct from His essence, or power, or existence. Thus also this term "wise" applied to man in some degree circumscribes and comprehends the thing signified; whereas this is not the case when it is applied to God; but it leaves the thing signified as incomprehended, and as exceeding the signification of the name. Hence it is evident that this term "wise" is not applied in the same way to God and to man. The same rule applies to other terms. Hence no name is predicated univocally of God and of creatures.

Neither, on the other hand, are names applied to God and creatures in a purely equivocal sense, as some have said. Because if that were so, it follows that from creatures nothing could be known or demonstrated about God at all; for the reasoning would always be exposed to the fallacy of equivocation. Such a view is against the philosophers, who proved many things about God, and also against what the Apostle says: "The invisible things of God are clearly seen being understood by the things that are made" (Romans 1:20). Therefore it must be said that these names are said of God and creatures in an analogous sense, i.e. according to proportion.

Now names are thus used in two ways: either according as many things are proportionate to one, thus for example "healthy" predicated of medicine and urine in relation and in proportion to health of a body, of which the former is the sign and the latter the cause: or according as one thing is proportionate to another, thus "healthy" is said of medicine and animal, since medicine is the cause of health in the animal body. And in this way some things are said of God and creatures analogically, and not in a purely equivocal nor in a purely univocal sense. For we can name God only from creatures (1). Thus whatever is said of God and creatures, is said according to the relation of a creature to God as its principle and cause, wherein all perfections of things pre-exist excellently. Now this mode of community of idea is a mean between pure equivocation and simple univocation. For in analogies the idea is not, as it is in univocals, one and the same, yet it is not totally diverse as in equivocals; but a term which is thus used in a multiple sense signifies various proportions to some one thing; thus "healthy" applied to urine signifies the sign of animal health, and applied to medicine signifies the cause of the same health.

Reply to Objection 1. Although equivocal predications must be reduced to univocal, still in actions, the non-univocal agent must precede the univocal agent. For the non-univocal agent is the universal cause of the whole species, as for instance the sun is the cause of the generation of all men; whereas the univocal agent is not the universal efficient cause of the whole species (otherwise it would be the cause of itself, since it is contained in the species), but is a particular cause of this individual which it places under the species by way of participation. Therefore the universal cause of the whole species is not an univocal agent; and the universal cause comes before the particular cause. But this universal agent, whilst it is not univocal, nevertheless is not altogether equivocal, otherwise it could not produce its own likeness, but rather it is to be called an analogical agent, as all univocal predications are reduced to one first non-univocal analogical predication, which is being.

Reply to Objection 2. The likeness of the creature to God is imperfect, for it does not represent one and the same generic thing (4, 3).

Reply to Objection 3. God is not the measure proportioned to things measured; hence it is not necessary that God and creatures should be in the same genus.

The arguments adduced in the contrary sense prove indeed that these names are not predicated univocally of God and creatures; yet they do not prove that they are predicated equivocally.

Article 6. Whether names predicated of God are predicated primarily of creatures?

Objection 1. It seems that names are predicated primarily of creatures rather than of God. For we name anything accordingly as we know it, since "names", as the Philosopher says, "are signs of ideas." But we know creatures before we know God. Therefore the names imposed by us are predicated primarily of creatures rather than of God.

Objection 2. Further, Dionysius says (Div. Nom. i): "We name God from creatures." But names transferred from creatures to God, are said primarily of creatures rather than of God, as "lion," "stone," and the like. Therefore all names applied to God and creatures are applied primarily to creatures rather than to God.

Objection 3. Further, all names equally applied to God and creatures, are applied to God as the cause of all creatures, as Dionysius says (De Mystica Theol.). But what is applied to anything through its cause, is applied to it secondarily, for "healthy" is primarily predicated of animal rather than of medicine, which is the cause of health. Therefore these names are said primarily of creatures rather than of God.

On the contrary, It is written, "I bow my knees to the Father, of our Lord Jesus Christ, of Whom all paternity in heaven and earth is named" (Ephesians 3:14-15); and the same applies to the other names applied to God and creatures. Therefore these names are applied primarily to God rather than to creatures.

I answer that, In names predicated of many in an analogical sense, all are predicated because they have reference to some one thing; and this one thing must be placed in the definition of them all. And since that expressed by the name is the definition, as the Philosopher says (Metaph. iv), such a name must be applied primarily to that which is put in the definition of such other things, and secondarily to these others according as they approach more or less to that first. Thus, for instance, "healthy" applied to animals comes into the definition of "healthy" applied to medicine, which is called healthy as being the cause of health in the animal; and also into the definition of "healthy" which is applied to urine, which is called healthy in so far as it is the sign of the animal's health. Thus all names applied metaphorically to God, are applied to creatures primarily rather than to God, because when said of God they mean only similitudes to such creatures. For as "smiling" applied to a field means only that the field in the beauty of its flowering is like the beauty of the human smile by proportionate likeness, so the name of "lion" applied to God means only that God manifests strength in His works, as a lion in his. Thus it is clear that applied to God the signification of names can be defined only from what is said of creatures. But to other names not applied to God in a metaphorical sense, the same rule would apply if they were spoken of God as the cause only, as some have supposed. For when it is said, "God is good," it would then only mean "God is the cause of the creature's goodness"; thus the term good applied to God would included in its meaning the creature's goodness. Hence "good" would apply primarily to creatures rather than to God. But as was shown above (Article 2), these names are applied to God not as the cause only, but also essentially. For the words, "God is good," or "wise," signify not only that He is the cause of wisdom or goodness, but that these exist in Him in a more excellent way. Hence as regards what the name signifies, these names are applied primarily to God rather than to creatures, because these perfections flow from God to creatures; but as regards the imposition of the names, they are primarily applied by us to creatures which we know first. Hence they have a mode of signification which belongs to creatures, as said above (Article 3).

Reply to Objection 1. This objection refers to the imposition of the name.

Reply to Objection 2. The same rule does not apply to metaphorical and to other names, as said above.

Reply to Objection 3. This objection would be valid if these names were applied to God only as cause, and not also essentially, for instance as "healthy" is applied to medicine.

Article 7. Whether names which imply relation to creatures are predicated of God temporally?

Objection 1. It seems that names which imply relation to creatures are not predicated of God temporally. For all such names signify the divine substance, as is universally held. Hence also Ambrose (De Fide i) that this name "Lord" is the name of power, which is the divine substance; and "Creator" signifies the action of God, which is His essence. Now the divine substance is not temporal, but eternal. Therefore these names are not applied to God temporally, but eternally.

Objection 2. Further, that to which something applies temporally can be described as made; for what is white temporally is made white. But to make does no apply to God. Therefore nothing can be predicated of God temporally.

Objection 3. Further, if any names are applied to God temporally as implying relation to creatures, the same rule holds good of all things that imply relation to creatures. But some names are spoken of God implying relation of God to creatures from eternity; for from eternity He knew and loved the creature, according to the word: "I have loved thee with an everlasting love" (Jeremiah 31:3). Therefore also other names implying relation to creatures, as "Lord" and "Creator," are applied to God from eternity.

Objection 4. Further, names of this kind signify relation. Therefore that relation must be something in God, or in the creature only. But it cannot be that it is something in the creature only, for in that case God would be called "Lord" from the opposite relation which is in creatures; and nothing is named from its opposite. Therefore the relation must be something in God also. But nothing temporal can be in God, for He is above time. Therefore these names are not applied to God temporally.

Objection 5. Further, a thing is called relative from relation; for instance lord from lordship, as white from whiteness. Therefore if the relation of lordship is not really in God, but only in idea, it follows that God is not really Lord, which is plainly false.

Objection 6. Further, in relative things which are not simultaneous in nature, one can exist without the other; as a thing knowable can exist without the knowledge of it, as the Philosopher says (Praedic. v). But relative things which are said of God and creatures are not simultaneous in nature. Therefore a relation can be predicated of God to the creature even without the existence of the creature; and thus these names "Lord" and "Creator" are predicated of God from eternity, and not temporally.

On the contrary, Augustine says (De Trin. v) that this relative appellation "Lord" is applied to God temporally.

I answer that, The names which import relation to creatures are applied to God temporally, and not from eternity.

To see this we must learn that some have said that relation is not a reality, but only an idea. But this is plainly seen to be false from the very fact that things themselves have a mutual natural order and habitude. Nevertheless it is necessary to know that since relation has two extremes, it happens in three ways that a relation is real or logical. Sometimes from both extremes it is an idea only, as when mutual order or habitude can only go between things in the apprehension of reason; as when we say a thing "the same as itself." For reason apprehending one thing twice regards it as two; thus it apprehends a certain habitude of a thing to itself. And the same applies to relations between "being" and "non-being" formed by reason, apprehending "non-being" as an extreme. The same is true of relations that follow upon an act of reason, as genus and species, and the like.

Now there are other relations which are realities as regards both extremes, as when for instance a habitude exists between two things according to some reality that belongs to both; as is clear of all relations, consequent upon quantity; as great and small, double and half, and the like; for quantity exists in both extremes: and the same applies to relations consequent upon action and passion, as motive power and the movable thing, father and son, and the like.

Again, sometimes a relation in one extreme may be a reality, while in the other extreme it is an idea only; and this happens whenever two extremes are not of one order; as sense and science refer respectively to sensible things and to intellectual things; which, inasmuch as they are realities existing in nature, are outside the order of sensible and intellectual existence. Therefore in science and in sense a real relation exists, because they are ordered either to the knowledge or to the sensible perception of things; whereas the things looked at in themselves are outside this order, and hence in them there is no real relation to science and sense, but only in idea, inasmuch as the intellect apprehends them as terms of the relations of science and sense. Hence the Philosopher says (Metaph. v) that they are called relative, not forasmuch as they are related to other things, but as others are related to them. Likewise for instance, "on the right" is not applied to a column, unless it stands as regards an animal on the right side; which relation is not really in the column, but in the animal.

Since therefore God is outside the whole order of creation, and all creatures are ordered to Him, and not conversely, it is manifest that creatures are really related to God Himself; whereas in God there is no real relation to creatures, but a relation only in idea, inasmuch as creatures are referred to Him. Thus there is nothing to prevent these names which import relation to the creature from being predicated of God temporally, not by reason of any change in Him, but by reason of the change of the creature; as a column is on the right of an animal, without change in itself, but by change in the animal.

Reply to Objection 1. Some relative names are imposed to signify the relative habitudes themselves, as "master" and "servant," "father," and "son," and the like, and these relatives are called predicamental [secundum esse]. But others are imposed to signify the things from which ensue certain habitudes, as the mover and the thing moved, the head and the thing that has a head, and the like: and these relatives are called transcendental [secundum dici]. Thus, there is the same two-fold difference in divine names. For some signify the habitude itself to the creature, as "Lord," and these do not signify the divine substance directly, but indirectly, in so far as they presuppose the divine substance; as dominion presupposes power, which is the divine substance. Others signify the divine essence directly, and consequently the corresponding habitudes, as "Saviour," "Creator," and suchlike; and these signify the action of God, which is His essence. Yet both names are said of God temporarily so far as they imply a habitude either principally or consequently, but not as signifying the essence, either directly or indirectly.

Reply to Objection 2. As relations applied to God temporally are only in God in our idea, so, "to become" or "to be made" are applied to God only in idea, with no change in Him, as for instance when we say, "Lord, Thou art become [Douay: 'hast been'] our refuge" (Psalm 89:1).

Reply to Objection 3. The operation of the intellect and the will is in the operator, therefore names signifying relations following upon the action of the intellect or will, are applied to God from eternity; whereas those following upon the actions proceeding according to our mode of thinking to external effects are applied to God temporally, as "Saviour," "Creator," and the like.

Reply to Objection 4. Relations signified by these names which are applied to God temporally, are in God only in idea; but the opposite relations in creatures are real. Nor is it incongruous that God should be denominated from relations really existing in the thing, yet so that the opposite relations in God should also be understood by us at the same time; in the sense that God is spoken of relatively to the creature, inasmuch as the creature is related to Him: thus the Philosopher says (Metaph. v) that the object is said to be knowable relatively because knowledge relates to it.

Reply to Objection 5. Since God is related to the creature for the reason that the creature is related to Him: and since the relation of subjection is real in the creature, it follows that God is Lord not in idea only, but in reality; for He is called Lord according to the manner in which the creature is subject to Him.

Reply to Objection 6. To know whether relations are simultaneous by nature or otherwise, it is not necessary by nature or otherwise of things to which they belong but the meaning of the relations themselves. For if one in its idea includes another, and vice versa, then they are simultaneous by nature: as double and half, father and son, and the like. But if one in its idea includes another, and not vice versa, they are not simultaneous by nature. This applies to science and its object; for the object knowable is considered as a potentiality, and the science as a habit, or as an act. Hence the knowable object in its mode of signification exists before science, but if the same object is considered in act, then it is simultaneous with science in act; for the object known is nothing as such unless it is known. Thus, though God is prior to the creature, still because the signification of Lord includes the idea of a servant and vice versa, these two relative terms, "Lord" and "servant," are simultaneous by nature. Hence, God was not "Lord" until He had a creature subject to Himself.

Article 8. Whether this name "God" is a name of the nature?

Objection 1. It seems that this name, "God," is not a name of the nature. For Damascene says (De Fide Orth. 1) that "God Theos is so called from the theein [which means to care of] and to cherish all things; or from the aithein, that is to burn, for our God is a fire consuming all malice; or from theasthai, which means to consider all things." But all these names belong to operation. Therefore this name "God" signifies His operation and not His nature.

Objection 2. Further, a thing is named by us as we know it. But the divine nature is unknown to us. Therefore this name "God" does not signify the divine nature.

On the contrary, Ambrose says (De Fide i) that "God" is a name of the nature.

I answer that, Whence a name is imposed, and what the name signifies are not always the same thing. For as we know substance from its properties and operations, so we name substance sometimes for its operation, or its property; e.g. we name the substance of a stone from its act, as for instance that it hurts the foot [loedit pedem]; but still this name is not meant to signify the particular action, but the stone's substance. The things, on the other hand, known to us in themselves, such as heat, cold, whiteness and the like, are not named from other things. Hence as regards such things the meaning of the name and its source are the same.

Because therefore God is not known to us in His nature, but is made known to us from His operations or effects, we name Him from these, as said in 1; hence this name "God" is a name of operation so far as relates to the source of its meaning. For this name is imposed from His universal providence over all things; since all who speak of God intend to name God as exercising providence over all; hence Dionysius says (Div. Nom. ii), "The Deity watches over all with perfect providence and goodness." But taken from this operation, this name "God" is imposed to signify the divine nature.

Reply to Objection 1. All that Damascene says refers to providence; which is the source of the signification of the name "God."

Reply to Objection 2. We can name a thing according to the knowledge we have of its nature from its properties and effects. Hence because we can know what stone is in itself from its property, this name "stone" signifies the nature of the stone itself; for it signifies the definition of stone, by which we know what it is, for the idea which the name signifies is the definition, as is said in Metaph. iv. Now from the divine effects we cannot know the divine nature in itself, so as to know what it is; but only by way of eminence, and by way of causality, and of negation as stated above (Question 12, Article 12). Thus the name "God" signifies the divine nature, for this name was imposed to signify something existing above all things, the principle of all things and removed from all things; for those who name God intend to signify all this.

Article 9. Whether this name "God" is communicable?

Objection 1. It seems that this name "God" is communicable. For whosoever shares in the thing signified by a name shares in the name itself. But this name "God" signifies the divine nature, which is communicable to others, according to the words, "He hath given us great [Vulgate: 'most great'] and precious promises, that by these we [Vulgate: 'ye'] may be made partakers of the divine nature" (2 Peter 1:4). Therefore this name "God" can be communicated to others.

Objection 2. Further, only proper names are not communicable. Now this name "God" is not a proper, but an appellative noun; which appears from the fact that it has a plural, according to the text, "I have said, You are gods" (Psalm 81:6). Therefore this name "God" is communicable.

Objection 3. Further, this name "God" comes from operation, as explained. But other names given to God from His operations or effects are communicable; as "good," "wise," and the like. Therefore this name "God" is communicable.

On the contrary, It is written: "They gave the incommunicable name to wood and stones" (Wisdom 14:21), in reference to the divine name. Therefore this name "God" is incommunicable.

I answer that, A name is communicable in two ways: properly, and by similitude. It is properly communicable in the sense that its whole signification can be given to many; by similitude it is communicable according to some part of the signification of the name. For instance this name "lion" is properly communicable to all things of the same nature as "lion"; by similitude it is communicable to those who participate in the nature of a lion, as for instance by courage, or strength, and those who thus participate are called lions metaphorically. To know, however, what names are properly communicable, we must consider that every form existing in the singular subject, by which it is individualized, is common to many either in reality, or in idea; as human nature is common to many in reality, and in idea; whereas the nature of the sun is not common to many in reality, but only in idea; for the nature of the sun can be understood as existing in many subjects; and the reason is because the mind understands the nature of every species by abstraction from the singular. Hence to be in one singular subject or in many is outside the idea of the nature of the species. So, given the idea of a species, it can be understood as existing in many. But the singular, from the fact that it is singular, is divided off from all others. Hence every name imposed to signify any singular thing is incommunicable both in reality and idea; for the plurality of this individual thing cannot be; nor can it be conceived in idea. Hence no name signifying any individual thing is properly communicable to many, but only by way of similitude; as for instance a person can be called "Achilles" metaphorically, forasmuch as he may possess something of the properties of Achilles, such as strength. On the other hand, forms which are individualized not by any "suppositum," but by and of themselves, as being subsisting forms, if understood as they are in themselves, could not be communicable either in reality or in idea; but only perhaps by way of similitude, as was said of individuals. Forasmuch as we are unable to understand simple self-subsisting forms as they really are, we understand them as compound things having forms in matter; therefore, as was said in the first article, we give them concrete names signifying a nature existing in some "suppositum." Hence, so far as concerns images, the same rules apply to names we impose to signify the nature of compound things as to names given to us to signify simple subsisting natures.

Since, then, this name "God" is given to signify the divine nature as stated above (Article 8), and since the divine nature cannot be multiplied as shown above (Question 11, Article 3), it follows that this name "God" is incommunicable in reality, but communicable in opinion; just in the same way as this name "sun" would be communicable according to the opinion of those who say there are many suns. Therefore, it is written: "You served them who by nature are not gods," (Galatians 4:8), and a gloss adds, "Gods not in nature, but in human opinion." Nevertheless this name "God" is communicable, not in its whole signification, but in some part of it by way of similitude; so that those are called gods who share in divinity by likeness, according to the text, "I have said, You are gods" (Psalm 81:6).

But if any name were given to signify God not as to His nature but as to His "suppositum," accordingly as He is considered as "this something," that name would be absolutely incommunicable; as, for instance, perhaps the Tetragrammaton among the Hebrew; and this is like giving a name to the sun as signifying this individual thing.

Reply to Objection 1. The divine nature is only communicable according to the participation of some similitude.

Reply to Objection 2. This name "God" is an appellative name, and not a proper name, for it signifies the divine nature in the possessor; although God Himself in reality is neither universal nor particular. For names do not follow upon the mode of being in things, but upon the mode of being as it is in our mind. And yet it is incommunicable according to the truth of the thing, as was said above concerning the name "sun."

Reply to Objection 3. These names "good," "wise," and the like, are imposed from the perfections proceeding from God to creatures; but they do not signify the divine nature, but rather signify the perfections themselves absolutely; and therefore they are in truth communicable to many. But this name "God" is given to God from His own proper operation, which we experience continually, to signify the divine nature.

Article 10. Whether this name "God" is applied to God univocally by nature, by participation, and according to opinion?

Objection 1. It seems that this name "God" is applied to God univocally by nature, by participation, and according to opinion. For where a diverse signification exists, there is no contradiction of affirmation and negation; for equivocation prevents contradiction. But a Catholic who says: "An idol is not God," contradicts a pagan who says: "An idol is God." Therefore GOD in both senses is spoken of univocally.

Objection 2. Further, as an idol is God in opinion, and not in truth, so the enjoyment of carnal pleasures is called happiness in opinion, and not in truth. But this name "beatitude" is applied univocally to this supposed happiness, and also to true happiness. Therefore also this name "God" is applied univocally to the true God, and to God also in opinion.

Objection 3. Further, names are called univocal because they contain one idea. Now when a Catholic says: "There is one God," he understands by the name God an omnipotent being, and one venerated above all; while the heathen understands the same when he says: "An idol is God." Therefore this name "God" is applied univocally to both.

On the contrary, The idea in the intellect is the likeness of what is in the thing as is said in Peri Herm. i. But the word "animal" applied to a true animal, and to a picture of one, is equivocal. Therefore this name "God" applied to the true God and to God in opinion is applied equivocally.

Further, No one can signify what he does not know. But the heathen does not know the divine nature. So when he says an idol is God, he does not signify the true Deity. On the other hand, A Catholic signifies the true Deity when he says that there is one God. Therefore this name "God" is not applied univocally, but equivocally to the true God, and to God according to opinion.

I answer that, This name "God" in the three aforesaid significations is taken neither univocally nor equivocally, but analogically. This is apparent from this reason: Univocal terms mean absolutely the same thing, but equivocal terms absolutely different; whereas in analogical terms a word taken in one signification must be placed in the definition of the same word taken in other senses; as, for instance, "being" which is applied to "substance" is placed in the definition of being as applied to "accident"; and "healthy" applied to animal is placed in the definition of healthy as applied to urine and medicine. For urine is the sign of health in the animal, and medicine is the cause of health.

The same applies to the question at issue. For this name "God," as signifying the true God, includes the idea of God when it is used to denote God in opinion, or participation. For when we name anyone god by participation, we understand by the name of god some likeness of the true God. Likewise, when we call an idol god, by this name god we understand and signify something which men think is God; thus it is manifest that the name has different meanings, but that one of them is comprised in the other significations. Hence it is manifestly said analogically.

Reply to Objection 1. The multiplication of names does not depend on the predication of the name, but on the signification: for this name "man," of whomsoever it is predicated, whether truly or falsely, is predicated in one sense. But it would be multiplied if by the name "man" we meant to signify different things; for instance, if one meant to signify by this name "man" what man really is, and another meant to signify by the same name a stone, or something else. Hence it is evident that a Catholic saying that an idol is not God contradicts the pagan asserting that it is God; because each of them uses this name GOD to signify the true God. For when the pagan says an idol is God, he does not use this name as meaning God in opinion, for he would then speak the truth, as also Catholics sometimes use the name in the sense, as in the Psalm, "All the gods of the Gentiles are demons" (Psalm 95:5).

The same remark applies to the Second and Third Objections. For these reasons proceed from the different predication of the name, and not from its various significations.

Reply to Objection 4. The term "animal" applied to a true and a pictured animal is not purely equivocal; for the Philosopher takes equivocal names in a large sense, including analogous names; because also being, which is predicated analogically, is sometimes said to be predicated equivocally of different predicaments.

Reply to Objection 5. Neither a Catholic nor a pagan knows the very nature of God as it is in itself; but each one knows it according to some idea of causality, or excellence, or remotion (12, 12). So a pagan can take this name "God" in the same way when he says an idol is God, as the Catholic does in saying an idol is not

God. But if anyone should be quite ignorant of God altogether, he could not even name Him, unless, perhaps, as we use names the meaning of which we know not.

## Article 11. Whether this name, HE WHO IS, is the most proper name of God?

Objection 1. It seems that this name HE WHO IS is not the most proper name of God. For this name "God" is an incommunicable name. But this name HE WHO IS, is not an incommunicable name. Therefore this name HE WHO IS is not the most proper name of God.

Objection 2. Further, Dionysius says (Div. Nom. iii) that "the name of good excellently manifests all the processions of God." But it especially belongs to God to be the universal principle of all things. Therefore this name "good" is supremely proper to God, and not this name HE WHO IS.

Objection 3. Further, every divine name seems to imply relation to creatures, for God is known to us only through creatures. But this name HE WHO IS imports no relation to creatures. Therefore this name HE WHO IS is not the most applicable to God.

On the contrary, It is written that when Moses asked, "If they should say to me, What is His name? what shall I say to them?" The Lord answered him, "Thus shalt thou say to them, HE WHO IS hath sent me to you" (Exodus 3:13-14). Therefore this name HE WHO IS most properly belongs to God.

I answer that, This name HE WHO IS is most properly applied to God, for three reasons:

First, because of its signification. For it does not signify form, but simply existence itself. Hence since the existence of God is His essence itself, which can be said of no other (3, 4), it is clear that among other names this one specially denominates God, for everything is denominated by its form.

Secondly, on account of its universality. For all other names are either less universal, or, if convertible with it, add something above it at least in idea; hence in a certain way they inform and determine it. Now our intellect cannot know the essence of God itself in this life, as it is in itself, but whatever mode it applies in determining what it understands about God, it falls short of the mode of what God is in Himself. Therefore the less determinate the names are, and the more universal and absolute they are, the more properly they are applied to God. Hence Damascene says (De Fide Orth. i) that, "HE WHO IS, is the principal of all names applied to God; for comprehending all in itself, it contains existence itself as an infinite and indeterminate sea of substance." Now by any other name some mode of substance is determined, whereas this name HE WHO IS, determines no mode of being, but is indeterminate to all; and therefore it denominates the "infinite ocean of substance."

Thirdly, from its consignification, for it signifies present existence; and this above all properly applies to God, whose existence knows not past or future, as Augustine says (De Trin. v).

Reply to Objection 1. This name HE WHO IS is the name of God more properly than this name "God," as regards its source, namely, existence; and as regards the mode of signification and consignification, as said above. But as regards the object intended by the name, this name "God" is more proper, as it is imposed to signify the divine nature; and still more proper is the Tetragrammaton, imposed to signify the substance of God itself, incommunicable and, if one may so speak, singular.

Reply to Objection 2. This name "good" is the principal name of God in so far as He is a cause, but not absolutely; for existence considered absolutely comes before the idea of cause.

Reply to Objection 3. It is not necessary that all the divine names should import relation to creatures, but it suffices that they be imposed from some perfections flowing from God to creatures. Among these the first is existence, from which comes this name, HE WHO IS.

Article 12. Whether affirmative propositions can be formed about God?

Objection 1. It seems that affirmative propositions cannot be formed about God. For Dionysius says (Coel. Hier. ii) that "negations about God are true; but affirmations are vague."

Objection 2. Further, Boethius says (De Trin. ii) that "a simple form cannot be a subject." But God is the most absolutely simple form, as shown (3): therefore He cannot be a subject. But everything about which an affirmative proposition is made is taken as a subject. Therefore an affirmative proposition cannot be formed about God.

Objection 3. Further, every intellect is false which understands a thing otherwise than as it is. But God has existence without any composition as shown above (Question 3, Article 7). Therefore since every affirmative intellect understands something as compound, it follows that a true affirmative proposition about God cannot be made.

On the contrary, What is of faith cannot be false. But some affirmative propositions are of faith; as that God is Three and One; and that He is omnipotent. Therefore true affirmative propositions can be formed about God.

I answer that, True affirmative propositions can be formed about God. To prove this we must know that in every true affirmative proposition the predicate and the subject signify in some way the same thing in reality, and different things in idea. And this appears to be the case both in propositions which have an accidental predicate, and in those which have an essential predicate. For it is manifest that "man" and "white" are the same in subject, and different in idea; for the idea of man is one thing, and that of whiteness is another. The same applies when I say, "man is an animal"; since the same thing which is man is truly animal; for in the same "suppositum" there is sensible nature by reason of which he is called animal, and the rational nature by reason of which he is called man; hence here again predicate and subject are the same as to "suppositum," but different as to idea. But in propositions where one same thing is predicated of itself, the same rule in some way applies, inasmuch as the intellect draws to the "suppositum" what it places in the subject; and what it places in the predicate it draws to the nature of the form existing in the "suppositum"; according to the saying that "predicates are to be taken formally, and subjects materially." To this diversity in idea corresponds the plurality of predicate and subject, while the intellect signifies the identity of the thing by the composition itself.

God, however, as considered in Himself, is altogether one and simple, yet our intellect knows Him by different conceptions because it cannot see Him as He is in Himself. Nevertheless, although it understands Him under different conceptions, it knows that one and the same simple object corresponds to its conceptions. Therefore the plurality of predicate and subject represents the plurality of idea; and the intellect represents the unity by composition.

Reply to Objection 1. Dionysius says that the affirmations about God are vague or, according to another translation, "incongruous," inasmuch as no name can be applied to God according to its mode of signification.

Reply to Objection 2. Our intellect cannot comprehend simple subsisting forms, as they really are in themselves; but it apprehends them as compound things in which there is something taken as subject and something that is inherent. Therefore it apprehends the simple form as a subject, and attributes something else to it.

Reply to Objection 3. This proposition, "The intellect understanding anything otherwise than it is, is false," can be taken in two senses, accordingly as this adverb "otherwise" determines the word "understanding" on the part of the thing understood, or on the part of the one who understands. Taken as referring to the thing understood, the proposition is true, and the meaning is: Any intellect which understands that the thing is otherwise than it is, is false. But this does not hold in the present case; because our intellect, when forming a proposition about God, does not affirm that He is composite, but that He is simple. But taken as referring to the one who understands, the proposition is false. For the mode of the intellect in understanding is different from the mode of the thing in its essence. Since it is clear that our intellect understands material things below itself in an immaterial manner; not that it understands them to be immaterial things; but its manner of understanding is immaterial. Likewise, when it understands simple things above itself, it understands them according to its own mode, which is in a composite manner; yet not so as to understand them to be composite things. And thus our intellect is not false in forming composition in its ideas concerning God.

## On the Eternity of the World
### By St. Thomas Aquinas

Let us assume, in accordance with the Catholic faith, that the world had a beginning in time. The question still arises whether the world could have always existed, and to explain the truth of this matter, we should first distinguish where we agree with our opponents from where we disagree with them. If someone holds that something besides God could have always existed, in the sense that there could be something always existing and yet not made by God, then we differ with him: such an abominable error is contrary not only to the faith but also to the teachings of the philosophers, who confess and prove that everything that in any way exists cannot exist unless it be caused by him who supremely and most truly has existence. However, someone may hold that there has always existed something that, nevertheless, had been wholly caused by God, and thus we ought to determine whether this position is tenable.

If it be impossible that something caused by God has always existed, it will be so either because God could not make something that has always existed or because such a thing could not be made, regardless of God's ability to make it. [3] As to the first, all parties agree that, in view of his infinite power, God could have made something that has always existed. [4] It remains to be seen, therefore, whether something that has always existed can be made.

If such a thing cannot be made, the impossibility will arise for one of two reasons: either because of an absence of a passive potentiality or because of some contradiction between the ideas involved. [5] In regard to the first, notice that before an angel is made, we may say, in a certain manner of speaking, that the angel cannot be made, [6] since no passive potentiality precedes its being, for an angel is not made from pre-existing matter. Nevertheless, God was able to make the angel, and he was able to cause the angel to be made, for God made it, and it was made. Therefore, if we understand "being made" or "being caused" as implying the pre-existence of a passive potentiality, then it should to be conceded, according to faith, that something caused cannot always exist, for it would then follow that a passive potentiality has always existed, and this is heretical. But since a passive potentiality need not precede in time whatever God may make, it does not follow that God could not have made something that has always existed.

In regard to the second, someone may hold that something that has always existed cannot be made because such a thing is self-contradictory, just as an affirmation and a denial cannot be made simultaneously true. Still, some people say that God can even make self-contradictories things, while others say God cannot make such things, for such things are actually nothing. Clearly, God cannot make such things come to be, for the assumption that such a thing exists immediately refutes itself. Nevertheless, if we allow that God can make such things come to be, the position is not heretical, though I believe it is false, just as the proposition that the past did not occur is false, about which Augustine says (XXVI Contra Faustum cap. 5), "Anyone who says, 'If God is omnipotent, let him make what has happened not to have happened,' does not realize that he is saying, 'If God is omnipotent, let him make true things false insofar as they are true.'" [PL 42, 481.] Nevertheless, certain great men have piously maintained that God can make past events not to have happened, and this was not reputed to be heretical.

We thus ought to determine whether there is any contradiction between these two ideas, namely, to be made by God and to have always existed. And, whatever may be the truth of this matter, it will not be heretical to say that God can make something created by him to have always existed, though I believe that if there were a contradiction involved in asserting this, the assertion would be false. However, if there is no contradiction involved, then it is neither false nor impossible that God could have made something that has always existed, and it will be an error to say otherwise. For, if there is no contradiction, we ought to admit that God could have made something that has always existed, for it would be clearly derogatory to the divine omnipotence, which exceeds every thought and power, to say that we creatures can conceive of something that God is unable to make. (Nor are sins an instance to the contrary, for, considered in themselves, they are nothing.) In this, therefore, the entire question consists: whether to be wholly created by God and not to have a beginning in time are contradictory terms.

That they are not contradictory can be shown as follows. If they are contradictory, this is for one or both of these two reasons: either because the agent cause must precede the effect in time, or because non-being must precede the effect in time, for we say that what God creates comes to be out of nothing.

First, we should show that it is not necessary that an agent cause, in this case God, precede in time that which he causes, if he should so will. This can be shown in several ways. First, no cause instantaneously producing its effect necessarily precedes the effect in time. God, however, is a cause that produces effects not through motion but instantaneously. Therefore, it is not necessary that he precede his effects in time. The first premise is proved inductively from all instantaneous changes, as, for example, with illumination and other such things. But the premise may be proved by reason as well.

For, at whatever instant a thing exists, at that instant it can begin to act, as is clear in the case of all things that come to be by generation: in the very instant at which there is fire, the fire heats. But in an instantaneous action, the beginning and the end of the action are simultaneous, indeed identical, as is clear in the case of all indivisible things. Hence, at whatever moment an agent instantaneously producing an effect exists, the end of its action can exist as well. The end of the action, however, is simultaneous with the thing made. Therefore, there is no contradiction if we suppose that a cause instantaneously producing an effect does not precede its effect in time. A contradiction does obtain if the cause involved is one that produces its effects through motion, for the beginning of the motion precedes in time the end of the motion. Since people are accustomed to considering the type of cause that produces effects through motion, they do not easily grasp that an agent cause may fail to precede its effect in time, and so, having limited experience, they easily make a false generalization.

Nor can the conclusion be avoided by saying that God is an agent cause that acts voluntarily, for neither the will nor the voluntary agent need precede its effect in time, unless the agent cause acts from deliberation, which we take to be absent in God.

Further, a cause that produces the whole substance of a thing does not, in producing a whole substance, act in a less perfect way than does a cause that produces just a form in producing the form. On the contrary, it acts in a much more perfect way, since it does not act by educing from the potentiality of matter, as do causes that merely produce forms. However, some causes that produce just forms are such that, whenever the cause exists, the form produced by it exists as well, as is clear in the case of illumination by the sun. Therefore, much more can God, who produces the whole substance of things, make something caused by him exist whenever he himself exists.

Further, if, granted a cause, its effect does not immediately exist as well, this can only be because something complementary to that cause is lacking: the complete cause and the thing caused are simultaneous. God, however, never lacks any kind of complementary cause in order to produce an effect. Therefore, at any instant at which God exists, so too can his effects, and thus God need not precede his effects in time.

Further, the will of the voluntary agent in no way diminishes his power, and this is especially true with God. But all those who try to answer the arguments of Aristotle (who held that something caused by God had always existed, since like always makes like) [7] say that the conclusion would follow if God were not a voluntary agent. Therefore, allowing that God is a voluntary agent, it still follows that he can make something that he has made never fail to exist. Thus, although God cannot make contradictories true, we have shown that there is no contradiction in saying that an agent cause does not precede its effect in time.

It remains to be seen, then, whether there is a contradiction in saying that something made has always existed, on the grounds that it may be necessary that its non-being precede it in time, for we say that it is made out of nothing. But that there is no contradiction here is shown by Anselm in his explanation of what it means to say that a creature is made out of nothing. He says (Monologion cap. 8), "The third sense in which we can say that something is made out of nothing is this: we understand that something is made, but that there is not something from which it is made. In a similar way, we say that someone who is sad without reason is sad about nothing. We can thus say that all things, except the Supreme Being, are made by him out of nothing in the sense that they are not made out of anything, and no absurdity results." On this understanding of the phrase "out of nothing," therefore, no temporal priority of non-being to being is posited, as there would be if there were first nothing and then later something.

Further, let us even suppose that the preposition "out of" imports some affirmative order of non-being to being, as if the proposition that the creature is made out of nothing meant that the creature is made after nothing. Then this expression "after" certainly implies order, but order is of two kinds: order of time and order of nature. If, therefore, the proper and the particular does not follow from the common and the universal, it will not necessarily follow that, because the creature is made after nothing, non-being is temporally prior to the being of the creature. Rather, it suffices that non-being be prior to being by nature. Now, whatever naturally pertains to something in itself is prior to what that thing only receives from another. A creature does not have being, however, except from another, for, considered in itself, every creature is nothing, and thus, with respect to the creature, non-being is prior to being by nature. Nor does it follow from the creature's always having existed that its being and non-being are ever simultaneous, as if the creature always existed but at some time nothing existed, for the priority is not one of time. Rather, the argument merely requires that the nature of the creature is such that, if the creature were left to itself, it would be nothing. For example, if we should say that the air has always been illuminated by the sun, it would be right to say that the air has always been made lucid by the sun. Thus, since anything that comes to be such-and-such comes to be such-and-such from being not such-and-such, we say that the air is made lucid from being non-lucid, or opaque, not because the air was once non-lucid or opaque, but because the air would be opaque if the sun did not illuminate it. This is clearly the case with the stars and those celestial bodies that are always illuminated by the sun.

Thus it is clear that there is no contradiction in saying that something made by God has always existed. Indeed, if there were some contradiction, it would be amazing that Augustine failed to see it, for exposing such a contradiction would be a most effective way of proving that the world is not eternal, and although Augustine offers many arguments against the eternity of the world in XI and XII De Civitate Dei, he never argues that his opponents' view is contradictory. On the contrary, Augustine seems to hint that there is no contradiction involved. Thus, speaking of the Platonists, he says (X De Civitate Dei cap. 31), "They somehow contemplate a beginning in causation rather than a beginning in time. Imagine, they say, a foot that has been in dust since eternity: a footprint has always been beneath it, and nobody would doubt that the footprint was made by the pressure of the foot. Though neither is prior in time to the other, yet one is made by the other. Likewise, they say, the world and the gods in it have always existed, just as he who made them always existed; yet nevertheless, they were made." [PL 41, 311] Nor does Augustine ever say that this cannot be understood; rather, he proceeds against the Platonists in a totally different way. He says (XI De Civitate Deicap. 4), "Those, however, who admit that the world was made by God but nevertheless want to hold that the world has a beginning in creation but not in time, so that, in some scarcely intelligible way, it has always been made by God, think that they are defending God against a charge of casual rashness."

[PL 41, 319][8] Their position is difficult to understand, however, only for the reason given above in the first argument.

How remarkable it would be that even the most noble of philosophers failed to see a contradiction in the idea that something made by God has always existed. Speaking against the Platonists, Augustine says (XI De Civitate Dei cap. 5), "Here we are contending with those who agree with us that God is the Creator of all bodies and all natures except himself," [PL 41, 320] and then, again about the Platonists, he adds (XI De Civitate Dei cap. 5), "These philosophers surpassed the rest in nobility and authority." [PL 41, 321] Augustine said this even after diligently considering their position that the world has always existed, for they nevertheless thought that it was made by God, and they saw no contradiction between these two ideas. Therefore, those who so subtly perceive the contradiction are solitary men, and with these does wisdom arise. [9]

Still, since certain authorities seem to argue on the side of such men, we ought to show that they base themselves on a weak foundation. Damascene says (I De Fide Orthodoxa cap. 8), "What is made out of nothing is by nature not such that it is coeternal to what has no causal principle and always exists." [PG 94, 814B] Likewise, Hugh of St. Victor says (De Sacramentis I-1 cap. 1), "The ineffable omnipotent power could not have anything coeternal beyond itself that would help it in making." [PL 176, 187B]

But the position of these and similar authorities is made clear by Boethius, who says (V De Consolatione prosa 6), "When some people hear that Plato thought this world neither had a beginning in time nor will ever have an end, they mistakenly conclude that the created world is coeternal with the Creator. However, to be led through the endless life Plato attributes to the world is one thing; to embrace simultaneously the whole presence of endless life is quite another, and it is this latter that is proper to the divine mind." [PL 63, 859B] Thus it does not follow, as some people object, that a creature, even if it had always existed, would be equal to God in duration. For, if "eternal" be understood in this sense, nothing can in any way be coeternal with God, for nothing but God is immutable. As Augustine says (XII De Civitate Dei cap. 15), [10] "Time, since it passes away by its mutability, cannot be coeternal with immutable eternity. Thus, even if the immortality of the angels does not pass away in time (it is neither past, as if it did not exist now; nor is it future, as if it did not yet exist), nevertheless, the angels' motions, by which moments of time are carried along from the future into the past, pass away. Therefore, angels cannot be coeternal with the Creator, in whose motion there is nothing which has been that is not now, nor anything which will later be that is not already." [PL 41, 364-365] Likewise, Augustine says (VIII Super Genesis ad Litteramcap. 23), "Since the nature of the Trinity is wholly unchangeable, it is eternal in such a way that nothing can be coeternal with it," [PL 34, 389] and he uses words to the same effect in XI Confessionum as well. [11]

Those who try to prove that the world could not have always existed even adduce arguments that the philosophers have considered and solved. Chief among these is the argument from the infinity of souls: if the world had always existed, these people argue, there would necessarily be an infinite number of souls. But this argument is not to the point, for God could have made the world without making men or creatures with souls, or he could have made men when in fact he did make them, even if he had made the rest of the world from eternity. In either case, an infinite number of souls would not remain after the bodies had passed away. Furthermore, it has not yet been demonstrated that God cannot cause an infinite number of things to exist simultaneously.

There are other arguments adduced as well, but I refrain from answering them at present, either because they have been suitably answered elsewhere, or because they are so weak that their very weakness lends probability to the opposing view.

NOTES:

[1] This translation follows the Leonine Edition of Aquinas's works, vol. 43 Sancti Thomae De Aquino Opera Omnia 85-89 (Rome 1976).

[2] All persons are licensed to reproduce this translation and the footnotes hereto for personal or educational purposes, provided that the notice of copyright above and this notice are included in their respective entireties in all copies. This license includes reproduction by a commercial entity engaged in the business of providing copying services if such reproduction is made at the behest of a person who would otherwise be licensed under the preceding sentence to reproduce this translation for personal or educational purposes.

[3] Aquinas means that the impossibility may be thought to arise either on the part of God, as if he were unable to make such a thing for lack of power, or on the part of the thing, as if such a thing could not be made because it lacks a pre-existing passive potentiality or because it is self-contradictory.

[4] That is, on the condition that such a thing can be made. In other words, all sides agree that the impossibility of something having always existed, if such there be, does not arise from some lack of power in God.

[5] That is, between "always having existed" and "having been made."

[6] In the sense that there was nothing existing before the angel that would become the angel, as the brass to be made into a statue exists before the statue and becomes the statue.

[7] See II De Generatione et Corruptione cap. 10, 336a 27-28.

[8] PL 41, 319. In the Leonine Edition, Aquinas does not quote the predicate of the independent clause; it does appear in the Parma Edition, and I have chosen to supply it.

[9] Said ironically, the sentence is quite out of character for Aquinas, who courteously conducted the bitterest disputations. Here he is probably alluding to the Vulgate text of Job 12:2, in which Job says, "You are solitary men, and with you wisdom shall die." The difference between "arises" (oritur) and "shall die" (morietur) is small.

[10] So in Aquinas. The chapter divisions in De Civitate Dei are, at this point, somewhat unclear, and, as the editors of the Leonine

Edition suggest, the quoted text is probably from cap. 16. In any event, the quoted material appears at PL 41, 364-365.
[11] See XI Confessionum cap. 30. PL 32, 826.


*Summa Theologica*

Question 19. The will of God

Article 1. Whether there is will in God?

Objection 1. It seems that there is not will in God. For the object of will is the end and the good. But we cannot assign to God any end. Therefore there is not will in God.

Objection 2. Further, will is a kind of appetite. But appetite, as it is directed to things not possessed, implies imperfection, which cannot be imputed to God. Therefore there is not will in God.

Objection 3. Further, according to the Philosopher (De Anima iii, 54), the will moves, and is moved. But God is the first cause of movement, and Himself is unmoved, as proved in Phys. viii, 49. Therefore there is not will in God.

On the contrary, The Apostle says (Romans 12:2): "That you may prove what is the will of God."

I answer that, There is will in God, as there is intellect: since will follows upon intellect. For as natural things have actual existence by their form, so the intellect is actually intelligent by its intelligible form. Now everything has this aptitude towards its natural form, that when it has it not, it tends towards it; and when it has it, it is at rest therein. It is the same with every natural perfection, which is a natural good. This aptitude to good in things without knowledge is called natural appetite. Whence also intellectual natures have a like aptitude as apprehended through its intelligible form; so as to rest therein when possessed, and when not possessed to seek to possess it, both of which pertain to the will. Hence in every intellectual being there is will, just as in every sensible being there is animal appetite. And so there must be will in God, since there is intellect in Him. And as His intellect is His own existence, so is His will.

Reply to Objection 1. Although nothing apart from God is His end, yet He Himself is the end with respect to all things made by Him. And this by His essence, for by His essence He is good, as shown above (Question 6, Article 3): for the end has the aspect of good.

Reply to Objection 2. Will in us belongs to the appetitive part, which, although named from appetite, has not for its only act the seeking what it does not possess; but also the loving and the delighting in what it does possess. In this respect will is said to be in God, as having always good which is its object, since, as already said, it is not distinct from His essence.

Reply to Objection 3. A will of which the principal object is a good outside itself, must be moved by another; but the object of the divine will is His goodness, which is His essence. Hence, since the will of God is His essence, it is not moved by another than itself, but by itself alone, in the same sense as understanding and willing are said to be movement. This is what Plato meant when he said that the first mover moves itself.

Article 2. Whether God wills things apart from Himself?

Objection 1. It seems that God does not will things apart from Himself. For the divine will is the divine existence. But God is not other than Himself. Therefore He does not will things other than Himself.

Objection 2. Further, the willed moves the willer, as the appetible the appetite, as stated in De Anima iii, 54. If, therefore, God wills anything apart from Himself, His will must be moved by another; which is impossible.

Objection 3. Further, if what is willed suffices the willer, he seeks nothing beyond it. But His own goodness suffices God, and completely satisfies His will. Therefore God does not will anything apart from Himself.

Objection 4. Further, acts of will are multiplied in proportion to the number of their objects. If, therefore, God wills Himself and things apart from Himself, it follows that the act of His will is manifold, and consequently His existence, which is His will. But this is impossible. Therefore God does not will things apart from Himself.

On the contrary, The Apostle says (1 Thessalonians 4:3): "This is the will of God, your sanctification."

I answer that, God wills not only Himself, but other things apart from Himself. This is clear from the comparison which we made above (Article 1). For natural things have a natural inclination not only towards their own proper good, to acquire it if not possessed, and, if possessed, to rest therein; but also to spread abroad their own good amongst others, so far as possible. Hence we see that every agent, in so far as it is perfect and in act, produces its like. It pertains, therefore, to the nature of the will to communicate as far as possible to others the good possessed; and especially does this pertain to the divine will, from which all perfection is derived in some kind of likeness. Hence, if natural things, in so far as they are perfect, communicate their good to others, much more does it appertain to the divine will to communicate by likeness its own good to others as much as possible. Thus, then, He wills both Himself to be, and other things to be; but Himself as the end, and other things as ordained to that end; inasmuch as it befits the divine goodness that other things should be partakers therein.

Reply to Objection 1. The divine will is God's own existence essentially, yet they differ in aspect, according to the different ways of understanding them and expressing them, as is clear from what has already been said (13, 4). For when we say that God exists, no relation to any other object is implied, as we do imply when we say that God wills. Therefore, although He is not anything apart from Himself, yet He does will things apart from Himself.

Reply to Objection 2. In things willed for the sake of the end, the whole reason for our being moved is the end, and this it is that moves the will, as most clearly appears in things willed only for the sake of the end. He who wills to take a bitter draught, in doing so wills nothing else than health; and this alone moves his will. It is different with one who takes a draught that is pleasant, which anyone may will to do, not only for the sake of health, but also for its own sake. Hence, although God wills things apart from Himself only for the sake of the end, which is His own goodness, it does not follow that anything else moves His will, except His goodness. So, as He understands things apart from Himself by understanding His own essence, so He wills things apart from Himself by willing His own goodness.

Reply to Objection 3. From the fact that His own goodness suffices the divine will, it does not follow that it wills nothing apart from itself, but rather that it wills nothing except by reason of its goodness. Thus, too, the divine intellect, though its perfection consists in its very knowledge of the divine essence, yet in that essence knows other things.

Reply to Objection 4. As the divine intellect is one, as seeing the many only in the one, in the same way the divine will is one and simple, as willing the many only through the one, that is, through its own goodness.

## Article 3. Whether whatever God wills He wills necessarily?

Objection 1. It seems that whatever God wills He wills necessarily. For everything eternal is necessary. But whatever God wills, He wills from eternity, for otherwise His will would be mutable. Therefore whatever He wills, He wills necessarily.

Objection 2. Further, God wills things apart from Himself, inasmuch as He wills His own goodness. Now God wills His own goodness necessarily. Therefore He wills things apart from Himself necessarily.

Objection 3. Further, whatever belongs to the nature of God is necessary, for God is of Himself necessary being, and the principle of all necessity, as above shown (2, 3). But it belongs to His nature to will whatever He wills; since in God there can be nothing over and above His nature as stated in Metaph. v, 6. Therefore whatever He wills, He wills necessarily.

Objection 4. Further, being that is not necessary, and being that is possible not to be, are one and the same thing. If, therefore, God does not necessarily will a thing that He wills, it is possible for Him not to will it, and therefore possible for Him to will what He does not will. And so the divine will is contingent upon one or the other of two things, and imperfect, since everything contingent is imperfect and mutable.

Objection 5. Further, on the part of that which is indifferent to one or the other of two things, no action results unless it is inclined to one or the other by some other power, as the Commentator [Averroes] says in Phys. ii. If, then, the Will of God is indifferent with regard to anything, it follows that His determination to act comes from another; and thus He has some cause prior to Himself.

Objection 6. Further, whatever God knows, He knows necessarily. But as the divine knowledge is His essence, so is the divine will. Therefore whatever God wills, He wills necessarily.

On the contrary, The Apostle says (Ephesians 1:11): "Who worketh all things according to the counsel of His will." Now, what we work according to the counsel of the will, we do not will necessarily. Therefore God does not will necessarily whatever He wills.

I answer that, There are two ways in which a thing is said to be necessary, namely, absolutely, and by supposition. We judge a thing to be absolutely necessary from the relation of the terms, as when the predicate forms part of the definition of the subject: thus it is absolutely necessary that man is an animal. It is the same when the subject forms part of the notion of the predicate; thus it is absolutely necessary that a number must be odd or even. In this way it is not necessary that Socrates sits: wherefore it is not necessary absolutely, though it may be so by supposition; for, granted that he is sitting, he must necessarily sit, as long as he is sitting. Accordingly as to things willed by God, we must observe that He wills something of absolute necessity: but this is not true of all that He wills. For the divine will has a necessary relation to the divine goodness, since that is its proper object. Hence God wills His own goodness necessarily, even as we will our own happiness necessarily, and as any other faculty has necessary relation to its proper and principal object, for instance the sight to color, since it tends to it by its own nature. But God wills things apart from Himself in so far as they are ordered to His own goodness as their end. Now in willing an end we do not necessarily will things that conduce to it, unless they are such that the end cannot be attained without them; as, we will to take food to preserve life, or to take ship in order to cross the sea. But we do not necessarily will things without which the end is attainable, such as a horse for a journey which we can take on foot, for we can make the journey without one. The same applies to other means. Hence, since the goodness of God is perfect, and can exist without other things inasmuch as no perfection can accrue to Him from them, it follows that His willing things apart from Himself is not absolutely necessary. Yet it can be necessary by supposition, for supposing that He wills a thing, then He is unable not to will it, as His will cannot change.

Reply to Objection 1. From the fact that God wills from eternity whatever He wills, it does not follow that He wills it necessarily; except by supposition.

Reply to Objection 2. Although God necessarily wills His own goodness, He does not necessarily will things willed on account of His goodness; for it can exist without other things.

Reply to Objection 3. It is not natural to God to will any of those other things that He does not will necessarily; and yet it is not unnatural or contrary to His nature, but voluntary.

Reply to Objection 4. Sometimes a necessary cause has a non-necessary relation to an effect; owing to a deficiency in the effect, and not in the cause. Even so, the sun's power has a non-necessary relation to some contingent events on this earth, owing to a defect not in the solar power, but in the effect that proceeds not necessarily from the cause. In the same way, that God does not necessarily will some of the things that He wills, does not result from defect in the divine will, but from a defect belonging to the nature of the thing willed, namely, that the perfect goodness of God can be without it; and such defect accompanies all created good.

Reply to Objection 5. A naturally contingent cause must be determined to act by some external power. The divine will, which by its nature is necessary, determines itself to will things to which it has no necessary relation.

Reply to Objection 6. As the divine essence is necessary of itself, so is the divine will and the divine knowledge; but the divine knowledge has a necessary relation to the thing known; not the divine will to the thing willed. The reason for this is that knowledge is of things as they exist in the knower; but the will is directed to things as they exist in themselves. Since then all other things have necessary existence inasmuch as they exist in God; but no absolute necessity so as to be necessary in themselves, in so far as they exist in themselves; it follows that God knows necessarily whatever He wills, but does not will necessarily whatever He wills.

Article 4. Whether the will of God is the cause of things?

Objection 1. It seems that the will of God is not the cause of things. For Dionysius says (Div. Nom. iv, 1): "As our sun, not by reason nor by pre-election, but by its very being, enlightens all things that can participate in its light, so the divine good by its very essence pours the rays of goodness upon everything that exists." But every voluntary agent acts by reason and pre-election. Therefore God does not act by will; and so His will is not the cause of things.

Objection 2. Further, The first in any order is that which is essentially so, thus in the order of burning things, that comes first which is fire by its essence. But God is the first agent. Therefore He acts by His essence; and that is His nature. He acts then by nature, and not by will. Therefore the divine will is not the cause of things.

Objection 3. Further, Whatever is the cause of anything, through being "such" a thing, is the cause by nature, and not by will. For fire is the cause of heat, as being itself hot; whereas an architect is the cause of a house, because he wills to build it. Now Augustine says (De Doctr. Christ. i, 32), "Because God is good, we exist." Therefore God is the cause of things by His nature, and not by His will.

Objection 4. Further, Of one thing there is one cause. But the created things is the knowledge of God, as said before (14, 8). Therefore the will of God cannot be considered the cause of things.

On the contrary, It is said (Wisdom 11:26), "How could anything endure, if Thou wouldst not?"

I answer that, We must hold that the will of God is the cause of things; and that He acts by the will, and not, as some have supposed, by a necessity of His nature. This can be shown in three ways:

First, from the order itself of active causes. Since both intellect and nature act for an end, as proved in Phys. ii, 49, the natural agent must have the end and the necessary means predetermined for it by some higher intellect; as the end and definite movement is predetermined for the arrow by the archer. Hence the intellectual and voluntary agent must precede the agent that acts by nature. Hence, since God is first in the order of agents, He must act by intellect and will.

This is shown, secondly, from the character of a natural agent, of which the property is to produce one and the same effect; for nature operates in one and the same way unless it be prevented. This is because the nature of the act is according to the nature of the agent; and hence as long as it has that nature, its acts will be in accordance with that nature; for every natural agent has a determinate being. Since, then, the Divine Being is undetermined, and contains in Himself the full perfection of being, it cannot be that He acts by a necessity of His nature, unless He were to cause something undetermined and indefinite in being: and that this is impossible has been already shown (7, 2). He does not, therefore, act by a necessity of His nature, but determined effects proceed from His own infinite perfection according to the determination of His will and intellect.

Thirdly, it is shown by the relation of effects to their cause. For effects proceed from the agent that causes them, in so far as they pre-exist in the agent; since every agent produces its like. Now effects pre-exist in their cause after the mode of the cause. Wherefore since the Divine Being is His own intellect, effects pre-exist in Him after the mode of intellect, and therefore proceed from Him after the same mode. Consequently, they proceed from Him after the mode of will, for His inclination to put in act what His intellect has conceived appertains to the will. Therefore the will of God is the cause of things.

Reply to Objection 1. Dionysius in these words does not intend to exclude election from God absolutely; but only in a certain sense, in so far, that is, as He communicates His goodness not merely to certain things, but to all; and as election implies a certain distinction.

Reply to Objection 2. Because the essence of God is His intellect and will, from the fact of His acting by His essence, it follows that He acts after the mode of intellect and will.

Reply to Objection 3. Good is the object of the will. The words, therefore, "Because God is good, we exist," are true inasmuch as His goodness is the reason of His willing all other things, as said before (2, ad 2).

Reply to Objection 4. Even in us the cause of one and the same effect is knowledge as directing it, whereby the form of the work is conceived, and will as commanding it, since the form as it is in the intellect only is not determined to exist or not to exist in the effect, except by the will. Hence, the speculative intellect has nothing to say to operation. But the power is cause, as executing the effect, since it denotes the immediate principle of operation. But in God all these things are one.

Article 5. Whether any cause can be assigned to the divine will?

Objection 1. It seems that some cause can be assigned to the divine will. For Augustine says (Qq. lxxxiii, 46): "Who would venture to say that God made all things irrationally?" But to a voluntary agent, what is the reason of operating, is the cause of willing. Therefore the will of God has some cause.

Objection 2. Further, in things made by one who wills to make them, and whose will is influenced by no cause, there can be no cause assigned except by the will of him who wills. But the will of God is the cause of all things, as has been already shown (4). If, then, there is no cause of His will, we cannot seek in any natural things any cause, except the divine will alone. Thus all science would be in vain, since science seeks to assign causes to effects. This seems inadmissible, and therefore we must assign some cause to the divine will.

Objection 3. Further, what is done by the willer, on account of no cause, depends simply on his will. If, therefore, the will of God has no cause, it follows that all things made depend simply on His will, and have no other cause. But this also is not admissible.

On the contrary, Augustine says (Qq. lxxxiii, 28): "Every efficient cause is greater than the thing effected." But nothing is greater than the will of God. We must not then seek for a cause of it.

I answer that, In no wise has the will of God a cause. In proof of which we must consider that, since the will follows from the intellect, there is cause of the will in the person who wills, in the same way as there is a cause of the understanding, in the person that understands. The case with the understanding is this: that if the premiss and its conclusion are understood separately from each other, the understanding the premiss is the cause that the conclusion is known. If the understanding perceive the conclusion in the premiss itself, apprehending both the one and the other at the same glance, in this case the knowing of the conclusion would not be caused by understanding the premisses, since a thing cannot be its own cause; and yet, it would be true that the thinker would understand the premisses to be the cause of the conclusion. It is the same with the will, with respect to which the end stands in the same relation to the means to the end, as do the premisses to the conclusion with regard to the understanding.

Hence, if anyone in one act wills an end, and in another act the means to that end, his willing the end will be the cause of his willing the means. This cannot be the case if in one act he wills both end and means; for a thing cannot be its own cause. Yet it will be true to say that he wills to order to the end the means to the end. Now as God by one act understands all things in His essence, so by one act He wills all things in His goodness. Hence, as in God to understand the cause is not the cause of His understanding the effect, for He understands the effect in the cause, so, in Him, to will an end is not the cause of His willing the means, yet He wills the ordering of the means to the end. Therefore, He wills this to be as means to that; but does not will this on account of that.

Reply to Objection 1. The will of God is reasonable, not because anything is to God a cause of willing, but in so far as He wills one thing to be on account of another.

Reply to Objection 2. Since God wills effects to proceed from definite causes, for the preservation of order in the universe, it is not unreasonable to seek for causes secondary to the divine will. It would, however, be unreasonable to do so, if such were considered as primary, and not as dependent on the will of God. In this sense Augustine says (De Trin. iii, 2): "Philosophers in their vanity have thought fit to attribute contingent effects to other causes, being utterly unable to perceive the cause that is shown above all others, the will of God."

Reply to Objection 3. Since God wills effects to come from causes, all effects that presuppose some other effect do not depend solely on the will of God, but on something else besides: but the first effect depends on the divine will alone. Thus, for example, we may say that God willed man to have hands to serve his intellect by their work, and intellect, that he might be man; and willed him to be man that he might enjoy Him, or for the completion of the universe. But this cannot be reduced to other created secondary ends. Hence such things depend on the simple will of God; but the others on the order of other causes.

Article 6. Whether the will of God is always fulfilled?

Objection 1. It seems that the will of God is not always fulfilled. For the Apostle says (1 Timothy 2:4): "God will have all men to be saved, and to come to the knowledge of the truth." But this does not happen. Therefore the will of God is not always fulfilled.

Objection 2. Further, as is the relation of knowledge to truth, so is that of the will to good. Now God knows all truth. Therefore He wills all good. But not all good actually exists; for much more good might exist. Therefore the will of God is not always fulfilled.

Objection 3. Further, since the will of God is the first cause, it does not exclude intermediate causes. But the effect of a first cause may be hindered by a defect of a secondary cause; as the effect of the motive power may be hindered by the weakness of the limb. Therefore the effect of the divine will may be hindered by a defect of the secondary causes. The will of God, therefore, is not always fulfilled.

On the contrary, It is said (Psalm 13:11): "God hath done all things, whatsoever He would."

I answer that, The will of God must needs always be fulfilled. In proof of which we must consider that since an effect is conformed to the agent according to its form, the rule is the same with active causes as with formal causes. The rule in forms is this: that although a thing may fall short of any particular form, it cannot fall short of the universal form. For though a thing may fail to be, for example, a man or a living being, yet it cannot fail to be a being. Hence the same must happen in active causes. Something may fall outside the order of any particular active cause, but not outside the order of the universal cause; under which all particular causes are included: and if any particular cause fails of its effect, this is because of the hindrance of some other particular cause, which is included in the order of the universal cause. Therefore an effect cannot possibly escape the order of the universal cause. Even in corporeal things this is clearly seen. For it may happen that a star is hindered from producing its effects; yet whatever effect does result, in corporeal things, from this hindrance of a corporeal cause, must be referred through intermediate causes to the universal influence of the first heaven. Since, then, the will of God is the universal cause of all things, it is impossible that the divine will should not produce its effect. Hence that which seems to depart from the divine will in one order, returns into it in another order; as does the sinner, who by sin falls away from the divine will as much as lies in him, yet falls back into the order of that will, when by its justice he is punished.

Reply to Objection 1. The words of the Apostle, "God will have all men to be saved," etc. can be understood in three ways.

First, by a restricted application, in which case they would mean, as Augustine says (De praed. sanct. i, 8: Enchiridion 103), "God wills all men to be saved that are saved, not because there is no man whom He does not wish saved, but because there is no man saved whose salvation He does not will."

Secondly, they can be understood as applying to every class of individuals, not to every individual of each class; in which case they mean that God wills some men of every class and condition to be saved, males and females, Jews and Gentiles, great and small, but not all of every condition.

Thirdly, according to Damascene (De Fide Orth. ii, 29), they are understood of the antecedent will of God; not of the consequent will. This distinction must not be taken as applying to the divine will itself, in which there is nothing antecedent nor consequent, but to the things willed.

To understand this we must consider that everything, in so far as it is good, is willed by God. A thing taken in its primary sense, and absolutely considered, may be good or evil, and yet when some additional circumstances are taken into account, by a consequent consideration may be changed into the contrary. Thus that a man should live is good; and that a man should be killed is evil, absolutely considered. But if in a particular case we add that a man is a murderer or dangerous to society, to kill him is a good; that he live is an evil. Hence it may be said of a just judge, that antecedently he wills all men to live; but consequently wills the murderer to be hanged. In the same way God antecedently wills all men to be saved, but consequently wills some to be damned, as His justice exacts. Nor do we will simply, what we will antecedently, but rather we will it in a qualified manner; for the will is directed to things as they are in themselves, and in themselves they exist under particular qualifications. Hence we will a thing simply inasmuch as we will it when all particular circumstances are considered; and this is what is meant by willing consequently. Thus it may be said that a just judge wills simply the hanging of a murderer, but in a qualified manner he would will him to live, to wit, inasmuch as he is a man. Such a qualified will may be called a willingness rather than an absolute will. Thus it is clear that whatever God simply wills takes place; although what He wills antecedently may not take place.

Reply to Objection 2. An act of the cognitive faculty is according as the thing known is in the knower; while an act of the appetite faculty is directed to things as they exist in themselves. But all that can have the nature of being and truth virtually exists in God, though it does not all exist in created things. Therefore God knows all truth; but does not will all good, except in so far as He wills Himself, in Whom all good virtually exists.

Reply to Objection 3. A first cause can be hindered in its effect by deficiency in the secondary cause, when it is not the universal first cause, including within itself all causes; for then the effect could in no way escape its order. And thus it is with the will of God, as said above.

Article 7. Whether the will of God is changeable?

Objection 1. It seems that the Will of God is changeable. For the Lord says (Genesis 6:7): "It repenteth Me that I have made man." But whoever repents of what he has done, has a changeable will. Therefore God has a changeable will.

Objection 2. Further, it is said in the person of the Lord: "I will speak against a nation and against a kingdom, to root out, and to pull down, and to destroy it; but if that nation shall repent of its evil, I also will repent of the evil that I have thought to do to them" (Jeremiah 18:7-8) Therefore God has a changeable will.

Objection 3. Further, whatever God does, He does voluntarily. But God does not always do the same thing, for at one time He ordered the law to be observed, and at another time forbade it. Therefore He has a changeable will.

Objection 4. Further, God does not will of necessity what He wills, as said before (3). Therefore He can both will and not will the same thing. But whatever can incline to either of two opposites, is changeable substantially; and that which can exist in a place or not in that place, is changeable locally. Therefore God is changeable as regards His will.

On the contrary, It is said: "God is not as a man, that He should lie, nor as the son of man, that He should be changed" (Numbers 23:19).

I answer that, The will of God is entirely unchangeable. On this point we must consider that to change the will is one thing; to will that certain things should be changed is another. It is possible to will a thing to be done now, and its contrary afterwards; and yet for the will to remain permanently the same: whereas the will would be changed, if one should begin to will what before he had not willed; or cease to will what he had willed before. This cannot happen, unless we presuppose change either in the knowledge or in the disposition of the substance of the willer. For since the will regards good, a man may in two ways begin to will a thing. In one way when that thing begins to be good for him, and this does not take place without a change in him. Thus when the cold weather begins, it becomes good to sit by the fire; though it was not so before. In another way when he knows for the first time that a thing is good for him, though he did not know it before; hence we take counsel in order to know what is good for us. Now it has already been shown that both the substance of God and His knowledge are entirely unchangeable (9, 1; 14, 15). Therefore His will must be entirely unchangeable.

Reply to Objection 1. These words of the Lord are to be understood metaphorically, and according to the likeness of our nature. For when we repent, we destroy what we have made; although we may even do so without change of will; as, when a man wills to make a thing, at the same time intending to destroy it later. Therefore God is said to have repented, by way of comparison with our mode of acting, in so far as by the deluge He destroyed from the face of the earth man whom He had made.

Reply to Objection 2. The will of God, as it is the first and universal cause, does not exclude intermediate causes that have power to produce certain effects. Since however all intermediate causes are inferior in power to the first cause, there are many things in the divine power, knowledge and will that are not included in the order of inferior causes. Thus in the case of the raising of Lazarus, one who looked only on inferior causes might have said: "Lazarus will not rise again," but looking at the divine first cause might have said: "Lazarus will rise again." And God wills both: that is, that in the order of the inferior cause a thing shall happen; but that in the order of the higher cause it shall not happen; or He may will conversely. We may say, then, that God sometimes declares that a thing shall happen according as it falls under the order of inferior causes, as of nature, or merit, which yet does not happen as not being in the designs of the divine and higher cause. Thus He foretold to Ezechias: "Take order with thy house, for thou shalt die, and not live" (Isaiah 38:1). Yet this did not take place, since from eternity it was otherwise disposed in the divine knowledge and will, which is unchangeable. Hence Gregory says (Moral. xvi, 5): "The sentence of God changes, but not His counsel"--that is to say, the counsel of His will. When therefore He says, "I also will repent," His words must be understood metaphorically. For men seem to repent, when they do not fulfill what they have threatened.

Reply to Objection 3. It does not follow from this argument that God has a will that changes, but that He sometimes wills that things should change.

Reply to Objection 4. Although God's willing a thing is not by absolute necessity, yet it is necessary by supposition, on account of the unchangeableness of the divine will, as has been said above (Article 3).

Article 8. Whether the will of God imposes necessity on the things willed?

Objection 1. It seems that the will of God imposes necessity on the things willed. For Augustine says (Enchiridion 103): "No one is saved, except whom God has willed to be saved. He must therefore be asked to will it; for if He wills it, it must necessarily be."

Objection 2. Further, every cause that cannot be hindered, produces its effect necessarily, because, as the Philosopher says (Phys. ii, 84) "Nature always works in the same way, if there is nothing to hinder it." But the will of God cannot be hindered. For the Apostle says (Romans 9:19): "Who resisteth His will?" Therefore the will of God imposes necessity on the things willed.

Objection 3. Further, whatever is necessary by its antecedent cause is necessary absolutely; it is thus necessary that animals should die, being compounded of contrary elements. Now things created by God are related to the divine will as to an antecedent cause, whereby they have necessity. For the conditional statement is true that if God wills a thing, it comes to pass; and every true conditional statement is necessary. It follows therefore that all that God wills is necessary absolutely.

On the contrary, All good things that exist God wills to be. If therefore His will imposes necessity on things willed, it follows that all good happens of necessity; and thus there is an end of free will, counsel, and all other such things.

I answer that, The divine will imposes necessity on some things willed but not on all. The reason of this some have chosen to assign to intermediate causes, holding that what God produces by necessary causes is necessary; and what He produces by contingent causes contingent. This does not seem to be a sufficient explanation, for two reasons.

First, because the effect of a first cause is contingent on account of the secondary cause, from the fact that the effect of the first cause is hindered by deficiency in the second cause, as the sun's power is hindered by a defect in the plant. But no defect of a secondary cause can hinder God's will from producing its effect.

Secondly, because if the distinction between the contingent and the necessary is to be referred only to secondary causes, this must be independent of the divine intention and will; which is inadmissible. It is better therefore to say that this happens on account of the efficacy of the divine will. For when a cause is efficacious to act, the effect follows upon the cause, not only as to the thing done, but also as to its manner of being done or of being. Thus from defect of active power in the seed it may happen that a child is born unlike its father in accidental points, that belong to its manner of being. Since then the divine will is perfectly efficacious, it follows not only that things are done, which God wills to be done, but also that they are done in the way that He wills. Now God wills some things to be done necessarily, some contingently, to the right ordering of things, for the building up of the universe. Therefore to some effects He has attached necessary causes, that cannot fail; but to others defectible and contingent causes, from which arise contingent effects. Hence it is not because the proximate causes are contingent that the effects willed by God happen contingently, but because God prepared contingent causes for them, it being His will that they should happen contingently.

Reply to Objection 1. By the words of Augustine we must understand a necessity in things willed by God that is not absolute, but conditional. For the conditional statement that if God wills a thing it must necessarily be, is necessarily true.

Reply to Objection 2. From the very fact that nothing resists the divine will, it follows that not only those things happen that God wills to happen, but that they happen necessarily or contingently according to His will.

Reply to Objection 3. Consequents have necessity from their antecedents according to the mode of the antecedents. Hence things effected by the divine will have that kind of necessity that God wills them to have, either absolute or conditional. Not all things, therefore, are absolute necessities.

Article 9. Whether God wills evils?

Objection 1. It seems that God wills evils. For every good that exists, God wills. But it is a good that evil should exist. For Augustine says (Enchiridion 95): "Although evil in so far as it is evil is not a good, yet it is good that not only good things should exist, but also evil things." Therefore God wills evil things.

Objection 2. Further, Dionysius says (Div. Nom. iv, 23): "Evil would conduce to the perfection of everything," i.e. the universe. And Augustine says (Enchiridion 10,11): "Out of all things is built up the admirable beauty of the universe, wherein even that which is called evil, properly ordered and disposed, commends the good more evidently in that good is more pleasing and praiseworthy when contrasted with evil." But God wills all that appertains to the perfection and beauty of the universe, for this is what God desires above all things in His creatures. Therefore God wills evil.

Objection 3. Further, that evil should exist, and should not exist, are contradictory opposites. But God does not will that evil should not exist; otherwise, since various evils do exist, God's will would not always be fulfilled. Therefore God wills that evil should exist.

On the contrary, Augustine says (Qq. 83,3): "No wise man is the cause of another man becoming worse. Now God surpasses all men in wisdom. Much less therefore is God the cause of man becoming worse; and when He is said to be the cause of a thing, He is said to will it." Therefore it is not by God's will that man becomes worse. Now it is clear that every evil makes a thing worse. Therefore God wills not evil things.

I answer that, Since the ratio of good is the ratio of appetibility, as said before (5, 1), and since evil is opposed to good, it is impossible that any evil, as such, should be sought for by the appetite, either natural, or animal, or by the intellectual appetite which is the will. Nevertheless evil may be sought accidentally, so far as it accompanies a good, as appears in each of the appetites. For a natural agent intends not privation or corruption, but the form to which is annexed the privation of some other form, and the generation of one thing, which implies the corruption of another. Also when a lion kills a stag, his object is food, to obtain which the killing of the animal is only the means. Similarly the fornicator has merely pleasure for his object, and the deformity of sin is only an accompaniment. Now the evil that accompanies one good, is the privation of another good. Never therefore would evil be sought after, not even accidentally, unless the good that accompanies the evil were more desired than the good of which the evil is the privation. Now God wills no good more than He wills His own goodness; yet He wills one good more than another. Hence He in no way wills the evil of sin, which is the privation of right order towards the divine good. The evil of natural defect, or of punishment, He does will, by willing the good to which such evils are attached. Thus in willing justice He wills punishment; and in willing the preservation of the natural order, He wills some things to be naturally corrupted.

Reply to Objection 1. Some have said that although God does not will evil, yet He wills that evil should be or be done, because, although evil is not a good, yet it is good that evil should be or be done. This they said because things evil in themselves are ordered to some good end; and this order they thought was expressed in the words "that evil should be or be done." This, however, is not correct; since evil is not of itself ordered to good, but accidentally. For it is beside the intention of the sinner, that any good should follow from his sin; as it was beside the intention of tyrants that the patience of the martyrs should shine forth from all their persecutions. It cannot therefore be said that such an ordering to good is implied in the statement that it is a good thing that evil should be or be done, since nothing is judged of by that which appertains to it accidentally, but by that which belongs to it essentially.

Reply to Objection 2. Evil does not operate towards the perfection and beauty of the universe, except accidentally, as said above (ad 1). Therefore Dionysius in saying that "evil would conduce to the perfection of the universe," draws a conclusion by reduction to an absurdity.

Reply to Objection 3. The statements that evil exists, and that evil exists not, are opposed as contradictories; yet the statements that anyone wills evil to exist and that he wills it not to be, are not so opposed; since either is affirmative. God therefore neither wills evil to be done, nor wills it not to be done, but wills to permit evil to be done; and this is a good.

Article 10. Whether God has free-will?

Objection 1. It seems that God has not free-will. For Jerome says, in a homily on the prodigal son [Ep. 146, ad Damas.]; "God alone is He who is not liable to sin, nor can be liable: all others, as having free-will, can be inclined to either side."

Objection 2. Further, free-will is the faculty of the reason and will, by which good and evil are chosen. But God does not will evil, as has been said (9). Therefore there is not free-will in God.

On the contrary, Ambrose says (De Fide ii, 3): "The Holy Spirit divideth unto each one as He will, namely, according to the free choice of the will, not in obedience to necessity."

I answer that, We have free-will with respect to what we will not of necessity, nor be natural instinct. For our will to be happy does not appertain to free-will, but to natural instinct. Hence other animals, that are moved to act by natural instinct, are not said to be moved by free-will. Since then God necessarily wills His own goodness, but other things not necessarily, as shown above (Article 3), He has free will with respect to what He does not necessarily will.

Reply to Objection 1. Jerome seems to deny free-will to God not simply, but only as regards the inclination to sin.

Reply to Objection 2. Since the evil of sin consists in turning away from the divine goodness, by which God wills all things, as above shown (De Fide ii, 3), it is manifestly impossible for Him to will the evil of sin; yet He can make choice of one of two opposites, inasmuch as He can will a thing to be, or not to be. In the same way we ourselves, without sin, can will to sit down, and not will to sit down.

Article 11. Whether the will of expression is to be distinguished in God?

Objection 1. It seems that the will of expression is not to be distinguished in God. For as the will of God is the cause of things, so is His wisdom. But no expressions are assigned to the divine wisdom. Therefore no expressions ought to be assigned to the divine will.

Objection 2. Further, every expression that is not in agreement with the mind of him who expresses himself, is false. If therefore the expressions assigned to the divine will are not in agreement with that will, they are false. But if they do agree, they are superfluous. No expressions therefore must be assigned to the divine will.

On the contrary, The will of God is one, since it is the very essence of God. Yet sometimes it is spoken of as many, as in the words of Psalm 110:2: "Great are the works of the Lord, sought out according to all His wills." Therefore sometimes the sign must be taken for the will.

I answer that, Some things are said of God in their strict sense; others by metaphor, as appears from what has been said before (13, 3). When certain human passions are predicated of the Godhead metaphorically, this is done because of a likeness in the effect. Hence a thing that is in us a sign of some passion, is signified metaphorically in God under the name of that passion. Thus with us it is usual for an angry man to punish, so that punishment becomes an expression of anger. Therefore punishment itself is signified by the word anger, when anger is attributed to God. In the same way, what is usually with us an expression of will, is sometimes metaphorically called will in God; just as when anyone lays down a precept, it is a sign that he wishes that precept obeyed. Hence a divine precept is sometimes called by metaphor the will of God, as in the words: "Thy will be done on earth, as it is in heaven" (Matthew 6:10). There is, however, this difference between will and anger, that anger is never attributed to God properly, since in its primary meaning it includes passion; whereas will is attributed to Him properly. Therefore in God there are distinguished will in its proper sense, and will as attributed to Him by metaphor. Will in its proper sense is called the will of good pleasure; and will metaphorically taken is the will of expression, inasmuch as the sign itself of will is called will.

Reply to Objection 1. Knowledge is not the cause of a thing being done, unless through the will. For we do not put into act what we know, unless we will to do so. Accordingly expression is not attributed to knowledge, but to will.

Reply to Objection 2. Expressions of will are called divine wills, not as being signs that God wills anything; but because what in us is the usual expression of our will, is called the divine will in God. Thus punishment is not a sign that there is anger in God; but it is called anger in Him, from the fact that it is an expression of anger in ourselves.

Article 12. Whether five expressions of will are rightly assigned to the divine will?

Objection 1. It seems that five expressions of will--namely, prohibition, precept, counsel, operation, and permission--are not rightly assigned to the divine will. For the same things that God bids us do by His precept or counsel, these He sometimes operates in us, and the same things that He prohibits, these He sometimes permits. They ought not therefore to be enumerated as distinct.

Objection 2. Further, God works nothing unless He wills it, as the Scripture says (Wisdom 11:26). But the will of expression is distinct from the will of good pleasure. Therefore operation ought not to be comprehended in the will of expression.

Objection 3. Further, operation and permission appertain to all creatures in common, since God works in them all, and permits some action in them all. But precept, counsel, and prohibition belong to rational creatures only. Therefore they do not come rightly under one division, not being of one order.

Objection 4. Further, evil happens in more ways than good, since "good happens in one way, but evil in all kinds of ways," as declared by the Philosopher (Ethic. ii, 6), and Dionysius (Div. Nom. iv, 22). It is not right therefore to assign one expression only in the case of evil--namely, prohibition--and two--namely, counsel and precept--in the case of good.

I answer that, By these signs we name the expression of will by which we are accustomed to show that we will something. A man may show that he wills something, either by himself or by means of another. He may show it by himself, by doing something either directly, or indirectly and accidentally. He shows it directly when he works in his own person; in that way the expression of his will is his own working. He shows it indirectly, by not hindering the doing of a thing; for what removes an impediment is called an accidental mover. In this respect the expression is called permission. He declares his will by means of another when he orders another to perform a work, either by insisting upon it as necessary by precept, and by prohibiting its contrary; or by persuasion, which is a part of counsel. Since in these ways the will of man makes itself known, the same five are sometimes denominated with regard to the divine will, as the expression of that will. That precept, counsel, and prohibition are called the will of God is clear from the words of Matthew 6:10: "Thy will be done on earth as it is in heaven." That permission and operation are called the will of God is clear from Augustine (Enchiridion 95), who says: "Nothing is done, unless the Almighty wills it to be done, either by permitting it, or by actually doing it."

Or it may be said that permission and operation refer to present time, permission being with respect to evil, operation with regard to good. Whilst as to future time, prohibition is in respect to evil, precept to good that is necessary and counsel to good that is of supererogation.

Reply to Objection 1. There is nothing to prevent anyone declaring his will about the same matter in different ways; thus we find many words that mean the same thing. Hence there is not reason why the same thing should not be the subject of precept, operation, and counsel; or of prohibition or permission.

Reply to Objection 2. As God may by metaphor be said to will what by His will, properly speaking, He wills not; so He may by metaphor be said to will what He does, properly speaking, will. Hence there is nothing to prevent the same thing being the object of the will of good pleasure, and of the will of expression. But operation is always the same as the will of good pleasure; while precept and counsel are not; both because the former regards the present, and the two latter the future; and because the former is of itself the effect of the will; the latter its effect as fulfilled by means of another.

Reply to Objection 3. Rational creatures are masters of their own acts; and for this reason certain special expressions of the divine will are assigned to their acts, inasmuch as God ordains rational creatures to act voluntarily and of themselves. Other creatures act only as moved by the divine operation; therefore only operation and permission are concerned with these.

Reply to Objection 4. All evil of sin, though happening in many ways, agrees in being out of harmony with the divine will. Hence with regard to evil, only one expression is assigned, that of prohibition. On the other hand, good stands in various relations to the divine goodness, since there are good deeds without which we cannot attain to the fruition of that goodness, and these are the subject of precept; and there are others by which we attain to it more perfectly, and these are the subject of counsel. Or it may be said that counsel is not only concerned with the obtaining of greater good; but also with the avoiding of lesser evils.

# Question 44. The procession of creatures from God, and of the first cause of all things

## Article 1. Whether it is necessary that every being be created by God?

Objection 1. It would seem that it is not necessary that every being be created by God. For there is nothing to prevent a thing from being without that which does not belong to its essence, as a man can be found without whiteness. But the relation of the thing caused to its cause does not appear to be essential to beings, for some beings can be understood without it; therefore they can exist without it; and therefore it is possible that some beings should not be created by God.

Objection 2. Further, a thing requires an efficient cause in order to exist. Therefore whatever cannot but exist does not require an efficient cause. But no necessary thing can not exist, because whatever necessarily exists cannot but exist. Therefore as there are many necessary things in existence, it appears that not all beings are from God.

Objection 3. Further, whatever things have a cause, can be demonstrated by that cause. But in mathematics demonstration is not made by the efficient cause, as appears from the Philosopher (Metaph. iii, text 3); therefore not all beings are from God as from their efficient cause.

On the contrary, It is said (Romans 11:36): "Of Him, and by Him, and in Him are all things."

I answer that, It must be said that every being in any way existing is from God. For whatever is found in anything by participation, must be caused in it by that to which it belongs essentially, as iron becomes ignited by fire. Now it has been shown above (Question 3, Article 4) when treating of the divine simplicity that God is the essentially self-subsisting Being; and also it was shown (11, 3,4) that subsisting being must be one; as, if whiteness were self-subsisting, it would be one, since whiteness is multiplied by its recipients. Therefore all beings apart from God are not their own being, but are beings by participation. Therefore it must be that all things which are diversified by the diverse participation of being, so as to be more or less perfect, are caused by one First Being, Who possesses being most perfectly.

Hence Plato said (Parmen. xxvi) that unity must come before multitude; and Aristotle said (Metaph. ii, text 4) that whatever is greatest in being and greatest in truth, is the cause of every being and of every truth; just as whatever is the greatest in heat is the cause of all heat.

Reply to Objection 1. Though the relation to its cause is not part of the definition of a thing caused, still it follows, as a consequence, on what belongs to its essence; because from the fact that a thing has being by participation, it follows that it is caused. Hence such a being cannot be without being caused, just as man cannot be without having the faculty of laughing. But, since to be caused does not enter into the essence of being as such, therefore is it possible for us to find a being uncaused.

Reply to Objection 2. This objection has led some to say that what is necessary has no cause (Phys. viii, text 46). But this is manifestly false in the demonstrative sciences, where necessary principles are the causes of necessary conclusions. And therefore Aristotle says (Metaph. v, text 6), that there are some necessary things which have a cause of their necessity. But the reason why an efficient cause is required is not merely because the effect is not necessary, but because the effect might not be if the cause were not. For this conditional proposition is true, whether the antecedent and consequent be possible or impossible.

Reply to Objection 3. The science of mathematics treats its object as though it were something abstracted mentally, whereas it is not abstract in reality. Now, it is becoming that everything should have an efficient cause in proportion to its being. And so, although the object of mathematics has an efficient cause, still, its relation to that cause is not the reason why it is brought under the consideration of the mathematician, who therefore does not demonstrate that object from its efficient cause.

Article 2. Whether primary matter is created by God?

Objection 1. It would seem that primary matter is not created by God. For whatever is made is composed of a subject and of something else (Phys. i, text 62). But primary matter has no subject. Therefore primary matter cannot have been made by God.

Objection 2. Further, action and passion are opposite members of a division. But as the first active principle is God, so the first passive principle is matter. Therefore God and primary matter are two principles divided against each other, neither of which is from the other.

Objection 3. Further, every agent produces its like, and thus, since every agent acts in proportion to its actuality, it follows that everything made is in some degree actual. But primary matter is only in potentiality, formally considered in itself. Therefore it is against the nature of primary matter to be a thing made.

On the contrary, Augustine says (Confess. xii, 7), Two "things hast Thou made, O Lord; one nigh unto Thyself"--viz. angels--"the other nigh unto nothing"--viz. primary matter.

I answer that, The ancient philosophers gradually, and as it were step by step, advanced to the knowledge of truth. At first being of grosser mind, they failed to realize that any beings existed except sensible bodies. And those among them who admitted movement, did not consider it except as regards certain accidents, for instance, in relation to rarefaction and condensation, by union and separation. And supposing as they did that corporeal substance itself was uncreated, they assigned certain causes for these accidental changes, as for instance, affinity, discord, intellect, or something of that kind. An advance was made when they understood that there was a distinction between the substantial form and matter, which latter they imagined to be uncreated, and when they perceived transmutation to take place in bodies in regard to essential forms. Such transmutations they attributed to certain universal causes, such as the oblique circle [The zodiac], according to Aristotle (De Gener. ii), or ideas, according to Plato. But we must take into consideration that matter is contracted by its form to a determinate species, as a substance, belonging to a certain species, is contracted by a supervening accident to a determinate mode of being; for instance, man by whiteness. Each of these opinions, therefore, considered "being" under some particular aspect, either as "this" or as "such"; and so they assigned particular efficient causes to things. Then others there were who arose to the consideration of "being," as being, and who assigned a cause to things, not as "these," or as "such," but as "beings."

Therefore whatever is the cause of things considered as beings, must be the cause of things, not only according as they are "such" by accidental forms, nor according as they are "these" by substantial forms, but also according to all that belongs to their being at all in any way. And thus it is necessary to say that also primary matter is created by the universal cause of things.

Reply to Objection 1. The Philosopher (Phys. i, text 62), is speaking of "becoming" in particular--that is, from form to form, either accidental or substantial. But here we are speaking of things according to their emanation from the universal principle of being; from which emanation matter itself is not excluded, although it is excluded from the former mode of being made.

Reply to Objection 2. Passion is an effect of action. Hence it is reasonable that the first passive principle should be the effect of the first active principle, since every imperfect thing is caused by one perfect. For the first principle must be most perfect, as Aristotle says (Metaph. xii, text 40).

Reply to Objection 3. The reason adduced does not show that matter is not created, but that it is not created without form; for though everything created is actual, still it is not pure act. Hence it is necessary that even what is potential in it should be created, if all that belongs to its being is created.

Article 3. Whether the exemplar cause is anything besides God?

Objection 1. It would seem that the exemplar cause is something besides God. For the effect is like its exemplar cause. But creatures are far from being like God. Therefore God is not their exemplar cause.

Objection 2. Further, whatever is by participation is reduced to something self-existing, as a thing ignited is reduced to fire, as stated above (Article 1). But whatever exists in sensible things exists only by participation of some species. This appears from the fact that in all sensible species is found not only what belongs to the species, but also individuating principles added to the principles of the species. Therefore it is necessary to admit self-existing species, as for instance, a "per se" man, and a "per se" horse, and the like, which are called the exemplars. Therefore exemplar causes exist besides God.

Objection 3. Further, sciences and definitions are concerned with species themselves, but not as these are in particular things, because there is no science or definition of particular things. Therefore there are some beings, which are beings or species not existing in singular things, and these are called exemplars. Therefore the same conclusion follows as above.

Objection 4. Further, this likewise appears from Dionysius, who says (Div. Nom. v) that self-subsisting being is before self-subsisting life, and before self-subsisting wisdom.

On the contrary, The exemplar is the same as the idea. But ideas, according to Augustine (QQ. 83, qu. 46), are "the master forms, which are contained in the divine intelligence." Therefore the exemplars of things are not outside God.

I answer that, God is the first exemplar cause of all things. In proof whereof we must consider that if for the production of anything an exemplar is necessary, it is in order that the effect may receive a determinate form. For an artificer produces a determinate form in matter by reason of the exemplar before him, whether it is the exemplar beheld externally, or the exemplar interiorily conceived in the mind. Now it is manifest that things made by nature receive determinate forms. This determination of forms must be reduced to the divine wisdom as its first principle, for divine wisdom devised the order of the universe, which order consists in the variety of things. And therefore we must say that in the divine wisdom are the types of all things, which types we have called ideas--i.e. exemplar forms existing in the divine mind (15, 1). And these ideas, though multiplied by their relations to things, in reality are not apart from the divine essence, according as the likeness to that essence can be shared diversely by different things. In this manner therefore God Himself is the first exemplar of all things. Moreover, in things created one may be called the exemplar of another by the reason of its likeness thereto, either in species, or by the analogy of some kind of imitation.

Reply to Objection 1. Although creatures do not attain to a natural likeness to God according to similitude of species, as a man begotten is like to the man begetting, still they do attain to likeness to Him, forasmuch as they represent the divine idea, as a material house is like to the house in the architect's mind.

Reply to Objection 2. It is of a man's nature to be in matter, and so a man without matter is impossible. Therefore although this particular man is a man by participation of the species, he cannot be reduced to anything self-existing in the same species, but to a superior species, such as separate substances. The same applies to other sensible things.

Reply to Objection 3. Although every science and definition is concerned only with beings, still it is not necessary that a thing should have the same mode in reality as the thought of it has in our understanding. For we abstract universal ideas by force of the active intellect from the particular conditions; but it is not necessary that the universals should exist outside the particulars in order to be their exemplars.

Reply to Objection 4. As Dionysius says (Div. Nom. iv), by "self-existing life and self-existing wisdom" he sometimes denotes God Himself, sometimes the powers given to things themselves; but not any self-subsisting things, as the ancients asserted.

Article 4. Whether God is the final cause of all things?

Objection 1. It would seem that God is not the final cause of all things. For to act for an end seems to imply need of the end. But God needs nothing. Therefore it does not become Him to act for an end.

Objection 2. Further, the end of generation, and the form of the thing generated, and the agent cannot be identical (Phys. ii, text 70), because the end of generation is the form of the thing generated. But God is the first agent producing all things. Therefore He is not the final cause of all things.

Objection 3. Further, all things desire their end. But all things do not desire God, for all do not even know Him. Therefore God is not the end of all things.

Objection 4. Further, the final cause is the first of causes. If, therefore, God is the efficient cause and the final cause, it follows that before and after exist in Him; which is impossible.

On the contrary, It is said (Proverbs 16:4): "The Lord has made all things for Himself."

I answer that, Every agent acts for an end: otherwise one thing would not follow more than another from the action of the agent, unless it were by chance. Now the end of the agent and of the patient considered as such is the same, but in a different way respectively. For the impression which the agent intends to produce, and which the patient intends to receive, are one and the same. Some things, however, are both agent and patient at the same time: these are imperfect agents, and to these it belongs to intend, even while acting, the acquisition of something. But it does not belong to the First Agent, Who is agent only, to act for the acquisition of some end; He intends only to communicate His perfection, which is His goodness; while every creature intends to acquire its own perfection, which is the likeness of the divine perfection and goodness. Therefore the divine goodness is the end of all things.

Reply to Objection 1. To act from need belongs only to an imperfect agent, which by its nature is both agent and patient. But this does not belong to God, and therefore He alone is the most perfectly liberal giver, because He does not act for His own profit, but only for His own goodness.

Reply to Objection 2. The form of the thing generated is not the end of generation, except inasmuch as it is the likeness of the form of the generator, which intends to communicate its own likeness; otherwise the form of the thing generated would be more noble than the generator, since the end is more noble than the means to the end.

Reply to Objection 3. All things desire God as their end, when they desire some good thing, whether this desire be intellectual or sensible, or natural, i.e. without knowledge; because nothing is good and desirable except forasmuch as it participates in the likeness to God.

Reply to Objection 4. Since God is the efficient, the exemplar and the final cause of all things, and since primary matter is from Him, it follows that the first principle of all things is one in reality. But this does not prevent us from mentally considering many things in Him, some of which come into our mind before others.

Question 45. The mode of emanation of things from the first principle

Article 1. Whether to create is to make something from nothing?

Objection 1. It would seem that to create is not to make anything from nothing. For Augustine says (Contra Adv. Leg. et Proph. i): "To make concerns what did not exist at all; but to create is to make something by bringing forth something from what was already."

Objection 2. Further, the nobility of action and of motion is considered from their terms. Action is therefore nobler from good to good, and from being to being, than from nothing to something. But creation appears to be the most noble action, and first among all actions. Therefore it is not from nothing to something, but rather from being to being.

Objection 3. Further, the preposition "from" [ex] imports relation of some cause, and especially of the material cause; as when we say that a statue is made from brass. But "nothing" cannot be the matter of being, nor in any way its cause. Therefore to create is not to make something from nothing.

On the contrary, On the text of Genesis 1, "In the beginning God created," etc., the gloss has, "To create is to make something from nothing."

I answer that, As said above (Question 44, Article 2), we must consider not only the emanation of a particular being from a particular agent, but also the emanation of all being from the universal cause, which is God; and this emanation we designate by the name of creation. Now what proceeds by particular emanation, is not presupposed to that emanation; as when a man is generated, he was not before, but man is made from "not-man," and white from "not-white." Hence if the emanation of the whole universal being from the first principle be considered, it is impossible that any being should be presupposed before this emanation. For nothing is the same as no being. Therefore as the generation of a man is from the "not-being" which is "not-man," so creation, which is the emanation of all being, is from the "not-being" which is "nothing."

Reply to Objection 1. Augustine uses the word creation in an equivocal sense, according as to be created signifies improvement in things; as when we say that a bishop is created. We do not, however, speak of creation in that way here, but as it is described above.

Reply to Objection 2. Changes receive species and dignity, not from the term "wherefrom," but from the term "whereto." Therefore a change is more perfect and excellent when the term "whereto" of the change is more noble and excellent, although the term "wherefrom," corresponding to the term "whereto," may be more imperfect: thus generation is simply nobler and more excellent than alteration, because the substantial form is nobler than the accidental form; and yet the privation of the substantial form, which is the term "wherefrom" in generation, is more imperfect than the contrary, which is the term "wherefrom" in alteration. Similarly creation is more perfect and excellent than generation and alteration, because the term "whereto" is the whole substance of the thing; whereas what is understood as the term "wherefrom" is simply not-being.

Reply to Objection 3. When anything is said to be made from nothing, this preposition "from" [ex] does not signify the material cause, but only order; as when we say, "from morning comes midday"--i.e. after morning is midday. But we must understand that this preposition "from" [ex] can comprise the negation implied when I say the word "nothing," or can be included in it. If taken in the first sense, then we affirm the order by stating the relation between what is now and its previous non-existence. But if the negation includes the preposition, then the order is denied, and the sense is, "It is made from nothing--i.e. it is not made from anything"--as if we were to say, "He speaks of nothing," because he does not speak of anything. And this is verified in both ways, when it is said, that anything is made from nothing. But in the first way this preposition "from" [ex] implies order, as has been said in this reply. In the second sense, it imports the material cause, which is denied.

Article 2. Whether God can create anything?

Objection 1. It would seem that God cannot create anything, because, according to the Philosopher (Phys. i, text 34), the ancient philosophers considered it as a commonly received axiom that "nothing is made from nothing." But the power of God does not extend to the contraries of first principles; as, for instance, that God could make the whole to be less than its part, or that affirmation and negation are both true at the same time. Therefore God cannot make anything from nothing, or create.

Objection 2. Further, if to create is to make something from nothing, to be created is to be made. But to be made is to be changed. Therefore creation is change. But every change occurs in some subject, as appears by the definition of movement: for movement is the act of what is in potentiality. Therefore it is impossible for anything to be made out of nothing by God.

Objection 3. Further, what has been made must have at some time been becoming. But it cannot be said that what is created, at the same time, is becoming and has been made, because in permanent things what is becoming, is not, and what has been made, already is: and so it would follow that something would be, and not be, at the same time. Therefore when anything is made, its becoming precedes its having been made. But this is impossible, unless there is a subject in which the becoming is sustained. Therefore it is impossible that anything should be made from nothing.

Objection 4. Further, infinite distance cannot be crossed. But infinite distance exists between being and nothing. Therefore it does not happen that something is made from nothing.

On the contrary, It is said (Genesis 1:1): "In the beginning God created heaven and earth."

I answer that, Not only is it not impossible that anything should be created by God, but it is necessary to say that all things were created by God, as appears from what has been said (44, 1). For when anyone makes one thing from another, this latter thing from which he makes is presupposed to his action, and is not produced by his action; thus the craftsman works from natural things, as wood or brass, which are caused not by the action of art, but by the action of nature. So also nature itself causes natural things as regards their form, but presupposes matter. If therefore God did only act from something presupposed, it would follow that the thing presupposed would not be caused by Him. Now it has been shown above (44, 1,2), that nothing can be, unless it is from God, Who is the universal cause of all being. Hence it is necessary to say that God brings things into being from nothing.

**Reply to Objection 1.** Ancient philosophers, as is said above (Question 44, Article 2), considered only the emanation of particular effects from particular causes, which necessarily presuppose something in their action; whence came their common opinion that "nothing is made from nothing." But this has no place in the first emanation from the universal principle of things.

**Reply to Objection 2.** Creation is not change, except according to a mode of understanding. For change means that the same something should be different now from what it was previously. Sometimes, indeed, the same actual thing is different now from what it was before, as in motion according to quantity, quality and place; but sometimes it is the same being only in potentiality, as in substantial change, the subject of which is matter. But in creation, by which the whole substance of a thing is produced, the same thing can be taken as different now and before only according to our way of understanding, so that a thing is understood as first not existing at all, and afterwards as existing. But as action and passion coincide as to the substance of motion, and differ only according to diverse relations (Phys. iii, text 20,21), it must follow that when motion is withdrawn, only diverse relations remain in the Creator and in the creature. But because the mode of signification follows the mode of understanding as was said above (Question 13, Article 1), creation is signified by mode of change; and on this account it is said that to create is to make something from nothing. And yet "to make" and "to be made" are more suitable expressions here than "to change" and "to be changed," because "to make" and "to be made" import a relation of cause to the effect, and of effect to the cause, and imply change only as a consequence.

**Reply to Objection 3.** In things which are made without movement, to become and to be already made are simultaneous, whether such making is the term of movement, as illumination (for a thing is being illuminated and is illuminated at the same time) or whether it is not the term of movement, as the word is being made in the mind and is made at the same time. In these things what is being made, is; but when we speak of its being made, we mean that it is from another, and was not previously. Hence since creation is without movement, a thing is being created and is already created at the same time.

Reply to Objection 4. This objection proceeds from a false imagination, as if there were an infinite medium between nothing and being; which is plainly false. This false imagination comes from creation being taken to signify a change existing between two forms.

Article 3. Whether creation is anything in the creature?

Objection 1. It would seem that creation is not anything in the creature. For as creation taken in a passive sense is attributed to the creature, so creation taken in an active sense is attributed to the Creator. But creation taken actively is not anything in the Creator, because otherwise it would follow that in God there would be something temporal. Therefore creation taken passively is not anything in the creature.

Objection 2. Further, there is no medium between the Creator and the creature. But creation is signified as the medium between them both: since it is not the Creator, as it is not eternal; nor is it the creature, because in that case it would be necessary for the same reason to suppose another creation to create it, and so on to infinity. Therefore creation is not anything in the creature.

Objection 3. Further, if creation is anything besides the created substance, it must be an accident belonging to it. But every accident is in a subject. Therefore a thing created would be the subject of creation, and so the same thing would be the subject and also the term of creation. This is impossible, because the subject is before the accident, and preserves the accident; while the term is after the action and passion whose term it is, and as soon as it exists, action and passion cease. Therefore creation itself is not any thing.

On the contrary, It is greater for a thing to be made according to its entire substance, than to be made according to its substantial or accidental form. But generation taken simply, or relatively, whereby anything is made according to the substantial or the accidental form, is something in the thing generated. Therefore much more is creation, whereby a thing is made according to its whole substance, something in the thing created.

I answer that, Creation places something in the thing created according to relation only; because what is created, is not made by movement, or by change. For what is made by movement or by change is made from something pre-existing. And this happens, indeed, in the particular productions of some beings, but cannot happen in the production of all being by the universal cause of all beings, which is God. Hence God by creation produces things without movement. Now when movement is removed from action and passion, only relation remains, as was said above (2, ad 2). Hence creation in the creature is only a certain relation to the Creator as to the principle of its being; even as in passion, which implies movement, is implied a relation to the principle of motion.

Reply to Objection 1. Creation signified actively means the divine action, which is God's essence, with a relation to the creature. But in God relation to the creature is not a real relation, but only a relation of reason; whereas the relation of the creature to God is a real relation, as was said above (Question 13, Article 7) in treating of the divine names.

Reply to Objection 2. Because creation is signified as a change, as was said above (2, ad 2), and change is a kind of medium between the mover and the moved, therefore also creation is signified as a medium between the Creator and the creature. Nevertheless passive creation is in the creature, and is a creature. Nor is there need of a further creation in its creation; because relations, or their entire nature being referred to something, are not referred by any other relations, but by themselves; as was also shown above (42, 1, ad 4), in treating of the equality of the Persons.

Reply to Objection 3. The creature is the term of creation as signifying a change, but is the subject of creation, taken as a real relation, and is prior to it in being, as the subject is to the accident. Nevertheless creation has a certain aspect of priority on the part of the object to which it is directed, which is the beginning of the creature. Nor is it necessary that as long as the creature is it should be created; because creation imports a relation of the creature to the Creator, with a certain newness or beginning.

Article 4. Whether to be created belongs to composite and subsisting things?

Objection 1. It would seem that to be created does not belong to composite and subsisting things. For in the book, De Causis (prop. iv) it is said, "The first of creatures is being." But the being of a thing created is not subsisting. Therefore creation properly speaking does not belong to subsisting and composite things.

Objection 2. Further, whatever is created is from nothing. But composite things are not from nothing, but are the result of their own component parts. Therefore composite things are not created.

Objection 3. Further, what is presupposed in the second emanation is properly produced by the first: as natural generation produces the natural thing, which is presupposed in the operation of art. But the thing supposed in natural generation is matter. Therefore matter, and not the composite, is, properly speaking, that which is created.

On the contrary, It is said (Genesis 1:1): "In the beginning God created heaven and earth." But heaven and earth are subsisting composite things. Therefore creation belongs to them.

I answer that, To be created is, in a manner, to be made, as was shown above (44, 2, ad 2,3). Now, to be made is directed to the being of a thing. Hence to be made and to be created properly belong to whatever being belongs; which, indeed, belongs properly to subsisting things, whether they are simple things, as in the case of separate substances, or composite, as in the case of material substances. For being belongs to that which has being-- that is, to what subsists in its own being. But forms and accidents and the like are called beings, not as if they themselves were, but because something is by them; as whiteness is called a being, inasmuch as its subject is white by it. Hence, according to the Philosopher (Metaph. vii, text 2) accident is more properly said to be "of a being" than "a being." Therefore, as accidents and forms and the like non-subsisting things are to be said to co-exist rather than to exist, so they ought to be called rather "concreated" than "created" things; whereas, properly speaking, created things are subsisting beings.

Reply to Objection 1. In the proposition "the first of created things is being," the word "being" does not refer to the subject of creation, but to the proper concept of the object of creation. For a created thing is called created because it is a being, not because it is "this" being, since creation is the emanation of all being from the Universal Being, as was said above (Article 1). We use a similar way of speaking when we say that "the first visible thing is color," although, strictly speaking, the thing colored is what is seen.

Reply to Objection 2. Creation does not mean the building up of a composite thing from pre-existing principles; but it means that the "composite" is created so that it is brought into being at the same time with all its principles.

Reply to Objection 3. This reason does not prove that matter alone is created, but that matter does not exist except by creation; for creation is the production of the whole being, and not only matter.

Article 5. Whether it belongs to God alone to create?

Objection 1. It would seem that it does not belong to God alone to create, because, according to the Philosopher (De Anima ii, text 34), what is perfect can make its own likeness. But immaterial creatures are more perfect than material creatures, which nevertheless can make their own likeness, for fire generates fire, and man begets man. Therefore an immaterial substance can make a substance like to itself. But immaterial substance can be made only by creation, since it has no matter from which to be made. Therefore a creature can create.

Objection 2. Further, the greater the resistance is on the part of the thing made, so much the greater power is required in the maker. But a "contrary" resists more than "nothing." Therefore it requires more power to make (something) from its contrary, which nevertheless a creature can do, than to make a thing from nothing. Much more therefore can a creature do this.

Objection 3. Further, the power of the maker is considered according to the measure of what is made. But created being is finite, as we proved above when treating of the infinity of God (7, 2,3,4). Therefore only a finite power is needed to produce a creature by creation. But to have a finite power is not contrary to the nature of a creature. Therefore it is not impossible for a creature to create.

On the contrary, Augustine says (De Trin. iii, 8) that neither good nor bad angels can create anything. Much less therefore can any other creatures.

I answer that, It sufficiently appears at the first glance, according to what precedes (1), that to create can be the action of God alone. For the more universal effects must be reduced to the more universal and prior causes. Now among all effects the most universal is being itself: and hence it must be the proper effect of the first and most universal cause, and that is God. Hence also it is said (De Causis prop., iii) that "neither intelligence nor the soul gives us being, except inasmuch as it works by divine operation." Now to produce being absolutely, not as this or that being, belongs to creation. Hence it is manifest that creation is the proper act of God alone.

It happens, however, that something participates the proper action of another, not by its own power, but instrumentally, inasmuch as it acts by the power of another; as air can heat and ignite by the power of fire. And so some have supposed that although creation is the proper act of the universal cause, still some inferior cause acting by the power of the first cause, can create. And thus Avicenna asserted that the first separate substance created by God created another after itself, and the substance of the world and its soul; and that the substance of the world creates the matter of inferior bodies. And in the same manner the Master says (Sent. iv, D, 5) that God can communicate to a creature the power of creating, so that the latter can create ministerially, not by its own power.

But such a thing cannot be, because the secondary instrumental cause does not participate the action of the superior cause, except inasmuch as by something proper to itself it acts dispositively to the effect of the principal agent. If therefore it effects nothing, according to what is proper to itself, it is used to no purpose; nor would there be any need of certain instruments for certain actions. Thus we see that a saw, in cutting wood, which it does by the property of its own form, produces the form of a bench, which is the proper effect of the principal agent. Now the proper effect of God creating is what is presupposed to all other effects, and that is absolute being. Hence nothing else can act dispositively and instrumentally to this effect, since creation is not from anything presupposed, which can be disposed by the action of the instrumental agent. So therefore it is impossible for any creature to create, either by its own power or instrumentally--that is, ministerially.

And above all it is absurd to suppose that a body can create, for no body acts except by touching or moving; and thus it requires in its action some pre-existing thing, which can be touched or moved, which is contrary to the very idea of creation.

Reply to Objection 1. A perfect thing participating any nature, makes a likeness to itself, not by absolutely producing that nature, but by applying it to something else. For an individual man cannot be the cause of human nature absolutely, because he would then be the cause of himself; but he is the cause of human nature being in the man begotten; and thus he presupposes in his action a determinate matter whereby he is an individual man. But as an individual man participates human nature, so every created being participates, so to speak, the nature of being; for God alone is His own being, as we have said above (7, 1,2). Therefore no created being can produce a being absolutely, except forasmuch as it causes "being" in "this": and so it is necessary to presuppose that whereby a thing is this thing, before the action whereby it makes its own likeness. But in an immaterial substance it is not possible to presuppose anything whereby it is this thing; because it is what it is by its form, whereby it has being, since it is a subsisting form. Therefore an immaterial substance cannot produce another immaterial substance like to itself as regards its being, but only as regards some added perfection; as we may say that a superior angel illuminates an inferior, as Dionysius says (Coel. Hier. iv, x). In this way even in heaven there is paternity, as the Apostle says (Ephesians 3:15): "From whom all paternity in heaven and on earth is named." From which evidently appears that no created being can cause anything, unless something is presupposed; which is against the very idea of creation.

Reply to Objection 2. A thing is made from its contrary indirectly (Phys. i, text 43), but directly from the subject which is in potentiality. And so the contrary resists the agent, inasmuch as it impedes the potentiality from the act which the agent intends to induce, as fire intends to reduce the matter of water to an act like to itself, but is impeded by the form and contrary dispositions, whereby the potentiality (of the water) is restrained from being reduced to act; and the more the potentiality is restrained, the more power is required in the agent to reduce the matter to act. Hence a much greater power is required in the agent when no potentiality pre-exists. Thus therefore it appears that it is an act of much greater power to make a thing from nothing, than from its contrary.

Reply to Objection 3. The power of the maker is reckoned not only from the substance of the thing made, but also from the mode of its being made; for a greater heat heats not only more, but quicker. Therefore although to create a finite effect does not show an infinite power, yet to create it from nothing does show an infinite power: which appears from what has been said (ad 2). For if a greater power is required in the agent in proportion to the distance of the potentiality from the act, it follows that the power of that which produces something from no presupposed potentiality is infinite, because there is no proportion between "no potentiality" and the potentiality presupposed by the power of a natural agent, as there is no proportion between "not being" and "being." And because no creature has simply an infinite power, any more than it has an infinite being, as was proved above (Question 7, Article 2), it follows that no creature can create.

## Article 6. Whether to create is proper to any person?

Objection 1. It would seem that to create is proper to some Person. For what comes first is the cause of what is after; and what is perfect is the cause of what is imperfect. But the procession of the divine Person is prior to the procession of the creature: and is more perfect, because the divine Person proceeds in perfect similitude of its principle; whereas the creature proceeds in imperfect similitude. Therefore the processions of the divine Persons are the cause of the processions of things, and so to create belongs to a Person.

Objection 2. Further, the divine Persons are distinguished from each other only by their processions and relations. Therefore whatever difference is attributed to the divine Persons belongs to them according to the processions and relations of the Persons. But the causation of creatures is diversely attributed to the divine Persons; for in the Creed, to the Father is attributed that "He is the Creator of all things visible and invisible"; to the Son is attributed that by Him "all things were made"; and to the Holy Ghost is attributed that He is "Lord and Life-giver." Therefore the causation of creatures belongs to the Persons according to processions and relations.

Objection 3. Further, if it be said that the causation of the creature flows from some essential attribute appropriated to some one Person, this does not appear to be sufficient; because every divine effect is caused by every essential attribute--viz. by power, goodness and wisdom--and thus does not belong to one more than to another. Therefore any determinate mode of causation ought not to be attributed to one Person more than to another, unless they are distinguished in creating according to relations and processions.

On the contrary, Dionysius says (Div. Nom. ii) that all things caused are the common work of the whole Godhead.

I answer that, To create is, properly speaking, to cause or produce the being of things. And as every agent produces its like, the principle of action can be considered from the effect of the action; for it must be fire that generates fire. And therefore to create belongs to God according to His being, that is, His essence, which is common to the three Persons. Hence to create is not proper to any one Person, but is common to the whole Trinity.

Nevertheless the divine Persons, according to the nature of their procession, have a causality respecting the creation of things. For as was said above (14, 8; 19, 4), when treating of the knowledge and will of God, God is the cause of things by His intellect and will, just as the craftsman is cause of the things made by his craft. Now the craftsman works through the word conceived in his mind, and through the love of his will regarding some object. Hence also God the Father made the creature through His Word, which is His Son; and through His Love, which is the Holy Ghost. And so the processions of the Persons are the type of the productions of creatures inasmuch as they include the essential attributes, knowledge and will.

Reply to Objection 1. The processions of the divine Persons are the cause of creation, as above explained.

Reply to Objection 2. As the divine nature, although common to the three Persons, still belongs to them in a kind of order, inasmuch as the Son receives the divine nature from the Father, and the Holy Ghost from both: so also likewise the power of creation, whilst common to the three Persons, belongs to them in a kind of order. For the Son receives it from the Father, and the Holy Ghost from both. Hence to be the Creator is attributed to the Father as to Him Who does not receive the power of creation from another. And of the Son it is said (John 1:3), "Through Him all things were made," inasmuch as He has the same power, but from another; for this preposition "through" usually denotes a mediate cause, or "a principle from a principle." But to the Holy Ghost,

Who has the same power from both, is attributed that by His sway He governs, and quickens what is created by the Father through the Son. Again, the reason for this particular appropriation may be taken from the common notion of the appropriation of the essential attributes. For, as above stated (39, 8, ad 3), to the Father is appropriated power which is chiefly shown in creation, and therefore it is attributed to Him to be the Creator. To the Son is appropriated wisdom, through which the intellectual agent acts; and therefore it is said: "Through Whom all things were made." And to the Holy Ghost is appropriated goodness, to which belong both government, which brings things to their proper end, and the giving of life--for life consists in a certain interior movement; and the first mover is the end, and goodness.

Reply to Objection 3. Although every effect of God proceeds from each attribute, each effect is reduced to that attribute with which it is naturally connected; thus the order of things is reduced to "wisdom," and the justification of the sinner to "mercy" and "goodness" poured out super-abundantly. But creation, which is the production of the very substance of a thing, is reduced to "power."

Article 7. Whether in creatures is necessarily found a trace of the Trinity?

Objection 1. It would seem that in creatures there is not necessarily found a trace of the Trinity. For anything can be traced through its traces. But the trinity of persons cannot be traced from the creatures, as was above stated (32, 1). Therefore there is no trace of the Trinity in creatures.

Objection 2. Further, whatever is in creatures is created. Therefore if the trace of the Trinity is found in creatures according to some of their properties, and if everything created has a trace of the Trinity, it follows that we can find a trace of the Trinity in each of these (properties): and so on to infinitude.

Objection 3. Further, the effect represents only its own cause. But the causality of creatures belongs to the common nature, and not to the relations whereby the Persons are distinguished and numbered. Therefore in the creature is to be found a trace not of the Trinity but of the unity of essence.

On the contrary, Augustine says (De Trin. vi, 10), that "the trace of the Trinity appears in creatures."

I answer that, Every effect in some degree represents its cause, but diversely. For some effects represent only the causality of the cause, but not its form; as smoke represents fire. Such a representation is called a "trace": for a trace shows that someone has passed by but not who it is. Other effects represent the cause as regards the similitude of its form, as fire generated represents fire generating; and a statue of Mercury represents Mercury; and this is called the representation of "image." Now the processions of the divine Persons are referred to the acts of intellect and will, as was said above (Article 27). For the Son proceeds as the word of the intellect; and the Holy Ghost proceeds as love of the will. Therefore in rational creatures, possessing intellect and will, there is found the representation of the Trinity by way of image, inasmuch as there is found in them the word conceived, and the love proceeding.

But in all creatures there is found the trace of the Trinity, inasmuch as in every creature are found some things which are necessarily reduced to the divine Persons as to their cause. For every creature subsists in its own being, and has a form, whereby it is determined to a species, and has relation to something else. Therefore as it is a created substance, it represents the cause and principle; and so in that manner it shows the Person of the Father, Who is the "principle from no principle." According as it has a form and species, it represents the Word as the form of the thing made by art is from the conception of the craftsman. According as it has relation of order, it represents the Holy Ghost, inasmuch as He is love, because the order of the effect to something else is from the will of the Creator. And therefore Augustine says (De Trin. vi 10) that the trace of the Trinity is found in every creature, according "as it is one individual," and according "as it is formed by a species," and according as it "has a certain relation of order." And to these also are reduced those three, "number," "weight," and "measure," mentioned in the Book of Wisdom (9:21). For "measure" refers to the substance of the thing limited by its principles, "number" refers to the species, "weight" refers to the order. And to these three are reduced the other three mentioned by Augustine (De Nat. Boni iii), "mode," "species," and "order," and also those he mentions (QQ. 83, qu. 18): "that which exists; whereby it is distinguished; whereby it agrees." For a thing exists by its substance, is distinct by its form, and agrees by its order. Other similar expressions may be easily reduced to the above.

Reply to Objection 1. The representation of the trace is to be referred to the appropriations: in which manner we are able to arrive at a knowledge of the trinity of the divine persons from creatures, as we have said (32, 1).

Reply to Objection 2. A creature properly speaking is a thing self-subsisting; and in such are the three above-mentioned things to be found. Nor is it necessary that these three things should be found in all that exists in the creature; but only to a subsisting being is the trace ascribed in regard to those three things.

Reply to Objection 3. The processions of the persons are also in some way the cause and type of creation; as appears from the above (Article 6).

Article 8. Whether creation is mingled with works of nature and art?

Objection 1. It would seem that creation is mingled in works of nature and art. For in every operation of nature and art some form is produced. But it is not produced from anything, since matter has no part in it. Therefore it is produced from nothing; and thus in every operation of nature and art there is creation.

Objection 2. Further, the effect is not more powerful than its cause. But in natural things the only agent is the accidental form, which is an active or a passive form. Therefore the substantial form is not produced by the operation of nature; and therefore it must be produced by creation.

Objection 3. Further, in nature like begets like. But some things are found generated in nature by a thing unlike to them; as is evident in animals generated through putrefaction. Therefore the form of these is not from nature, but by creation; and the same reason applies to other things.

Objection 4. Further, what is not created, is not a creature. If therefore in nature's productions there were not creation, it would follow that nature's productions are not creatures; which is heretical.

On the contrary, Augustine (Super Gen. v, 6,14,15) distinguishes the work of propagation, which is a work of nature, from the work of creation.

I answer that, The doubt on this subject arises from the forms which, some said, do not come into existence by the action of nature, but previously exist in matter; for they asserted that forms are latent. This arose from ignorance concerning matter, and from not knowing how to distinguish between potentiality and act. For because forms pre-exist in matter, "in potentiality," they asserted that they pre-exist "simply." Others, however, said that the forms were given or caused by a separate agent by way of creation; and accordingly, that to each operation of nature is joined creation. But this opinion arose from ignorance concerning form. For they failed to consider that the form of the natural body is not subsisting, but is that by which a thing is. And therefore, since to be made and to be created belong properly to a subsisting thing alone, as shown above (Article 4), it does not belong to forms to be made or to be created, but to be "concreated." What, indeed, is properly made by the natural agent is the "composite," which is made from matter.

Hence in the works of nature creation does not enter, but is presupposed to the work of nature.

Reply to Objection 1. Forms begin to be actual when the composite things are made, not as though they were made "directly," but only "indirectly."

Reply to Objection 2. The active qualities in nature act by virtue of substantial forms: and therefore the natural agent not only produces its like according to quality, but according to species.

Reply to Objection 3. For the generation of imperfect animals, a universal agent suffices, and this is to be found in the celestial power to which they are assimilated, not in species, but according to a kind of analogy. Nor is it necessary to say that their forms are created by a separate agent. However, for the generation of perfect animals the universal agent does not suffice, but a proper agent is required, in the shape of a univocal generator.

Reply to Objection 4. The operation of nature takes place only on the presupposition of created principles; and thus the products of nature are called creatures.

# Question 46. The beginning of the duration of creatures

## Article 1. Whether the universe of creatures always existed?

Objection 1. It would seem that the universe of creatures, called the world, had no beginning, but existed from eternity. For everything which begins to exist, is a possible being before it exists: otherwise it would be impossible for it to exist. If therefore the world began to exist, it was a possible being before it began to exist. But possible being is matter, which is in potentiality to existence, which results from a form, and to non-existence, which results from privation of form. If therefore the world began to exist, matter must have existed before the world. But matter cannot exist without form: while the matter of the world with its form is the world. Therefore the world existed before it began to exist: which is impossible.

Objection 2. Further, nothing which has power to be always, sometimes is and sometimes is not; because so far as the power of a thing extends so long is exists. But every incorruptible thing has power to be always; for its power does not extend to any determinate time. Therefore no incorruptible thing sometimes is, and sometimes is not: but everything which has a beginning at some time is, and at some time is not; therefore no incorruptible thing begins to exist. But there are many incorruptible things in the world, as the celestial bodies and all intellectual substances. Therefore the world did not begin to exist.

Objection 3. Further, what is unbegotten has no beginning. But the Philosopher (Phys. i, text 82) proves that matter is unbegotten, and also (De Coelo et Mundo i, text 20) that the heaven is unbegotten. Therefore the universe did not begin to exist.

Objection 4. Further, a vacuum is where there is not a body, but there might be. But if the world began to exist, there was first no body where the body of the world now is; and yet it could be there, otherwise it would not be there now. Therefore before the world there was a vacuum; which is impossible.

Objection 5. Further, nothing begins anew to be moved except through either the mover or the thing moved being otherwise than it was before. But what is otherwise now than it was before, is moved. Therefore before every new movement there was a previous movement. Therefore movement always was; and therefore also the thing moved always was, because movement is only in a movable thing.

Objection 6. Further, every mover is either natural or voluntary. But neither begins to move except by some pre-existing movement. For nature always moves in the same manner: hence unless some change precede either in the nature of the mover, or in the movable thing, there cannot arise from the natural mover a movement which was not there before. And the will, without itself being changed, puts off doing what it proposes to do; but this can be only by some imagined change, at least on the part of time. Thus he who wills to make a house tomorrow, and not today, awaits something which will be tomorrow, but is not today; and at least awaits for today to pass, and for tomorrow to come; and this cannot be without change, because time is the measure of movement. Therefore it remains that before every new movement, there was a previous movement; and so the same conclusion follows as before.

Objection 7. Further, whatever is always in its beginning, and always in its end, cannot cease and cannot begin; because what begins is not in its end, and what ceases is not in its beginning. But time always is in its beginning and end, because there is no time except "now" which is the end of the past and the beginning of the future. Therefore time cannot begin or end, and consequently neither can movement, the measure of what is time.

Objection 8. Further, God is before the world either in the order of nature only, or also by duration. If in the order of nature only, therefore, since God is eternal, the world also is eternal. But if God is prior by duration; since what is prior and posterior in duration constitutes time, it follows that time existed before the world, which is impossible.

Objection 9. Further, if there is a sufficient cause, there is an effect; for a cause to which there is no effect is an imperfect cause, requiring something else to make the effect follow. But God is the sufficient cause of the world; being the final cause, by reason of His goodness, the exemplar cause by reason of His wisdom, and the efficient cause, by reason of His power as appears from the above (44, 2,3,4). Since therefore God is eternal, the world is also eternal.

Objection 10. Further, eternal action postulates an eternal effect. But the action of God is His substance, which is eternal. Therefore the world is eternal.

On the contrary, It is said (John 17:5), "Glorify Me, O Father, with Thyself with the glory which I had before the world was"; and (Proverbs 8:22), "The Lord possessed Me in the beginning of His ways, before He made anything from the beginning."

I answer that, Nothing except God can be eternal. And this statement is far from impossible to uphold: for it has been shown above (Question 19, Article 4) that the will of God is the cause of things. Therefore things are necessary, according as it is necessary for God to will them, since the necessity of the effect depends on the necessity of the cause (Metaph. v, text 6). Now it was shown above (Question 19, Article 3), that, absolutely speaking, it is not necessary that God should will anything except Himself. It is not therefore necessary for God to will that the world should always exist; but the world exists forasmuch as God wills it to exist, since the being of the world depends on the will of God, as on its cause.

It is not therefore necessary for the world to be always; and hence it cannot be proved by demonstration.

Nor are Aristotle's reasons (Phys. viii) simply, but relatively, demonstrative--viz. in order to contradict the reasons of some of the ancients who asserted that the world began to exist in some quite impossible manner. This appears in three ways.

Firstly, because, both in Phys. viii and in De Coelo i, text 101, he premises some opinions, as those of Anaxagoras, Empedocles and Plato, and brings forward reasons to refute them.

Secondly, because wherever he speaks of this subject, he quotes the testimony of the ancients, which is not the way of a demonstrator, but of one persuading of what is probable.

Thirdly, because he expressly says (Topic. i, 9), that there are dialectical problems, about which we have nothing to say from reason, as, "whether the world is eternal."

Reply to Objection 1. Before the world existed it was possible for the world to be, not, indeed, according to a passive power which is matter, but according to the active power of God; and also, according as a thing is called absolutely possible, not in relation to any power, but from the sole habitude of the terms which are not repugnant to each other; in which sense possible is opposed to impossible, as appears from the Philosopher (Metaph. v, text 17).

Reply to Objection 2. Whatever has power always to be, from the fact of having that power, cannot sometimes be and sometimes not be; but before it received that power, it did not exist.

Hence this reason which is given by Aristotle (De Coelo i, text 120) does not prove simply that incorruptible things never began to exist; but that they did not begin by the natural mode whereby things generated and corruptible begin.

Reply to Objection 3. Aristotle (Phys. i, text 82) proves that matter is unbegotten from the fact that it has not a subject from which to derive its existence; and (De Coelo et Mundo i, text 20) he proves that heaven is ungenerated, forasmuch as it has no contrary from which to be generated. Hence it appears that no conclusion follows either way, except that matter and heaven did not begin by generation, as some said, especially about heaven. But we say that matter and heaven were produced into being by creation, as appears above (44, 1, ad 2).

Reply to Objection 4. The notion of a vacuum is not only "in which is nothing," but also implies a space capable of holding a body and in which there is not a body, as appears from Aristotle (Phys. iv, text 60). Whereas we hold that there was no place or space before the world was.

Reply to Objection 5. The first mover was always in the same state: but the first movable thing was not always so, because it began to be whereas hitherto it was not. This, however, was not through change, but by creation, which is not change, as said above (45, 2, as 2). Hence it is evident that this reason, which Aristotle gives (Phys. viii), is valid against those who admitted the existence of eternal movable things, but not eternal movement, as appears from the opinions of Anaxagoras and Empedocles. But we hold that from the moment that movable things began to exist movement also existed.

Reply to Objection 6. The first agent is a voluntary agent. And although He had the eternal will to produce some effect, yet He did not produce an eternal effect. Nor is it necessary for some change to be presupposed, not even on account of imaginary time. For we must take into consideration the difference between a particular agent, that presupposes something and produces something else, and the universal agent, who produces the whole. The particular agent produces the form, and presupposes the matter; and hence it is necessary that it introduce the form in due proportion into a suitable matter. Hence it is correct to say that it introduces the form into such matter, and not into another, on account of the different kinds of matter. But it is not correct to say so of God Who produces form and matter together: whereas it is correct to say of Him that He produces matter fitting to the form and to the end. Now, a particular agent presupposes time just as it presupposes matter. Hence it is correctly described as acting in time "after" and not in time "before," according to an imaginary succession of time after time. But the universal agent who produces the thing and time also, is not correctly described as acting now, and not before, according to an imaginary succession of time succeeding time, as if time were presupposed to His action; but He must be considered as giving time to His effect as much as and when He willed, and according to what was fitting to demonstrate His power. For the world leads more evidently to the knowledge of the divine creating power, if it was not always, than if it had always been; since everything which was not always manifestly has a cause; whereas this is not so manifest of what always was.

Reply to Objection 7. As is stated (Phys. iv, text 99), "before" and "after" belong to time, according as they are in movement. Hence beginning and end in time must be taken in the same way as in movement. Now, granted the eternity of movement, it is necessary that any given moment in movement be a beginning and an end of movement; which need not be if movement be a beginning. The same applies to the "now" of time. Thus it appears that the idea of the instant "now," as being always the beginning and end of time, presupposes the eternity of time and movement. Hence Aristotle brings forward this reason (Phys. viii, text 10) against those who asserted the eternity of time, but denied the eternity of movement.

Reply to Objection 8. God is prior to the world by priority of duration. But the word "prior" signifies priority not of time, but of eternity. Or we may say that it signifies the eternity of imaginary time, and not of time really existing; thus, when we say that above heaven there is nothing, the word "above" signifies only an imaginary place, according as it is possible to imagine other dimensions beyond those of the heavenly body.

Reply to Objection 9. As the effect follows from the cause that acts by nature, according to the mode of its form, so likewise it follows from the voluntary agent, according to the form preconceived and determined by the agent, as appears from what was said above (19, 4; 41, 2). Therefore, although God was from eternity the sufficient cause of the world, we should not say that the world was produced by Him, except as preordained by His will--that is, that it should have being after not being, in order more manifestly to declare its author.

Reply to Objection 10. Given the action, the effect follows according to the requirement of the form, which is the principle of action. But in agents acting by will, what is conceived and preordained is to be taken as the form, which is the principle of action. Therefore from the eternal action of God an eternal effect did not follow; but such an effect as God willed, an effect, to wit, which has being after not being.

Article 2. Whether it is an article of faith that the world began?

Objection 1. It would seem that it is not an article of faith but a demonstrable conclusion that the world began. For everything that is made has a beginning of its duration. But it can be proved demonstratively that God is the effective cause of the world; indeed this is asserted by the more approved philosophers. Therefore it can be demonstratively proved that the world began.

Objection 2. Further, if it is necessary to say that the world was made by God, it must therefore have been made from nothing or from something. But it was not made from something; otherwise the matter of the world would have preceded the world; against which are the arguments of Aristotle (De Coelo i), who held that heaven was ungenerated. Therefore it must be said that the world was made from nothing; and thus it has being after not being. Therefore it must have begun.

Objection 3. Further, everything which works by intellect works from some principle, as appears in all kinds of craftsmen. But God acts by intellect: therefore His work has a principle. The world, therefore, which is His effect, did not always exist.

Objection 4. Further, it appears manifestly that certain arts have developed, and certain countries have begun to be inhabited at some fixed time. But this would not be the case if the world had been always. Therefore it is manifest that the world did not always exist.

Objection 5. Further, it is certain that nothing can be equal to God. But if the world had always been, it would be equal to God in duration. Therefore it is certain that the world did not always exist.

Objection 6. Further, if the world always was, the consequence is that infinite days preceded this present day. But it is impossible to pass through an infinite medium. Therefore we should never have arrived at this present day; which is manifestly false.

Objection 7. Further, if the world was eternal, generation also was eternal. Therefore one man was begotten of another in an infinite series. But the father is the efficient cause of the son (Phys. ii, text 5). Therefore in efficient causes there could be an infinite series, which is disproved (Metaph. ii, text 5).

Objection 8. Further, if the world and generation always were, there have been an infinite number of men. But man's soul is immortal: therefore an infinite number of human souls would actually now exist, which is impossible. Therefore it can be known with certainty that the world began, and not only is it known by faith.

On the contrary, The articles of faith cannot be proved demonstratively, because faith is of things "that appear not" (Hebrews 11:1). But that God is the Creator of the world: hence that the world began, is an article of faith; for we say, "I believe in one God," etc. And again, Gregory says (Hom. i in Ezech.), that Moses prophesied of the past, saying, "In the beginning God created heaven and earth": in which words the newness of the world is stated. Therefore the newness of the world is known only by revelation; and therefore it cannot be proved demonstratively.

I answer that, By faith alone do we hold, and by no demonstration can it be proved, that the world did not always exist, as was said above of the mystery of the Trinity (32, 1). The reason of this is that the newness of the world cannot be demonstrated on the part of the world itself. For the principle of demonstration is the essence of a thing. Now everything according to its species is abstracted from "here" and "now"; whence it is said that universals are everywhere and always. Hence it cannot be demonstrated that man, or heaven, or a stone were not always. Likewise neither can it be demonstrated on the part of the efficient cause, which acts by will. For the will of God cannot be investigated by reason, except as regards those things which God must will of necessity; and what He wills about creatures is not among these, as was said above (Question 19, Article 3). But the divine will can be manifested by revelation, on which faith rests. Hence that the world began to exist is an object of faith, but not of demonstration or science. And it is useful to consider this, lest anyone, presuming to demonstrate what is of faith, should bring forward reasons that are not cogent, so as to give occasion to unbelievers to laugh, thinking that on such grounds we believe things that are of faith.

Reply to Objection 1. As Augustine says (De Civ. Dei xi, 4), the opinion of philosophers who asserted the eternity of the world was twofold. For some said that the substance of the world was not from God, which is an intolerable error; and therefore it is refuted by proofs that are cogent. Some, however, said that the world was eternal, although made by God. For they hold that the world has a beginning, not of time, but of creation, so that in a certain hardly intelligible way it was always made. "And they try to explain their meaning thus (De Civ. Dei x, 31): for as, if the foot were always in the dust from eternity, there would always be a footprint which without doubt was caused by him who trod on it, so also the world always was, because its Maker always existed." To understand this we must consider that the efficient cause, which acts by motion, of necessity precedes its effect in time; because the effect is only in the end of the action, and every agent must be the principle of action. But if the action is instantaneous and not successive, it is not necessary for the maker to be prior to the thing made in duration as appears in the case of illumination. Hence they say that it does not follow necessarily if God is the active cause of the world, that He should be prior to the world in duration; because creation, by which He produced the world, is not a successive change, as was said above (Question 45, Article 2).

Reply to Objection 2. Those who would say that the world was eternal, would say that the world was made by God from nothing, not that it was made after nothing, according to what we understand by the word creation, but that it was not made from anything; and so also some of them do not reject the word creation, as appears from Avicenna (Metaph. ix, text 4).

Reply to Objection 3. This is the argument of Anaxagoras (as quoted in Phys. viii, text 15). But it does not lead to a necessary conclusion, except as to that intellect which deliberates in order to find out what should be done, which is like movement. Such is the human intellect, but not the divine intellect (14, 7,12).

Reply to Objection 4. Those who hold the eternity of the world hold that some region was changed an infinite number of times, from being uninhabitable to being inhabitable and "vice versa," and likewise they hold that the arts, by reason of various corruptions and accidents, were subject to an infinite variety of advance and decay. Hence Aristotle says (Meteor. i), that it is absurd from such particular changes to hold the opinion of the newness of the whole world.

Reply to Objection 5. Even supposing that the world always was, it would not be equal to God in eternity, as Boethius says (De Consol. v, 6); because the divine Being is all being simultaneously without succession; but with the world it is otherwise.

Reply to Objection 6. Passage is always understood as being from term to term. Whatever bygone day we choose, from it to the present day there is a finite number of days which can be passed through. The objection is founded on the idea that, given two extremes, there is an infinite number of mean terms.

Reply to Objection 7. In efficient causes it is impossible to proceed to infinity "per se"--thus, there cannot be an infinite number of causes that are "per se" required for a certain effect; for instance, that a stone be moved by a stick, the stick by the hand, and so on to infinity. But it is not impossible to proceed to infinity "accidentally" as regards efficient causes; for instance, if all the causes thus infinitely multiplied should have the order of only one cause, their multiplication being accidental, as an artificer acts by means of many hammers accidentally, because one after the other may be broken. It is accidental, therefore, that one particular hammer acts after the action of another; and likewise it is accidental to this particular man as generator to be generated by another man; for he generates as a man, and not as the son of another man. For all men generating hold one grade in efficient causes--viz. the grade of a particular generator. Hence it is not impossible for a man to be generated by man to infinity; but such a thing would be impossible if the generation of this man depended upon this man, and on an elementary body, and on the sun, and so on to infinity.

Reply to Objection 8. Those who hold the eternity of the world evade this reason in many ways. For some do not think it impossible for there to be an actual infinity of souls, as appears from the Metaphysics of Algazel, who says that such a thing is an accidental infinity. But this was disproved above (Question 7, Article 4). Some say that the soul is corrupted with the body. And some say that of all souls only one will remain. But others, as Augustine says [Serm. xiv, De Temp. 4,5; De Haeres., haeres. 46; De Civ. Dei xii. 13, asserted on this account a circuit of souls--viz. that souls separated from their bodies return again thither after a course of time; a fuller consideration of which matters will be given later (75, 2; 118, 6). But be it noted that this argument considers only a particular case. Hence one might say that the world was eternal, or least some creature, as an angel, but not man. But we are considering the question in general, as to whether any creature can exist from eternity.

Article 3. Whether the creation of things was in the beginning of time?

Objection 1. It would seem that the creation of things was not in the beginning of time. For whatever is not in time, is not of any part of time. But the creation of things was not in time; for by the creation the substance of things was brought into being; and time does not measure the substance of things, and especially of incorporeal things. Therefore creation was not in the beginning of time.

Objection 2. Further, the Philosopher proves (Phys. vi, text 40) that everything which is made, was being made; and so to be made implies a "before" and "after." But in the beginning of time, since it is indivisible, there is no "before" and "after." Therefore, since to be created is a kind of "being made," it appears that things were not created in the beginning of time.

Objection 3. Further, even time itself is created. But time cannot be created in the beginning of time, since time is divisible, and the beginning of time is indivisible. Therefore, the creation of things was not in the beginning of time.

On the contrary, It is said (Genesis 1:1): "In the beginning God created heaven and earth."

I answer that, The words of Genesis, "In the beginning God created heaven and earth," are expounded in a threefold sense in order to exclude three errors. For some said that the world always was, and that time had no beginning; and to exclude this the words "In the beginning" are expounded--viz. "of time." And some said that there are two principles of creation, one of good things and the other of evil things, against which "In the beginning" is expounded--"in the Son." For as the efficient principle is appropriated to the Father by reason of power, so the exemplar principle is appropriated to the Son by reason of wisdom, in order that, as it is said (Psalm 103:24), "Thou hast made all things in wisdom," it may be understood that God made all things in the beginning--that is, in the Son; according to the word of the Apostle (Colossians 1:16), "In Him"--viz. the Son--"were created all things." But others said that corporeal things were created by God through the medium of spiritual creation; and to exclude this it is expounded thus: "In the beginning"--i.e. before all things--"God created heaven and earth." For four things are stated to be created together--viz. the empyrean heaven, corporeal matter, by which is meant the earth, time, and the angelic nature.

Reply to Objection 1. Things are said to be created in the beginning of time, not as if the beginning of time were a measure of creation, but because together with time heaven and earth were created.

Reply to Objection 2. This saying of the Philosopher is understood "of being made" by means of movement, or as the term of movement. Because, since in every movement there is "before" and "after," before any one point in a given movement--that is, whilst anything is in the process of being moved and made, there is a "before" and also an "after," because what is in the beginning of movement or in its term is not in "being moved." But creation is neither movement nor the term of movement, as was said above (45, 2,3). Hence a thing is created in such a way that it was not being created before.

Reply to Objection 3. Nothing is made except as it exists. But nothing exists of time except "now." Hence time cannot be made except according to some "now"; not because in the first "now" is time, but because from it time begins.

# The Book of Job
(RSV)

Job.1

[1] There was a man in the land of Uz, whose name was Job; and that man was blameless and upright, one who feared God, and turned away from evil.

[2] There were born to him seven sons and three daughters.

[3] He had seven thousand sheep, three thousand camels, five hundred yoke of oxen, and five hundred she-asses, and very many servants; so that this man was the greatest of all the people of the east.

[4] His sons used to go and hold a feast in the house of each on his day; and they would send and invite their three sisters to eat and drink with them.

[5] And when the days of the feast had run their course, Job would send and sanctify them, and he would rise early in the morning and offer burnt offerings according to the number of them all; for Job said, "It may be that my sons have sinned, and cursed God in their hearts." Thus Job did continually.

[6] Now there was a day when the sons of God came to present themselves before the LORD, and Satan also came among them.

[7] The LORD said to Satan, "Whence have you come?" Satan answered the LORD, "From going to and fro on the earth, and from walking up and down on it."

[8] And the LORD said to Satan, "Have you considered my servant Job, that there is none like him on the earth, a blameless and upright man, who fears God and turns away from evil?"

[9] Then Satan answered the LORD, "Does Job fear God for nought?

[10] Hast thou not put a hedge about him and his house and all that he has, on every side? Thou hast blessed the work of his hands, and his possessions have increased in the land.

[11] But put forth thy hand now, and touch all that he has, and he will curse thee to thy face."

[12] And the LORD said to Satan, "Behold, all that he has is in your power; only upon himself do not put forth your hand." So Satan went forth from the presence of the LORD.

[13] Now there was a day when his sons and daughters were eating and drinking wine in their eldest brother's house;

[14] and there came a messenger to Job, and said, "The oxen were plowing and the asses feeding beside them;

[15] and the Sabe'ans fell upon them and took them, and slew the servants with the edge of the sword; and I alone have escaped to tell you."

[16] While he was yet speaking, there came another, and said, "The fire of God fell from heaven and burned up the sheep and the servants, and consumed them; and I alone have escaped to tell you."

[17] While he was yet speaking, there came another, and said, "The Chalde'ans formed three companies, and made a raid upon the camels and took them, and slew the servants with the edge of the sword; and I alone have escaped to tell you."

[18] While he was yet speaking, there came another, and said, "Your sons and daughters were eating and drinking wine in their eldest brother's house;

[19] and behold, a great wind came across the wilderness, and struck the four corners of the house, and it fell upon the young people, and they are dead; and I alone have escaped to tell you."

[20] Then Job arose, and rent his robe, and shaved his head, and fell upon the ground, and worshiped.

[21] And he said, "Naked I came from my mother's womb, and naked shall I return; the LORD gave, and the LORD has taken away; blessed be the name of the LORD."

[22] In all this Job did not sin or charge God with wrong.

Job.2

[1] Again there was a day when the sons of God came to present themselves before the LORD, and Satan also came among them to present himself before the LORD.

[2] And the LORD said to Satan, "Whence have you come?" Satan answered the LORD, "From going to and fro on the earth, and from walking up and down on it."

[3] And the LORD said to Satan, "Have you considered my servant Job, that there is none like him on the earth, a blameless and upright man, who fears God and turns away from evil? He still holds fast his integrity, although you moved me against him, to destroy him without cause."

[4] Then Satan answered the LORD, "Skin for skin! All that a man has he will give for his life.

[5] But put forth thy hand now, and touch his bone and his flesh, and he will curse thee to thy face."

[6] And the LORD said to Satan, "Behold, he is in your power; only spare his life."

[7] So Satan went forth from the presence of the LORD, and afflicted Job with loathsome sores from the sole of his foot to the crown of his head.

[8] And he took a potsherd with which to scrape himself, and sat among the ashes.

[9] Then his wife said to him, "Do you still hold fast your integrity? Curse God, and die."

[10] But he said to her, "You speak as one of the foolish women would speak. Shall we receive good at the hand of God, and shall we not receive evil?" In all this Job did not sin with his lips.

[11] Now when Job's three friends heard of all this evil that had come upon him, they came each from his own place, Eli'phaz the Te'manite, Bildad the Shuhite, and Zophar the Na'amathite. They made an appointment together to come to condole with him and comfort him.

[12] And when they saw him from afar, they did not recognize him; and they raised their voices and wept; and they rent their robes and sprinkled dust upon their heads toward heaven.

[13] And they sat with him on the ground seven days and seven nights, and no one spoke a word to him, for they saw that his suffering was very great.

Job.3

[1] After this Job opened his mouth and cursed the day of his birth.
[2] And Job said:
[3] "Let the day perish wherein I was born,
and the night which said,
`A man-child is conceived.'
[4] Let that day be darkness!
May God above not seek it,
nor light shine upon it.
[5] Let gloom and deep darkness claim it.
Let clouds dwell upon it;
let the blackness of the day terrify it.
[6] That night -- let thick darkness seize it!
let it not rejoice among the days of the year,
let it not come into the number of the months.
[7] Yea, let that night be barren;
let no joyful cry be heard in it.
[8] Let those curse it who curse the day,
who are skilled to rouse up Levi'athan.
[9] Let the stars of its dawn be dark;
let it hope for light, but have none,
nor see the eyelids of the morning;
[10] because it did not shut the doors of my mother's womb,
nor hide trouble from my eyes.
[11] "Why did I not die at birth,
come forth from the womb and expire?
[12] Why did the knees receive me?
Or why the breasts, that I should suck?
[13] For then I should have lain down and been quiet;
I should have slept; then I should have been at rest,
[14] with kings and counselors of the earth
who rebuilt ruins for themselves,
[15] or with princes who had gold,
who filled their houses with silver.

[16] Or why was I not as a hidden untimely birth,
as infants that never see the light?
[17] There the wicked cease from troubling,
and there the weary are at rest.
[18] There the prisoners are at ease together;
they hear not the voice of the taskmaster.
[19] The small and the great are there,
and the slave is free from his master.
[20] "Why is light given to him that is in misery,
and life to the bitter in soul,
[21] who long for death, but it comes not,
and dig for it more than for hid treasures;
[22] who rejoice exceedingly,
and are glad, when they find the grave?
[23] Why is light given to a man whose way is hid,
whom God has hedged in?
[24] For my sighing comes as my bread,
and my groanings are poured out like water.
[25] For the thing that I fear comes upon me,
and what I dread befalls me.
[26] I am not at ease, nor am I quiet;
I have no rest; but trouble comes."

...

Job.32

[1] So these three men ceased to answer Job, because he was
righteous in his own eyes.
[2] Then Eli'hu the son of Bar'achel the Buzite, of the family of
Ram, became angry. He was angry at Job because he justified
himself rather than God;
[3] he was angry also at Job's three friends because they had found
no answer, although they had declared Job to be in the wrong.
[4] Now Eli'hu had waited to speak to Job because they were older
than he.

[5] And when Eli'hu saw that there was no answer in the mouth of these three men, he became angry.

[6] And Eli'hu the son of Bar'achel the Buzite answered:
"I am young in years,
and you are aged;
therefore I was timid and afraid
to declare my opinion to you.

[7] I said, `Let days speak,
and many years teach wisdom.'

[8] But it is the spirit in a man,
the breath of the Almighty, that makes him understand.

[9] It is not the old that are wise,
nor the aged that understand what is right.

[10] Therefore I say, `Listen to me;
let me also declare my opinion.'

[11] "Behold, I waited for your words,
I listened for your wise sayings,
while you searched out what to say.

[12] I gave you my attention,
and, behold, there was none that confuted Job,
or that answered his words, among you.

[13] Beware lest you say, `We have found wisdom;
God may vanquish him, not man.'

[14] He has not directed his words against me,
and I will not answer him with your speeches.

[15] "They are discomfited, they answer no more;
they have not a word to say.

[16] And shall I wait, because they do not speak,
because they stand there, and answer no more?

[17] I also will give my answer;
I also will declare my opinion.

[18] For I am full of words,
the spirit within me constrains me.

[19] Behold, my heart is like wine that has no vent;
like new wineskins, it is ready to burst.

[20] I must speak, that I may find relief;

I must open my lips and answer.
[21] I will not show partiality to any person
or use flattery toward any man.
[22] For I do not know how to flatter,
else would my Maker soon put an end to me.

Job.33

[1] "But now, hear my speech, O Job,
and listen to all my words.
[2] Behold, I open my mouth;
the tongue in my mouth speaks.
[3] My words declare the uprightness of my heart,
and what my lips know they speak sincerely.
[4] The spirit of God has made me,
and the breath of the Almighty gives me life.
[5] Answer me, if you can;
set your words in order before me; take your stand.
[6] Behold, I am toward God as you are;
I too was formed from a piece of clay.
[7] Behold, no fear of me need terrify you;
my pressure will not be heavy upon you.
[8] "Surely, you have spoken in my hearing,
and I have heard the sound of your words.
[9] You say, `I am clean, without transgression;
I am pure, and there is no iniquity in me.
[10] Behold, he finds occasions against me,
he counts me as his enemy;
[11] he puts my feet in the stocks,
and watches all my paths.'
[12] "Behold, in this you are not right. I will answer you.
God is greater than man.
[13] Why do you contend against him,
saying, `He will answer none of my words'?
[14] For God speaks in one way,
and in two, though man does not perceive it.

[15] In a dream, in a vision of the night,
when deep sleep falls upon men,
while they slumber on their beds,
[16] then he opens the ears of men,
and terrifies them with warnings,
[17] that he may turn man aside from his deed,
and cut off pride from man;
[18] he keeps back his soul from the Pit,
his life from perishing by the sword.
[19] "Man is also chastened with pain upon his bed,
and with continual strife in his bones;
[20] so that his life loathes bread,
and his appetite dainty food.
[21] His flesh is so wasted away that it cannot be seen;
and his bones which were not seen stick out.
[22] His soul draws near the Pit,
and his life to those who bring death.
[23] If there be for him an angel,
a mediator, one of the thousand,
to declare to man what is right for him;
[24] and he is gracious to him, and says,
`Deliver him from going down into the Pit,
I have found a ransom;
[25] let his flesh become fresh with youth;
let him return to the days of his youthful vigor';
[26] then man prays to God, and he accepts him,
he comes into his presence with joy.
He recounts to men his salvation,
[27] and he sings before men, and says:
`I sinned and perverted what was right,
and it was not requited to me.
[28] He has redeemed my soul from going down into the Pit,
and my life shall see the light.'
[29] "Behold, God does all these things,
twice, three times, with a man,
[30] to bring back his soul from the Pit,

that he may see the light of life.
[31] Give heed, O Job, listen to me;
be silent, and I will speak.
[32] If you have anything to say, answer me;
speak, for I desire to justify you.
[33] If not, listen to me;
be silent, and I will teach you wisdom."

Job.34

[1] Then Eli'hu said:
[2] "Hear my words, you wise men,
and give ear to me, you who know;
[3] for the ear tests words
as the palate tastes food.
[4] Let us choose what is right;
let us determine among ourselves what is good.
[5] For Job has said, `I am innocent,
and God has taken away my right;
[6] in spite of my right I am counted a liar;
my wound is incurable, though I am without transgression.'
[7] What man is like Job,
who drinks up scoffing like water,
[8] who goes in company with evildoers
and walks with wicked men?
[9] For he has said, `It profits a man nothing
that he should take delight in God.'
[10] "Therefore, hear me, you men of understanding,
far be it from God that he should do wickedness,
and from the Almighty that he should do wrong.
[11] For according to the work of a man he will requite him,
and according to his ways he will make it befall him.
[12] Of a truth, God will not do wickedly,
and the Almighty will not pervert justice.
[13] Who gave him charge over the earth
and who laid on him the whole world?

[14] If he should take back his spirit to himself,
and gather to himself his breath,
[15] all flesh would perish together,
and man would return to dust.
[16] "If you have understanding, hear this;
listen to what I say.
[17] Shall one who hates justice govern?
Will you condemn him who is righteous and mighty,
[18] who says to a king, `Worthless one,'
and to nobles, `Wicked man';
[19] who shows no partiality to princes,
nor regards the rich more than the poor,
for they are all the work of his hands?
[20] In a moment they die;
at midnight the people are shaken and pass away,
and the mighty are taken away by no human hand.
[21] "For his eyes are upon the ways of a man,
and he sees all his steps.
[22] There is no gloom or deep darkness
where evildoers may hide themselves.
[23] For he has not appointed a time for any man
to go before God in judgment.
[24] He shatters the mighty without investigation,
and sets others in their place.
[25] Thus, knowing their works,
he overturns them in the night, and they are crushed.
[26] He strikes them for their wickedness
in the sight of men,
[27] because they turned aside from following him,
and had no regard for any of his ways,
[28] so that they caused the cry of the poor to come to him,
and he heard the cry of the afflicted --
[29] When he is quiet, who can condemn?
When he hides his face, who can behold him,
whether it be a nation or a man? --
[30] that a godless man should not reign,

that he should not ensnare the people.
[31] "For has any one said to God,
`I have borne chastisement; I will not offend any more;
[32] teach me what I do not see;
if I have done iniquity, I will do it no more'?
[33] Will he then make requital to suit you,
because you reject it?
For you must choose, and not I;
therefore declare what you know.
[34] Men of understanding will say to me,
and the wise man who hears me will say:
[35] `Job speaks without knowledge,
his words are without insight.'
[36] Would that Job were tried to the end,
because he answers like wicked men.
[37] For he adds rebellion to his sin;
he claps his hands among us,
and multiplies his words against God."

Job.35

[1] And Eli'hu said:
[2] "Do you think this to be just?
Do you say, `It is my right before God,'
[3] that you ask, `What advantage have I?
How am I better off than if I had sinned?'
[4] I will answer you
and your friends with you.
[5] Look at the heavens, and see;
and behold the clouds, which are higher than you.
[6] If you have sinned, what do you accomplish against him?
And if your transgressions are multiplied, what do you do to him?
[7] If you are righteous, what do you give to him;
or what does he receive from your hand?
[8] Your wickedness concerns a man like yourself,
and your righteousness a son of man.

[9] "Because of the multitude of oppressions people cry out;
they call for help because of the arm of the mighty.
[10] But none says, `Where is God my Maker,
who gives songs in the night,
[11] who teaches us more than the beasts of the earth,
and makes us wiser than the birds of the air?'
[12] There they cry out, but he does not answer,
because of the pride of evil men.
[13] Surely God does not hear an empty cry,
nor does the Almighty regard it.
[14] How much less when you say that you do not see him,
that the case is before him, and you are waiting for him!
[15] And now, because his anger does not punish,
and he does not greatly heed transgression,
[16] Job opens his mouth in empty talk,
he multiplies words without knowledge."

Job.36

[1] And Eli'hu continued, and said:
[2] "Bear with me a little, and I will show you,
for I have yet something to say on God's behalf.
[3] I will fetch my knowledge from afar,
and ascribe righteousness to my Maker.
[4] For truly my words are not false;
one who is perfect in knowledge is with you.
[5] "Behold, God is mighty, and does not despise any;
he is mighty in strength of understanding.
[6] He does not keep the wicked alive,
but gives the afflicted their right.
[7] He does not withdraw his eyes from the righteous,
but with kings upon the throne
he sets them for ever, and they are exalted.
[8] And if they are bound in fetters
and caught in the cords of affliction,
[9] then he declares to them their work

and their transgressions, that they are behaving arrogantly.
[10] He opens their ears to instruction,
and commands that they return from iniquity.
[11] If they hearken and serve him,
they complete their days in prosperity,
and their years in pleasantness.
[12] But if they do not hearken, they perish by the sword,
and die without knowledge.
[13] "The godless in heart cherish anger;
they do not cry for help when he binds them.
[14] They die in youth,
and their life ends in shame.
[15] He delivers the afflicted by their affliction,
and opens their ear by adversity.
[16] He also allured you out of distress
into a broad place where there was no cramping,
and what was set on your table was full of fatness.
[17] "But you are full of the judgment on the wicked;
judgment and justice seize you.
[18] Beware lest wrath entice you into scoffing;
and let not the greatness of the ransom turn you aside.
[19] Will your cry avail to keep you from distress,
or all the force of your strength?
[20] Do not long for the night,
when peoples are cut off in their place.
[21] Take heed, do not turn to iniquity,
for this you have chosen rather than affliction.
[22] Behold, God is exalted in his power;
who is a teacher like him?
[23] Who has prescribed for him his way,
or who can say, `Thou hast done wrong'?
[24] "Remember to extol his work,
of which men have sung.
[25] All men have looked on it;
man beholds it from afar.
[26] Behold, God is great, and we know him not;

the number of his years is unsearchable.
[27] For he draws up the drops of water,
he distils his mist in rain
[28] which the skies pour down,
and drop upon man abundantly.
[29] Can any one understand the spreading of the clouds,
the thunderings of his pavilion?
[30] Behold, he scatters his lightning about him,
and covers the roots of the sea.
[31] For by these he judges peoples;
he gives food in abundance.
[32] He covers his hands with the lightning,
and commands it to strike the mark.
[33] Its crashing declares concerning him,
who is jealous with anger against iniquity.

Job.37

[1] "At this also my heart trembles,
and leaps out of its place.
[2] Hearken to the thunder of his voice
and the rumbling that comes from his mouth.
[3] Under the whole heaven he lets it go,
and his lightning to the corners of the earth.
[4] After it his voice roars;
he thunders with his majestic voice
and he does not restrain the lightnings when his voice is heard.
[5] God thunders wondrously with his voice;
he does great things which we cannot comprehend.
[6] For to the snow he says, `Fall on the earth';
and to the shower and the rain, `Be strong.'
[7] He seals up the hand of every man,
that all men may know his work.
[8] Then the beasts go into their lairs,
and remain in their dens.
[9] From its chamber comes the whirlwind,

and cold from the scattering winds.
[10] By the breath of God ice is given,
and the broad waters are frozen fast.
[11] He loads the thick cloud with moisture;
the clouds scatter his lightning.
[12] They turn round and round by his guidance,
to accomplish all that he commands them
on the face of the habitable world.
[13] Whether for correction, or for his land,
or for love, he causes it to happen.
[14] "Hear this, O Job;
stop and consider the wondrous works of God.
[15] Do you know how God lays his command upon them,
and causes the lightning of his cloud to shine?
[16] Do you know the balancings of the clouds,
the wondrous works of him who is perfect in knowledge,
[17] you whose garments are hot
when the earth is still because of the south wind?
[18] Can you, like him, spread out the skies,
hard as a molten mirror?
[19] Teach us what we shall say to him;
we cannot draw up our case because of darkness.
[20] Shall it be told him that I would speak?
Did a man ever wish that he would be swallowed up?
[21] "And now men cannot look on the light
when it is bright in the skies,
when the wind has passed and cleared them.
[22] Out of the north comes golden splendor;
God is clothed with terrible majesty.
[23] The Almighty -- we cannot find him;
he is great in power and justice,
and abundant righteousness he will not violate.
[24] Therefore men fear him;
he does not regard any who are wise in their own conceit."

Job.38

[1] Then the LORD answered Job out of the whirlwind:
[2] "Who is this that darkens counsel by words without knowledge?
[3] Gird up your loins like a man,
I will question you, and you shall declare to me.
[4] "Where were you when I laid the foundation of the earth?
Tell me, if you have understanding.
[5] Who determined its measurements -- surely you know!
Or who stretched the line upon it?
[6] On what were its bases sunk,
or who laid its cornerstone,
[7] when the morning stars sang together,
and all the sons of God shouted for joy?
[8] "Or who shut in the sea with doors,
when it burst forth from the womb;
[9] when I made clouds its garment,
and thick darkness its swaddling band,
[10] and prescribed bounds for it,
and set bars and doors,
[11] and said, `Thus far shall you come, and no farther,
and here shall your proud waves be stayed'?
[12] "Have you commanded the morning since your days began,
and caused the dawn to know its place,
[13] that it might take hold of the skirts of the earth,
and the wicked be shaken out of it?
[14] It is changed like clay under the seal,
and it is dyed like a garment.
[15] From the wicked their light is withheld,
and their uplifted arm is broken.
[16] "Have you entered into the springs of the sea,
or walked in the recesses of the deep?
[17] Have the gates of death been revealed to you,
or have you seen the gates of deep darkness?
[18] Have you comprehended the expanse of the earth?

Declare, if you know all this.
[19] "Where is the way to the dwelling of light,
and where is the place of darkness,
[20] that you may take it to its territory
and that you may discern the paths to its home?
[21] You know, for you were born then,
and the number of your days is great!
[22] "Have you entered the storehouses of the snow,
or have you seen the storehouses of the hail,
[23] which I have reserved for the time of trouble,
for the day of battle and war?
[24] What is the way to the place where the light is distributed,
or where the east wind is scattered upon the earth?
[25] "Who has cleft a channel for the torrents of rain,
and a way for the thunderbolt,
[26] to bring rain on a land where no man is,
on the desert in which there is no man;
[27] to satisfy the waste and desolate land,
and to make the ground put forth grass?
[28] "Has the rain a father,
or who has begotten the drops of dew?
[29] From whose womb did the ice come forth,
and who has given birth to the hoarfrost of heaven?
[30] The waters become hard like stone,
and the face of the deep is frozen.
[31] "Can you bind the chains of the Plei'ades,
or loose the cords of Orion?
[32] Can you lead forth the Maz'zaroth in their season,
or can you guide the Bear with its children?
[33] Do you know the ordinances of the heavens?
Can you establish their rule on the earth?
[34] "Can you lift up your voice to the clouds,
that a flood of waters may cover you?
[35] Can you send forth lightnings, that they may go
and say to you, `Here we are'?
[36] Who has put wisdom in the clouds,

or given understanding to the mists?
[37] Who can number the clouds by wisdom?
Or who can tilt the waterskins of the heavens,
[38] when the dust runs into a mass
and the clods cleave fast together?
[39] "Can you hunt the prey for the lion,
or satisfy the appetite of the young lions,
[40] when they crouch in their dens,
or lie in wait in their covert?
[41] Who provides for the raven its prey,
when its young ones cry to God,
and wander about for lack of food?

Job.39

[1] "Do you know when the mountain goats bring forth?
Do you observe the calving of the hinds?
[2] Can you number the months that they fulfil,
and do you know the time when they bring forth,
[3] when they crouch, bring forth their offspring,
and are delivered of their young?
[4] Their young ones become strong, they grow up in the open;
they go forth, and do not return to them.
[5] "Who has let the wild ass go free?
Who has loosed the bonds of the swift ass,
[6] to whom I have given the steppe for his home,
and the salt land for his dwelling place?
[7] He scorns the tumult of the city;
he hears not the shouts of the driver.
[8] He ranges the mountains as his pasture,
and he searches after every green thing.
[9] "Is the wild ox willing to serve you?
Will he spend the night at your crib?
[10] Can you bind him in the furrow with ropes,
or will he harrow the valleys after you?
[11] Will you depend on him because his strength is great,

and will you leave to him your labor?
[12] Do you have faith in him that he will return,
and bring your grain to your threshing floor?
[13] "The wings of the ostrich wave proudly;
but are they the pinions and plumage of love?
[14] For she leaves her eggs to the earth,
and lets them be warmed on the ground,
[15] forgetting that a foot may crush them,
and that the wild beast may trample them.
[16] She deals cruelly with her young, as if they were not hers;
though her labor be in vain, yet she has no fear;
[17] because God has made her forget wisdom,
and given her no share in understanding.
[18] When she rouses herself to flee,
she laughs at the horse and his rider.
[19] "Do you give the horse his might?
Do you clothe his neck with strength?
[20] Do you make him leap like the locust?
His majestic snorting is terrible.
[21] He paws in the valley, and exults in his strength;
he goes out to meet the weapons.
[22] He laughs at fear, and is not dismayed;
he does not turn back from the sword.
[23] Upon him rattle the quiver,
the flashing spear and the javelin.
[24] With fierceness and rage he swallows the ground;
he cannot stand still at the sound of the trumpet.
[25] When the trumpet sounds, he says `Aha!'
He smells the battle from afar,
the thunder of the captains, and the shouting.
[26] "Is it by your wisdom that the hawk soars,
and spreads his wings toward the south?
[27] Is it at your command that the eagle mounts up
and makes his nest on high?
[28] On the rock he dwells and makes his home
in the fastness of the rocky crag.

[29] Thence he spies out the prey;
his eyes behold it afar off.
[30] His young ones suck up blood;
and where the slain are, there is he."

Job.40

[1] And the LORD said to Job:
[2] "Shall a faultfinder contend with the Almighty?
He who argues with God, let him answer it."
[3] Then Job answered the LORD:
[4] "Behold, I am of small account; what shall I answer thee?
I lay my hand on my mouth.
[5] I have spoken once, and I will not answer;
twice, but I will proceed no further."
[6] Then the LORD answered Job out of the whirlwind:
[7] "Gird up your loins like a man;
I will question you, and you declare to me.
[8] Will you even put me in the wrong?
Will you condemn me that you may be justified?
[9] Have you an arm like God,
and can you thunder with a voice like his?
[10] "Deck yourself with majesty and dignity;
clothe yourself with glory and splendor.
[11] Pour forth the overflowings of your anger,
and look on every one that is proud, and abase him.
[12] Look on every one that is proud, and bring him low;
and tread down the wicked where they stand.
[13] Hide them all in the dust together;
bind their faces in the world below.
[14] Then will I also acknowledge to you,
that your own right hand can give you victory.
[15] "Behold, Be'hemoth,
which I made as I made you;
he eats grass like an ox.
[16] Behold, his strength in his loins,

and his power in the muscles of his belly.
[17] He makes his tail stiff like a cedar;
the sinews of his thighs are knit together.
[18] His bones are tubes of bronze,
his limbs like bars of iron.
[19] "He is the first of the works of God;
let him who made him bring near his sword!
[20] For the mountains yield food for him
where all the wild beasts play.
[21] Under the lotus plants he lies,
in the covert of the reeds and in the marsh.
[22] For his shade the lotus trees cover him;
the willows of the brook surround him.
[23] Behold, if the river is turbulent he is not frightened;
he is confident though Jordan rushes against his mouth.
[24] Can one take him with hooks,
or pierce his nose with a snare?

Job.41

[1] "Can you draw out Levi'athan with a fishhook,
or press down his tongue with a cord?
[2] Can you put a rope in his nose,
or pierce his jaw with a hook?
[3] Will he make many supplications to you?
Will he speak to you soft words?
[4] Will he make a covenant with you
to take him for your servant for ever?
[5] Will you play with him as with a bird,
or will you put him on leash for your maidens?
[6] Will traders bargain over him?
Will they divide him up among the merchants?
[7] Can you fill his skin with harpoons,
or his head with fishing spears?
[8] Lay hands on him;
think of the battle; you will not do it again!

[9] Behold, the hope of a man is disappointed;
he is laid low even at the sight of him.
[10] No one is so fierce that he dares to stir him up.
Who then is he that can stand before me?
[11] Who has given to me, that I should repay him?
Whatever is under the whole heaven is mine.
[12] "I will not keep silence concerning his limbs,
or his mighty strength, or his goodly frame.
[13] Who can strip off his outer garment?
Who can penetrate his double coat of mail?
[14] Who can open the doors of his face?
Round about his teeth is terror.
[15] His back is made of rows of shields,
shut up closely as with a seal.
[16] One is so near to another
that no air can come between them.
[17] They are joined one to another;
they clasp each other and cannot be separated.
[18] His sneezings flash forth light,
and his eyes are like the eyelids of the dawn.
[19] Out of his mouth go flaming torches;
sparks of fire leap forth.
[20] Out of his nostrils comes forth smoke,
as from a boiling pot and burning rushes.
[21] His breath kindles coals,
and a flame comes forth from his mouth.
[22] In his neck abides strength,
and terror dances before him.
[23] The folds of his flesh cleave together,
firmly cast upon him and immovable.
[24] His heart is hard as a stone,
hard as the nether millstone.
[25] When he raises himself up the mighty are afraid;
at the crashing they are beside themselves.
[26] Though the sword reaches him, it does not avail;
nor the spear, the dart, or the javelin.

[27] He counts iron as straw,
and bronze as rotten wood.
[28] The arrow cannot make him flee;
for him slingstones are turned to stubble.
[29] Clubs are counted as stubble;
he laughs at the rattle of javelins.
[30] His underparts are like sharp potsherds;
he spreads himself like a threshing sledge on the mire.
[31] He makes the deep boil like a pot;
he makes the sea like a pot of ointment.
[32] Behind him he leaves a shining wake;
one would think the deep to be hoary.
[33] Upon earth there is not his like,
a creature without fear.
[34] He beholds everything that is high;
he is king over all the sons of pride."

Job.42

[1] Then Job answered the LORD:
[2] "I know that thou canst do all things,
and that no purpose of thine can be thwarted.
[3] `Who is this that hides counsel without knowledge?'
Therefore I have uttered what I did not understand,
things too wonderful for me, which I did not know.
[4] `Hear, and I will speak;
I will question you, and you declare to me.'
[5] I had heard of thee by the hearing of the ear,
but now my eye sees thee;
[6] therefore I despise myself,
and repent in dust and ashes."
[7] After the LORD had spoken these words to Job, the LORD said
to Eli'phaz the Te'manite: "My wrath is kindled against you and
against your two friends; for you have not spoken of me what is
right, as my servant Job has.

[8] Now therefore take seven bulls and seven rams, and go to my servant Job, and offer up for yourselves a burnt offering; and my servant Job shall pray for you, for I will accept his prayer not to deal with you according to your folly; for you have not spoken of me what is right, as my servant Job has."

[9] So Eli'phaz the Te'manite and Bildad the Shuhite and Zophar the Na'amathite went and did what the LORD had told them; and the LORD accepted Job's prayer.

[10] And the LORD restored the fortunes of Job, when he had prayed for his friends; and the LORD gave Job twice as much as he had before.

[11] Then came to him all his brothers and sisters and all who had known him before, and ate bread with him in his house; and they showed him sympathy and comforted him for all the evil that the LORD had brought upon him; and each of them gave him a piece of money and a ring of gold.

[12] And the LORD blessed the latter days of Job more than his beginning; and he had fourteen thousand sheep, six thousand camels, a thousand yoke of oxen, and a thousand she-asses.

[13] He had also seven sons and three daughters.

[14] And he called the name of the first Jemi'mah; and the name of the second Kezi'ah; and the name of the third Ker'en-hap'puch.

[15] And in all the land there were no women so fair as Job's daughters; and their father gave them inheritance among their brothers.

[16] And after this Job lived a hundred and forty years, and saw his sons, and his sons' sons, four generations.

[17] And Job died, an old man, and full of days.

## Summa Theologica I

Question 22. The providence of God

Article 1. Whether providence can suitably be attributed to God?

Objection 1. It seems that providence is not becoming to God. For providence, according to Tully (De Invent. ii), is a part of prudence. But prudence, since, according to the Philosopher (Ethic. vi, 5,9,18), it gives good counsel, cannot belong to God, Who never has any doubt for which He should take counsel. Therefore providence cannot belong to God.

Objection 2. Further, whatever is in God, is eternal. But providence is not anything eternal, for it is concerned with existing things that are not eternal, according to Damascene (De Fide Orth. ii, 29). Therefore there is no providence in God.

Objection 3. Further, there is nothing composite in God. But providence seems to be something composite, because it includes both the intellect and the will. Therefore providence is not in God.

On the contrary, It is said (Wisdom 14:3): "But Thou, Father, governest all things by providence [Vulg. But 'Thy providence, O Father, governeth it.']."

I answer that, It is necessary to attribute providence to God. For all the good that is in created things has been created by God, as was shown above (Question 6, Article 4). In created things good is found not only as regards their substance, but also as regards their order towards an end and especially their last end, which, as was said above, is the divine goodness (21, 4). This good of order existing in things created, is itself created by God. Since, however, God is the cause of things by His intellect, and thus it behooves that the type of every effect should pre-exist in Him, as is clear from what has gone before (19, 4), it is necessary that the type of the order of things towards their end should pre-exist in the divine mind: and the type of things ordered towards an end is, properly speaking, providence. For it is the chief part of prudence, to which two other parts are directed--namely, remembrance of the past, and understanding of the present; inasmuch as from the remembrance of what is past and the understanding of what is present, we gather how to provide for the future. Now it belongs to prudence, according to the Philosopher (Ethic. vi, 12), to direct other things towards an end whether in regard to oneself--as for instance, a man is said to be prudent, who orders well his acts towards the end of life--or in regard to others subject to him, in a family, city or kingdom; in which sense it is said (Matthew 24:45), "a faithful and wise servant, whom his lord hath appointed over his family." In this way prudence or providence may suitably be attributed to God. For in God Himself there can be nothing ordered towards an end, since He is the last end. This type of order in things towards an end is therefore in God called providence. Whence Boethius says (De Consol. iv, 6) that "Providence is the divine type itself, seated in the Supreme Ruler; which disposeth all things": which disposition may refer either to the type of the order of things towards an end, or to the type of the order of parts in the whole.

Reply to Objection 1. According to the Philosopher (Ethic. vi, 9,10), "Prudence is what, strictly speaking, commands all that 'ebulia' has rightly counselled and 'synesis' rightly judged" [Cf. I-II, 57, 6]. Whence, though to take counsel may not be fitting to God, from the fact that counsel is an inquiry into matters that are doubtful, nevertheless to give a command as to the ordering of things towards an end, the right reason of which He possesses, does belong to God, according to Psalm 148:6: "He hath made a decree, and it shall not pass away." In this manner both prudence and providence belong to God. Although at the same time it may be said that the very reason of things to be done is called counsel in God; not because of any inquiry necessitated, but from the certitude of the knowledge, to which those who take counsel come by inquiry. Whence it is said: "Who worketh all things according to the counsel of His will" (Ephesians 1:11).

Reply to Objection 2. Two things pertain to the care of providence--namely, the "reason of order," which is called providence and disposition; and the execution of order, which is termed government. Of these, the first is eternal, and the second is temporal.

Reply to Objection 3. Providence resides in the intellect; but presupposes the act of willing the end. Nobody gives a precept about things done for an end; unless he will that end. Hence prudence presupposes the moral virtues, by means of which the appetitive faculty is directed towards good, as the Philosopher says. Even if Providence has to do with the divine will and intellect equally, this would not affect the divine simplicity, since in God both the will and intellect are one and the same thing, as we have said above (Article 19).

Article 2. Whether everything is subject to the providence of God?

Objection 1. It seems that everything is not subject to divine providence. For nothing foreseen can happen by chance. If then everything was foreseen by God, nothing would happen by chance. And thus hazard and luck would disappear; which is against common opinion.

Objection 2. Further, a wise provider excludes any defect or evil, as far as he can, from those over whom he has a care. But we see many evils existing. Either, then, God cannot hinder these, and thus is not omnipotent; or else He does not have care for everything.

Objection 3. Further, whatever happens of necessity does not require providence or prudence. Hence, according to the Philosopher (Ethic. vi, 5,9, 10,11): "Prudence is the right reason of things contingent concerning which there is counsel and choice." Since, then, many things happen from necessity, everything cannot be subject to providence.

Objection 4. Further, whatsoever is left to itself cannot be subject to the providence of a governor. But men are left to themselves by God in accordance with the words: "God made man from the beginning, and left him in the hand of his own counsel" (Sirach 15:14). And particularly in reference to the wicked: "I let them go according to the desires of their heart" (Psalm 80:13). Everything, therefore, cannot be subject to divine providence.

Objection 5. Further, the Apostle says (1 Corinthians 9:9): "God doth not care for oxen [Vulg. 'Doth God take care for oxen?']": and we may say the same of other irrational creatures. Thus everything cannot be under the care of divine providence.

On the contrary, It is said of Divine Wisdom: "She reacheth from end to end mightily, and ordereth all things sweetly" (Wisdom 8:1).

I answer that, Certain persons totally denied the existence of providence, as Democritus and the Epicureans, maintaining that the world was made by chance. Others taught that incorruptible things only were subject to providence and corruptible things not in their individual selves, but only according to their species; for in this respect they are incorruptible. They are represented as saying (Job 22:14): "The clouds are His covert; and He doth not consider our things; and He walketh about the poles of heaven." Rabbi Moses, however, excluded men from the generality of things corruptible, on account of the excellence of the intellect which they possess, but in reference to all else that suffers corruption he adhered to the opinion of the others.

We must say, however, that all things are subject to divine providence, not only in general, but even in their own individual selves. This is made evident thus. For since every agent acts for an end, the ordering of effects towards that end extends as far as the causality of the first agent extends. Whence it happens that in the effects of an agent something takes place which has no reference towards the end, because the effect comes from a cause other than, and outside the intention of the agent. But the causality of God, Who is the first agent, extends to all being, not only as to constituent principles of species, but also as to the individualizing principles; not only of things incorruptible, but also of things corruptible. Hence all things that exist in whatsoever manner are necessarily directed by God towards some end; as the Apostle says: "Those things that are of God are well ordered [Vulg.'Those powers that are, are ordained of God': 'Quae autem sunt, a Deo ordinatae sunt.' St. Thomas often quotes this passage, and invariably reads: 'Quae a Deo sunt, ordinata sunt.']" (Romans 13:1). Since, therefore, as the providence of God is nothing less than the type of the order of things towards an end, as we have said; it necessarily follows that all things, inasmuch as they participate in existence, must likewise be subject to divine providence. It has also been shown (14, 6, 11) that God knows all things, both universal and particular. And since His knowledge may be compared to the things themselves, as the knowledge of art to the objects of art, all things must of necessity come under His ordering; as all things wrought by art are subject to the ordering of that art.

Reply to Objection 1. There is a difference between universal and particular causes. A thing can escape the order of a particular cause; but not the order of a universal cause. For nothing escapes the order of a particular cause, except through the intervention and hindrance of some other particular cause; as, for instance, wood may be prevented from burning, by the action of water. Since then, all particular causes are included under the universal cause, it could not be that any effect should take place outside the range of that universal cause. So far then as an effect escapes the order of a particular cause, it is said to be casual or fortuitous in respect to that cause; but if we regard the universal cause, outside whose range no effect can happen, it is said to be foreseen. Thus, for instance, the meeting of two servants, although to them it appears a chance circumstance, has been fully foreseen by their master, who has purposely sent to meet at the one place, in such a way that the one knows not about the other.

Reply to Objection 2. It is otherwise with one who has care of a particular thing, and one whose providence is universal, because a particular provider excludes all defects from what is subject to his care as far as he can; whereas, one who provides universally allows some little defect to remain, lest the good of the whole should be hindered. Hence, corruption and defects in natural things are said to be contrary to some particular nature; yet they are in keeping with the plan of universal nature; inasmuch as the defect in one thing yields to the good of another, or even to the universal good: for the corruption of one is the generation of another, and through this it is that a species is kept in existence. Since God, then, provides universally for all being, it belongs to His providence to permit certain defects in particular effects, that the perfect good of the universe may not be hindered, for if all evil were prevented, much good would be absent from the universe. A lion would cease to live, if there were no slaying of animals; and there would be no patience of martyrs if there were no tyrannical persecution. Thus Augustine says (Enchiridion 2): "Almighty God would in no wise permit evil to exist in His works, unless He were so almighty and so good as to produce good even from evil." It would appear that it was on account of these two arguments to which we have just replied, that some were persuaded to consider corruptible things--e.g. casual and evil things--as removed from the care of divine providence.

Reply to Objection 3. Man is not the author of nature; but he uses natural things in applying art and virtue to his own use. Hence human providence does not reach to that which takes place in nature from necessity; but divine providence extends thus far, since God is the author of nature. Apparently it was this argument that moved those who withdrew the course of nature from the care of divine providence, attributing it rather to the necessity of matter, as Democritus, and others of the ancients.

Reply to Objection 4. When it is said that God left man to himself, this does not mean that man is exempt from divine providence; but merely that he has not a prefixed operating force determined to only the one effect; as in the case of natural things, which are only acted upon as though directed by another towards an end; and do not act of themselves, as if they directed themselves towards an end, like rational creatures, through the possession of free will, by which these are able to take counsel and make a choice. Hence it is significantly said: "In the hand of his own counsel." But since the very act of free will is traced to God as to a cause, it necessarily follows that everything happening from the exercise of free will must be subject to divine providence. For human providence is included under the providence of God, as a particular under a universal cause. God, however, extends His providence over the just in a certain more excellent way than over the wicked; inasmuch as He prevents anything happening which would impede their final salvation. For "to them that love God, all things work together unto good" (Romans 8:28). But from the fact that He does not restrain the wicked from the evil of sin, He is said to abandon them: not that He altogether withdraws His providence from them; otherwise they would return to nothing, if they were not preserved in existence by His providence. This was the reason that had weight with Tully, who withdrew from the care of divine providence human affairs concerning which we take counsel.

Reply to Objection 5. Since a rational creature has, through its free will, control over its actions, as was said above (Question 19, Article 10), it is subject to divine providence in an especial manner, so that something is imputed to it as a fault, or as a merit; and there is given it accordingly something by way of punishment or reward. In this way, the Apostle withdraws oxen from the care of God: not, however, that individual irrational creatures escape the care of divine providence; as was the opinion of the Rabbi Moses.

## Article 3. Whether God has immediate providence over everything?

Objection 1. It seems that God has not immediate providence over all things. For whatever is contained in the notion of dignity, must be attributed to God. But it belongs to the dignity of a king, that he should have ministers; through whose mediation he provides for his subjects. Therefore much less has God Himself immediate providence over all things.

Objection 2. Further, it belongs to providence to order all things to an end. Now the end of everything is its perfection and its good. But it appertains to every cause to direct its effect to good; wherefore every active cause is a cause of the effect of providence. If therefore God were to have immediate providence over all things, all secondary causes would be withdrawn.

Objection 3. Further, Augustine says (Enchiridion 17) that, "It is better to be ignorant of some things than to know them, for example, vile things": and the Philosopher says the same (Metaph. xii, 51). But whatever is better must be assigned to God. Therefore He has not immediate providence over bad and vile things.

On the contrary, It is said (Job 34:13): "What other hath He appointed over the earth? or whom hath He set over the world which He made?" On which passage Gregory says (Moral. xxiv, 20): "Himself He ruleth the world which He Himself hath made."

I answer that, Two things belong to providence--namely, the type of the order of things foreordained towards an end; and the execution of this order, which is called government. As regards the first of these, God has immediate providence over everything, because He has in His intellect the types of everything, even the smallest; and whatsoever causes He assigns to certain effects, He gives them the power to produce those effects. Whence it must be that He has beforehand the type of those effects in His mind. As to the second, there are certain intermediaries of God's providence; for He governs things inferior by superior, not on account of any defect in His power, but by reason of the abundance of His goodness; so that the dignity of causality is imparted even to creatures. Thus Plato's opinion, as narrated by Gregory of Nyssa (De Provid. viii, 3), is exploded. He taught a threefold providence.

First, one which belongs to the supreme Deity, Who first and foremost has provision over spiritual things, and thus over the whole world as regards genus, species, and universal causes. The second providence, which is over the individuals of all that can be generated and corrupted, he attributed to the divinities who circulate in the heavens; that is, certain separate substances, which move corporeal things in a circular direction. The third providence, over human affairs, he assigned to demons, whom the Platonic philosophers placed between us and the gods, as Augustine tells us (De Civ. Dei, 1, 2: viii, 14).

Reply to Objection 1. It pertains to a king's dignity to have ministers who execute his providence. But the fact that he has not the plan of those things which are done by them arises from a deficiency in himself. For every operative science is the more perfect, the more it considers the particular things with which its action is concerned.

Reply to Objection 2. God's immediate provision over everything does not exclude the action of secondary causes; which are the executors of His order, as was said above (19, 5, 8).

Reply to Objection 3. It is better for us not to know low and vile things, because by them we are impeded in our knowledge of what is better and higher; for we cannot understand many things simultaneously; because the thought of evil sometimes perverts the will towards evil. This does not hold with God, Who sees everything simultaneously at one glance, and whose will cannot turn in the direction of evil.

Article 4. Whether providence imposes any necessity on things foreseen?

Objection 1. It seems that divine providence imposes necessity upon things foreseen. For every effect that has a "per se" cause, either present or past, which it necessarily follows, happens from necessity; as the Philosopher proves (Metaph. vi, 7). But the providence of God, since it is eternal, pre-exists; and the effect flows from it of necessity, for divine providence cannot be frustrated. Therefore divine providence imposes a necessity upon things foreseen.

Objection 2. Further, every provider makes his work as stable as he can, lest it should fail. But God is most powerful. Therefore He assigns the stability of necessity to things provided.

Objection 3. Further, Boethius says (De Consol. iv, 6): "Fate from the immutable source of providence binds together human acts and fortunes by the indissoluble connection of causes." It seems therefore that providence imposes necessity upon things foreseen.

On the contrary, Dionysius says that (Div. Nom. iv, 23) "to corrupt nature is not the work of providence." But it is in the nature of some things to be contingent. Divine providence does not therefore impose any necessity upon things so as to destroy their contingency.

I answer that, Divine providence imposes necessity upon some things; not upon all, as some formerly believed. For to providence it belongs to order things towards an end. Now after the divine goodness, which is an extrinsic end to all things, the principal good in things themselves is the perfection of the universe; which would not be, were not all grades of being found in things. Whence it pertains to divine providence to produce every grade of being. And thus it has prepared for some things necessary causes, so that they happen of necessity; for others contingent causes, that they may happen by contingency, according to the nature of their proximate causes.

Reply to Objection 1. The effect of divine providence is not only that things should happen somehow; but that they should happen either by necessity or by contingency. Therefore whatsoever divine providence ordains to happen infallibly and of necessity happens infallibly and of necessity; and that happens from contingency, which the plan of divine providence conceives to happen from contingency.

Reply to Objection 2. The order of divine providence is unchangeable and certain, so far as all things foreseen happen as they have been foreseen, whether from necessity or from contingency.

Reply to Objection 3. That indissolubility and unchangeableness of which Boethius speaks, pertain to the certainty of providence, which fails not to produce its effect, and that in the way foreseen; but they do not pertain to the necessity of the effects. We must remember that properly speaking "necessary" and "contingent" are consequent upon being, as such. Hence the mode both of necessity and of contingency falls under the foresight of God, who provides universally for all being; not under the foresight of causes that provide only for some particular order of things.

*Summma Theologica* I

Question 23. Predestination

Article 1. Whether men are predestined by God?

Objection 1. It seems that men are not predestined by God, for Damascene says (De Fide Orth. ii, 30): "It must be borne in mind that God foreknows but does not predetermine everything, since He foreknows all that is in us, but does not predetermine it all." But human merit and demerit are in us, forasmuch as we are the masters of our own acts by free will. All that pertains therefore to merit or demerit is not predestined by God; and thus man's predestination is done away.

Objection 2. Further, all creatures are directed to their end by divine providence, as was said above (22, 1, 2). But other creatures are not said to be predestined by God. Therefore neither are men.

Objection 3. Further, the angels are capable of beatitude, as well as men. But predestination is not suitable to angels, since in them there never was any unhappiness (miseria); for predestination, as Augustine says (De praedest. sanct. 17), is the "purpose to take pity [miserendi]" [See 22, 3]. Therefore men are not predestined.

Objection 4. Further, the benefits God confers upon men are revealed by the Holy Ghost to holy men according to the saying of the Apostle (1 Corinthians 2:12): "Now we have received not the spirit of this world, but the Spirit that is of God: that we may know the things that are given us from God." Therefore if man were predestined by God, since predestination is a benefit from God, his predestination would be made known to each predestined; which is clearly false.

On the contrary, It is written (Romans 8:30): "Whom He predestined, them He also called."

I answer that, It is fitting that God should predestine men. For all things are subject to His providence, as was shown above (Question 22, Article 2). Now it belongs to providence to direct things towards their end, as was also said (22, 1, 2). The end towards which created things are directed by God is twofold; one which exceeds all proportion and faculty of created nature; and this end is life eternal, that consists in seeing God which is above the nature of every creature, as shown above (Question 12, Article 4). The other end, however, is proportionate to created nature, to which end created being can attain according to the power of its nature. Now if a thing cannot attain to something by the power of its nature, it must be directed thereto by another; thus, an arrow is directed by the archer towards a mark. Hence, properly speaking, a rational creature, capable of eternal life, is led towards it, directed, as it were, by God. The reason of that direction pre-exists in God; as in Him is the type of the order of all things towards an end, which we proved above to be providence. Now the type in the mind of the doer of something to be done, is a kind of pre-existence in him of the thing to be done. Hence the type of the aforesaid direction of a rational creature towards the end of life eternal is called predestination. For to destine, is to direct or send. Thus it is clear that predestination, as regards its objects, is a part of providence.

Reply to Objection 1. Damascene calls predestination an imposition of necessity, after the manner of natural things which are predetermined towards one end. This is clear from his adding: "He does not will malice, nor does He compel virtue." Whence predestination is not excluded by Him.

Reply to Objection 2. Irrational creatures are not capable of that end which exceeds the faculty of human nature. Whence they cannot be properly said to be predestined; although improperly the term is used in respect of any other end.

Reply to Objection 3. Predestination applies to angels, just as it does to men, although they have never been unhappy. For movement does not take its species from the term "wherefrom" but from the term "whereto." Because it matters nothing, in respect of the notion of making white, whether he who is made white was before black, yellow or red. Likewise it matters nothing in respect of the notion of predestination whether one is predestined to life eternal from the state of misery or not. Although it may be said that every conferring of good above that which is due pertains to mercy; as was shown previously (21, 3 and 4).

Reply to Objection 4. Even if by a special privilege their predestination were revealed to some, it is not fitting that it should be revealed to everyone; because, if so, those who were not predestined would despair; and security would beget negligence in the predestined.

Article 2. Whether predestination places anything in the predestined?

Objection 1. It seems that predestination does place something in the predestined. For every action of itself causes passion. If therefore predestination is action in God, predestination must be passion in the predestined.

Objection 2. Further, Origen says on the text, "He who was predestined," etc. (Romans 1:4): "Predestination is of one who is not; destination, of one who is." And Augustine says (De Praed. Sanct.): "What is predestination but the destination of one who is?" Therefore predestination is only of one who actually exists; and it thus places something in the predestined.

Objection 3. Further, preparation is something in the thing prepared. But predestination is the preparation of God's benefits, as Augustine says (De Praed. Sanct. ii, 14). Therefore predestination is something in the predestined.

Objection 4. Further, nothing temporal enters into the definition of eternity. But grace, which is something temporal, is found in the definition of predestination. For predestination is the preparation of grace in the present; and of glory in the future. Therefore predestination is not anything eternal. So it must needs be that it is in the predestined, and not in God; for whatever is in Him is eternal.

On the contrary, Augustine says (De Praed. Sanct. ii, 14) that "predestination is the foreknowledge of God's benefits." But foreknowledge is not in the things foreknown, but in the person who foreknows them. Therefore, predestination is in the one who predestines, and not in the predestined.

I answer that, Predestination is not anything in the predestined; but only in the person who predestines. We have said above that predestination is a part of providence. Now providence is not anything in the things provided for; but is a type in the mind of the provider, as was proved above (Question 22, Article 1). But the execution of providence which is called government, is in a passive way in the thing governed, and in an active way in the governor. Whence it is clear that predestination is a kind of type of the ordering of some persons towards eternal salvation, existing in the divine mind. The execution, however, of this order is in a passive way in the predestined, but actively in God. The execution of predestination is the calling and magnification; according to the Apostle (Romans 8:30): "Whom He predestined, them He also called and whom He called, them He also magnified [Vulg. 'justified']."

Reply to Objection 1. Actions passing out to external matter imply of themselves passion--for example, the actions of warming and cutting; but not so actions remaining in the agent, as understanding and willing, as said above (14, 2; 18, 3, ad 1). Predestination is an action of this latter class. Wherefore, it does not put anything in the predestined. But its execution, which passes out to external things, has an effect in them.

Reply to Objection 2. Destination sometimes denotes a real mission of someone to a given end; thus, destination can only be said of someone actually existing. It is taken, however, in another sense for a mission which a person conceives in the mind; and in this manner we are said to destine a thing which we firmly propose in our mind. In this latter way it is said that Eleazar "determined not to do any unlawful things for the love of life" (2 Maccabees 6:20). Thus destination can be of a thing which does not exist. Predestination, however, by reason of the antecedent nature it implies, can be attributed to a thing which does not actually exist; in whatsoever way destination is accepted.

Reply to Objection 3. Preparation is twofold: of the patient in respect to passion and this is in the thing prepared; and of the agent to action, and this is in the agent. Such a preparation is predestination, and as an agent by intellect is said to prepare itself to act, accordingly as it preconceives the idea of what is to be done. Thus, God from all eternity prepared by predestination, conceiving the idea of the order of some towards salvation.

Reply to Objection 4. Grace does not come into the definition of predestination, as something belonging to its essence, but inasmuch as predestination implies a relation to grace, as of cause to effect, and of act to its object. Whence it does not follow that predestination is anything temporal.

Article 3. Whether God reprobates any man?

Objection 1. It seems that God reprobates no man. For nobody reprobates what he loves. But God loves every man, according to (Wisdom 11:25): "Thou lovest all things that are, and Thou hatest none of the things Thou hast made." Therefore God reprobates no man.

Objection 2. Further, if God reprobates any man, it would be necessary for reprobation to have the same relation to the reprobates as predestination has to the predestined. But predestination is the cause of the salvation of the predestined. Therefore reprobation will likewise be the cause of the loss of the reprobate. But this false. For it is said (Hosea 13:9): "Destruction is thy own, O Israel; Thy help is only in Me." God does not, then, reprobate any man.

Objection 3. Further, to no one ought anything be imputed which he cannot avoid. But if God reprobates anyone, that one must perish. For it is said (Ecclesiastes 7:14): "Consider the works of God, that no man can correct whom He hath despised." Therefore it could not be imputed to any man, were he to perish. But this is false. Therefore God does not reprobate anyone.

On the contrary, It is said (Malachi 1:2-3): "I have loved Jacob, but have hated Esau."

I answer that, God does reprobate some. For it was said above (Article 1) that predestination is a part of providence. To providence, however, it belongs to permit certain defects in those things which are subject to providence, as was said above (Question 22, Article 2). Thus, as men are ordained to eternal life through the providence of God, it likewise is part of that providence to permit some to fall away from that end; this is called reprobation. Thus, as predestination is a part of providence, in regard to those ordained to eternal salvation, so reprobation is a part of providence in regard to those who turn aside from that end. Hence reprobation implies not only foreknowledge, but also something more, as does providence, as was said above (Question 22, Article 1). Therefore, as predestination includes the will to confer grace and glory; so also reprobation includes the will to permit a person to fall into sin, and to impose the punishment of damnation on account of that sin.

Reply to Objection 1. God loves all men and all creatures, inasmuch as He wishes them all some good; but He does not wish every good to them all. So far, therefore, as He does not wish this particular good--namely, eternal life--He is said to hate or reprobated them.

Reply to Objection 2. Reprobation differs in its causality from predestination. This latter is the cause both of what is expected in the future life by the predestined--namely, glory--and of what is received in this life--namely, grace. Reprobation, however, is not the cause of what is in the present--namely, sin; but it is the cause of abandonment by God. It is the cause, however, of what is assigned in the future--namely, eternal punishment. But guilt proceeds from the free-will of the person who is reprobated and deserted by grace. In this way, the word of the prophet is true-- namely, "Destruction is thy own, O Israel."

Reply to Objection 3. Reprobation by God does not take anything away from the power of the person reprobated. Hence, when it is said that the reprobated cannot obtain grace, this must not be understood as implying absolute impossibility: but only conditional impossibility: as was said above (Question 19, Article 3), that the predestined must necessarily be saved; yet a conditional necessity, which does not do away with the liberty of choice. Whence, although anyone reprobated by God cannot acquire grace, nevertheless that he falls into this or that particular sin comes from the use of his free-will. Hence it is rightly imputed to him as guilt.

Article 4. Whether the predestined are chosen by God?

Objection 1. It seems that the predestined are not chosen by God. For Dionysius says (Div. Nom. iv, 1) that as the corporeal sun sends his rays upon all without selection, so does God His goodness. But the goodness of God is communicated to some in an especial manner through a participation of grace and glory. Therefore God without any selection communicates His grace and glory; and this belongs to predestination.

Objection 2. Further, election is of things that exist. But predestination from all eternity is also of things which do not exist. Therefore, some are predestined without election.

Objection 3. Further, election implies some discrimination. Now God "wills all men to be saved" (1 Timothy 2:4). Therefore, predestination which ordains men towards eternal salvation, is without election.

On the contrary, It is said (Ephesians 1:4): "He chose us in Him before the foundation of the world."

I answer that, Predestination presupposes election in the order of reason; and election presupposes love. The reason of this is that predestination, as stated above (Article 1), is a part of providence. Now providence, as also prudence, is the plan existing in the intellect directing the ordering of some things towards an end; as was proved above (Question 22, Article 2). But nothing is directed towards an end unless the will for that end already exists. Whence the predestination of some to eternal salvation presupposes, in the order of reason, that God wills their salvation; and to this belong both election and love:--love, inasmuch as He wills them this particular good of eternal salvation; since to love is to wish well to anyone, as stated above (20, 2, 3):--election, inasmuch as He wills this good to some in preference to others; since He reprobates some, as stated above (Article 3). Election and love, however, are differently ordered in God, and in ourselves: because in us the will in loving does not cause good, but we are incited to love by the good which already exists; and therefore we choose someone to love, and so election in us precedes love. In God, however, it is the reverse. For His will, by which in loving He wishes good to someone, is the cause of that good possessed by some in preference to others. Thus it is clear that love precedes election in the order of reason, and election precedes predestination. Whence all the predestinate are objects of election and love.

Reply to Objection 1. If the communication of the divine goodness in general be considered, God communicates His goodness without election; inasmuch as there is nothing which does not in some way share in His goodness, as we said above (Question 6, Article 4). But if we consider the communication of this or that particular good, He does not allot it without election; since He gives certain goods to some men, which He does not give to others. Thus in the conferring of grace and glory election is implied.

Reply to Objection 2. When the will of the person choosing is incited to make a choice by the good already pre-existing in the object chosen, the choice must needs be of those things which already exist, as happens in our choice. In God it is otherwise; as was said above (Question 20, Article 2). Thus, as Augustine says (De Verb. Ap. Serm. 11): "Those are chosen by God, who do not exist; yet He does not err in His choice."

Reply to Objection 3. God wills all men to be saved by His antecedent will, which is to will not simply but relatively; and not by His consequent will, which is to will simply.

Article 5. Whether the foreknowledge of merits is the cause of predestination?

Objection 1. It seems that foreknowledge of merits is the cause of predestination. For the Apostle says (Romans 8:29): "Whom He foreknew, He also predestined." Again a gloss of Ambrose on Romans 9:15: "I will have mercy upon whom I will have mercy" says: "I will give mercy to him who, I foresee, will turn to Me with his whole heart." Therefore it seems the foreknowledge of merits is the cause of predestination.

Objection 2. Further, Divine predestination includes the divine will, which by no means can be irrational; since predestination is "the purpose to have mercy," as Augustine says (De Praed. Sanct. ii, 17). But there can be no other reason for predestination than the foreknowledge of merits. Therefore it must be the cause of reason of predestination.

Objection 3. Further, "There is no injustice in God" (Romans 9:14). Now it would seem unjust that unequal things be given to equals. But all men are equal as regards both nature and original sin; and inequality in them arises from the merits or demerits of their actions. Therefore God does not prepare unequal things for men by predestinating and reprobating, unless through the foreknowledge of their merits and demerits.

On the contrary, The Apostle says (Titus 3:5): "Not by works of justice which we have done, but according to His mercy He saved us." But as He saved us, so He predestined that we should be saved. Therefore, foreknowledge of merits is not the cause or reason of predestination.

I answer that, Since predestination includes will, as was said above (Article 4), the reason of predestination must be sought for in the same way as was the reason of the will of God. Now it was shown above (Question 19, Article 5), that we cannot assign any cause of the divine will on the part of the act of willing; but a reason can be found on the part of the things willed; inasmuch as God wills one thing on account of something else. Wherefore nobody has been so insane as to say that merit is the cause of divine predestination as regards the act of the predestinator. But this is the question, whether, as regards the effect, predestination has any cause; or what comes to the same thing, whether God pre-ordained that He would give the effect of predestination to anyone on account of any merits.

Accordingly there were some who held that the effect of predestination was pre-ordained for some on account of pre-existing merits in a former life. This was the opinion of Origen, who thought that the souls of men were created in the beginning, and according to the diversity of their works different states were assigned to them in this world when united with the body. The Apostle, however, rebuts this opinion where he says (Romans 9:11-12): "For when they were not yet born, nor had done any good or evil . . . not of works, but of Him that calleth, it was said of her: The elder shall serve the younger."

Others said that pre-existing merits in this life are the reason and cause of the effect of predestination. For the Pelagians taught that the beginning of doing well came from us; and the consummaion from God: so that it came about that the effect of predestination was granted to one, and not to another, because the one made a beginning by preparing, whereas the other did not. But against this we have the saying of the Apostle (2 Corinthians 3:5), that "we are not sufficient to think anything of ourselves as of ourselves." Now no principle of action can be imagined previous to the act of thinking. Wherefore it cannot be said that anything begun in us can be the reason of the effect of predestination.

And so others said that merits following the effect of predestination are the reason of predestination; giving us to understand that God gives grace to a person, and pre-ordains that He will give it, because He knows beforehand that He will make good use of that grace, as if a king were to give a horse to a soldier because he knows he will make good use of it. But these seem to have drawn a distinction between that which flows from grace, and that which flows from free will, as if the same thing cannot come from both. It is, however, manifest that what is of grace is the effect of predestination; and this cannot be considered as the reason of predestination, since it is contained in the notion of predestination. Therefore, if anything else in us be the reason of predestination, it will outside the effect of predestination. Now there is no distinction between what flows from free will, and what is of predestination; as there is not distinction between what flows from a secondary cause and from a first cause. For the providence of God produces effects through the operation of secondary causes, as was above shown (22, 3). Wherefore, that which flows from free-will is also of predestination. We must say, therefore, that the effect of predestination may be considered in a twofold light--in one way, in particular; and thus there is no reason why one effect of predestination should not be the reason or cause of another; a subsequent effect being the reason of a previous effect, as its final cause; and the previous effect being the reason of the subsequent as its meritorious cause, which is reduced to the disposition of the matter. Thus we might say that God pre-ordained to give glory on account of merit, and that He pre-ordained to give grace to merit glory. In another way, the effect of predestination may be considered in general. Thus, it is impossible that the whole of the effect of predestination in general should have any cause as coming from us; because whatsoever is in man disposing him towards salvation, is all included under the effect of predestination; even the preparation for grace. For neither does this happen otherwise than by divine help, according to the prophet Jeremias (Lamentations 5:21): "convert us, O Lord, to Thee, and we shall be converted." Yet predestination has in this way, in regard to its effect, the goodness of God for its reason; towards which the whole effect of predestination is directed as to an end; and from which it proceeds, as from its first moving principle.

Reply to Objection 1. The use of grace foreknown by God is not the cause of conferring grace, except after the manner of a final cause; as was explained above.

Reply to Objection 2. Predestination has its foundation in the goodness of God as regards its effects in general. Considered in its particular effects, however, one effect is the reason of another; as already stated.

Reply to Objection 3. The reason for the predestination of some, and reprobation of others, must be sought for in the goodness of God. Thus He is said to have made all things through His goodness, so that the divine goodness might be represented in things. Now it is necessary that God's goodness, which in itself is one and undivided, should be manifested in many ways in His creation; because creatures in themselves cannot attain to the simplicity of God. Thus it is that for the completion of the universe there are required different grades of being; some of which hold a high and some a low place in the universe. That this multiformity of grades may be preserved in things, God allows some evils, lest many good things should never happen, as was said above (Question 22, Article 2). Let us then consider the whole of the human race, as we consider the whole universe. God wills to manifest His goodness in men; in respect to those whom He predestines, by means of His mercy, as sparing them; and in respect of others, whom he reprobates, by means of His justice, in punishing them. This is the reason why God elects some and rejects others. To this the Apostle refers, saying (Romans 9:22-23): "What if God, willing to show His wrath [that is, the vengeance of His justice], and to make His power known, endured [that is, permitted] with much patience vessels of wrath, fitted for destruction; that He might show the riches of His glory on the vessels of mercy, which He hath prepared unto glory" and (2 Timothy 2:20): "But in a great house there are not only vessels of gold and silver; but also of wood and of earth; and some, indeed, unto honor, but some unto dishonor." Yet why He chooses some for glory, and reprobates others, has no reason, except the divine will. Whence Augustine says (Tract. xxvi. in Joan.): "Why He draws one, and another He draws not, seek not to judge, if thou dost not wish to err." Thus too, in the things of nature, a reason can be assigned, since primary matter is altogether uniform, why one part of it was fashioned by God from the beginning under the form of fire, another under the form of earth, that there might be a diversity of species in things of nature. Yet why this particular part of matter is under this particular form, and that under another, depends upon the simple will of God; as from the simple will of the artificer it depends that this stone is in part of the wall, and that in another; although the plan requires that some stones should be in this place, and some in that place. Neither on this account can there be said to be injustice in God, if He prepares unequal lots for not unequal things. This would be altogether contrary to the notion of justice, if the effect of predestination were granted as a debt, and not gratuitously. In things which are given gratuitously, a person can give more or less, just as he pleases (provided he deprives nobody of his due), without any infringement of justice. This is what the master of the house said: "Take what is thine, and go thy way. Is it not lawful for me to do what I will?" (Matthew 20:14-15).

Article 6. Whether predestination is certain?

Objection 1. It seems that predestination is not certain. Because on the words "Hold fast that which thou hast, that no one take thy crown," (Apocalypse 3:11), Augustine says (De Corr. et Grat. 15): "Another will not receive, unless this one were to lose it." Hence the crown which is the effect of predestination can be both acquired and lost. Therefore predestination cannot be certain.

Objection 2. Further, granted what is possible, nothing impossible follows. But it is possible that one predestined--e.g. Peter--may sin and then be killed. But if this were so, it would follow that the effect of predestination would be thwarted. This then, is not impossible. Therefore predestination is not certain.

Objection 3. Further, whatever God could do in the past, He can do now. But He could have not predestined whom He hath

425

predestined. Therefore now He is able not to predestine him. Therefore predestination is not certain.

On the contrary, A gloss on Romans 8:29: "Whom He foreknew, He also predestinated", says: "Predestination is the foreknowledge and preparation of the benefits of God, by which whosoever are freed will most certainly be freed."

I answer that, Predestination most certainly and infallibly takes effect; yet it does not impose any necessity, so that, namely, its effect should take place from necessity. For it was said above (Article 1), that predestination is a part of providence. But not all things subject to providence are necessary; some things happening from contingency, according to the nature of the proximate causes, which divine providence has ordained for such effects. Yet the order of providence is infallible, as was shown above (Question 22, Article 4). So also the order of predestination is certain; yet free-will is not destroyed; whence the effect of predestination has its contingency. Moreover all that has been said about the divine knowledge and will (14, 13; 19, 4) must also be taken into consideration; since they do not destroy contingency in things, although they themselves are most certain and infallible.

Reply to Objection 1. The crown may be said to belong to a person in two ways; first, by God's predestination, and thus no one loses his crown: secondly, by the merit of grace; for what we merit, in a certain way is ours; and thus anyone may lose his crown by mortal sin. Another person receives that crown thus lost, inasmuch as he takes the former's place. For God does not permit some to fall, without raising others; according to Job 34:24: "He shall break in pieces many and innumerable, and make others to stand in their stead." Thus men are substituted in the place of the fallen angels; and the Gentiles in that of the Jews. He who is substituted for another in the state of grace, also receives the crown of the fallen in that in eternal life he will rejoice at the good the other has done, in which life he will rejoice at all good whether done by himself or by others.

Reply to Objection 2. Although it is possible for one who is predestinated considered in himself to die in mortal sin; yet it is not possible, supposed, as in fact it is supposed. that he is predestinated. Whence it does not follow that predestination can fall short of its effect.

Reply to Objection 3. Since predestination includes the divine will as stated above (Article 4): and the fact that God wills any created thing is necessary on the supposition that He so wills, on account of the immutability of the divine will, but is not necessary absolutely; so the same must be said of predestination. Wherefore one ought not to say that God is able not to predestinate one whom He has predestinated, taking it in a composite sense, thought, absolutely speaking, God can predestinate or not. But in this way the certainty of predestination is not destroyed.

Article 7. Whether the number of the predestined is certain?

Objection 1. It seems that the number of the predestined is not certain. For a number to which an addition can be made is not certain. But there can be an addition to the number of the predestined as it seems; for it is written (Deuteronomy 1:11): "The Lord God adds to this number many thousands," and a gloss adds, "fixed by God, who knows those who belong to Him." Therefore the number of the predestined is not certain.

Objection 2. Further, no reason can be assigned why God pre-ordains to salvation one number of men more than another. But nothing is arranged by God without a reason. Therefore the number to be saved pre-ordained by God cannot be certain.

Objection 3. Further, the operations of God are more perfect than those of nature. But in the works of nature, good is found in the majority of things; defect and evil in the minority. If, then, the number of the saved were fixed by God at a certain figure, there would be more saved than lost. Yet the contrary follows from Matthew 7:13-14: "For wide is the gate, and broad the way that leadeth to destruction, and many there are who go in thereat. How narrow is the gate, and strait is the way that leadeth to life; and few there are who find it!" Therefore the number of those pre-ordained by God to be saved is not certain.

On the contrary, Augustine says (De Corr. et Grat. 13): "The number of the predestined is certain, and can neither be increased nor diminished."

I answer that, The number of the predestined is certain. Some have said that it was formally, but not materially certain; as if we were to say that it was certain that a hundred or a thousand would be saved; not however these or those individuals. But this destroys the certainty of predestination; of which we spoke above (Article 6). Therefore we must say that to God the number of the predestined is certain, not only formally, but also materially. It must, however, be observed that the number of the predestined is said to be certain to God, not by reason of His knowledge, because, that is to say, He knows how many will be saved (for in this way the number of drops of rain and the sands of the sea are certain to God); but by reason of His deliberate choice and determination. For the further evidence of which we must remember that every agent intends to make something finite, as is clear from what has been said above when we treated of the infinite (7, 2, 3). Now whosoever intends some definite measure in his effect thinks out some definite number in the essential parts, which are by their very nature required for the perfection of the whole. For of those things which are required not principally, but only on account of something else, he does not select any definite number "per se"; but he accepts and uses them in such numbers as are necessary on account of that other thing. For instance, a builder thinks out the definite measurements of a house, and also the definite number of rooms which he wishes to make in the house; and definite measurements of the walls and roof; he does not, however, select a definite number of stones, but accepts and uses just so many as are sufficient for the required measurements of the wall. So also must we consider concerning God in regard to the whole universe, which is His effect. For He pre-ordained the measurements of the whole of the universe, and what number would befit the essential parts of that universe--that is to say, which have in some way been ordained in perpetuity; how many spheres, how many stars, how many elements, and how many species. Individuals, however, which undergo corruption, are not ordained as it were chiefly for the good of the universe, but in a secondary way, inasmuch as the good of the species is preserved through them. Whence, although God knows the total number of individuals, the number of oxen, flies and such like, is not pre-ordained by God "per se"; but divine providence produces just so many as are sufficient for the preservation of the species. Now of all creatures the rational creature is chiefly ordained for the good of the universe, being as such incorruptible; more especially those who attain to eternal happiness, since they more immediately reach the ultimate end. Whence the number of the predestined is certain to God; not only by way of knowledge, but also by way of a principal pre-ordination.

It is not exactly the same thing in the case of the number of the reprobate, who would seem to be pre-ordained by God for the good of the elect, in whose regard "all things work together unto good" (Romans 8:28). Concerning the number of all the predestined, some say that so many men will be saved as angels fell; some, so many as there were angels left; others, as many as the number of angels created by God. It is, however, better to say that, "to God alone is known the number for whom is reserved eternal happiness [From the 'secret' prayer of the missal, 'pro vivis et defunctis.']"

Reply to Objection 1. These words of Deuteronomy must be taken as applied to those who are marked out by God beforehand in respect to present righteousness. For their number is increased and diminished, but not the number of the predestined.

Reply to Objection 2. The reason of the quantity of any one part must be judged from the proportion of that part of the whole. Thus in God the reason why He has made so many stars, or so many species of things, or predestined so many, is according to the proportion of the principal parts to the good of the whole universe.

Reply to Objection 3. The good that is proportionate to the common state of nature is to be found in the majority; and is wanting in the minority. The good that exceeds the common state of nature is to be found in the minority, and is wanting in the majority. Thus it is clear that the majority of men have a sufficient knowledge for the guidance of life; and those who have not this knowledge are said to be half-witted or foolish; but they who attain to a profound knowledge of things intelligible are a very small minority in respect to the rest. Since their eternal happiness, consisting in the vision of God, exceeds the common state of nature, and especially in so far as this is deprived of grace through the corruption of original sin, those who are saved are in the minority. In this especially, however, appears the mercy of God, that He has chosen some for that salvation, from which very many in accordance with the common course and tendency of nature fall short.

Article 8. Whether predestination can be furthered by the prayers of the saints?

Objection 1. It seems that predestination cannot be furthered by the prayers of the saints. For nothing eternal can be preceded by anything temporal; and in consequence nothing temporal can help towards making something else eternal. But predestination is eternal. Therefore, since the prayers of the saints are temporal, they cannot so help as to cause anyone to become predestined. Predestination therefore is not furthered by the prayers of the saints.

Objection 2. Further, as there is no need of advice except on account of defective knowledge, so there is not need of help except through defective power. But neither of these things can be said of God when He predestines. Whence it is said: "Who hath helped the Spirit of the Lord? [Vulgate: 'Who hath known the mind of the Lord?'] Or who hath been His counsellor?" (Romans 11:34). Therefore predestination cannot be furthered by the prayers of the saints.

Objection 3. Further, if a thing can be helped, it can also be hindered. But predestination cannot be hindered by anything. Therefore it cannot be furthered by anything.

On the contrary, It is said that "Isaac besought the Lord for his wife because she was barren; and He heard him and made Rebecca to conceive" (Genesis 25:21). But from that conception Jacob was born, and he was predestined. Now his predestination would not have happened if he had never been born. Therefore predestination can be furthered by the prayers of the saints.

I answer that, Concerning this question, there were different errors. Some, regarding the certainty of divine predestination, said that prayers were superfluous, as also anything else done to attain salvation; because whether these things were done or not, the predestined would attain, and the reprobate would not attain, eternal salvation. But against this opinion are all the warnings of Holy Scripture, exhorting us to prayer and other good works.

Others declared that the divine predestination was altered through prayer. This is stated to have the opinion of the Egyptians, who thought that the divine ordination, which they called fate, could be frustrated by certain sacrifices and prayers. Against this also is the authority of Scripture. For it is said: "But the triumpher in Israel will not spare and will not be moved to repentance" (1 Samuel 15:29); and that "the gifts and the calling of God are without repentance" (Romans 11:29).

Wherefore we must say otherwise that in predestination two things are to be considered--namely, the divine ordination; and its effect. As regards the former, in no possible way can predestination be furthered by the prayers of the saints. For it is not due to their prayers that anyone is predestined by God. As regards the latter, predestination is said to be helped by the prayers of the saints, and by other good works; because providence, of which predestination is a part, does not do away with secondary causes but so provides effects, that the order of secondary causes falls also under providence. So, as natural effects are provided by God in such a way that natural causes are directed to bring about those natural effects, without which those effects would not happen; so the salvation of a person is predestined by God in such a way, that whatever helps that person towards salvation falls under the order of predestination; whether it be one's own prayers or those of another; or other good works, and such like, without which one would not attain to salvation. Whence, the predestined must strive after good works and prayer; because through these means predestination is most certainly fulfilled. For this reason it is said: "Labor more that by good works you may make sure your calling and election" (2 Peter 1:10).

Reply to Objection 1. This argument shows that predestination is not furthered by the prayers of the saints, as regards the preordination.

Reply to Objection 2. One is said to be helped by another in two ways; in one way, inasmuch as he receives power from him: and to be helped thus belongs to the weak; but this cannot be said of

God, and thus we are to understand, "Who hath helped the Spirit of the Lord?" In another way one is said to be helped by a person through whom he carries out his work, as a master through a servant. In this way God is helped by us; inasmuch as we execute His orders, according to 1 Corinthians 3:9: "We are God's co-adjutors." Nor is this on account of any defect in the power of God, but because He employs intermediary causes, in order that the beauty of order may be preserved in the universe; and also that He may communicate to creatures the dignity of causality.

Reply to Objection 3. Secondary causes cannot escape the order of the first universal cause, as has been said above (Question 19, Article 6), indeed, they execute that order. And therefore predestination can be furthered by creatures, but it cannot be impeded by them.

## *Summa Theologica* I-II

### Question 9. That which moves the will

### Article 1. Whether the will is moved by the intellect?

Objection 1. It would seem that the will is not moved by the intellect. For Augustine says on Psalm 118:20: "My soul hath coveted to long for Thy justifications: The intellect flies ahead, the desire follows sluggishly or not at all: we know what is good, but deeds delight us not." But it would not be so, if the will were moved by the intellect: because movement of the movable results from motion of the mover. Therefore the intellect does not move the will.

Objection 2. Further, the intellect in presenting the appetible object to the will, stands in relation to the will, as the imagination in representing the appetible will to the sensitive appetite. But the imagination, does not remove the sensitive appetite: indeed sometimes our imagination affects us no more than what is set before us in a picture, and moves us not at all (De Anima ii, 3). Therefore neither does the intellect move the will.

Objection 3. Further, the same is not mover and moved in respect of the same thing. But the will moves the intellect; for we exercise the intellect when we will. Therefore the intellect does not move the will.

On the contrary, The Philosopher says (De Anima iii, 10) that "the appetible object is a mover not moved, whereas the will is a mover moved."

I answer that, A thing requires to be moved by something in so far as it is in potentiality to several things; for that which is in potentiality needs to be reduced to act by something actual; and to do this is to move. Now a power of the soul is seen to be in potentiality to different things in two ways: first, with regard to acting and not acting; secondly, with regard to this or that action. Thus the sight sometimes sees actually, and sometimes sees not: and sometimes it sees white, and sometimes black. It needs therefore a mover in two respects, viz. as to the exercise or use of the act, and as to the determination of the act. The first of these is on the part of the subject, which is sometimes acting, sometimes not acting: while the other is on the part of the object, by reason of which the act is specified.

The motion of the subject itself is due to some agent. And since every agent acts for an end, as was shown above (Question 1, Article 2), the principle of this motion lies in the end. And hence it is that the art which is concerned with the end, by its command moves the art which is concerned with the means; just as the "art of sailing commands the art of shipbuilding" (Phys. ii, 2). Now good in general, which has the nature of an end, is the object of the will. Consequently, in this respect, the will moves the other powers of the soul to their acts, for we make use of the other powers when we will. For the end and perfection of every other power, is included under the object of the will as some particular good: and always the art or power to which the universal end belongs, moves to their acts the arts or powers to which belong the particular ends included in the universal end. Thus the leader of an army, who intends the common good--i.e. the order of the whole army--by his command moves one of the captains, who intends the order of one company.

On the other hand, the object moves, by determining the act, after the manner of a formal principle, whereby in natural things actions are specified, as heating by heat. Now the first formal principle is universal "being" and "truth," which is the object of the intellect. And therefore by this kind of motion the intellect moves the will, as presenting its object to it.

Reply to Objection 1. The passage quoted proves, not that the intellect does not move, but that it does not move of necessity.

Reply to Objection 2. Just as the imagination of a form without estimation of fitness or harmfulness, does not move the sensitive appetite; so neither does the apprehension of the true without the aspect of goodness and desirability. Hence it is not the speculative intellect that moves, but the practical intellect (De Anima iii, 9).

Reply to Objection 3. The will moves the intellect as to the exercise of its act; since even the true itself which is the perfection of the intellect, is included in the universal good, as a particular good. But as to the determination of the act, which the act derives from the object, the intellect moves the will; since the good itself is apprehended under a special aspect as contained in the universal true. It is therefore evident that the same is not mover and moved in the same respect.

Article 2. Whether the will is moved by the sensitive appetite?

Objection 1. It would seem that the will cannot be moved by the sensitive appetite. For "to move and to act is more excellent than to be passive," as Augustine says (Gen. ad lit. xii, 16). But the sensitive appetite is less excellent than the will which is the intellectual appetite; just as sense is less excellent than intellect. Therefore the sensitive appetite does not move the will.

Objection 2. Further, no particular power can produce a universal effect. But the sensitive appetite is a particular power, because it follows the particular apprehension of sense. Therefore it cannot cause the movement of the will, which movement is universal, as following the universal apprehension of the intellect.

Objection 3. Further, as is proved in Phys. viii, 5, the mover is not moved by that which it moves, in such a way that there be reciprocal motion. But the will moves the sensitive appetite, inasmuch as the sensitive appetite obeys the reason. Therefore the sensitive appetite does not move the will.

On the contrary, It is written (James 1:14): "Every man is tempted by his own concupiscence, being drawn away and allured." But man would not be drawn away by his concupiscence, unless his will were moved by the sensitive appetite, wherein concupiscence resides. Therefore the sensitive appetite moves the will.

I answer that, As stated above (Article 1), that which is apprehended as good and fitting, moves the will by way of object. Now, that a thing appear to be good and fitting, happens from two causes: namely, from the condition, either of the thing proposed, or of the one to whom it is proposed. For fitness is spoken of by way of relation; hence it depends on both extremes. And hence it is that taste, according as it is variously disposed, takes to a thing in various ways, as being fitting or unfitting. Wherefore as the Philosopher says (Ethic. iii, 5): "According as a man is, such does the end seem to him."

Now it is evident that according to a passion of the sensitive appetite man is changed to a certain disposition. Wherefore according as man is affected by a passion, something seems to him fitting, which does not seem so when he is not so affected: thus that seems good to a man when angered, which does not seem good when he is calm. And in this way, the sensitive appetite moves the will, on the part of the object.

Reply to Objection 1. Nothing hinders that which is better simply and in itself, from being less excellent in a certain respect. Accordingly the will is simply more excellent than the sensitive appetite: but in respect of the man in whom a passion is predominant, in so far as he is subject to that passion, the sensitive appetite is more excellent.

Reply to Objection 2. Men's acts and choices are in reference to singulars. Wherefore from the very fact that the sensitive appetite is a particular power, it has great influence in disposing man so that something seems to him such or otherwise, in particular cases.

Reply to Objection 3. As the Philosopher says (Polit. i, 2), the reason, in which resides the will, moves, by its command, the irascible and concupiscible powers, not, indeed, "by a despotic sovereignty," as a slave is moved by his master, but by a "royal and politic sovereignty," as free men are ruled by their governor, and can nevertheless act counter to his commands. Hence both irascible and concupiscible can move counter to the will: and accordingly nothing hinders the will from being moved by them at times.

Article 3. Whether the will moves itself?

Objection 1. It would seem that the will does not move itself. For every mover, as such, is in act: whereas what is moved, is in potentiality; since "movement is the act of that which is in potentiality, as such" [Aristotle, Phys. iii, 1. Now the same is not in potentiality and in act, in respect of the same. Therefore nothing moves itself. Neither, therefore, can the will move itself.

Objection 2. Further, the movable is moved on the mover being present. But the will is always present to itself. If, therefore, it moved itself, it would always be moving itself, which is clearly false.

Objection 3. Further, the will is moved by the intellect, as stated above (Article 1). If, therefore, the will move itself, it would follow that the same thing is at once moved immediately by two movers; which seems unreasonable. Therefore the will does not move itself.

On the contrary, The will is mistress of its own act, and to it belongs to will and not to will. But this would not be so, had it not the power to move itself to will. Therefore it moves itself.

I answer that, As stated above (Article 1), it belongs to the will to move the other powers, by reason of the end which is the will's object. Now, as stated above (Question 8, Article 2), the end is in things appetible, what the principle is in things intelligible. But it is evident that the intellect, through its knowledge of the principle, reduces itself from potentiality to act, as to its knowledge of the conclusions; and thus it moves itself. And, in like manner, the will, through its volition of the end, moves itself to will the means.

Reply to Objection 1. It is not in respect of the same that the will moves itself and is moved: wherefore neither is it in act and in potentiality in respect of the same. But forasmuch as it actually wills the end, it reduces itself from potentiality to act, in respect of the means, so as, in a word, to will them actually.

Reply to Objection 2. The power of the will is always actually present to itself; but the act of the will, whereby it wills an end, is not always in the will. But it is by this act that it moves itself. Accordingly it does not follow that it is always moving itself.

Reply to Objection 3. The will is moved by the intellect, otherwise than by itself. By the intellect it is moved on the part of the object: whereas it is moved by itself, as to the exercise of its act, in respect of the end.

Article 4. Whether the will is moved by an exterior principle?

Objection 1. It would seem that the will is not moved by anything exterior. For the movement of the will is voluntary. But it is essential to the voluntary act that it be from an intrinsic principle, just as it is essential to the natural act. Therefore the movement of the will is not from anything exterior.

Objection 2. Further, the will cannot suffer violence, as was shown above (Question 6, Article 4). But the violent act is one "the principle of which is outside the agent" [Aristotle, Ethic. iii, 1. Therefore the will cannot be moved by anything exterior.

Objection 3. Further, that which is sufficiently moved by one mover, needs not to be moved by another. But the will moves itself sufficiently. Therefore it is not moved by anything exterior.

On the contrary, The will is moved by the object, as stated above (Article 1). But the object of the will can be something exterior, offered to the sense. Therefore the will can be moved by something exterior.

I answer that, As far as the will is moved by the object, it is evident that it can be moved by something exterior. But in so far as it is moved in the exercise of its act, we must again hold it to be moved by some exterior principle.

For everything that is at one time an agent actually, and at another time an agent in potentiality, needs to be moved by a mover. Now it is evident that the will begins to will something, whereas previously it did not will it. Therefore it must, of necessity, be moved by something to will it. And, indeed, it moves itself, as stated above (Article 3), in so far as through willing the end it reduces itself to the act of willing the means. Now it cannot do this without the aid of counsel: for when a man wills to be healed, he begins to reflect how this can be attained, and through this reflection he comes to the conclusion that he can be healed by a physician: and this he wills. But since he did not always actually will to have health, he must, of necessity, have begun, through something moving him, to will to be healed. And if the will moved itself to will this, it must, of necessity, have done this with the aid of counsel following some previous volition. But this process could not go on to infinity. Wherefore we must, of necessity, suppose that the will advanced to its first movement in virtue of the instigation of some exterior mover, as Aristotle concludes in a chapter of the Eudemian Ethics (vii, 14).

Reply to Objection 1. It is essential to the voluntary act that its principle be within the agent: but it is not necessary that this inward principle be the first principle unmoved by another. Wherefore though the voluntary act has an inward proximate principle, nevertheless its first principle is from without. Thus, too, the first principle of the natural movement is from without, that, to wit, which moves nature.

Reply to Objection 2. For an act to be violent it is not enough that its principle be extrinsic, but we must add "without the concurrence of him that suffers violence." This does not happen when the will is moved by an exterior principle: for it is the will that wills, though moved by another. But this movement would be violent, if it were counter to the movement of the will: which in the present case is impossible; since then the will would will and not will the same thing.

Reply to Objection 3. The will moves itself sufficiently in one respect, and in its own order, that is to say as proximate agent; but it cannot move itself in every respect, as we have shown. Wherefore it needs to be moved by another as first mover.

Article 5. Whether the will is moved by a heavenly body?

Objection 1. It would seem that the human will is moved by a heavenly body. For all various and multiform movements are reduced, as to their cause, to a uniform movement which is that of the heavens, as is proved in Phys. viii, 9. But human movements are various and multiform, since they begin to be, whereas previously they were not. Therefore they are reduced, as to their cause, to the movement of the heavens, which is uniform according to its nature.

Objection 2. Further, according to Augustine (De Trin. iii, 4) "the lower bodies are moved by the higher." But the movements of the human body, which are caused by the will, could not be reduced to the movement of the heavens, as to their cause, unless the will too were moved by the heavens. Therefore the heavens move the human will.

Objection 3. Further, by observing the heavenly bodies astrologers foretell the truth about future human acts, which are caused by the will. But this would not be so, if the heavenly bodies could not move man's will. Therefore the human will is moved by a heavenly body.

On the contrary, Damascene says (De Fide Orth. ii, 7) that "the heavenly bodies are not the causes of our acts." But they would be, if the will, which is the principle of human acts, were moved by the heavenly bodies. Therefore the will is not moved by the heavenly bodies.

I answer that, It is evident that the will can be moved by the heavenly bodies in the same way as it is moved by its object; that is to say, in so far as exterior bodies, which move the will, through being offered to the senses, and also the organs themselves of the sensitive powers, are subject to the movements of the heavenly bodies.

But some have maintained that heavenly bodies have an influence on the human will, in the same way as some exterior agent moves the will, as to the exercise of its act. But this is impossible. For the "will," as stated in De Anima iii, 9, "is in the reason." Now the reason is a power of the soul, not bound to a bodily organ: wherefore it follows that the will is a power absolutely incorporeal and immaterial. But it is evident that no body can act on what is incorporeal, but rather the reverse: because things incorporeal and immaterial have a power more formal and more universal than any corporeal things whatever. Therefore it is impossible for a heavenly body to act directly on the intellect or will. For this reason Aristotle (De Anima iii, 3) ascribed to those who held that intellect differs not from sense, the theory that "such is the will of men, as is the day which the father of men and of gods bring on" [Odyssey xviii. 135 (referring to Jupiter, by whom they understand the entire heavens). For all the sensitive powers, since they are acts of bodily organs, can be moved accidentally, by the heavenly bodies, i.e. through those bodies being moved, whose acts they are.

But since it has been stated (2) that the intellectual appetite is moved, in a fashion, by the sensitive appetite, the movements of the heavenly bodies have an indirect bearing on the will; in so far as the will happens to be moved by the passions of the sensitive appetite.

Reply to Objection 1. The multiform movements of the human will are reduced to some uniform cause, which, however, is above the intellect and will. This can be said, not of any body, but of some superior immaterial substance. Therefore there is no need for the movement of the will to be referred to the movement of the heavens, as to its cause.

Reply to Objection 2. The movements of the human body are reduced, as to their cause, to the movement of a heavenly body, in so far as the disposition suitable to a particular movement, is somewhat due to the influence of heavenly bodies; also, in so far as the sensitive appetite is stirred by the influence of heavenly bodies; and again, in so far as exterior bodies are moved in accordance with the movement of heavenly bodies, at whose presence, the will begins to will or not to will something; for instance, when the body is chilled, we begin to wish to make the fire. But this movement of the will is on the part of the object offered from without: not on the part of an inward instigation.

Reply to Objection 3. As stated above (Cf. I, 84, 6,7) the sensitive appetite is the act of a bodily organ. Wherefore there is no reason why man should not be prone to anger or concupiscence, or some like passion, by reason of the influence of heavenly bodies, just as by reason of his natural complexion. But the majority of men are led by the passions, which the wise alone resist. Consequently, in the majority of cases predictions about human acts, gathered from the observation of heavenly bodies, are fulfilled. Nevertheless, as Ptolemy says (Centiloquium v), "the wise man governs the stars"; which is a though to say that by resisting his passions, he opposes his will, which is free and nowise subject to the movement of the heavens, to such like effects of the heavenly bodies.

Or, as Augustine says (Gen. ad lit. ii, 15): "We must confess that when the truth is foretold by astrologers, this is due to some most hidden inspiration, to which the human mind is subject without knowing it. And since this is done in order to deceive man, it must be the work of the lying spirits."

Article 6. Whether the will is moved by God alone, as exterior principle?

Objection 1. It would seem that the will is not moved by God alone as exterior principle. For it is natural that the inferior be moved by its superior: thus the lower bodies are moved by the heavenly bodies. But there is something which is higher than the will of man and below God, namely, the angel. Therefore man's will can be moved by an angel also, as exterior principle.

Objection 2. Further, the act of the will follows the act of the intellect. But man's intellect is reduced to act, not by God alone, but also by the angel who enlightens it, as Dionysius says (Coel.

Hier. iv). For the same reason, therefore, the will also is moved by an angel.

Objection 3. Further, God is not the cause of other than good things, according to Genesis 1:31: "God saw all the things that He had made, and they were very good." If, therefore man's will were moved by God alone, it would never be moved to evil: and yet it is the will whereby "we sin and whereby we do right," as Augustine says (Retract. i, 9).

On the contrary, It is written (Philippians 2:13): "It is God Who worketh in us" [Vulg.'you'] "both to will and to accomplish."

I answer that, The movement of the will is from within, as also is the movement of nature. Now although it is possible for something to move a natural thing, without being the cause of the thing moved, yet that alone, which is in some way the cause of a thing's nature, can cause a natural movement in that thing. For a stone is moved upwards by a man, who is not the cause of the stone's nature, but this movement is not natural to the stone; but the natural movement of the stone is caused by no other than the cause of its nature. Wherefore it is said in Phys. vii, 4, that the generator moves locally heavy and light things. Accordingly man endowed with a will is sometimes moved by something that is not his cause; but that his voluntary movement be from an exterior principle that is not the cause of his will, is impossible.

Now the cause of the will can be none other than God. And this is evident for two reasons. First, because the will is a power of the rational soul, which is caused by God alone, by creation, as was stated in the I, 90, 2. Secondly, it is evident from the fact that the will is ordained to the universal good. Wherefore nothing else can be the cause of the will, except God Himself, Who is the universal good: while every other good is good by participation, and is some particular good, and a particular cause does not give a universal inclination. Hence neither can primary matter, which is potentiality to all forms, be created by some particular agent.

Reply to Objection 1. An angel is not above man in such a way as to be the cause of his will, as the heavenly bodies are the causes of natural forms, from which result the natural movements of natural bodies.

Reply to Objection 2. Man's intellect is moved by an angel, on the part of the object, which by the power of the angelic light is proposed to man's knowledge. And in this way the will also can be moved by a creature from without, as stated above (Article 4).

Reply to Objection 3. God moves man's will, as the Universal Mover, to the universal object of the will, which is good. And without this universal motion, man cannot will anything. But man determines himself by his reason to will this or that, which is true or apparent good. Nevertheless, sometimes God moves some specially to the willing of something determinate, which is good; as in the case of those whom He moves by grace, as we shall state later on (109, 2).

Question 10. The manner in which the will is moved

Article 1. Whether the will is moved to anything naturally?

Objection 1. It would seem that the will is not moved to anything naturally. For the natural agent is condivided with the voluntary agent, as stated at the beginning of Phys. ii, 1. Therefore the will is not moved to anything naturally.

Objection 2. Further, that which is natural is in a thing always: as "being hot" is in fire. But no movement is always in the will. Therefore no movement is natural to the will.

Objection 3. Further, nature is determinate to one thing: whereas the will is referred to opposites. Therefore the will wills nothing naturally.

On the contrary, The movement of the will follows the movement of the intellect. But the intellect understands some things naturally. Therefore the will, too, wills some things naturally.

I answer that, As Boethius says (De Duabus Nat.) and the Philosopher also (Metaph. v, 4) the word "nature" is used in a manifold sense. For sometimes it stands for the intrinsic principle in movable things. In this sense nature is either matter or the material form, as stated in Phys. ii, 1. In another sense nature stands for any substance, or even for any being. And in this sense, that is said to be natural to a thing which befits it in respect of its substance. And this is that which of itself is in a thing. Now all things that do not of themselves belong to the thing in which they are, are reduced to something which belongs of itself to that thing, as to their principle. Wherefore, taking nature in this sense, it is necessary that the principle of whatever belongs to a thing, be a natural principle. This is evident in regard to the intellect: for the principles of intellectual knowledge are naturally known. In like manner the principle of voluntary movements must be something naturally willed.

Now this is good in general, to which the will tends naturally, as does each power to its object; and again it is the last end, which stands in the same relation to things appetible, as the first principles of demonstrations to things intelligible: and, speaking generally, it is all those things which belong to the willer according to his nature. For it is not only things pertaining to the will that the will desires, but also that which pertains to each power, and to the entire man. Wherefore man wills naturally not only the object of the will, but also other things that are appropriate to the other powers; such as the knowledge of truth, which befits the intellect; and to be and to live and other like things which regard the natural well-being; all of which are included in the object of the will, as so many particular goods.

Reply to Objection 1. The will is distinguished from nature as one kind of cause from another; for some things happen naturally and some are done voluntarily. There is, however, another manner of causing that is proper to the will, which is mistress of its act, besides the manner proper to nature, which is determinate to one thing. But since the will is founded on some nature, it is necessary that the movement proper to nature be shared by the will, to some extent: just as what belongs to a previous cause is shared by a subsequent cause. Because in every thing, being itself, which is from nature, precedes volition, which is from the will. And hence it is that the will wills something naturally.

Reply to Objection 2. In the case of natural things, that which is natural, as a result of the form only, is always in them actually, as heat is in fire. But that which is natural as a result of matter, is not always in them actually, but sometimes only in potentiality: because form is act, whereas matter is potentiality. Now movement is "the act of that which is in potentiality" (Aristotle, Phys. iii, 1). Wherefore that which belongs to, or results from, movement, in regard to natural things, is not always in them. Thus fire does not always move upwards, but only when it is outside its own place. [The Aristotelian theory was that fire's proper place is the fiery heaven, i.e. the Empyrean.] And in like manner it is not necessary that the will (which is reduced from potentiality to act, when it wills something), should always be in the act of volition; but only when it is in a certain determinate disposition. But God's will, which is pure act, is always in the act of volition.

Reply to Objection 3. To every nature there is one thing corresponding, proportionate, however, to that nature. For to nature considered as a genus, there corresponds something one generically; and to nature as species there corresponds something one specifically; and to the individualized nature there corresponds some one individual. Since, therefore, the will is an immaterial power like the intellect, some one general thing corresponds to it, naturally which is the good; just as to the intellect there corresponds some one general thing, which is the true, or being, or "what a thing is." And under good in general are included many particular goods, to none of which is the will determined.

Article 2. Whether the will is moved, of necessity, by its object?

Objection 1. It seems that the will is moved, of necessity, by its object. For the object of the will is compared to the will as mover to movable, as stated in De Anima iii, 10. But a mover, if it be sufficient, moves the movable of necessity. Therefore the will can be moved of necessity by its object.

Objection 2. Further, just as the will is an immaterial power, so is the intellect: and both powers are ordained to a universal object, as stated above (01, ad 3). But the intellect is moved, of necessity, by its object: therefore the will also, by its object.

Objection 3. Further, whatever one wills, is either the end, or something ordained to an end. But, seemingly, one wills an end necessarily: because it is like the principle in speculative matters, to which principle one assents of necessity. Now the end is the reason for willing the means; and so it seems that we will the means also necessarily. Therefore the will is moved of necessity by its object.

On the contrary, The rational powers, according to the Philosopher (Metaph. ix, 2) are directed to opposites. But the will is a rational power, since it is in the reason, as stated in De Anima iii, 9. Therefore the will is directed to opposites. Therefore it is not moved, of necessity, to either of the opposites.

449

I answer that, The will is moved in two ways: first, as to the exercise of its act; secondly, as to the specification of its act, derived from the object. As to the first way, no object moves the will necessarily, for no matter what the object be, it is in man's power not to think of it, and consequently not to will it actually. But as to the second manner of motion, the will is moved by one object necessarily, by another not. For in the movement of a power by its object, we must consider under what aspect the object moves the power. For the visible moves the sight, under the aspect of color actually visible. Wherefore if color be offered to the sight, it moves the sight necessarily: unless one turns one's eyes away; which belongs to the exercise of the act. But if the sight were confronted with something not in all respects colored actually, but only so in some respects, and in other respects not, the sight would not of necessity see such an object: for it might look at that part of the object which is not actually colored, and thus it would not see it. Now just as the actually colored is the object of sight, so is good the object of the will. Wherefore if the will be offered an object which is good universally and from every point of view, the will tends to it of necessity, if it wills anything at all; since it cannot will the opposite. If, on the other hand, the will is offered an object that is not good from every point of view, it will not tend to it of necessity. And since lack of any good whatever, is a non-good, consequently, that good alone which is perfect and lacking in nothing, is such a good that the will cannot not-will it: and this is Happiness. Whereas any other particular goods, in so far as they are lacking in some good, can be regarded as non-goods: and from this point of view, they can be set aside or approved by the will, which can tend to one and the same thing from various points of view.

Reply to Objection 1. The sufficient mover of a power is none but that object that in every respect presents the aspect of the mover of that power. If, on the other hand, it is lacking in any respect, it will not move of necessity, as stated above.

Reply to Objection 2. The intellect is moved, of necessity, by an object which is such as to be always and necessarily true: but not by that which may be either true or false--viz. by that which is contingent: as we have said of the good.

Reply to Objection 3. The last end moves the will necessarily, because it is the perfect good. In like manner whatever is ordained to that end, and without which the end cannot be attained, such as "to be" and "to live," and the like. But other things without which the end can be gained, are not necessarily willed by one who wills the end: just as he who assents to the principle, does not necessarily assent to the conclusions, without which the principles can still be true.

Article 3. Whether the will is moved, of necessity, by the lower appetite?

Objection 1. It would seem that the will is moved of necessity by a passion of the lower appetite. For the Apostle says (Romans 7:19): "The good which I will I do not; but the evil which I will not, that I do": and this is said by reason of concupiscence, which is a passion. Therefore the will is moved of necessity by a passion.

Objection 2. Further, as stated in Ethic. iii, 5, "according as a man is, such does the end seem to him." But it is not in man's power to cast aside a passion once. Therefore it is not in man's power not to will that to which the passion inclines him.

Objection 3. Further, a universal cause is not applied to a particular effect, except by means of a particular cause: wherefore the universal reason does not move save by means of a particular estimation, as stated in De Anima iii, 11. But as the universal reason is to the particular estimation, so is the will to the sensitive appetite. Therefore the will is not moved to will something particular, except through the sensitive appetite. Therefore, if the sensitive appetite happen to be disposed to something, by reason of a passion, the will cannot be moved in a contrary sense.

On the contrary, It is written (Genesis 4:7): "Thy lust [Vulg. 'The lust thereof'] shall be under thee, and thou shalt have dominion over it." Therefore man's will is moved of necessity by the lower appetite.

I answer that, As stated above (Question 9, Article 2), the passion of the sensitive appetite moves the will, in so far as the will is moved by its object: inasmuch as, to wit, man through being disposed in such and such a way by a passion, judges something to be fitting and good, which he would not judge thus were it not for the passion. Now this influence of a passion on man occurs in two ways. First, so that his reason is wholly bound, so that he has not the use of reason: as happens in those who through a violent access of anger or concupiscence become furious or insane, just as they may from some other bodily disorder; since such like passions do not take place without some change in the body. And of such the same is to be said as of irrational animals, which follow, of necessity, the impulse of their passions: for in them there is neither movement of reason, nor, consequently, of will.

Sometimes, however, the reason is not entirely engrossed by the passion, so that the judgment of reason retains, to a certain extent, its freedom: and thus the movement of the will remains in a certain degree. Accordingly in so far as the reason remains free, and not subject to the passion, the will's movement, which also remains, does not tend of necessity to that whereto the passion inclines it. Consequently, either there is no movement of the will in that man, and the passion alone holds its sway: or if there be a movement of the will, it does not necessarily follow the passion.

Reply to Objection 1. Although the will cannot prevent the movement of concupiscence from arising, of which the Apostle says: "The evil which I will not, that I do--i.e. I desire"; yet it is in the power of the will not to will to desire or not to consent to concupiscence. And thus it does not necessarily follow the movement of concupiscence.

Reply to Objection 2. Since there is in man a twofold nature, intellectual and sensitive; sometimes man is such and such uniformly in respect of his whole soul: either because the sensitive part is wholly subject to this reason, as in the virtuous; or because reason is entirely engrossed by passion, as in a madman. But sometimes, although reason is clouded by passion, yet something of this reason remains free. And in respect of this, man can either repel the passion entirely, or at least hold himself in check so as not to be led away by the passion. For when thus disposed, since man is variously disposed according to the various parts of the soul, a thing appears to him otherwise according to his reason, than it does according to a passion.

Reply to Objection 3. The will is moved not only by the universal good apprehended by the reason, but also by good apprehended by sense. Wherefore he can be moved to some particular good independently of a passion of the sensitive appetite. For we will and do many things without passion, and through choice alone; as is most evident in those cases wherein reason resists passion.

Article 4. Whether the will is moved of necessity by the exterior mover which is God?

Objection 1. It would seem that the will is moved of necessity by God. For every agent that cannot be resisted moves of necessity. But God cannot be resisted, because His power is infinite; wherefore it is written (Romans 9:19): "Who resisteth His will?" Therefore God moves the will of necessity.

Objection 2. Further, the will is moved of necessity to whatever it wills naturally, as stated above (02, ad 3). But "whatever God does in a thing is natural to it," as Augustine says (Contra Faust. xxvi,

3). Therefore the will wills of necessity everything to which God moves it.

Objection 3. Further, a thing is possible, if nothing impossible follows from its being supposed. But something impossible follows from the supposition that the will does not will that to which God moves it: because in that case God's operation would be ineffectual. Therefore it is not possible for the will not to will that to which God moves it. Therefore it wills it of necessity.

On the contrary, It is written (Sirach 15:14): "God made man from the beginning, and left him in the hand of his own counsel." Therefore He does not of necessity move man's will.

I answer that, As Dionysius says (Div. Nom. iv) "it belongs to Divine providence, not to destroy but to preserve the nature of things." Wherefore it moves all things in accordance with their conditions; so that from necessary causes through the Divine motion, effects follow of necessity; but from contingent causes, effects follow contingently. Since, therefore, the will is an active principle, not determinate to one thing, but having an indifferent relation to many things, God so moves it, that He does not determine it of necessity to one thing, but its movement remains contingent and not necessary, except in those things to which it is moved naturally.

Reply to Objection 1. The Divine will extends not only to the doing of something by the thing which He moves, but also to its being done in a way which is fitting to the nature of that thing. And therefore it would be more repugnant to the Divine motion, for the will to be moved of necessity, which is not fitting to its nature; than for it to be moved freely, which is becoming to its nature.

Reply to Objection 2. That is natural to a thing, which God so works in it that it may be natural to it: for thus is something becoming to a thing, according as God wishes it to be becoming. Now He does not wish that whatever He works in things should be natural to them, for instance, that the dead should rise again. But this He does wish to be natural to each thing--that it be subject to the Divine power.

Reply to Objection 3. If God moves the will to anything, it is incompatible with this supposition, that the will be not moved thereto. But it is not impossible simply. Consequently it does not follow that the will is moved by God necessarily.

READING QUESTIONS

## 1. Plato & Aristotle; Being & Becoming; The Wise Man

1. What is the context of the metaphysical discussion in Plato's Timaeus? What does this mean?

2. How does Timaeus set up the dichotomy between being and becoming? Is this a true dichotomy?

3. What is the significance of Timaeus's claim that the good is self-diffusing?

4. How is time defined in the Timaeus?

5. Explain Aristotle's opening line of the Metaphysics in detail.

6. How do sense, memory, experience and universals relate to each other according to Aristotle?

7. What is the source of philosophical thinking according to Aristotle? What is required for it?

8. What are the six attributes of the wise man and how does Metaphysics satisfy all of them?

9. How does myth relate to philosophy according to Aristotle?

10. Why is metaphysics the "most divine" science?

11. Where does metaphysics begin? Where does it end?

## 2. Aristotle and the Other Guys

12. Describe Aristotle's historical survey of previous thinkers' teaching on causes. Which cause was discovered first and why? Which came afterward and why? Why does he make this survey?

13. What was the problem of all the earlier thinkers in general according to Aristotle?

14. How does Aristotle account for Plato's thinking? What thinkers is he related to and how?

15. How does Aristotle reply to the materialists?

16. How does Aristotle reply to Plato?

17. What is the difference between metaphysics and the "special sciences?"

18. What is the significance of Aristotle's claim that unity and being are coextensive?

19. In what ways is substance "prior to" accident?

20. What are the four senses of substance?

21. How can we today understand Aristotle's references to forces "in matter" and "imperfect forms?"

22. What is the difference between the part of a definition and the part of a thing?

23. How is a definition with different parts really one?

24. What is the difference between "one" and "a heap?"

25. Why are accidents not being in the full sense?

### 3. Aristotle's God

26. What is the significance of the claim that causes and principles are analogically similar? What does this tell us about God?

27. What is God's essence according to Aristotle?

28. How does Aristotle prove that there must be a God?

29. What is Aristotle's God? Describe him.

30. What is the nature of Divine Thought according to Aristotle?

### 4. Thomas Aquinas – A Bunch of Stuff

31. What are the first things conceived by the intellect according to Thomas? Why is it so important to understand them precisely?

32. What is the relationship between nature and operation and what does this mean?

33. How are form and matter related to the individual? How do form and matter contribute to individuality?

34. Is the universal one or many? How might Thomas respond to a nominalist?

35. What does the intellect cause in things? What does this mean in regard to the nominalist argument?

36. What metaphor does Thomas use to illustrate his response to nominalism? Explain it.

37. What is the definition of a cause? Explain it.

38. What is Thomas's argument that there is a real distinction between existence and essence?

39. How does the distinction between existence and essence apply to: God, angels, human beings.

40. What is the significance of the image of the Phoenix Thomas uses?

41. What is the relationship between essence and accidents? What does this mean for epistemology?

42. Why can there be no definition of God?

43. Describe all the transcendentals and how they are connected to being.

44. Is the Beautiful a transcendental? Why or why not?

## 5. Proofs for God's Existence

1. What is Anselm's proof for God's existence?

2. On what grounds does Aquinas reject Anselm's proof for God's existence?

3. What are the two objections to the existence of God for Aquinas, and how does he answer them?

4. What are Thomas's "five ways" to prove God's existence? What do they tell us about God's essence?

5. How does Thomas show that God's essence and existence are identical? (3 ways)

6. What does it mean that we speak of God "analogically?" What is this contrasted with?

## 6. God Stuff

7. What is the connection between God's goodness and his efficient causality?

8. How do we know that God is "in" all things?

9. In what ways is God "in" all things? (3 ways) What is the significance of each?

10. How do we know that God is immutable? (3 ways)

11. What is the difference between eternity and aveternity?

12. How do we know that God is One? (3 ways)

17. Why is "he who is" the most proper name for God? (3 reasons)

## 7. Creation

18. How do we know that God can act by will, and not only by necessity? (3 ways)

19. How does the reality that God acts by both necessity and free will provide a response to Ockham?

20. Is it possible for the world to be created but to always have existed? Why or why not?

21. Is creation a change? Why or why not?

22. What is "creation in the creature?"

23. What is the difference between being "created" and being "con-created?"

24. Why can only God create?

25. How is an instrumental cause used?

26. Why is it more evident that there is a God if the universe had a temporal beginning?

## 8. Evil

27. What does the introduction to the book of Job tell us about the role of evil in God's plan?

28. What is the difference between natural and moral evil, and what do they have in common?

29. What do the cycles of speeches in Job tell us about our understanding of God's plan?

30. What is the message of God's speeches to Job? What about his two responses?

31. What is the significance of the numbering of the goods Job receives at the end of the book?

32. How does God incorporate evil into his providential plan according to Aquinas?

## 9. Free Will

33. How does free will exist within providence?

34. What does free will have to do with the dignity of causality?

35. What is the difference between a necessary mode of causality and a contingent mode?

36. Why do very few people know whether they are predestined?

37. Why is it not unjust for God to save some and condemn others?

38. What is the difference between particular and general providence? What causes each?

39. How do prayers and good works contribute to salvation?

40. How does Anselm show that no temptation forces us to sin unwillingly?

41. In what way is the will moved by a "heavenly body?" In what way is it not?

42. Is the will moved of necessity by its object? By the lower appetite? Why or why not?

Made in the USA
Las Vegas, NV
20 December 2022